JOHN MILTON
Paradise Lost: Books IX–X

THE CAMBRIDGE MILTON FOR
SCHOOLS AND COLLEGES

GENERAL EDITOR: J. B. BROADBENT

JOHN MILTON

Paradise Lost: Books IX–X

Edited by

J. MARTIN EVANS

Stanford University, California

They wondered why the fruit had been forbidden;
It taught them nothing new. They hid their pride,
But did not listen much when they were chidden;
They knew exactly what to do outside.

They left: immediately the memory faded
Of all they'd learnt; they could not understand
The dogs now who, before, had always aided;
The stream was dumb with whom they'd always planned.

They wept and quarrelled: freedom was so wild.
In front, maturity, as he ascended,
Retired like a horizon from the child;

The dangers and the punishments grew greater;
And the way back by angels was defended
Against the poet and the legislator.

W. H. Auden *In time of war* 1950

CAMBRIDGE
UNIVERSITY PRESS

CAMBRIDGE
UNIVERSITY PRESS

University Printing House, Cambridge CB2 8BS, United Kingdom

Cambridge University Press is part of the University of Cambridge.

It furthers the University's mission by disseminating knowledge in the pursuit of education, learning and research at the highest international levels of excellence.

Information on this title: education.cambridge.org

© Cambridge University Press 1973

First published 1973
27th printing 2016

Printed in the United Kingdom by Printondemand-worldwide, Peterborough

A catalogue record for this publication is available from the British Library

ISBN 978-0-521-20067-7 Paperback

Acknowledgements

Like every editor of Milton I am in debt to the accumulated wisdom of all my predecessors, but I should like to acknowledge the help I received from four editions in particular: A. W. Verity *Paradise Lost Books IX and X* 1896, E. M. W. Tillyard *Paradise Lost Books IX and X* 1961, M. Y. Hughes *Paradise Lost* 1962, J. Carey and A. Fowler *The Poems of John Milton* 1968.

I am grateful to Helen Pinkerton for permission to quote from her poem *Error pursued*.

Acknowledgements for permission to quote poetry are due to the following publishers: Faber and Faber Ltd and Oxford University Press (New York) for Edwin Muir, *One foot in Eden* (*Collected Poems* 1965); Faber and Faber Ltd and Random House for W. H. Auden, *In time of war* (*Collected Shorter Poems* 1950); Secker and Warburg for W. R. Rodgers *The fall* (*Europa, the bull and other poems* 1952); *Saturday Review* for Robinson Jeffers, *Original sin* (*Saturday Review of Literature* 1948).

I wish to dedicate this new edition of Books IX and X to the two English masters who first taught me to enjoy Milton when I was in the sixth form of Cardiff High School for Boys: Dr D. Elwyn Williams and Mr Glyn Dennis-Jones.

J. M. EVANS

Contents

Preface to the Cambridge Milton

We have also considered him as a poet, and such he was, if ever human nature could boast it had produced one...in expounding him we have therefore always given, as well as we were enabled, a poetic sense...for a poem, such a one as this especially, is not to be read, and construed, as an Act of Parliament, or a mathematical dissertation: the things of the spirit are spiritually discerned.

JONATHAN RICHARDSON father and son *Explanatory notes and remarks on Paradise Lost* 1734

This volume is part of the Cambridge Milton series. It can be used independently but we assume that you refer as appropriate to two other volumes in particular:

John Milton: introductions. A collaborative volume listed under the general editor's name. For Milton's life, times, ideas; music, visual arts, science, the Bible in relation to his poetry; a long essay on *Milton in literary history* and *General introduction to the early poems.* (Each early poem will also have a specific introduction in its own volume.)

Paradise Lost: introduction. J. B. Broadbent. General introduction to the poem as a whole with chapters on myth and ritual; epic; history of publication; ideology; structures; allusion; language; syntax; rhetoric; minor components of epic; similes; rhythm; style. This volume also contains a full list of resources (books, art, music etc.); a chronology of the Bible and biblical writings, epics, and other versions of the material of *PL* (this section constitutes a list of materials for projects); and a table of the contents of *PL* with cross-references.

Paradise regained and *Samson agonistes*: their volumes will have self-contained introductions.

Examining, teaching, study

Milton's poems need more annotation to achieve a given degree of comprehension and pleasure than most others. Shakespeare, Donne, Blake, Yeats all demand annotation; but they arouse interest more immediately than Milton does, and so motivate study. This difficulty does not lie in the idleness of the reader or his ignorance: it was felt by Dr Johnson (admittedly a slothful man, but also a learned one and himself an editor). *PL* was one of the first English poems to be annotated. In 1695, twenty-one years after Milton died, Patrick Hume published his *Annotations... Wherein the Texts of Sacred Writ Relating to the Poem, are Quoted; The Parallel Places and Imitations of the Most Excellent Homer and Virgil, Cited and Compared; All the Obscure Parts Render'd in Phrases More Familiar; The Old and Obsolete Words, with Their Originals, Explain'd and Made Easie...* As editors we are all guilty, like Hume, of answering the wrong questions. As examiners, we're guilty of asking them. Milton's poetry is worth using in education because it is difficult; but we have to attend to the right kind of difficulty. In *PL* the serious difficulties are not the surface obscurities of

> nor to which transform'd
> *Ammonian Jove*, or *Capitoline* was seen,
> Hee with *Olympias*, this with her who bore
> *Scipio* the highth of *Rome*.   IX 507

They are the grave issues of sin, death, 'all our woe', grace, the use of beauty and strength, 'conjugal love'. Those are also the interesting things. But they tend to get left out of editions, and exam papers, because they are more suitable for discussion than for notes and tests.

The best elementary exam on *PL* that I have seen was set in the summer of 1968 on *PL* IV and IX. It asked for either an essay, or a series of shorter answers on a printed passage: so two sorts of candidate were each given a decent chance to show their best. The essay topic was large yet crucial: in effect, did Adam and Eve *have* to fall? No nonsense about Satan's 'character' dragged in from the Shakespeare paper, or invitations to be romantic about Milton's soul. The printed passage was from Satan's soliloquy on arriving in Paradise, and the candidates were told so. Four questions directed the candidate to specific locales – 'What do the phraseology and form of these four lines tell you about Satan's own nature?' for instance. The fifth asked for the passage to be related to its parallel in Book IX. In short, the candidates' memory and attention were being helped; but they were being asked seriously difficult questions.

This edition of Milton

The texts are based on the latest editions published in his lifetime: i.e. chiefly *Poems of Mr John Milton, both English and Latin* (the earlier poems) 1645; and the second edition of *PL* 1674. But the text has no authority as such.

The spelling has been modernized (except where it would completely alter pronunciation, e.g. *anow* has been changed to *enow* but not to *enough*).

Stress marks (´) have been added where Milton seems to have intended a stress unusual for us, e.g. *óbscene*. Grave accents (`) have been added to indicate voiced syllables in such cases as *blessèd* and in unfamiliar names, e.g. *Atè*. Milton distinguished between stressed and unstressed forms of *hee, he, their, thir*, etc. These have all been reduced to their normal modern forms.

Milton showed much elision of *e*'s, e.g. 'th'obscene dread of Moab's sons', 'th'heavens'. These have been omitted too because the elision comes more naturally if we read it with our usual neutral *e* sounds in such cases, than if we try to say *thóbscene* or *theavens*.

On the other hand, Milton's punctuation has been left almost untouched. It is not the same as ours, but you soon get used to it, and to tamper would alter the rhythm. In particular, modern punctuation would interrupt the flow of ideas. For example, a passage about Eve's hair:

> She as a veil down to the slender waist
> Her unadornèd golden tresses wore
> Disshevelled, but in wanton ringlets waved
> As the vine curls her tendrils, which implied
> Subjection, but required with gentle sway,
> And by her yielded, by him best received,
> Yielded with coy submission, modest pride,
> And sweet reluctant amorous delay.   *PL* IV 304

Pause at each punctuation mark. Pause at all awkward line-changes, e.g. 'implied/Subjection' puts a pause equal to a whole stress between the lines. Let all neutral vowels stay neutral, e.g. *tendrils, required, yielded*. Run over unstressed words as in ordinary speech, e.g. 'She as a veil' is nearly elided as 'She's a

3

veil'; but give all stressed syllables their full value. Don't be officious with the syntax: its sense is impressionistic rather than logical. The words implied–required–yielded–received are set in a pattern which represents a relationship, not a grammar: Eve's hair implies subjection; Adam requires that subjection of her, gently; she does actually yield – also perhaps gently; and he receives it, takes it back again – and then she goes on yielding it, her yielding and her reluctance to yield both an expression of love, her *delay* the rhyming answer to his *sway* (= power). It is not a sentence but a dance.

Milton's meanings are often etymological, e.g. *disshevelled* does not mean unkempt but let down without coiffure; *reluctant* does not mean unwilling but resistant; these meanings will emerge more easily if the words are dwelt on and given their full syllabic value – *dis-shevelled, re-luctant*. Reading Hopkins helps because he uses words etymologically. But do not elocute. Actors' voices have a particularly bad effect on Milton because his language is hardly ever beautiful or emotive – it is stiff and thoughtful, or colloquial and definite:

> The leaf was darkish, and had prickles on it,
> But in another country, as he said,
> Bore a bright golden flower, but not in this soil.
>
> *Comus* 631

>   but all sat mute,
> Pondering the danger with deep thoughts; and each
> In other's countenance read his own dismay
> Astonished.   *PL* 11 420

In the second passage there, one might emphasize the emotions of dismay and astonishment; but as a matter of fact, *astonished* means *dismayed*; and what matters is the shape, the structure of the lines; it is that, not expressiveness, which represents the fallen angels' bafflement. The structure runs: an angel – another angel – own dismay – more dismay. It is better to read with an eye to semantics than to histrionics; and to read as Milton did (with a provincial accent, rather harshly, with something of a sarcastic note, rolling his *r*'s) than with elegance.

The series will supersede A. W. Verity's Pitt Press edition of Milton's poetry published from Cambridge 1891 *et seq.* It is designed for use by the individual student, and the class, and the teacher, in schools and colleges, from about the beginning of the sixth form to the end of the first postgraduate year course in England. Introductions and notes aim to provide enough material

for the reader to work on for himself, but nothing of a profession-
ally academic kind. We hope that if any volume of text is
prescribed for examination, some of its contents will not be set,
but left for the student to explore at will.

In the face of the syllabus – heavy for many subjects – 'adventures of
ideas' in wider fields, and the time-consuming operations of developing
independence of thought. . . will be undertaken 'at risk'.

> Report of the Welsh Committee of the Schools Council, in
> Schools Council Working Paper 20, *Sixth form examining
> methods*, HMSO 1968.

This edition assumes that risk.

J.B.B.

Introduction to Paradise Lost IX—X

Like Virgil's *Aeneid* Milton's epic contains twelve books and begins *in medias res*, in the middle of events. In strictly arithmetical terms this means that Book IX initiates the last sixth of the story, not, as its position in the poem implies, the last third. We are beginning almost *in ultimas res*. Look at what has happened so far (for a more detailed summary see the 'contents of *PL* with some cross-references' in the *PL: introduction* in this series): Satan has rebelled against God and after a three-day war been cast down from heaven into hell with all his followers; God has created the universe and placed Adam and Eve in the garden of Eden; Satan in the meantime has roused his fallen angels in hell, built Pandemonium, and undertaken to voyage to earth to see if that part of God's empire might be vulnerable; God has noticed him escaping from hell, foretold the fall of man and accepted the Son's offer to atone for human wickedness; Satan has arrived in paradise, eavesdropped on Adam and Eve and been arrested by Ithuriel and Zephon while he was trying to infect Eve's imagination as she slept; Raphael has descended to the garden of Eden to tell Adam and Eve about Satan's rebellion and the creation of the universe; Adam in turn has told Raphael about his own experiences, the creation of Eve, and his subsequent infatuation with her; and Raphael has just returned to heaven with these final admonitions:

> But I can now no more; the parting sun
> Beyond the earth's green cape and verdant isles
> Hespérian sets, my signal to depart.
> Be strong, live happy, and love, but first of all
> Him whom to love is to obey, and keep
> His great command; take heed lest passion sway
> Thy judgement to do aught, which else free will
> Would not admit; thine and of all thy sons
> The weal or woe in thee is placed; beware.

> I in thy persevering shall rejoice,
> And all the blest; stand fast; to stand or fall
> Free in thine own arbitrament it lies.
> Perfect within, no outward aid require;
> And all temptation to transgress repel.
>   So saying, he arose; whom Adam thus
> Followed with benediction. 'Since to part,
> Go heavenly guest, ethereal messenger,
> Sent from whose sovereign goodness I adore.
> Gentle to me and affable hath been
> Thy condescension, and shall be honoured ever
> With grateful memory: thou to mankind
> Be good and friendly still, and oft return.'
>   So parted they, the angel up to heaven
> From the thick shade, and Adam to his bower.

                                                    VIII 630–53

All that remains is for Adam and Eve to eat the forbidden fruit
and suffer the consequences.

Yet in spite of all this, Books IX–X don't feel conclusive,
climactic or even penultimate. They feel central, pivotal, transi-
tional. One reason is that the dynamics of *PL* are more complex
than the simple calculations we began with allow. The fulcrum
of the poem doesn't necessarily coincide with its mathematical
middle, or vice-versa; we must take into account weight as well
as length, the shape and content of the plot as well as its duration.
Another reason is that the fall and condemnation of man, the
original crime and punishment, really are the crux of the story
both in the epic and in the original biblical source:

IX

Now the serpent was more subtle than any beast of the field which the
Lord God had made. And he said unto the woman, Yea, hath God said,
Ye shall not eat of every tree of the garden?

And the woman said unto the serpent, We may eat of the fruit of the
trees of the garden:

But of the fruit of the tree which is in the midst of the garden, God hath
said, Ye shall not eat of it, neither shall ye touch it, lest ye die.

And the serpent said unto the woman, Ye shall not surely die:

For God doth know that in the day ye eat thereof, then your eyes shall
be opened, and ye shall be as gods, knowing good and evil.

And when the woman saw that the tree was good for food, and that it
was pleasant to the eyes, and a tree to be desired to make one wise, she
took of the fruit thereof, and did eat, and gave also unto her husband
with her; and he did eat.

And the eyes of them both were opened, and they knew that they
were naked; and they sewed fig leaves together, and made themselves
aprons.

And they heard the voice of the Lord God walking in the garden in the cool of the day: and Adam and his wife hid themselves from the presence of the Lord God amongst the trees of the garden.

And the Lord God called unto Adam and said unto him, Where art thou?

And he said, I heard thy voice in the garden, and I was afraid, because I was naked; and I hid myself.

And he said, Who told thee that thou wast naked? Hast thou eaten of the tree whereof I commanded thee that thou shouldst not eat?

And the man said, The woman whom thou gavest to be with me, she gave me of the tree, and I did eat.

And the Lord God said unto the woman, What is this that thou hast done? And the woman said, The serpent beguiled me, and I did eat.

And the Lord God said unto the serpent, Because thou hast done this, thou art cursed above all cattle, and above every beast of the field; upon thy belly shalt thou go, and dust shalt thou eat all the days of thy life:

And I will put enmity between thee and the woman, and between thy seed and her seed; it shall bruise thy head, and thou shalt bruise his heel.

Unto the woman he said, I will greatly multiply thy sorrow and thy conception; in sorrow thou shalt bring forth children; and thy desire shall be to thy husband, and he shall rule over thee.

And unto Adam he said, Because thou hast hearkened unto the voice of thy wife, and hast eaten of the tree, of which I commanded thee, saying, Thou shalt not eat of it: cursed is the ground for thy sake; in sorrow shalt thou eat of it all the days of thy life;

Thorns also and thistles shall it bring forth to thee; and thou shalt eat the herb of the field;

In the sweat of thy face shalt thou eat bread, till thou return unto the ground; for out of it wast thou taken; for dust thou art, and unto dust shalt thou return.

And Adam called his wife's name Eve; because she was the mother of all living.

Unto Adam also and to his wife did the Lord God make coats of skins, and clothed them. *Genesis* iii 1–21

These laconic verses can be read in a number of ways – theologically as a means of reconciling the imperfection of the creation with the perfection of the creator (see commentary *p.* 24), anthropologically as a racial memory of the transition from the fruit-gathering to the crop-cultivating stage of our evolution (see topics p. 170), or psychologically as an account of the onset of sexuality (see topics p. 168) – but in every case they fulfil what Claude Lévi-Strauss and the structuralists believe to be the basic function of myth: the mediation between opposites, good and evil, forest and field, innocence and experience. Milton, who wanted to 'assert eternal providence And justify the ways of God to men' (I 25), read the story theologically. But as a poet he could not help responding to it mythically as well, so beneath the overt doctrinal meaning we can often sense other structures operating in the language, imagery and allusion. Here is a chart of some of them. It may help to suggest just how 'central, pivotal and transitional' this part of the poem really is.

	Pre-fall	Fall	Post-fall
	before – prime (IX 200, 395, 940)	then – now	after – end (X 720)
	morning – Lucifer (X 425)	noon	evening – Hesperus (IX 49)
	beginning of day		beginning of night
TIME	spring	summer	autumn
	childhood	adolescence	adulthood
	daughter	Eve	mother
	golden age	disaster	later ages
	forest – bower, enclosure	emergence	fields
	wild nature – Oreads, Dryads	technology	cultivated nature – Pales, Pomona
	raw	fire	cooked
STATE	nature – real	unpremeditated verse	art – feigned
	innocence	knowledge	experience
	sinlessness	sin	sinfulness
	immortality	forbidden fruit	mortality
	virginity – Diana	intercourse	sexuality – Venus
	erect – serpent, reason, penis	curse, abuse, orgasm	fallen – prone, powerless, flaccid

Commentary: Book IX

IX 1–47 *Prologue*

The introduction to Book IX marks a crucial turning point both in the action and in Milton's treatment of it. The other prefaces in the poem have all been prayers addressed to the 'heavenly muse' (I), 'holy light' (III), or 'Urania' (VII). This one is a manifesto addressed directly to the audience. Its abrupt conversational opening, 'No more of talk', takes us almost by surprise after the sonorous invocations we have come to expect. Book VII, for instance, began:

> Descend from heaven, Urania, by that name
> If rightly thou art called, whose voice divine
> Following, above the Olympian hill I soar,
> Above the flight of Pegaséan wing.

There is nothing so lofty in the present passage. Even when the same aspiring image appears in the final few lines the mundane idiom keeps it earthbound:

> unless an age too late, or cold
> Climate, or years damp my intended wing
> Depressed, and much they may, if all be mine,
> Not hers who brings it nightly to my ear.   44–7

This is the voice of a man speaking to men, not of 'a poet, soaring in the high regions of his fancies with his garland and singing robes about him' (*Church-gov* II 1). Throughout the entire preface the tone is colloquial and the syntax elaborately casual: phrases and clauses are loosely strung together with scarcely any main verbs to govern them. Book IX, we sense, is going to be dramatic rather than epic in conception. Milton has changed his 'notes to tragic' (6) and during the five 'acts' which follow he will observe the classical unities as strictly as any Greek playwright. Here he is delivering the prologue.

   The prologue to a play, however, is usually retrospective; it tells us what took place before the curtain rises. The prologue to Book IX of *PL* is prospective; it tells us what is going to take place from now on. The opening few lines, it is true, look back for a moment at man's brief experience of innocence, but only to emphasize the physical and spiritual solitude his disobedience will bring with it. By eating the forbidden fruit instead of the 'rural repast' of Eden's other trees Adam will break off for ever the 'venial discourse' (4–5) he once enjoyed with his heavenly visitors (see V–VIII). The voice of God or angel will come now to rebuke, sentence, and finally expel him from the happy garden. The first two words, 'No more', state the theme of the whole book.

Like all good manifestoes, then, the introduction to Book IX announces a revolution: the only main verb in the first 42 lines is 'change'. And not just Adam's. Milton promises to revolutionize our idea of heroic action. The just anger of the Christian God, he claims, is 'not less but more heroic' (14) than the tantrums of the pagan gods and heroes celebrated in classical epic – so in a sense the theme of the whole book is also going to be 'more'. The episodes cited certainly don't reflect any great credit on the characters involved in them. As Aristotle noticed, Achilles' pursuit of Hector 'about Troy wall' (16) in Homer's *Iliad* verges on the ludicrous, while Turnus' rage when Aeneas stole his bride-to-be, Lavinia, in Virgil's *Aeneid* served only to bring about his own death. Neptune's persecution of Odysseus in Homer's *Odyssey* may have been justified by the Greeks' desecration of his temple during the siege of Troy, but Odysseus reached home in spite of it. Juno's hatred of Aeneas, on the other hand, was based on little more than pique because she lost a celestial beauty contest with his mother, Venus (see *PL* V 381). The conclusion we are supposed to draw is clear. The wrath of Milton's God is neither vain nor implacable. He does not destroy or perplex his enemies; he judges and ultimately forgives them.

The terms of the pagan side of the comparison are so carefully structured, however, that they invite us to consider other parallels as well. The diagram opposite suggests some of the possibilities. Two particularly interesting points emerge from this analysis. First, the allusion to Turnus is the odd man out in the pattern. After the reference to Achilles, the protagonist of the *Iliad*, we expect a balancing reference to Aeneas, the protagonist of the *Aeneid*. Instead we encounter Turnus, the antagonist, in the equivalent position to Achilles. Aeneas is present by implication only, as the un-named object of Turnus' rage. What is more, all the other objects of rage are identified, 'his foe', 'the Greek' and 'Cytherea's son'. Turnus' enemy is not, and we sense the omission.

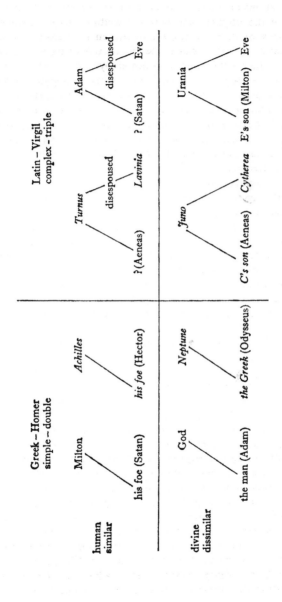

Greek – Homer
simple – double

Latin – Virgil
complex – triple

human similar

Milton
his foe (Satan)

Achilles
his foe (Hector)

Turnus
disespoused
?(Aeneas)

Lavinia

Adam
disespoused
? (Satan)

Eve

divine dissimilar

God
the man (Adam)

Neptune
the Greek (Odysseus)

Juno
C's son (Aeneas)

Cytherea

Urania
E's son (Milton)

Eve

Why do you think Milton violated the otherwise perfect symmetry of the structure in this one instance? Are we intended to wonder, perhaps, at whom Adam's rage 'for Eve disespoused' should be directed? Or does Milton want us to question the true status of Aeneas in Virgil's epic, and hence the meaning of the frequent allusions to him in *PL* (see 1001n)? This brings us to the second point. The character equations created by the parallels uncover ambiguities in all the major characters. Adam, for example, is related to both a villain, Turnus, and a hero, Odysseus; Eve to both a wife, Lavinia, and a mother, Cytherea (see topics, p. 174); Satan to both a victor, Aeneas, and a victim, Hector. Only Milton is related to two heroes, Achilles and Aeneas.

Having put Homer and Virgil in their place, Milton goes on in lines 27–41 to dispose of a more recent species of epic, the medieval and renaissance chivalric romance, which in the 17th century also came under the general heading of 'heroic' poetry – at one time Milton had considered writing one himself (see 26n). Their stories, to begin with, were secular fiction, 'fabled knights In battles feigned' (30); his is scriptural fact. They described war and carnage, 'races and games' (33); he portrays 'the better fortitude Of patience and heroic martyrdom' (31). They delighted in the outward luxury of courtly ceremony; he reveals the inner simplicity of the Christian life. His theme is 'higher' (42) in true value.

These attacks on false heroism define the real thing largely by implication. Milton is content to ridicule his rivals and let the reader draw his own conclusions. As a result the dominant impression is negative: 'not less...heroic', 'not sedulous', 'not that which' (14, 27, 40). The corresponding positives are only hinted at: 'more heroic', 'better fortitude', 'higher argument' (14, 31, 42). We learn more about what Milton is not going to do than about what he is going to do. With one all-important exception: the role he plays in the contest. For the writing of an epic poem is itself a heroic venture (see topics p. 154), and no one is more aware of this than Milton. So in lines 20–6 he invites us to compare his relationship to his 'celestial patroness' (21) with that of Odysseus and Aeneas to Neptune and Juno. Where they were 'perplexed' (19) he is inspired; indeed he claims to be no more than his muse's secretary, taking down by dictation the words she whispers to him while he sleeps. After the fall man may not be able to converse directly with the inhabitants of heaven but he can at least hear their voices.

It is this thought that consoles him in lines 41–7 when he pits himself against the heroes he has just repudiated. Unlike them he lives in a relatively late age in the history of the world; unlike them he lives in a cold northern climate; unlike them he is no longer in his prime. But one final difference outweighs all the others: unlike them he is guided by the sacred muse, eternally vigorous. She will give him the strength to see his quest through to its conclusion. So after pausing to reflect on the nature and magnitude of his subject, he draws in his breath for the final burst of creativity which will carry him through to the end of Book XII.

IX 48–191 *Satan*

Argument. Satan having compassed the earth, with meditated guile returns as a mist by night into paradise, enters into the serpent sleeping.

One of the major issues at stake in Satan's rebellion against God in Book V was his claim that he was self-created. He was, of course, nothing of the kind, either literally or literarily. Literally, God made him. Literarily, he was bred by a misinterpretation out of a misunderstanding. For his namesake in the *OT* was simply a kind of celestial district attorney, responsible for seeking out and prosecuting human weakness (e.g. *Job*). The proud antagonist of omnipotence is the offspring of a quite separate tradition, based on Isaiah's prophecy of the downfall of Babylon:

How art thou fallen from heaven, O Lucifer, son of the morning! how art thou cut down to the ground, which didst weaken the nations!

For thou has said in thine heart, I will ascend into heaven, I will exalt my throne above the stars of God: I will sit also upon the mount of the congregation in the sides of the north:

I will ascend above the heights of the clouds; I will be like the Most High.

Yet thou shalt be brought down to hell, to the sides of the pit.

xiv 12–15

Originally this was an astral myth about the disappearance of the morning star, Venus, at daybreak (see 49n), but by the 1st century AD it was being interpreted as an account of the Devil's attempt to overthrow the hierarchy of heaven and by the end of the 3rd century it had been combined with the following passage from *Ezekiel* to produce the legend of the beautiful angel corrupted by ambition:

Thou art the anointed cherub that covereth; and I have set thee so; thou wast upon the holy mountain of God; thou hast walked up and down in the midst of the stones of fire.

> Thou wast perfect in thy ways from the day that thou wast created, till
> iniquity was found in thee...
>
> Thine heart was lifted up because of thy beauty; thou hast corrupted
> thy wisdom by reason of thy brightness: I will cast thee to the ground, I
> will lay thee before kings, that they may behold thee.   xxviii 14–17

As a result, the figure Milton inherited as the villain of *PL* has
two very different aspects. As Lucifer he is arrogant, daring,
magniloquent, charismatic – a hero. As Satan he is cunning,
devious, sophistical, persuasive – a tempter. In Books I–II he is
almost pure Lucifer. Here in Book IX, however, he is almost pure
Satan. The proud warrior who had dared all the powers of heaven
and hell now re-enters the poem as a furtive intruder, slipping into
Eden under cover of darkness and immediately looking for a
disguise to hide in. C. S. Lewis believes that this change should
be interpreted morally as a continuation of the Devil's fall (*A
preface to PL* 1942 repr 1960 pp. 99–100), but we should also
remember that the pattern Lewis traces was already built into the
Devil's character; the fact that the rebel became a seducer came to
Milton as one of the givens of the story.

So did the fact that the seducer chose to disguise himself as a
snake. In *Genesis* itself there is no suggestion that the serpent was
anything other than it seemed. Why it wanted man to eat of the
tree of knowledge is never explained, though when the myth was
first written down in the 9th or 10th century BC no explanation
may have been needed. For in the ancient Near East snakes were
regarded with an uneasy mixture of fear and reverence (see also
topics p. 158). On the one hand they were often poisonous; on the
other they appeared to be immortal, shedding their skins every
spring. The combination suggested that they were semi-divine
beings, and the subtle serpent of *Genesis* may simply have been
a rival of Jehovah's. But when in the 1st century AD it was
associated with the figure of Lucifer–Satan the question of its
identity and motive took on a completely different aspect. In St
Augustine's words:

This Lucifer, striving to insinuate his sly seductions into the minds of
man whose fidelity he envied, since he himself had fallen, chose for his
spokesman a serpent in the terrestrial paradise, where all the animals of
earth were living in harmless subjection to Adam and Eve. It was suited
for the task because it was a slimy and slippery beast that could slither
and twist on its tortuous way. So, subjecting it to his diabolical design
by the powerful presence of his angelic nature and misusing it as his
instrument, he, at first, parleyed cunningly with the woman as with the
weaker part of that human society, hoping gradually to gain the whole.
City of God xiv 11 tr Gerald G. Walsh *et al* 1958 repr 1962.

The only remaining problem was why the devil bothered to use a
disguise at all. Why not accost Eve in his own person? Because, the
theologians reasoned, his appearance would have frightened her.
Milton, however, was still not satisfied. With his ability to change
shape at will the devil could have taken the form of any of the
animals in Eden. Why, then, did he choose the serpent? St
Augustine's answer quoted above is a moralist's. Milton's is a
poet's:

> for in the wily snake
> Whatever sleights none would suspicious mark,
> As from his wit and native subtlety
> Proceeding, which in other beasts observed
> Doubt might beget of diabolic power
> Active within beyond the sense of brute.
>
> IX 91–6, but see X 867–72

The tempter's strategy is conceived from the inside out rather
than vice-versa.

Nevertheless Satan has serious misgivings about degrading
himself in this way. He is descending two steps in the chain of
being, from superhuman angel to subhuman animal:

> O foul descent! that I who erst contended
> With gods to sit the highest, am now constrained
> Into a beast, and mixed with bestial slime,
> This essence to incarnate and imbrute,
> That to the heighth of deity aspired. IX 163–7

Richard Bentley, the editor of the 1732 edition of *PL*, objected
to 'incarnate': 'Milton would not use thus the word *incarnate*;
he knew a higher essence, than seraphical, was afterwards
incarnated.' But that is exactly Milton's point, as a contemporary
American poet, Helen Pinkerton, has seen:

> Satan in Eden was 'constrain'd
> Into a beast'.
> All of the proud, like him, are pained
> And you not least,
> To wear the flesh of which we all are made.
>
> It was a means for him and Christ.
> Shrewder than we,
> Each knew for what he sacrificed.
> Carnality
> Destroys when not accepted and allayed.
>
> *Error pursued* Iowa City 1959

As the tempter in *PL* becomes 'incarnate' in order to corrupt man
we are thus reminded that Christ will become incarnate in order

to save him. The prelude to the fall parodies the first stage of the redemption.

Before insinuating himself into the reptile Satan pauses for a moment to look around him. It is the first time we have heard him soliloquize since Book IV, when he had contemplated the beauty of Eden and the innocence of his future victims. Here too he offers a poignant tribute to God's handiwork. But as he describes the universe (see below p. 48 and topics p. 183), and analyses the chain of 'gradual life' (112) extending upwards from the vegetable and the animal to the human, his perversity begins to assert itself. For the basis of his eulogy is the inferiority of heaven to earth. God, he assumes, learns by experience like one of his creatures; so the world, having been built with 'second thoughts' (101), must be an improvement on the older model above it. This principle turns the natural hierarchy upside down: men, in this case, would be superior to angels, the angels superior to God. Satan has invented the value system that prizes novelty above all else.

A second, more fundamental perversity emerges shortly afterwards. Having declared in an earlier soliloquy 'Evil be thou my good' (IV 110), Satan discovers that he is compelled to accept the converse: good be thou my evil. As a result the delights of Eden bring him nothing but anguish (119–23). He has become the prisoner of his own slogans, and as he speaks his awareness of the orderly perfection of the creation is transformed into an intense compulsion to destroy it. Like the villains of renaissance tragedy, of whom he is both the successor and the prototype (see topics p. 157), he must corrupt what he cannot possess (124–30).

Here if anywhere in the poem Milton plumbs the depths of the Satanic dilemma, for in this passage the Devil reveals the most terrible irony of all: evil is not just destructive, it is self-destructive. So his quest to bring misery on mankind also involves bringing further misery on himself (171–3). There is a kind of twisted altruism in this admission, 'the religious passion in reverse' as W. H. Auden calls it (*The enchafèd flood* 1951). The saint does good not for any benefit it will bring him but simply because it is good. The Devil does evil not for the sake of any relief it will bring him but simply because it is evil. The possibility of 'mastering heaven's supreme' (125) is a hollow echo of the Luciferan boasts we heard in Books I–II, mentioned in a despairing parenthesis more for the sake of form than anything else. The real motive now is not hope but naked self-consuming hatred.

The rest of the speech consists of a series of attempts to explain it away, as if Satan were unable to face his own desperation for more than a moment. First he seeks consolation in the 'glory' (135) he will win in hell for destroying in one day what it took God six days to create. This in turn reminds him that the creation cancelled out his earlier feat of persuading his followers to revolt (see 141n) and here he finds a plausible excuse for his assault on man. Since God made Adam and Eve to replace the fallen angels, what more reasonable than to prevent these earth-born upstarts from occupying 'our room' (148)? At last he has found a motive which will conceal from him the hideous truth he glimpsed at the beginning of his speech (see topics p. 157). Now he can brush aside despair and concentrate all his energy on his envy of 'this new favourite Of heaven' (175). For the first time in the poem, man is the direct object of Satan's hatred, and his speech ends in a protracted hiss of spite.

But Milton hasn't finished with Satan yet. As the Devil enters the serpent a final irony emerges:

> in at his mouth
> The Devil entered, and his brutal sense,
> In heart or head, possessing soon inspired
> With act intelligential; but his sleep
> Disturbed not, waiting close the approach of morn.
>
> 187–91

Coming to these lines fresh from Milton's account of how the divine muse inspired him during the night, dictating to him the words he would recite next morning to his secretary, we are again reminded of the contrast between Satan's destructiveness and God's creativity. A poet possessed by the Holy Spirit is an apt commentator on a snake possessed by the Devil.

IX 192–411 *Adam and Eve*

Argument. Adam and Eve in the morning go forth to their labours, which Eve proposes to divide in several places, each labouring apart: Adam consents not, alleging the danger, lest that enemy, of whom they were forewarned, should attempt her found alone: Eve loath to be thought not circumspect or firm enough, urges her going apart, the rather desirous to make trial of her strength; Adam at last yields.

Life and energy come flooding back into the poem as the dawn of 'sacred light' (192) dispels the 'midnight vapour' (159) of the previous scene. Satan's 'dark intent' (162) gives way to the 'silent praise' (195) of nature's choir, his 'black mist low creeping' (180) to the 'morning incense' (194) of the flowers. For it is 'prime' (200), the canonical hour, and the morning service is in progress in God's cathedral (surprisingly, it sounds like a Catholic one). The priests who lead it with their 'vocal worship' (198) are Adam and Eve. Milton doesn't tell us what words they are singing, but he has no need to; we have already heard their orisons in VI 53–208. Then they had proceeded to their 'rural work' (V 211) together. Now they are going to divide their labour, and themselves.

No reason is given in *Genesis* for Adam's absence during his wife's temptation, so Milton has to invent one. This is not as easy as it sounds. He can't, for instance, let Eve wander off on her own quite by chance. If she and Adam are to be responsible for the fall they must also be responsible for the conditions which made it possible. The kind of misfortune which led to the deaths of Romeo and Juliet has no place in paradise (see topics p. 153). Satan may think he finds Eve alone by 'hap' (421) but Milton impresses on us that it is nothing of the kind. By prefacing the temptation with a long debate about the dangers of working apart he ensures that Adam and Eve decide to do so only when they have considered all the relevant facts. Neither of them can plead later that the fall was the result of sheer bad luck.

What they can plead, and do, is that it was all the other's fault. Adam blames Eve for the 'strange Desire of wandering' (1135) which came over her; she blames him for not being 'firm and fixed' (1160) enough in his dissent. Both are right, for as Milton no doubt knew from his own considerable experience in these matters, it is a rare marital dispute in which either partner is wholly blameless or at fault. The first pair, we should remember, are not just the father and mother of the human race; they are its prototypes. More particularly, their marriage is the prototype of all future marriages – hence Adam's bitter predictions in X 898–908. If the present scene works properly, then, we should feel we are overhearing the paradigm of every squabble between husband and wife that has taken place since.

It works brilliantly. The dramatists of the restoration were masters of this kind of domestic sparring, but few of them rendered its cuts and thrusts as vividly as Milton does here. Despite their formality the speeches sound as if they had been written for the stage. The narrative commentary is scarcely necessary. We can hear the 'sweet austere composure' (272) of

Eve's second speech, for instance, in the carefully controlled structure of her opening sentence, just as we can hear the resentment beneath it emerging in the clumsy construction of the next one, then taking over completely in the nagging word-play and grammatical confusion of the last few lines (see 282n, 285n, 288n). A little later on we would know without being told so that Adam is speaking 'fervently' (342) from his abrupt form of address (see 342n), his curt syntax, and his sinewy argument, so unlike the flat moralizing of his first 'mild' (226) speech. Each change of mood is reflected by a corresponding shift in the style. As the prologue has suggested it would be, the entire conception is dramatic.

The arguments themselves revolve around the central question in any marriage: the relationship between the sexes. And although our knowledge of the outcome might incline us to take Adam's side at the outset, as the debate continues it becomes increasingly difficult to take sides at all. Eve's initial proposal for increasing their productivity seems perfectly sensible, for example, yet it contains within it an implicit criticism of her conduct from this point onwards. The language she uses in 205–12 echoes Adam's advice in Book IV:

> With first approach of light, we must be risen,
> And at our *pleasant labour*, to reform
> Yon flowery arbours, yonder alleys green,
> Our walk at noon, with branches *overgrown*,
> That *mock* our scant manuring, and require
> *More hands* than ours to lop their *wanton growth*.
>
> IV 624–9 (my italics)

The point of the parallel – with Milton's parallels there is always a point – is that Eve had then replied:

> Unargued I obey; so God ordains,
> God is thy law, thou mine: to know no more
> Is woman's happiest knowledge and her praise.   IV 636–8

Here in Book IX she will no longer be content to obey 'unargued'. On the contrary, she will insist on her independence, moral and intellectual, seeking her 'happiest knowledge and her praise' in her own unaided ability to resist temptation.

But what, we may ask, is wrong with that? When, in her penultimate speech, she observes that their virtue is suspect if it cannot stand alone, she is only repeating what Milton himself had said in *Areopagitica*:

I cannot praise a fugitive and cloistered virtue, unexercised and unbreathed, that never sallies out and sees her adversary, but slinks out of the race, where that immortal garland is to be run for, not without dust and heat.

Adam, surely, is being over-protective in wanting to keep his wife by his side, and Eve is quite right to demand a chance to put her virtue to the test by sallying out to see the adversary. As she asks:

> what is faith, love, virtue unassayed
> Alone, without exterior help sustained? 335–6

This is a very difficult case to answer in terms of modern assumptions. Believing as we do in sexual democracy we are not unduly disturbed that Eve should sound like a suffragette claiming equal rights for women. Milton, however, was not a sexual democrat, and from the moment he first introduced them he has been reminding us that Adam and Eve are:

> Not equal, as their sex not equal seemed;
> For contemplation he and valour formed,
> For softness she and sweet attractive grace,
> He for God only, she for God in him. IV 296–9

With the possible exception of Shakespeare, who very often makes his heroines morally and intellectually superior to his heroes, almost every writer in the 16th and 17th centuries would have agreed, in theory if not in practice. Even Shakespeare gave Katherina the following speech of advice to her fellow wives at the end of *The taming of the shrew*:

> Thy husband is thy lord, thy life, thy keeper,
> Thy head, thy sovereign...
> Such duty as the subject owes the prince
> Even such a woman oweth to her husband;
> And when she is froward, peevish, sullen sour,
> And not obedient to her husband's will,
> What is she but a foul contending rebel
> And graceless traitor to her loving lord? v ii 146–60

Outside marriage the situation was altogether different. As the heirs of the courtly love tradition, the poets of the renaissance continued to extol their mistresses in terms which implied exactly the opposite kind of relationship to the one Katherina describes: woman was the queen, man the loyal and adoring servant. But woe betide the mistress who expected the same treatment when she became a wife, for as soon as the wedding took place St Paul's dictum came into effect: 'the head of the woman is the man'. Only a handful of poems written in this period celebrate the love of husband for wife – Spenser's *Epithalamion* and Donne's

Valediction forbidding mourning are perhaps the most famous examples. The vast majority still preserve the feudal assumption that romance is by definition extra-marital.

So when Eve takes umbrage at the mere suggestion that she is Adam's inferior, a 17th-century reader would have realized at once that something is wrong. She is beginning to get above herself, and it is Adam's clear duty to remind her of her place. The reason he doesn't, and the reason we find it so difficult to be sorry he doesn't, is that his feelings for her are more like a lover's than a husband's (see 310n). In Book VIII he told Raphael that:

> All higher knowledge in her presence falls
> Degraded, wisdom in discourse with her
> Looses discountenanced, and like folly shows;
> Authority and reason on her wait,
> As one intended first, not after made
> Occasionally; and to consummate all,
> Greatness of mind and nobleness their seat
> Build in her loveliest, and create an awe
> About her, as a guard angelic placed.   VIII 551–9

No courtly poet praised his mistress more extravagantly. As a result he cannot bring himself to assert his authority here in Book IX without spoiling the effect by letting her have her own way in any case. As she leaves him, accompanied by his 'ardent look' (397) and the poet's helpless prophecies of doom, she may still be technically 'sinless' (659), for he has given his 'permission' (378), but Milton has made it clear that both in their different ways have failed.

IX 412–838 *The fall of Eve*

Argument. The serpent finds her alone; his subtle approach, first gazing, then speaking, with much flattery extolling Eve above all other creatures. Eve wondering to hear the serpent speak, asks how he attained to human speech and such understanding not till now; the serpent answers, that by tasting of a certain tree in the garden he attained both to speech and reason, till then void of both: Eve requires him to bring her to that tree, and finds it to be the tree of knowledge forbidden: the serpent now grown bolder, with many wiles and arguments induces her at length to eat; she pleased with the taste deliberates awhile whether to import thereof to Adam or not...

Genesis does not mention a 'fall' as such, and the unknown author who first wrote down the story of Adam and Eve in the 9th or 10th century BC would probably have been surprised by the doctrine that was read into it a thousand years later. The word itself denotes some kind of descent, either literal, like Satan's drop from heaven to hell, or metaphorical, like the ruin of a tragic hero (see topics p. 152). Most *OT* scholars are agreed, however, that the original myth was intended to describe exactly the opposite process – the ascent of primitive man from ignorance to knowledge (see topics p. 171). The serpent was another Prometheus; Jehovah another Zeus, determined to prevent his creatures from becoming like him; the tree of knowledge another symbol of the arts of civilization. But the divine fire could burn man as well as warm him. 'In much wisdom' wrote Ecclesiastes 'is much grief: and he that increaseth knowledge increaseth sorrow' (i 18). Thus while Adam was still a child he had a child's innocence of his own nakedness. When his eyes were opened, adult awareness made him ashamed of his genitals, and his first invention was the skirt of fig-leaves. Like Wordsworth's *Ode on intimations of immortality* the third chapter of *Genesis* is about growing up with all its ambiguities and anxieties (see topics p. 168).

Thanks largely to the influence of St Paul, Christian theologians interpreted the story very differently. They found in it the explanation not of human science but of human wickedness. The disobedience of Adam and Eve was what Milton calls the 'mortal sin Original' (1003), mortal because it was committed by men and made them liable to death, original because it was the source of all subsequent sins. For the first pair contained within them 'the whole included race' (416), and when they fell all their descendants fell with them:

For we all existed in that one man, since, taken together, we were the one man who fell into sin through the woman who was made out of him before sin existed. Although the specific form by which each of us was to live was not yet created and assigned, our nature was already present in the seed from which we were to spring. And because this nature has been soiled by sin and doomed to death and justly condemned, no man was to be born of man in any other condition.   St Augustine *City of God* xiii 14

It was the violation of the tree of knowledge in the garden of Eden, then, that made necessary Christ's sacrifice on the tree of Calvary. In St Paul's words:

For as by one man's disobedience many were made sinners, so by the obedience of one shall many be made righteous. *Romans* v 19; cf. *PR* I 1

For since by man came death, by man came also the resurrection of the dead.
For as in Adam all die, even so in Christ shall all be made alive.
I Corinthians xv 21

This second version of the myth with its more idealistic view of God and man raises many problems in the interpretation of the rest of the story, but none is more tricky than that posed by the tree of knowledge. Milton's Satan sees the difficulty immediately:

> One fatal tree there stands of knowledge called,
> Forbidden them to taste: knowledge forbidden?
> Suspicious, reasonless. Why should their Lord
> Envy them that? Can it be sin to know,
> Can it be death? And do they only stand
> By ignorance, is that their happy state,
> The proof of their obedience and their faith?   IV 514–20

The answer was provided by St Augustine, who explained that the forbidden tree was called the tree of the knowledge of good and evil, 'to signify by this name the consequence of their discovering both what good they would experience if they kept the prohibition and what evil if they transgressed it' (*On the merits and forgiveness of sins* ii 35 tr M. Dods 1871). The fruit had no supernatural properties of any kind; it conferred neither scientific nor moral knowledge, and the only reason God forbade man to eat of it was to show him the need for obedience. This is Milton's position in *PL*. In Adam's words, the tree is just the 'sign of our obedience' (IV 428) and the only kind of knowledge it offers is of 'good lost and evil got' (IX 1072). Satan, as usual, has misunderstood God's intentions.

These two opposing definitions of innocence, and thus of God, man, and the forbidden tree, clash head on as the serpent tempts Eve here in Book IX. Indeed the whole scene hinges on which definition she will choose to believe. Milton himself, of course, is deeply committed to the 'descent' theory. Satan, who has to pretend that the 'fall' is no such thing, naturally opts for the older 'ascent' theory with its emphasis on man's primitive condition, God's envious nature, and the tree's 'sciential' (837) powers. The last point is the key to the others. If he can persuade Eve that the apple is not just a moral barometer but a magic potion which will change her into a goddess, then the rest should be easy. Everything depends on convincing her that there is more to the fruit than Adam told her.

As it turns out, his disguise is what does the trick, though not in the way he had planned. His original motive for hiding in the serpent was to avoid rousing Eve's suspicion; she would attribute any 'sleights' (92) she noticed to the serpent's subtlety, or so he hoped. In fact her very first reaction is to question how even a snake can talk (553–7). This is a critical moment for Satan. He clearly hadn't anticipated such a response, and his carefully planned strategy seems to have broken down during its first test. But he has always been a better tactician than strategist, and he meets the crisis with a brilliant piece of improvisation. The fruit of 'a goodly tree far distant' (576), he tells her, gave him the ability to both think and speak. Subsequently it proves to be the tree of knowledge, but Satan is too clever to name it just yet. First he wants to build up Eve's anticipation. When she realizes later that the magic tree is the only one in the garden which she is not allowed to taste she will be bitterly disappointed, and his arguments for ignoring the prohibition will sound all the more convincing to her. Like a good salesman, he doesn't mention the price until his customer is really interested in buying.

The claim that the forbidden fruit made him semi-human is the basis of Satan's entire case for eating it. It gives Eve apparent proof of the tree's potency, it suggests the possibility of undergoing 'proportional ascent' (936) herself, and it allows him to prepare the ground for his second lie: man's alleged state of deprivation. For the contemptuous references to the 'rude' (544), 'low' (572) beasts who couldn't reach the fruit imply long before Satan actually says so that Adam and Eve are also 'low and ignorant' (704). The apple becomes a 'cure' (776).

His flattery is designed to have the same effect. The earlier 'town and country' simile has already established him as a London beau leering at an innocent village girl (see topics p. 166), and now he begins to court her with all the hyperbole of a renaissance love poet. Her looks are a 'heaven' (534), her beauty is 'celestial' (540) and she herself should be 'a goddess among gods, adored and served By angels numberless' (547). Eating the forbidden fruit served only to heighten his appreciation of her (603–9). These lines sum up a whole tradition of love poetry, from Sidney's courtly sonnets to Donne's idolatrous songs and Marvell's plaints to his coy mistress. The reluctant wife of the previous scene has got her wish: now that she is free of her husband – Satan dismisses him in a parenthesis (546) – she really is being treated as a mistress.

Like the 'cruel and fair' lady of that tradition (see IV 769–70), however, she rejects her suitor's compliments (615). Satan, it appears, has miscalculated by laying it on too thick. But this is just the point: call a corporal 'sir' for long enough and he will begin to wonder why he hasn't been made an officer. Satan knows exactly what he is doing here, and his 'overpraising' is quite deliberate. Indeed, coming directly after what Eve considered to be Adam's underpraising, it is doubly effective. By the time she arrives at the forbidden tree she is feeling thoroughly badly done by. It is only at this stage that the temptation begins in *Genesis*:

> Now the serpent was more subtle than any beast of the field which the Lord God had made. And he said unto the woman, Yea hath God said, Ye shall not eat of every tree of the garden?
> And the woman said unto the serpent, We may eat of the fruit of the trees of the garden;
> But of the fruit of the tree which is in the midst of the garden, God hath said, Ye shall not eat of it, neither shall ye touch it, lest ye die.
>
> iii 1–3

We can measure the effectiveness of Satan's non-biblical prologue by the fact that when he and Eve repeat these words almost verbatim (see 656n, 661n) in *PL*, they sound quite different. Satan asks his question in mock-surprise, rubbing salt in the wound with his addition, 'Yet lords declared of all in earth or air?' (658), and the disappointment in Eve's voice as she replies is almost audible. The battle is already half over. All that remains is to take advantage of her disgruntlement by offering her some plausible reasons for doing what she wants to.

As Satan proceeds to do so the mood shifts from romantic to epic. The ardent lover of the first part of the scene turns into an indignant orator, another Demosthenes urging the Athenians to stand up for their liberty. The God of Christianity becomes the 'gods' of classical mythology (see 708n), providence is replaced by 'fate' (see 689n), and 'virtue' reverts to its pagan sense of courage (see 694n). Eve is being given a chance to fulfil the pseudo-heroic ambitions she revealed in her earlier tiff with Adam – not by resisting temptation but by giving in to it.

In classical epic, however, heroism is a male prerogative. The women – Helen, Penelope, Dido, Lavinia – are either temptresses or victims. It is the men – Achilles, Odysseus, Aeneas – who defy the 'ire' (18, 692) of the envious gods. As the word 'virtue' implies (694), Eve is being invited to betray her own nature. Satan is too good a psychologist to be unaware of this, and throughout his speech he simultaneously provides her with arguments which appeal to the less militant aspects of her character. Eating the fruit is a 'petty trespass' (693) as well as an act of 'dauntless virtue' (694); it will lead to 'happier life' (697) as well as the 'pain Of death denounced' (694); the gods will

27

'praise' (693) as well as 'envy' (729) her; and she will prove her valour by defying a threat which is really empty. In short, she can be a heroine without taking any risks. Eve by this time is too excited and confused to notice the glaring contradictions in Satan's reasoning, but she still has to talk herself into taking his advice. Her hesitance is conveyed by the structure of the verse itself, a slow crescendo of question and answer which brings her closer to the tree with every cycle. She reaches out her 'rash hand' – or it reaches out of its own accord (see 780n) – only when she has convinced herself that there is nothing to be afraid of.

At this juncture another interpretation of the tree of knowledge makes its impact on the scene. Rabbinical commentators had suggested that the forbidden tree may have been a vine, and as Eve eats of it here she grows 'heightened as with wine' (793). Tipsily she promises to worship it each morning, pretends God hasn't even seen her taste it, and then pauses to savour her superiority to Adam (817–21). But the possibility that God really has seen her eat the fruit brings her up short. If he carries out the threat of death then Adam might live on to marry 'another Eve' (828). That must be prevented at all costs; if she is to die, Adam must die with her:

> So dear I love him, that with him all deaths
> I could endure, without him live no life. 832

The double-think of this final couplet (see 833n) is worthy of Satan. She loves her husband so dearly that she is going to kill him. She makes it sound, of course, as if Adam is in danger of death and she is nobly deciding to sacrifice herself with him. Yet as she has just admitted, there is no question of her living on 'without him'. What she is determined to forestall is the possibility of his living on without her. Her real motives have been turned inside out, and as she goes off to meet Adam it is as if a new character had suddenly entered the poem. In the contest between the myth and the doctrine of the 'fall' which has been going on throughout the scene the doctrine has the final word.

IX 838–999 *The fall of Adam*

Argument...[Eve] at last brings him of the fruit, relates what persuaded her to eat thereof: Adam at first amazed, but perceiving her lost, resolves through vehemence of love to perish with her; and extenuating the trespass eats also of the fruit.

It was 'by one man's disobedience', wrote St Paul, that 'many were made sinners' (*Romans* v 19), not one woman's. The fall of Adam, therefore, must have been even graver than the fall of Eve. Milton's problem was that in *Genesis* the fall of Eve comes first, and is treated in far greater detail. At this point of the story he had to describe a second act of disobedience without letting it seem either repetitious or anti-climactic. His solution to the problem also derives from St Paul:

> I suffer not a woman to teach, nor to usurp authority over the man but to be in silence.
> For Adam was first formed, then Eve.
> And Adam was not deceived, but the woman being deceived was in the transgression.   *I Timothy* ii 12–14

Ironically enough this passage appears to prove just the opposite of what Milton needed. Eve, it implies, was really to blame, for it was she who succumbed to the wiles of the tempter. But as St Augustine realized, these verses could bear another interpretation:

> So, too, we must believe that Adam transgressed the law of God, not because he was deceived into believing that the lie was true, but because in obedience to a social compulsion he yielded to Eve, as husband to wife, as the only man in the world to the only woman. It was not without reason that the Apostle wrote: 'Adam was not deceived but the woman was deceived.' He means, no doubt, that Eve accepted the serpent's word as true, whereas Adam refused to be separated from his partner even in a union of sin – not, of course, that he was, on that account, any less guilty, since he sinned knowingly and deliberately. That is why the Apostle does not say: 'He did not sin' but 'he was not deceived.'... The distinction is here made between those who, like Adam, sin with full knowledge and those who are deceived because they do not know that what they are doing is a sin. It is this distinction which gives meaning to the statement: 'Adam was not deceived.'   *City of God* xiv 11

Thus Milton insists that Adam is 'in the transgression' precisely because he is 'not deceived' (998), because he sins with his eyes open. His wife was 'by some fair appearing good surprised' (354), as he had warned her she might be, but he willingly chooses what he knows to be evil. Her failure was primarily intellectual; his is moral.

Not that Eve doesn't try to deceive him. The tree of knowledge, she declares excitedly, is not deadly after all. Its fruit has made her divine (877–85). After her soliloquy in the previous scene the bland hypocrisy of this speech is only too obvious. Far from despising godhead 'unshared' with Adam, she intended to 'keep the odds of knowledge in my power Without copartner' (820);

far from seeking to avoid 'different degree', she welcomed the chance of becoming 'sometime Superior' (824); and far from wanting to make her husband divine, she decided to ensure his mortality. For the first time in the poem their discourse has been contaminated with lies.

Adam, however, is 'not deceived'. He totally ignores her assurances that the forbidden fruit is harmless, and responds instead to the fears which had been running through her mind before they met. She had been preoccupied by the thought of his living on with 'another Eve' (828); he rejects the idea out of hand (911–13). She had resolved to make him die with her; he voluntarily agrees to do so (906–10). It is almost as if he had read her thoughts.

Adam, then, eats the apple not out of pride or ambition but, as the Argument states, out of love. Naturally we find it hard to disapprove of Adam's decision, but Milton doesn't necessarily want us to, at least not yet. On the contrary his whole strategy depends on our complicity with Adam, first because Adam is our prototype, and second because according to the doctrine of original sin the entire human race was involved in the fall (see above p. 24). The moment we applaud Adam's action we are directly implicated in it ourselves. Eve tempts us all.

As a result, Milton's sneer about Adam's being 'fondly over-come by female charm' (999) shocks us. It is meant to. By challenging our response to what we have just read it forces us to look back and wonder whether in fact we haven't been taken in. If the strategy has been successful we should not only participate in Adam's disobedience; we should be willing to regret it in retrospect. What allows us to do so is Eve's murderous soliloquy and her deceitful speech immediately afterwards. It is one thing for a husband to choose to die with his wife rather than live on with another woman; it is quite another for him to make this choice for the sake of a wife who has already made up her mind that he isn't going to survive anyway. Adam no doubt acts out of love when he decides to die with Eve, but the Eve he loves is already dead: Satan has 'disespoused' him. The woman who threatens that unless he eats the fruit he will soon find himself a mere human married to a goddess is herself 'another Eve'.

Up to this point Adam has broken only his 'inward silence' (895). Now that he has made up his mind what to do he is ready to talk aloud. By this time Eve must be feeling rather uneasy, so he hastens to reassure her by accepting all the arguments she has just used. He pretends, and we have heard enough to know it really is a pretence, that the fruit may indeed raise them both to godhead and that God may indeed let their trespass go unpunished. In a desperate attempt at jocularity he even makes up a little speech for the Devil. It has the authentic Satanic ring (948–50). God, he concludes, must let them live on in order to save face. But no sooner has he said this than he gives the game away by allowing his true motive for eating the fruit to emerge (952–4). The feelings he revealed in his 'soliloquy' are too powerful to be suppressed for long, and in the final lines of this speech they rise back to the surface in a great paean of love.

Eve jubilantly accepts his sacrifice for what it is, even though this involves admitting that they are united in 'one guilt, one crime' (971). Realizing her slip, she quickly covers it up with a qualification (see 972n) and goes on to crown her earlier lies with the most blatant of all (977–81). If there were still any doubt in our minds about the effect of the fruit these lines would remove it for good. Eve has become the type of all those evil temptresses of epic and romance who offer their victims a poisoned cup with a smile of reassurance on their lips.

From a psychological point of view this has been by far the richest scene in the poem so far. Even the minutely observed argument earlier in Book IX seems flat by comparison. For the dialogue here has a third dimension which was absent then: the thoughts lying behind the actual speeches. Before the fall Adam and Eve said what they thought; there was no gap between word and meaning. In the state of innocence everything was still simple in the best sense of the term (see 161n) and if the conversations seemed flat it was because the whole person was speaking in unison. This is why good moral characters tend to make bad literary characters and vice-versa. Complexity, Milton implies, is the result of the fall.

IX 1000–1189 *Shame*

Argument. The effects thereof in them both; they seek to cover their nakedness; then fall to variance and accusation of one another.

The universe of *PL* is whole. Like a healthy organism and a good poem it contains neither more nor less than it needs to work efficiently. God's 'creating hand Nothing imperfect or deficient left Of all that he created' (344). Like a healthy organism too it has its own internal logic. The parts which form the whole are inter-dependent, and as soon as a new element is introduced or an old one removed the entire structure is affected by the change. So when Eve first sinned:

> Earth felt the wound, and nature from her seat
> Sighing through all her works gave signs of woe,
> That all was lost. 782–4

Now that Adam has sinned as well:

> Earth trembled from her entrails, as again
> In pangs, and nature gave a second groan,
> Sky loured and muttering thunder, some sad drops
> Wept at completing of the mortal sin
> Original. 1000–4

A 17th-century reader would not have been surprised to see earth and nature behaving as if they were human, for in 1667 the pathetic fallacy had not yet been fully exposed (see A. Z. Butler 'The pathetic fallacy in *PL*' *Essays in honor of W. C. Curry* 1954). Despite the attacks of Bacon, Hobbes and the scientists of the Royal Society, the idea still persisted that the force which held the universe together was analogy. The correspondences between the 'little world of man' (*Lear* III i 10) and the great world of nature were real, not metaphorical, and by exploring them a poet was simply acknowledging the harmony of the creation. They could work, of course, in both directions; resemblance is not a one-way street. If rain can 'weep', tears can 'rain', so when Milton comes to describe the effects of the fall on Adam and Eve he is able to reverse his initial equation: 'nor only tears Rained at their eyes...' (1121). They experience a tempest in the mind, an exact counterpart of the thunderstorm at the beginning of the scene and the still more violent storm to come in Book x.

Both kinds of tempest consist of a disturbance in the divinely ordered processes of nature. Milton illustrates it in 1127–31 with yet another popular renaissance correspondence, that between the human body and the body politic. To understand what is happening here we have to go back to Adam's explanation of the ideal relationship between will, understanding and appetite earlier in the story. Just before she left him he told Eve that:

> God left free the will, for what obeys
> Reason is free, and reason he made right,
> But bid her well beware, and still erect,
> Lest by some fair appearing good surprised
> She dictate false, and misinform the will
> To do what God expressly hath forbid. 351–6

In terms of the political image implicit in 1127–31, reason (or understanding – the terms are interchangeable) is parliament, will is the civil service, and the passions (or appetite) are the common people. Usually it was the other way round, with will as king and reason as parliament, but Milton was a parliamentarian so reason is 'sovereign'. When the common people have a request to make they petition parliament, which in turn instructs the civil service whether or not to implement it. What went wrong during Eve's fall was that parliament was deceived by a specious request; in Adam's case the civil service disregarded parliament's instructions. As a result a revolution now takes place, and the structure of man's internal government is turned upside down. The people overthrow parliament and take direct control of the civil service. Appetite rules supreme and the will ignores the advice of reason. Thus Eve's rebellion against Adam and Adam's against God cause a corresponding breakdown of authority within them. In Brutus's words:

> the state of man
> Like to a little kingdom, suffers then
> The nature of an insurrection.   *Julius Caesar* II i 67–9

The triad of appetite, will and reason dominates the entire scene as Milton shows first one and then the others turning corrupt. He begins with appetite. Like 'new wine' (1008) the forbidden fruit quite literally intoxicates Adam and Eve as they swallow it. Adam in particular talks and acts (see 1017–26) as if he were drunk (Eve had her turn in the previous scene). The lurching rhythms created by the swaying caesura and run-over lines, the convoluted syntax, the over-elaborate jokes (see 1017n), and the petty bravado are those of a man who has had one drink too many. So are the tipsy advances he makes to Eve in the next lines. He proposes to 'enjoy' (1032) her, and Milton describes their love-making in terms which suggest gluttony as well as lust: 'Her hand he seized...they their fill of love and love's disport Took largely' (1037–43). Eve, as the ambiguous referent of 'bounty' confirms (see 1033n), has become a thing, a piece of fruit to be devoured like the apple. The fallen pair may think they are becoming gods, but the language of the poem insists that they are turning into animals.

The corruption of appetite is followed almost immediately by the corruption of will. Adam's eyes are opened, as the serpent had promised they would be, but only to his own moral nakedness. His immediate instinct, therefore, is to hide (1080–90). As in so

33

many cases, a parallel scene before the fall brings this one into sharper focus. When they had woken up in Book v Adam and Eve emerged from their bower to praise their Creator in a hymn which included the following lines:

> His praise ye winds, that from four quarters blow,
> Breathe soft or loud; and wave your tops, ye pines,
> With every plant, in sign of worship wave.   v 192–4

Here in Book IX that hymn has been replaced by a dirge, worship by fear. Nature has become a means of concealing man from God rather than revealing God to man, a hide-out rather than a church. In his guilt and shame Adam is consciously turning his will away from his Creator, and he will be unable to pray again until he learns to repent.

Finally reason itself is corrupted as the married calm which should exist between husband and wife is shattered by their first real quarrel. Like the argument they had before they separated it is prototypical. Now that the decision they took together has proved to be wrong, neither of them is prepared to take the blame for it. Eve, her accent no longer 'sweet', reproaches Adam for failing to exert his masculine authority; he, his words no longer 'healing', reproaches her for failing to restrain her feminine curiosity and pride. It is a brilliantly observed account of mutual recrimination; each speech contains just enough truth to strike home. As we saw earlier, both are at least partially justified in their criticisms of each other. The trouble is that neither is 'self-condemning' (1188). The understanding, whose function is to make moral distinctions, has been debased until it can detect only what is wrong in someone else. Adam and Eve do not reason here; they rationalize, using their understanding for self-defence rather than self-analysis. We are left with a vision of endless accusations and counter-accusations, a 'vain contest' (1189) which can end only when they both confess their respective sins and unite in repentance. The achievement of this state of penitence will be one of the major themes of Book X.

Commentary: Book X

X 1-91 *Heaven*

Argument. Man's transgression known, the guardian angels forsake paradise, and return up to heaven to approve their vigilance, and are approved, God declaring that the entrance of Satan could not be by them prevented.

After the intensity of Book IX, the explosive variety of Book X threatens to burst the poem open at the seams. The dramatic unities which had governed events in Eden suddenly disintegrate: time ceases to be continuous, slipping backwards with each 'meanwhile' (1, 229, 585) to bring another aspect of the story up to date; place jumps from heaven to earth to hell and back again as the repercussions of the fall spread to the limits of the universe; action splits into a series of overlapping episodes which hustle all the major characters on and off stage in less than 600 lines. It is as if the violent forces released by Adam's sin had invaded the structure of the narrative itself. Even the narrator's voice has changed. In Book IX it was often stern, but it did not lack compassion. Now it is harsh and querulous, scolding the fallen pair for their forgetfulness (12) and bullying the reader with strident rhetorical questions (5-7, 15). As one of the sons Adam expects to curse him (733-6), Milton may well be angry with his ancestor. The tones we hear at the start of Book X, however, transcend merely human indignation. The poet has begun to sound like his God (see topics p. 178).

Admittedly it is a difficult moment for both of them. When the guardian angels return to heaven, their 'unwelcome news' (21) afflicts the entire populace with 'dim sadness' (23). The downcast faces look odd in a setting which is supposed to be eternally joyful, so Milton pretends that grief isn't unhappy at all provided it is mixed with pity. God knows better. At least he tries to cheer everyone up, though in a rather curious way:

> Assembled angels, and ye powers returned
> From unsuccessful charge, be not dismayed,

> Nor troubled at these tidings from the earth,
> Which your sincerest care could not prevent,
> Foretold so lately what would come to pass,
> When first this tempter crossed the gulf from hell.   34–9

Not, one would have thought, an announcement likely to restore celestial morale, yet this blunt exposure of their own uselessness seems to set the sentries' minds at ease. It has the opposite effect on us. If the fall was inevitable, we want to ask, why bother to take such strenuous precautions against it? And if God knew all along that Adam and Eve were going to disobey him, why get so angry with them when they do? An omniscient and omnipotent deity, after all, doesn't make mistakes; whatever he says will happen must happen, and what must happen is nobody's fault (except, possibly, the deity's – see 41n, 72n). Gabriel and his companions are relieved of any blame for letting Satan slip past them for the very good reason that they could not stop divine predictions coming true. How, then, could man? (See topics pp. 176–8.)

The more theologically minded devils had puzzled over this problem while they were waiting in hell for their leader's return, but 'found no end, in wandering mazes lost' (II 561). Perhaps to prevent such fruitless speculations from going on in heaven, God had revealed the solution shortly afterwards: Adam and Eve would not be able to claim that his foreknowledge compelled them to sin because

> they themselves decreed
> Their own revolt, not I: if I foreknew,
> Foreknowledge had no influence on their fault,
> Which had no less proved certain unforeknown.
>
> III 116–19

By reminding his nervous angels of this speech here in Book x God is able to excuse them and accuse man at one stroke (40–7). The trouble with these arguments is not just their defensiveness – a character who keeps protesting his innocence of a crime no one has mentioned is bound to arouse suspicion sooner or later – but their failure to *show* how divine prescience can be reconciled with human freedom. The two concepts appear to be mutually exclusive: either God has foreknowledge or man has free will. It is not very helpful to be told simply that both alternatives are true.

On the other hand there is one all-important fact which makes it easier to take God's word for it now than on the earlier occasion: the fall itself has taken place in the meantime. In Book III, before the event, the theory has to be judged on its own merits. In

Book x, after the event, the theory can be tested against the practice preceding it. If Milton has succeeded in convincing us that Adam and Eve were morally responsible for their actions when they ate the forbidden fruit, then we may be willing to suspend our philosophical objections by an act of poetic faith.

But this is not the end of our difficulties, for God goes on to gloat, in some of the ugliest lines in the poem (see 53n), over the punishment he is about to inflict on the unsuspecting culprits. Mocking their hopes for 'acquittance' (53), he identifies himself exclusively with the demands of justice. The quality of mercy seems to have no place in heaven until he turns to the Son (58–62). Again the parallel scene in Book III is the key to this one. There as here the Father had insisted that man should be condemned to death for his offence:

> He with his whole posterity must die,
> Die he or justice must; unless for him
> Some other able, and as willing, pay
> The rigid satisfaction, death for death.   III 209–12

There as here the Son had promised to settle man's 'account' (cf. 501n) with his ferocious creditor by repaying the debt himself. The contrast is unfortunate. The Father, perpetually shrouded in thunder-clouds, turns out to be the implacable Jehovah of the *OT*, claiming an eye for an eye, a tooth for a tooth, while the Son stands for the more distinctively Christian values of forgiveness and compassion preached by the Jesus of the *NT*. Orthodox theology may unite both figures in the Trinity, but in *PL* the two are so clearly distinguished from each other that they exist as independent characters. As a result Milton's heaven seems to be ruled by an irate Shylock whose thirst for vengeance has constantly to be tempered by a more attractive and charitable Portia.

X 92–228 *Judgement*

Argument. He sends his Son to judge the transgressors, who descends and gives sentence accordingly; then in pity clothes them both, and reascends.

We return to earth and the text of *Genesis* (see 178n) as the Son descends to pass judgement. The preceding scene, whatever its defects, is helpful here. Without it, Christ's enquiries would suggest, as they do in the biblical version of the episode, that he really can't understand why his creatures are hiding from him or how they came to realize they are naked. After the earlier discussion in heaven, however, we are well aware that he is not as ignorant as he pretends to be. He knows the answers to his questions before he asks them, and from his point of view the whole interrogation is unnecessary. But not from Adam and Eve's, which is what matters at this juncture. Divine as well as human justice must be seen to be done, especially by the judged. So although man's crime has already been detected and his sentence already fixed, there still has to be a trial. Otherwise the fallen pair might never escape from the cycle of mutual recrimination in which we left them at the end of Book ix. Before they can either forgive or be forgiven they must both accept their full share of the blame. This is exactly what the Son's cross-examination is intended to achieve: the offenders are being given a chance to plead guilty.

Adam takes it rather grudgingly. His immediate reaction is to prevaricate (116), and even when Christ challenges him directly he still refuses to give a straight answer. Instead he worries aloud about accusing Eve (125–31). The Adam of *Genesis* had no such misgivings, and many critics have remarked that Milton's reluctant witness is by far the more attractive figure. So he is if we take his words at face value, but should we? We have just been told that 'Love was not in their looks, either to God Or to each other' (111), which hardly squares with the sentiments Adam expresses here, while the 'calamitous constraint' (132) he uses as an excuse for implicating his wife turns out to be nothing more compelling than his unwillingness to bear all the punishment himself. We may well suspect that his high-sounding professions of loyalty are merely a rhetorical gesture calculated to make the forthcoming disclosure seem less ungallant.

In any case, when God's omniscience provides a further reason for abandoning his noble intentions, Adam proceeds to accuse Eve with a vengeance. And not just Eve. His account of her creation clearly implies that the whole thing was really the Creator's fault in the first place:

> This woman whom thou mad'st to be my help,
> And gav'st me as thy perfect gift, so good,
> So fit, so acceptable, so divine,
> That from her hand I could suspect no ill,
> And what she did, whatever in itself,
> Her doing seemed to justify the deed;
> She gave me of the tree, and I did eat.   137–43

Between subject and verb rises a crescendo of relative phrases and clauses all designed to drown out the final guilty monosyllables.

Ironically, though, Adam reveals a good deal about the nature of
his sin in the process of trying to misrepresent it. In Book VIII he
had confessed to Raphael that ever since he first saw Eve:

> when I approach
> Her loveliness, so absolute she seems
> And in herself complete, so well to know
> Her own, that what she wills to do or say,
> Seems wisest, virtuousest, discreetest, best.   546–50

The angel had replied with a stern warning against letting female
charm usurp male authority:

> oft times nothing profits more
> Than self esteem, grounded on just and right
> Well managed; of that skill the more thou know'st,
> The more she will acknowledge thee her head,
> And to realities yield all her shows.   571–5

This is the burden of Christ's rebuke here in Book X. By failing
to know himself (see 156n), and thus allowing Eve's beauty rather
than God's law to govern him, Adam has turned the natural order
upside down: his fall was an act of idolatry (see 139n).

Eve does not have to be lectured about her offence because,
unlike her husband, she makes no excuse for it: 'The serpent me
beguiled and I did eat' (162). Her candour is refreshing after all
Adam's evasions, and it leaves Christ free to pronounce judgement
without further ado – since the serpent was just the Devil's
instrument there is no point in asking it anything; now that it is
no longer possessed, it couldn't reply anyway.

Following the chronology of the temptation, Christ begins with
the tempter (175–81). In the biblical story this was probably the
least important of the three curses. It explained merely why snakes
crawl on the ground and why men are afraid of them. By the time
Milton came to write *PL*, however, the concluding phrase had
acquired a second meaning, which referred not to the serpent but
to its former occupant. Satan was being told that Jesus, the 'seed'
of Mary, would 'bruise' his head by rising from his grave in
triumph after the crucifixion. Interpreted in this way the sentence
was really a *protevangelium*, the original prophecy of man's
redemption and the Devil's defeat. The 'mysterious terms' (173)
of the condemnation contained within them the promise of
eventual redemption. For the moment neither Adam nor Satan
fully understands the hidden significance of Christ's words. Adam
later guesses the identity of his tempter (see 1030n), but not until

Michael explains it to him does he find out how the serpent's head is going to be crushed (XII 386–435). Satan realizes at once that the curse applies to him, but he is clearly thinking of a physical bruise when he jokes about it with his followers in hell (494–500). To ensure that we don't make the same mistake Milton pauses to cite a whole series of *NT* passages recording the fulfilment of the Son's enigmatic prophecy. Although the fallen pair are not yet aware of their judge's mercy, the biblical allusions see to it that we are.

Divine mercy is also the theme of the next episode, the clothing of Adam and Eve:

> Nor he their outward only with the skins
> Of beasts, but inward nakedness, much more
> Opprobrious, with his robe of righteousness,
> Arraying covered from his Father's sight. 220–3

Our initial response, perhaps, is that the Father must be rather prudish, but if we remember how nakedness was described on an earlier occasion the passage begins to appear in a rather different light. As a result of the fall, Milton told us in Book IX, Adam and Eve were stripped of their spiritual and moral perfections:

> innocence, that as a veil
> Had shadowed them from knowing ill, was gone,
> Just confidence, and native righteousness
> And honour from about them, naked left
> To guilty shame. 1054–8

The key word in both cases is 'righteousness', the state of virtue in which man was created. When he sinned his guilt and shame made him so abhorrent to his Creator that before he could be restored to grace he had to make himself presentable again. But he was unable to accomplish this on his own; once lost, righteousness was irretrievable. Only Christ could cover up the deformity of human wickedness by cloaking it with his 'robe of righteousness', the miraculous armour which in Spenser's *Fairy queen* turned a 'clownish young man' into a 'gentle knight'. Thus something profoundly important is happening at the end of this scene; Adam and Eve may not know it, but the process of redemption is already under way.

X 229–409 *Sin and Death*

Argument. Sin and Death sitting till then at the gates of hell, by wondrous sympathy feeling the success of Satan in this new world, and the sin by man there committed, resolve to sit no longer confined in hell, but to follow Satan their sire up to the place of man: to make the way easier from hell to this world to and fro, they pave a broad highway or bridge over chaos, according to the track that Satan first made; then preparing for earth, they meet him proud of his success returning to hell; their mutual gratulation.

As the Son returns to heaven Milton takes us in the opposite direction, down to the gates of hell where Sin and Death have been waiting since the end of Book II. Their names alone are enough to suggest how radically they differ from the other characters in the poem. Although Adam and Eve, for instance, represent the whole human race, they still remain two individual human beings, a man and a woman rather than Man and Woman. Even the Devil, who is portrayed as the source of all wickedness, never loses his concrete identity as Satan; he may be 'the evil one' (IX 463) but he is never simply Evil. Sin and Death, on the contrary, have no concrete identities; only abstract ones. They are not so much persons as personifications, ideas with bodies, hovering halfway between concept and object. We might expect to meet such figures in the symbolic landscape of a work like the *Fairy queen* (indeed, Sin bears a striking resemblance to Spenser's Error with her snaky tail and brood of hell-hounds – see topics p. 180) but many critics from Addison on have felt that they are out of place in the literal universe of *PL*. Dr Johnson, for example, wrote in his *Life of Milton* that although to 'exalt causes into agents, to invest abstract ideas with form, and to animate them with activity, has always been the right of poetry', to 'give them any material agency is to make them allegorical no longer, but to shock the mind by ascribing effects to nonentity'. In support of Dr Johnson's objections one might cite the evidence of Milton's dramatic drafts for the poem (see topics p. 153) which included a large number of similar abstractions: Justice, Mercy, Conscience, Faith, Hope and Charity etc. Several of these subsequently appeared in the epic, but always in non-allegorical form; Conscience became the disembodied voice in Adam's soliloquy (see below p. 53) while Justice and Mercy evolved into the Father and Son (see above p. 37). Sin and Death, it is tempting to assume, are simply undigested remnants of those earlier plans, in Johnson's words two 'airy beings' who never quite materialized.

In fact they are the products of a literary tradition far older than Milton's dramatic drafts or the 16th-century romance, a tradition which stems from man's primaeval fear of the night and what it may contain. Satan's offspring are creatures from the outer darkness, a region of the imagination beyond the light of a communal campfire or the consciousness of an individual mind (see topics p. 180). As Johnson realized, they are 'nonentities'; as he did not realize, they are nonentities which are in the process of becoming entities (cf. 586n). In Book II Death was just a shape:

> If shape it might be called that shape had none
> Distinguishable in member, joint, or limb,
> Or substance might be called that shadow seemed.   667–9

Here in Book X he begins as a 'shade' (249) but by 280 he has acquired a 'nostril' and in 601 he is a 'vast unhide-bound corpse' complete with 'maw'. As he and his mother make their way across the 'unreal' (471) limbo of chaos, in which Milton has so far insulated them, it is as if two monsters were about to break out of a nightmare into waking reality.

The theological ancestry of Sin and Death is straightforward by comparison. It derives from a brief verse in the *NT*: 'When lust hath conceived, it bringeth forth sin: and sin, when it is finished, bringeth forth death' (*James* i 15). Substitute Satan for lust and this is an accurate summary of the genesis of Sin and Death as the former relates it to her father in *PL* II 755–67. Sin's account of her Minerva-like origin foreshadows the births of Eve and Christ later in the poem. Eve, who in her husband's words is the 'best image of myself' (v 95), was formed from Adam's rib after God had 'opened my left side' (VIII 465); Christ was begotten by the Father out of his own substance in the 'radiant image of his glory' (III 63). The correspondences are too close to be accidental. Sin, they imply, is multi-dimensional; apart from being the Devil's wife and daughter she may also be a second Eve with Death or Satan as her Adam, or an infernal Christ with Death and Satan making up the Trinity.

Milton exploits both possibilities in the present scene. At the outset he takes us back to the situation just before the fall (229). What follows, therefore, takes place at the same time as the events we saw unfolding in Eden in Book IX. While Sin is asking her partner 'why sit we here each other viewing Idly' (235) Eve is warning hers that since:

```
        so near each other thus all day
    Our task we choose, what wonder if so near
    Looks intervene and smiles...which intermits
    Our day's work brought to little          IX 220-4
```

While Sin feels 'Wings growing, and dominion given me large
Beyond this deep' (244) Adam and Eve imagine 'Divinity within
them breeding wings Wherewith to scorn the earth' (IX 1010).
And while Death is relishing the 'savour of death' (269) Adam
is joking about his wife's savour (IX 1019) and proposing to
'enjoy' (IX 1032) her. The effect coincides with the cause, and
as the 'hellish pair' (585) prepare to occupy paradise we keep
catching glimpses of the 'human pair' (IX 197) above them simul-
taneously engaged in the process of losing it (see also 249n, 265n,
390n).

When Sin and Death start building the bridge, however, a
second and still more insistent analogy emerges. In Book VII
Christ had created our universe by marking out its boundaries
with his compass and then bringing life and order to the formless
matter inside:

```
              on the watery calm
    His brooding wings the spirit of God outspread,
    And vital virtue infused, and vital warmth
    Throughout the fluid mass, but downward purged
    The black tartareous cold infernal dregs
    Adverse to life: then founded, then conglobed
    Like things to like, the rest to several place
    Disparted, and between spun out the air,
    And earth self-balanced on her centre hung.     VII 234-42
```

His counterpart, aided in turn by her 'shadow' (264), now pro-
ceeds to do exactly the opposite (X 282-96). Virtue and warmth
give way to petrification and cold, the harmony of like things to
the violent collision of opposites, the architect's compass to the
destroyer's mace. Sin and Death perform what amounts to an
anti-creation, using the dregs Christ had rejected to build not the
earth suspended from heaven but an arch of soil chained to hell
(for a more detailed analysis of the parallel see E. M. W. Tillyard
'The causeway from hell to the world in the tenth book of *PL*'
Studies in philology XXXVIII 1941).

Two of Milton's soaring periods, each anchored by an epic
simile, carry the highway out over the abyss. The first span comes
to rest on the image of an arctic wasteland, the second on a
punning allusion to the crossing of the Hellespont (313n).
Initially these comparisons seem simple enough. As Sin and Death

pile up the flotsam from the sea of chaos they are like polar winds driving the ice-floes together; as they build their causeway to a world they plan to enslave they are like the emperor of Persia constructing his pontoon bridge across the Bosphorus 'the liberty of Greece to yoke' (307). But when we look at them more closely both similes turn out to be more complex than this. To begin with, one contradicts the other: the ice-floes 'stop' (291) the passage from Europe to Asia; Xerxes' boats 'Europe with Asia joined' (310). The latter function seems more appropriate in the context until we remember that the road from hell is going to be a road *to* hell so far as man is concerned. From his point of view the causeway really is an obstacle, standing between him and heaven. What is more, as the reference to Xerxes implies, the bridge-builders themselves are in for a surprise. Soon after he reached Greece the would-be conqueror suffered a disastrous defeat in the battle of Salamis, and Milton soon confirms that Sin and Death are also going to meet an overwhelming reverse when God hurls them back to hell to 'stop' up its gates for ever (629–37). The arch from hell to earth is not as 'triumphal' (390) as they imagine.

No such thoughts occur to Satan when he views the 'monument' (258) his children have erected to him. Intoxicated by Sin's flattery (see 354n) and his own recent success he feels as powerful as God:

> You two this way, among these numerous orbs
> All yours, right down to paradise descend;
> There dwell and reign in bliss, thence on the earth
> Dominion exercise and in the air,
> Chiefly on man, sole lord of all declared,
> Him first make sure your thrall, and lastly kill.
> My substitutes I send ye, and create
> Plenipotent on earth.   397–404

The roles Sin and Death have played earlier in the scene here coalesce in a final blasphemy. For now that their parody of the creation is complete, Satan addresses them as if he were the Creator introducing another Adam and Eve to the garden of Eden. His instructions are a distorted echo of God's commandments in *Genesis* i 28:

Be fruitful and multiply, and replenish the earth, and subdue it: and have dominion over the fish of the sea, and over the fowl of the air, and over every living thing that moveth upon the earth.

(cf. *PL* VII 530–4; VIII 319–41)

Man's successors come to paradise to kill, not to multiply, to enthrall rather than to govern. Their 'dominion' is clearly going to be a reign of terror.

x 410–584 *Hell*

Argument. Satan arrives at Pandemonium, in full assembly relates with boasting his success against man; instead of applause is entertained with a general hiss by all his audience, transformed with himself also suddenly into serpents, according to his doom given in paradise; then deluded with a show of the forbidden tree springing up before them, they greedily reaching to take of the fruit, chew dust and bitter ashes.

The myths of Greece and Rome are full of transformations (see topics p. 182). Ovid collected the most famous of them in his *Metamorphoses*, and any of Milton's readers who, like him, had studied that work at school might well have been struck by the similarity between Satan's fate at this point of *PL* and that of a character like Actaeon who was turned into a stag because he spied on Diana while she was bathing (see IX 424n). It is strange to find God behaving like the capricious deities of classical legend, especially when we recall how clearly he was distinguished from them in the prologue to Book IX. The practical joke he plays on the fallen angels seems merely spiteful, a display of sorcery rather than an act of divine justice. One could argue, of course, that he is just carrying out the exact terms of the Son's curse on the serpent – the tempter really does grovel on his belly and eat the dust 'according to his doom' (517) – but their real meaning, we already know, is 'mysterious'; Christ himself will inflict the sentence when he redeems mankind. In comparison with that spiritual victory this physical vengeance is petty as well as unnecessary. The Almighty did not have to be so literal.

F. R. Leavis has called the episode a 'pantomime trick' ('Mr Eliot and Milton' in *The common pursuit* 1952 p. 26). His phrase accurately describes not only the childishness but also the theatricality of the action in this scene. For there is more than a hint of melodrama about the 'exploding hiss' which greets the Devil's exit (see 546n), while his slow-motion tumble verges on farce (see 513n). Not all the theatricals are God's however. From the moment he arrived back in hell Satan has been carefully setting the stage for his triumphant reappearance in Pandemonium. This is to be the grand finale of the one-man show he has been giving ever since Book I, and he uses every device he knows to make it as sensational as possible. First he slips into the council chamber in disguise; then, so that no one will notice him mounting his throne, he becomes invisible; finally, when he has paused to take stock of the spectators, he bursts upon them in a dazzling explosion of light. It is pure pantomime, the entrance of the demon-king, but it works (452–9).

What follows is, by any standards, a virtuoso 'performance' (see 502n). During the course of the poem Satan has played a bewildering variety of parts, but in this speech he manages to combine his three favourite ones, the religious (saviour), the epic (hero), and the commercial (adventurer). He begins by announcing that he has returned from earth 'to lead ye forth Triumphant out of this infernal pit' (463). The Devil is proposing to harrow his own hell, to do for his followers what Christ was traditionally believed to have done for men when he descended into hell after the crucifixion to release the souls of the just from their bondage. Satan's impersonation of the Son, which started in Book II with his offer to undertake the journey to earth, continued in Book IX with his 'incarnation' in the serpent (see above p. 17) and culminated in the same book with the 'conversion' of Eve (see IX 713n), has run its full course. He has lived out a grotesque parody of Christ's redemptive mission in the act of creating the need for it.

Having exhausted the role of saviour, he next strikes the pose of an epic hero, a weary Aeneas relating his 'adventure hard' (468) to Dido and her court, a travel-worn Odysseus re-united with his family (469–72). This involves some rather skilful editing, for not all his perils were as great as he would like his audience to believe. He has to exaggerate, for instance, the hazards he encountered on his way to Eden (see 478n) and leave out altogether his humiliating arrest by Ithuriel and Zephon when he got there. The fallen angels, who last saw their 'mighty chief' (455) at his most heroic as he set off on his lonely quest, may not be aware of the gap between the rhetoric and the reality, but we should be.

In order to deal with the temptation itself Satan slips into yet a third role. His 'voyage' (II 426, 919; X 366, 471) across the 'gulf' (II 441; X 39, 253, 366) of chaos has been accompanied throughout by similes drawn from the familiar 17th-century world of merchant-adventurers 'on the trading flood' (II 640). Earth in turn has been consistently described as the 'new world' (II 403, 867; X 257, 377), which in the renaissance, of course, meant America, the land where:

46

> Columbus found the American so girt
> With feathered cincture, naked else and wild
> Among the trees on isles and woody shores.   IX 1116–18

It is only natural, then, that Satan should present himself as the 'great adventurer' his followers have been waiting for, newly returned 'from the search Of foreign worlds' (x 440). The language he uses in 480–501 reduces the fall of man to a shrewd piece of business by history's first colonist. Like the settlers who bought Manhattan island from the Indians, Satan thinks he has got a bargain, a 'world' in exchange for a 'bruise'. The ignorant natives, he sneers, were willing to sell out for an apple. The 'account' (see 501n) he presents is almost all profit.

Satan has worked hard for the applause he now expects to break out. During the last part of his speech in particular he has played quite blatantly to the gallery, milking the audience for every gasp of astonishment – 'the more to increase Your wonder' – and snigger of amusement – 'worth your laughter' – he can squeeze out of them. But at this point a still greater showman intervenes to add a surprise epilogue. The metamorphosis may be melodramatic, but it is a fitting climax to the theatricals we have just witnessed. The quick-change artist undergoes one final transformation which at one stroke negates all his previous roles: the mock-saviour turns into the serpent the real saviour will bruise; the pseudo-hero turns into the traditional monstrous opponent of the epic warrior; the shady merchant is forced to swallow his own rotten fruit. Whatever we think of the morality of God's pantomime trick, its ironies are satisfying.

X 585–719 *Discord*

Argument. The proceedings of Sin and Death; God foretells the final victory of his Son over them, and the renewing of all things; but for the present commands his angels to make several alterations in the heavens and elements.

The vision of insatiable appetite gorging itself on inedible food grows still more complex as the action moves back to paradise. For while the devils are being teased with imitation fruit in hell, Death is already looking forward to a real feast on earth. The role in which Satan cast him during their recent encounter, and which Adam confirms in 815, adds an extra dimension to his appearance here: a second Adam has come to take possession of the garden and its occupants (see 591n). This time, however, there are no

47

forbidden trees and the menu is no longer strictly vegetarian (603–9). Sin's parody of Eve's domestic duties (V 303–39) and God's orders to man (VIII 319–41) reminds us that Eden's new master comes as a predator rather than a gardener, a hunter whose favourite dish is human flesh (see topics p. 181). When she ate the fruit Eve 'knew not eating death' (IX 792). Now the biter is going to be bit – literally.

In the very next speech God reveals that this will also be true of Sin and Death: fattened like pigs on the world's 'draff and filth' (630), they themselves are destined to be eaten by 'the mouth of hell' (636). And just as the soot and cinders choked the spell-bound devils, so Sin and Death will stick in the 'ravenous jaws' (637) they were originally appointed to guard. Once again they will serve as porters, blocking for ever the passage to their father's kingdom. The simple fact that the fall consisted of tasting forbidden food generates a rich progression of oral images which illustrate not only the self-consuming nature of sin but also the mysterious ironies of God's 'eternal providence' (I 25).

So far the narrative has dealt exclusively with moral evil (Sin) and its penalty (Death). But the fall was supposed to account for physical evil as well, for pain, disease, deformity and such natural disasters as earthquakes, floods and droughts. In the renaissance all these phenomena were generally attributed to the malign influence of the stars, so in order to explain them Milton proceeds to describe the effect of Adam's disobedience on the cosmic system which God had created in Book VII. Essentially it was an idealized version of the Ptolemaic universe, with the earth at the centre surrounded by the spheres of the seven planets and the fixed stars beyond them, then the crystalline sphere, and finally the *primum mobile*, the outer skin which kept the whole mechanism in motion (see III 481–3 and topics p. 184). What distinguished it from the Ptolemaic scheme was its perfect symmetry. The sun's path, for example, followed the equator, giving Eden a climate of eternal spring with days and nights of equal length. The courses of the other planets were also planned in such a way that their influence on the earth was purely beneficial (see IX 104–13). Our world was the focal point of a harmonious combination of stellar forces, all designed to make human life as agreeable as possible.

On God's instructions, the angels now set about disrupting this orderly arrangement. They begin by tipping the sun's orbit (or, to allow for the Copernican hypothesis, the earth's axis) 23.5° out of line with the celestial equator, to produce the extremes of heat and cold the world has suffered ever since. Then they change the courses of the planets so that their influence becomes more harmful than benign (see topics p. 183). Finally, they replace the 'gentle airs' (93) which had fanned the garden of Eden with the 'adverse blast' (701) of the ten winds. It seems strange at first that Milton should spend so much time on the last item, but he does so for a good reason. Before the creation in Book VII the Son had looked out over

> the vast immeasurable abyss
> Outrageous as a sea, dark, wasteful, wild,
> Up from the bottom turned by furious winds
> And surging waves, as mountains to assault
> Heaven's heighth, and with the centre mix the pole.
>
> 211-15

And when Sin and Death were constructing their causeway they were compared to 'polar winds blowing adverse' (289). The blustering winds which in the present scene 'confound Sea, air, and shore' (665) are the symbols of anarchy (cf. *Lear* III ii 1). As the storms 'rend the woods and seas upturn' (700) we seem to be witnessing a reversion to chaos. Chaos, we may remember, from Book II, is a place of 'endless wars' where the four elements are 'mixed confusedly' and 'thus must ever fight' (II 897-914). The collisions of 'sideral blast' (x 693) brought about by the angels hint at the same kind of perpetual warfare, but the still more violent maelstrom of 'thwart' (703) winds leaves us in no doubt. Everything has suddenly become 'counter' (see 231n), and we can begin to understand why, when Eve ate the apple, 'nature from her seat Sighing through all her works gave signs of woe' (IX 782). God has capped the figurative anti-creation of Sin and Death with a literal anti-creation of his own.

The only trouble is that unlike the actions of Sin and Death God's destructive outburst appears to have no direct connection with the fall. Satan had assumed that if he could corrupt man 'all this will soon Follow, as to him linked in weal or woe' (IX 132); and Adam had made the same point later when he was trying to cheer up Eve (IX 938-43). But the mere fact that God has to send his angels to mutilate the universe denies the whole idea of the interdependence of man and nature which Satan and Adam affirmed and which was so richly elaborated at the end of Book IX. The only suggestion of any such link here in Book X is when the sun turns aside his course 'as from Thyestean banquet' (688), but by this time we know the angels have given it a push.

Consequently the dislocation of the cosmos appears to be the result of nothing more than God's bad temper. Because the actors have performed badly the manager has ordered the theatre to be dismantled. As the workmen obey him they might well be embarrassed to recall a comment they made just after the creation was completed: 'to create Is greater than created to destroy' (VII 606).

X 720–862 *Despair*

Argument. Adam more and more perceiving his fallen condition heavily bewails...

A soliloquy is the speech of a lonely man. Satan, the loneliest character in *PL*, has more of them than anyone else. God, who is perfectly self-sufficient, has none. This is Adam's first because it is the first time he has been really alone. Before Eve was created to keep him company he could converse with his Maker, but now that he is estranged from both he has no one to talk to except himself. His isolation, as the hostile animals emphasize, is total.

To a 17th-century Puritan Adam's predicament would have been all too familiar. Conscious only of his own guilt on the one hand and of 'justice divine' (857) on the other, he is clearly suffering from a severe attack of despair. Defined in theological rather than psychological terms, this is the state of a man who realizes he is wicked but ignores or denies the saving power of God's grace. The heroes of the other two great Protestant epics of the period, Spenser's *Fairy queen* and Bunyan's *Pilgrim's progress*, both succumb to it during their quests for holiness and have to be reminded of Christ's promise to redeem them before they can go on (see topics p. 186). Adam, having received the promise in 'mysterious terms', must first recognize it for what it is. For the moment he is trapped, like Satan, in the sterile solitude of 'the hell within him' (IV 20).

Adam himself links his plight with the Devil's when he declares towards the end of his speech that he is 'To Satan only like both crime and doom' (841). We know this is an exaggeration from a distinction God made before the fall:

> The first sort by their own suggestion fell,
> Self-tempted, self-depraved: man falls deceived
> By the other first; man therefore shall find grace,
> The other none.   III 129–32

But the comparison is still useful, for despite these basic differences the fallen angel and the fallen man share many of the same agonies before their fates diverge. In particular they share the claustrophobic sense of confinement which Satan expresses in his first soliloquy:

> Which way shall I fly
> Infinite wrath and infinite despair?
> Which way I fly is hell; myself am hell.   IV 73-5

As Milton observes:

> within him hell
> He brings, and round about him, nor from hell
> One step no more than from himself can fly.   IV 20-2

Several critics have suggested that Adam, on the contrary, succeeds in groping his way out of his inner darkness as his speech progresses. (See, for instance, K. Svendsen 'Adam's soliloquy in Book x of *PL*' *College English* 1949.) If there is any such development it is hard to detect, for the speech does not really progress at all. It consists, rather, of a series of false starts which keep circling back 'with dreadful revolution' (814) to the point of departure, the guilty self at the centre:

> all my evasions vain,
> And reasonings, though through mazes, lead me still
> But to my own conviction: first and last
> On me, me only, as the source and spring
> Of all corruption, all the blame lights due.   829-33

Anyone who has been lost in a maze will know what Adam is talking about here. Every path he tries turns out to be a cul-de-sac; over and over again he is forced to retrace his steps and start afresh. His insistent questions – almost half the speech is in the interrogative – twist and turn in desperation, but each 'yet' and 'but' – nine sentences begin with one or the other – signals another dead end. The whole frustrating process is re-enacted grammatically by Adam's habit of making himself the object of his own verbs; his speech is so reflexive that it contains as many *me*s as *I*s. Even the syntax is a vicious circle (e.g. 738-41). Like the characters in Sartre's *No exit*, he is engaged in a hopeless search for the way out of a hell without doors.

The image of the labyrinth explains the disorientation of his thinking throughout the soliloquy. His arguments repeatedly lead him into 'strange contradiction' (799): light is 'heavy' (741), death is 'living' (788), finite is infinite (802), the thanks of his unborn sons are 'execration' (737) and they will 'bless' him for disinheriting them (821). The laws of nature embodied in the scholastic axioms he clutches at so frantically (see 805n) have been suspended. The anarchy which had been loosed on the universe in the previous scene now invades Adam's interior world. He is caught in the eye of an intellectual as well as a physical storm.

The most horrifying contradiction of all is that in addition to claustrophobia he is also in the grip of the opposite neurosis, agoraphobia. Again Satan anticipates him:

> And in the lowest deep a lower deep
> Still threatening to devour me opens wide
> To which the hell I suffer seems a heaven.   IV 76–8

The Devil's feeling of vertigo has its counterpart here in Adam's vision of a bottomless 'abyss of fears' (842). A finite mind is dizzied by the prospect of infinity, but this is what Adam has to face as he contemplates the meaning of 'death'. Before the fall he could dismiss it in a frivolous aside: 'So near grows death to life, what e'er death is, Some dreadful thing no doubt' (IV 425). Now that he is 'mortal doomed' (796) it begins to occur to him just how 'dreadful' it might be, not 'one stroke, as I supposed, Bereaving sense, but endless misery' (809). Variations of this idea have been recurring every 10 lines or so since he started to speak: 'lasting woes (742)...endless woes (754)...deathless pain (775)...living death (788)...deathless death' (798). The dilemma is a familiar one in renaissance drama. Hamlet was haunted by the fear that 'in that sleep of death what dreams may come...Must give us pause' (III i 66). Marlowe's Faustus, threatened with eternal damnation, cried:

> Yet for Christ's sake, whose blood hath ransomed me,
> Impose some end to my incessant pain;
> Let Faustus live in hell a thousand years,
> A hundred thousand, and at last be saved.   v ii 1959–62

Adam, still unaware of even the possibility of salvation, cannot make the same prayer. His only consolation is an Aristotelian formula (see 805n).

As the father of the human race he has another aspect of eternity to consider: the effect of his sin on his descendants, who now come back to reproach him like the ghosts of the victims in an Elizabethan tragedy: 'Ill fare our ancestor impure, For this we may thank Adam' (735). Like his successor in Laurence

Binyon's *The death of Adam* 1904, he realizes that he has damned 'the whole included race' (IX 416):

> What is this thing that I have done, what doom,
> What boundless and irrevocable doom,
> My children, have I wakened for you all?
> O could I see the end, but end is none.
> My thoughts are carried from me, and they faint,
> As birds that come from out the farthest sky,
> Voyaging to a home far, far beyond,
> Sink in our valley on a drooping wing
> Quite wearied out, yea, we have seen them sink,
> So my thoughts faint within my bosom old;
> The vision is too vast, I am afraid.

What distinguishes him from Satan, and so hints at the possibility of his recovery, is his reaction to this idea. Rather than seeking 'league' (IV 375) with them in hell he wants to save them by bearing all the wrath himself (see 832n). Conscience, whose insistent voice corrects his most blatant errors (see 842n), points out at once that his wish is 'Fond' (834), but merely by having it Adam has shown his capacity for pity. It is this quality which in the following scene will enable him to forgive Eve and thus take the first step towards redemption.

X 863–1104 *Repentance*

Argument...[Adam] rejects the condolement of Eve; she persists and at length appeases him: then to evade the curse likely to fall on their offspring, proposes to Adam violent ways which he approves not, but conceiving better hope, puts her in mind of the late promise made them, that her seed should be revenged on the serpent, and exhorts her with him to seek peace of the offended Deity, by repentance and supplication.

In his *Christian doctrine* Milton defined the 'progressive steps in repentance' as 'conviction of sin, contrition, confession, departure from evil, conversion to good' (I 19). At the moment Adam is still at the stage of 'conviction' (831) and seems likely to remain there. Conscience has succeeded only in reducing him to despair and self-pity. Before he can go any further some external force must intervene. Ironically it turns out to be the same force that led him to sin in the first place: Eve. We don't hear the 'soft words' (865) she speaks to him at the beginning of the scene, only the hysterical tirade they provoke in response (see 883n). The effect is to make Adam's abuse sound even more vicious than it might if we knew what prompted it, and many critics have concluded that Milton

53

rather than Adam must be the speaker here, venting on women in general the personal spite he felt as a result of his unhappy marriage with Mary Powell. This kind of autobiographical reading (other famous examples are Samson's denunciations of his fellow countrymen, and Christ's recollections of his youth in *PR*) raises, of course, the whole question of an author's relationship to the characters he creates. To what extent can he use them as mouthpieces for his own feelings without destroying the dramatic illusion? Or, to approach the problem from the opposite end, how can we tell when he is doing so? The answer to the second question is that we can't if he does it cleverly enough. For however closely the character's sentiments might correspond to what we know of his creator's, we have no reason to suspect ventriloquism unless the speech sounds wrong, wrong coming from that particular person or wrong coming at that particular time. Like any other author Milton is free to use his hero as Satan used the serpent, so long as the audience remains unaware of it.

What we have to decide, then, is whether Adam's onslaught on his wife is in character. Clearly it is exaggerated (see 876n). If we are to believe him, the entire blame for the fall is Eve's; the one mistake he will admit to is having trusted her (880n). But surely this is exactly the reaction we might have expected in the circumstances. Red Cross Knight was rescued from despair by Una, a personification of divine truth (see topics p. 186); Christian, by a key symbolizing the promise of divine grace (see topics, p. 186). Eve, however, is no Una and she carries no magic key. All she can bring her husband is a mirror image of his own guilt. Naturally he wants to smash it. The pent-up anger and remorse which could find no outlet during his soliloquy are suddenly released in a breathless succession of insults and accusations directed at his 'other self' (see 128n), the prototype of all women (see IX 1183n). It is the catharsis he had been seeking in the previous scene (see 719n), a chance to cleanse himself at last of the conflicting passions inside him. Far from striking a false note, his invective rings absolutely true.

Eve's reply has been called 'one of the most resplendent human occasions the poem has to offer' (J. Carey *Milton* 1969 p. 103) and so it is. As she pleads with Adam (914–36) it is as if the temptation scene were being played over but in reverse. In Book IX she had thanked him for refusing to live on without her, then boasted that she would 'sustain alone The worst' if she really thought the fruit were fatal, and finally 'embraced him' weeping for joy (IX 961–91). Now she embraces him again, weeping for grief, begs him not to desert her, and undertakes to keep the promise she made before she gave him the apple. The good temptation is an echo of the evil one (see 947n), and by giving in to it Adam begins the process of regeneration. If he can forgive Eve, God can forgive them both. His 'peaceful words' (946) reveal that his catharsis is complete; self-pity and fear have given way to compassion and a subdued kind of resolution. No longer does he recoil, as he did during the judgement, at the thought of bearing all the punishment himself. On the contrary, he wishes 'That on my head all might be visited, Thy frailty and infirmer sex forgiven' (955). The care he expressed for his descendants during his soliloquy has been extended to include Eve.

From this point on she serves a rather different function, that of devil's advocate. We are reminded not so much of the temptation itself as of the argument preceding it. For once again Eve starts making practical suggestions for improving their lot, and once again they will lead to disaster should Adam accept them. But he has learned his lesson. To remain childless or to commit suicide, as she proposes, would be 'acts Of contumacy' (1026). By rejecting them he regains the authority he had abdicated in Book IX, and with it comes the dawning recognition that there was more involved in the judgement than he realized. Looking back on it he sees that Christ's curse on the serpent was really meant for Satan (see 1030n). He sees too that his judge spoke 'Without wrath or reviling' (1048). For the first time since the fall he begins to feel hopeful. God may have afflicted them with cold, but he has also shown them how to keep themselves warm by making fire. Science, which in the original version of the myth was the gift of the tree of knowledge (see topics pp. 170–71), proves to be a means of repairing the physical effects of the fall. Still more important, however, he has learned how to repair its spiritual effects (see 1087n):

> What better can we do, than to the place
> Repairing where he judged us, prostrate fall
> Before him reverent, and there confess
> Humbly our faults, and pardon beg, with tears
> Watering the ground, and with our sighs the air
> Frequenting, sent from hearts contrite, in sign
> Of sorrow unfeigned, and humiliation meek.   1086–92

This is one of the most important moments in the poem, and Milton emphasizes it by repeating the passage word for word in the final lines of the book. Thanks to Eve, Adam has achieved contrition and is proposing to make confession. By the opening of Book XI they are both repentant:

> Thus they in lowliest plight repentant stood
> Praying,...

Something bad has happened in EDEN and its worse

Book IX

NO MORE OF TALK where God or angel guest
With man, as with his friend, familiar used
To sit indulgent, and with him partake
Rural repast, permitting him the while
Venial discourse unblamed: I now must change   5
Those notes to tragic; foul distrust, and breach
Disloyal on the part of man, revolt,
And disobedience: on the part of heaven
Now alienated, distance and distaste,
Anger and just rebuke, and judgement given,   10
That brought into this world a world of woe,
Sin and her shadow Death, and Misery
Death's harbinger: sad task, yet argument
Not less but more heroic than the wrath
Of stern Achílles on his foe pursued   15
Thrice fugitive about Troy wall; or rage
Of Turnus for Lavínia disespoused,
Or Neptune's ire or Juno's, that so long
Perplexed the Greek and Cýtheréa's son;
If answerable style I can obtain   20
Of my celestial patroness, who deigns

2 familiar like a member of the family.   **3 indulgent** kind.   **5 Venial**
innocent.   **6 tragic** see topics p. 152.   **11 world of woe** cf. I 3; XI 627.
The cumulative syntax and insistent front-rhymes on **dis** in 6–10 build
up to this climax.   **12 Sin…Death** real characters; see II 648; X 229ff.
13 harbinger forerunner. **sad task**, the phrase Raphael used in
V 564 to introduce his subject (**argument**), Satan's rebellion. The falls of
angels and men are linked at the outset.   **15 foe…Greek…Cýtheréa's
son** the Trojan hero Hector, the Greek hero Odysseus, and Venus's son,
the Roman hero Aeneas, respectively. The last two were **Perplexed**
(literally, entangled) by Neptune and Juno; see commentary p. 12.
20 answerable corresponding (to the more heroic subject).   **21 patron-
ess** M's sacred muse, Urania, traditionally the muse of astronomy, but

57

Her nightly visitation unimplored,
And dictates to me slumbering, or inspires
Easy my unpremeditated verse:
Since first this subject for heroic song   25
Pleased me long choosing, and beginning late;
Not sedulous by nature to indite
Wars, hitherto the only argument
Heroic deemed, chief maistrie to dissect
With long and tedious havoc fabled knights   30
In battles feigned; the better fortitude
Of patience and heroic martyrdom
Unsung; or to describe races and games,
Or tilting furniture, emblazoned shields,
Impreses quaint, capárisons and steeds;   35
Bases and tinsel trappings, gorgeous knights
At joust and tournament; then marshalled feast
Served up in hall with sewers, and séneschals;
The skill of artifice or office mean,
Not that which justly gives heroic name   40
To person or to poem. Me of these
Nor skilled nor studious, higher argument

here associated with the Holy Spirit (cf. prologues to I, VII). The periphrasis
distinguishes her from terrestrial patronesses such as John Donne's, Lucy
Countess of Bedford.   **22 nightly** cf. VII 29. M dictated each fresh
passage of *PL* early in the morning.   **24 unpremeditated** like Adam and
Eve's morning hymn in V 149. As a Puritan M believed that 'to imprison
and confine by force into a Pinfold of set words those two unimprisonable
things, our prayers and that divine spirit of utterance that moves them, is a
tyranny' (*Eikonoklastes* XVI).   **26 long choosing** as a young man M had
declared his intention of writing an epic, possibly about King Arthur,
but he did not start serious work on *PL* until late middle age. The following
attack on chivalric romance explains why he changed subjects.   **27 indite**
relate; like **maistrie** (mastery) archaic, evocative of medieval poetry.
34 tilting furniture equipment for jousting, including shields decorated
(**emblazoned**) with coats of arms, ingenious emblems (**Impreses quaint**),
equestrian trappings (**capárisons**), and protective skirts (**Bases**) worn by
horses or riders. The tripping rhythms and technical jargon mock the
whole affair; cf. I 763–6.   **37 marshalled feast** cf. 'Rural repast' in 4.
The marshal seated the guests in order of precedence, the **sewer** served
them, and the **séneschal** was chief steward. Their menial duties (**office
mean**) and the **artifice** of chivalric equipment are all that romance
amounts to.   **41 Me** to me.

Remains, sufficient of itself to raise
That name, unless an age too late, or cold
Climate, or years damp my intended wing   45
Depressed, and much they may, if all be mine,
Not hers who brings it nightly to my ear.

   The sun was sunk, and after him the star
Of Hesperus, whose office is to bring
Twilight upon the earth, short arbiter   50
'Twixt day and night, and now from end to end
Night's hemisphere had veiled the horizon round:
When Satan who late fled before the threats
Of Gabriel out of Eden, now improved
In meditated fraud and malice, bent   55
On man's destruction, maugre what might hap
Of heavier on himself, fearless returned.
By night he fled, and at midnight returned
From compassing the earth, cautious of day,
Since Úriel regent of the sun descried   60
His entrance, and forewarned the Cherubim
That kept their watch; thence full of anguish driven,
The space of seven continued nights he rode
With darkness, thrice the equinoctial line
He circled, four times crossed the car of night 65

43 raise That name bestow the title of heroic on *PL*.   **44 too late** see
commentary p. 15.   **45 damp**... prevent his inspiration from soaring
as high as he intends.   **49 Hesperus** Venus, the evening star, the inter-
mediary (**arbiter**) between day and night.   **52 hemisphere** M imagines
night as a half-sphere, darkening one side of the earth as it revolves.
53 late recently. In IV 874ff. Satan was expelled by Gabriel and his fellow
angels from the garden of Eden, but not before he had overheard Adam
telling Eve about the prohibition of the tree of knowledge. Now he is
improved in fraud because he knows how to bring about the fall.   **56
maugre** regardless of anything worse that might happen to him.   **57
returned** after the hovering alliterative phrases before it, the final verb
pounces with Satan.   **60 Úriel** literally = divine fire, the angel of the sun
who gave the alarm in IV 555 when Satan first approached the earth.
63 rode With darkness Satan orbits the earth seven times, always keeping
on the dark side. He follows the equator, travelling from east to west ahead
of the sun, for 3 nights; then the four major circles of longitude
(**colúres**) for 4. He crosses the world, but not in benediction.

*Satan is determined
to get his plan right*

From pole to pole, travérsing each colúre;
On the eighth returned, and on the coast averse
From entrance or cherubic watch, by stealth
Found unsuspected way. There was a place,
Now not, though sin, not time, first wrought the   70
    change,
Where Tigris at the foot of paradise
Into a gulf shot under ground, till part
Rose up a fountain by the tree of life;
In with the river sunk, and with it rose
Satan involved in rising mist, then sought   75
Where to lie hid; sea he had searched and land
From Eden over Pontus, and the pool
Mæótis, up beyond the river Ob;
Downward as far antarctic; and in length
West from Oróntès to the ocean barred   80
At Dárien, thence to the land where flows
Ganges and Indus: thus the orb he roamed
Siberience   With narrow search; and with inspection deep
Considered every creature, which of all
Most opportune might serve his wiles, and found   85
The serpent subtlest beast of all the field.
Him after long debate, irresolute
Of thoughts revolved, his final sentence chose

67 **coast averse** the opposite side of Eden from the entrance, which
was guarded by the cherubim.   70 **Now not** thanks to the fall; see XI
829ff.   71 **Tigris** one of the four rivers watering Eden, which was thought
to lie in Mesopotamia.   72 **Into ... shot under** the trochees plunge the
river downwards; cf. the river Alph in Coleridge's *Kubla Khan*.   75
involved wrapped in.   77 **From Eden** ... cf. Satan's travels in
62–6. From Eden he went north via the Black Sea (**Pontus**) and the
Sea of Azof (**pool Maeótis**) up past the Siberian river **Ob**, then down the
other side of the world to the Antarctic. From east to west he travelled from
the river **Oróntès** in Syria along the Mediterranean and across the Atlantic
to the isthmus of Panama (**Dárien**), then over the Pacific to the **Ganges**
in India and the **Indus**, a river near Eden. Satan hovers over the waters
like the spirit of God in VII 210–39 and *Genesis* i.   83 **narrow** close.
86 **subtlest** see *Genesis* iii 1. Understand 'to be' after **serpent**.   87
Him ... chose the inverted word-order, with the long gap between
object and verb, enacts Satan's indecision as he wavers between the vari-
ous thoughts going round in his mind.   88 **sentence** decision, but

Fit vessel, fittest imp of fraud, in whom
To enter, and his dark suggestions hide   90
From sharpest sight: for in the wily snake,
Whatever sleights none would suspicious mark,
As from his wit and native subtlety
Proceeding, which in other beasts observed
Doubt might beget of diabolic power   95
Active within beyond the sense of brute.
Thus he resolved, but first from inward grief
His bursting passion into plaints thus poured:
    'O earth, how like to heaven, if not preferred
More justly, seat worthier of gods, as built   100
With second thoughts, reforming what was old!
For what God after better worse would build?
Terrestrial heaven, danced round by other heavens
That shine, yet bear their bright officious lamps,
Light above light, for thee alone, as seems,   105
In thee concentring all their precious beams
Of sacred influence: as God in heaven
Is centre, yet extends to all, so thou
Centring receiv'st from all those orbs; in thee,
Not in themselves, all their known virtue appears   110
Productive in herb, plant, and nobler birth
Of creatures animate with gradual life

later his condemnation (to take the form of a snake). **89 imp**
either instrument or shoot. In the latter case the metaphor implies
that Eden now has a new gardener. But he cultivates unnatural strains by
grafting the serpent like a scion on to his own deceptive nature. **91 wily**
the devious syntax mimes Satan's guile: Adam and Eve would attribute
any tricks (**sleights**) they noticed to the serpent's subtlety whereas in a
less clever animal the same tricks might create the suspicion (**doubt**) that it
was possessed by a devilish force operating inside it, beyond the capacity
of a mere beast. But see Adam's comments in X 869ff.   **99 preferred** to
be preferred. Satan has to inflate the value of the earth to make it an
adequate substitute for the heaven he has lost. During the temptation
(546–8) he will amplify the idea that it is a **seat** (home) more worthy of
gods (note the plural).   **103 heavens** stars: their dance was a traditional
symbol of harmony (cf. Sir John Davies's *Orchestra*).   **104 officious**
dutiful.   **106 concentring** focusing. This phenomenon puzzled Adam
in VIII 15–38; Raphael explained it in VIII 66ff. See topics p. 183.   **110**
virtue productive power.   **112 gradual** ascending in steps: see V 469ff.

Of growth, sense, reason, all summed up in man.
With what delight could I have walked thee round,
If I could joy in aught, sweet interchange   115
Of hill, and valley, rivers, woods and plains,
Now land, now sea, and shores with forest crowned,
Rocks, dens, and caves; but I in none of these
Find place or refuge; and the more I see
Pleasures about me, so much more I feel   120
Torment within me, as from the hateful siege
Of contraries; all good to me becomes
Bane, and in heaven much worse would be my state.
But neither here seek I, no nor in heaven
To dwell, unless by mastering heaven's supreme;   125
Nor hope to be myself less miserable
By what I seek, but others to make such
As I, though thereby worse to me redound:
For only in destroying I find ease
To my relentless thoughts; and him destroyed,   130
Or won to what may work his utter loss,
For whom all this was made, all this will soon
Follow, as to him linked in weal or woe;
In woe then; that destruction wide may range:
To me shall be the glory sole among   135
The infernal powers, in one day to have marred
What he Almighty styled, six nights and days
Continued making, and who knows how long

116 Of hill... Satan's echo of Adam's description of Eden in VIII 262–3 and 275 invites us to compare their responses to nature. **119 place or refuge** Satan can find nowhere to exist, or to hide. Like Adam after the fall (1088–90) he sees nature as a means of concealing himself from God rather than of revealing God to him. **121 hateful siege** the good surrounding Satan besieges the evil inside him. **123 Bane** woe, or, more specifically, poison. The unexpected stress emphasizes the contrast with **good.** Note the wrenched accent throughout this speech. **128 redound** recoil (literally, flow back upon). Satan experiences this backlash throughout the poem (see III 85; VII 57), Adam only when he has fallen (x 739). **130 him destroyed**... when man has been destroyed or lured into doing something that will bring complete ruin on him. The ablative absolute construction places the fall already in the past. **136 one day** Satan's boast that he will take only one day to destroy what God took six days to

Before had been contriving, though perhaps
Not longer than since I in one night freed   140
From servitude inglorious well-nigh half
The angelic name, and thinner left the throng
Of his adorers: he to be avenged,
And to repair his numbers thus impaired,
Whether such virtue spent of old now failed   145
More angels to create, if they at least
Are his created, or to spite us more,
Determined to advance into our room
A creature formed of earth, and him endow,
Exalted from so base original,   150
With heavenly spoils, our spoils: what he decreed
He effected; man he made, and for him built
Magnificent this world, and earth his seat,
Him lord pronounced, and, O indignity!
Subjected to his service angel wings,   155
And flaming ministers to watch and tend
Their earthy charge: of these the vigilance
I dread, and to elude, thus wrapped in mist
Of midnight vapour glide obscure, and pry
In every bush and brake, where hap may find   160
The serpent sleeping, in whose mazy folds

make, tails off, as his boasts have a habit of doing, into qualification. He wonders how long God had been planning the creation and concludes, wrongly, that he did not begin to contrive it until Satan's revolt left gaps in the angelic ranks.   **141 half** in fact Satan had persuaded only one third of the angelic **name** (order) to rebel; see II 692.   **144 repair...** **impaired** a typical Satanic play on words; cf. VI 562–7. Satan's way of using language tends to blur distinctions.   **145 spent** implies God created men rather than angels to take the place of the rebels because his creative energy (**virtue**) was exhausted or diminished. But this concedes what Satan had denied during his revolt (V 853–63), that God created the angels in the first place. The **if** clause in the next line tries to put the cat back in the bag.   **150 base original** lowly origin, referring to the dust from which Adam was made (*Genesis* II 7).   **151 spoils** Satan still thinks of the universe as a battleground. He cannot admit that God gave him anything. **153 world** in *PL* this always means universe as opposed to the **earth**. **156 flaming ministers** the fiery cherubim who guard Eden.   **160 hap** chance. Like Sin and Death, Satan is a great believer in luck; see X 260–1 n. **161 mazy** like **perplex** always a sinister word in *PL*; cf. II 561; X 830. Physical and mental tangles are the result of sin; good is direct and clear.

To hide me, and the dark intent I bring.
O foul descent! that I who erst contended
With gods to sit the highest, am now constrained
Into a beast, and mixed with bestial slime,   165
This essence to incarnate and imbrúte,
That to the height of deity aspired;
But what will not ambition and revenge
Descend to? Who aspires must down as low
As high he soared, obnoxious first or last   170
To basest things. Revenge, at first though sweet,
Bitter ere long back on itself recoils;
Let it; I reck not, so it light well aimed,
Since higher I fall short, on him who next
Provokes my envy, this new favourite   175
Of heaven, this man of clay, son of despite,
Whom us the more to spite his Maker raised
From dust: spite then with spite is best repaid.'
    So saying, through each thicket dank or dry,
Like a black mist low creeping, he held on   180
His midnight search, where soonest he might find
The serpent: him fast sleeping soon he found
In labyrinth of many a round self-rolled,
His head the midst, well stored with subtle wiles:
Not yet in horrid shade or dismal den,   185
Nor nocent yet, but on the grassy herb
Fearless unfeared he slept: in at his mouth

163 erst formerly.   **164 constrained** compressed as well as forced into; cf. x 511ff.   **166 essence** M explains in i 425 that angelic essence is 'uncompounded...Not tied or manacled with joint or limb'. Thus for Satan **incarnate = imbrúte**; see commentary p. 17.   **169 Who aspires** whoever aspires (to the **height of deity** in 167).   **170 obnoxious** vulnerable.   **172 recoils** cf. the cannon image in iv 17. Satan doesn't care (**reck**) if he is knocked down so long as his shot hits the target, man (since **higher** heaven is beyond his range). For Satan's actual artillery see vi 469ff.   **175 favourite** casts Adam as Duke of Buckingham to God's James I.   **176 son of despite** like **man of clay** (made out of clay and therefore pliable) this phrase has a second meaning: as well as being a despicable creature in himself man is the offspring of God's spite towards Satan.   **180 mist** cf. the cherubim in xii 628ff.   **185 horrid** bristling; **dismal** sinister.   **186 nocent** harmful: **herb** grass.

The Devil entered, and his brutal sense,
In heart or head, possessing soon inspired
With act intelligential; but his sleep   190
Disturbed not, waiting close the approach of morn.

Now whenas sacred light began to dawn
In Eden on the humid flowers, that breathed
Their morning incense, when all things that breathe,
From the earth's great altar send up silent praise   195
To the Creator, and his nostrils fill
With grateful smell, forth came the human pair
And joined their vocal worship to the choir
Of creatures wanting voice; that done partake
The season, prime for sweetest scents and airs: 200
Then cómmune how that day they best may ply
Their growing work: for much their work outgrew
The hands' dispatch of two gardening so wide.
And Eve first to her husband thus began:
    'Adam, well may we labour still to dress   205
This garden, still to tend plant, herb and flower,
Our pleasant task enjoined, but till more hands
Aid us, the work under our labour grows,
Luxurious by restraint; what we by day
Lop overgrown, or prune, or prop, or bind,   210

188 **brutal** animal, as opposed to **intelligential** (rational) in 190.
191 **close** in hiding, or intently.   192 **whenas** when; **sacred** because
associated with God (see *Genesis* i 3, *Matthew* v, *John* i; in *PL* see
especially III 1ff.).   196 **nostrils** M usually avoids such anthropo-
morphisms; the action of the flowers reverses *Genesis* ii where God
breathes into his creatures' nostrils.   197 **grateful** pleasant.   199 **wanting**
lacking; cf. 553ff. The voiceless choir anticipates the paradox of Keats'
Grecian urn: it utters **silent praise**. **partake The season** savour
the time of day, the early morning, which is best (**prime**) for smelling the
scents of the flowers. Before the fall there were no seasons in the modern
sense (see X 677–80), simply an eternal spring.   201 **cómmune** discuss. The
shifting tenses from 192 on create a sense of timelessness which involves
us in these events.   205 **Adam** the first time Eve addresses him without
any formal titles, and the first time she starts a conversation. She will also
have the last word.   206 **still** continually.   207 **enjoined** prescribed (in
Genesis ii). Before the fall work is purely pleasurable (cf. X 201–5); **more
hands** children.

One night or two with wanton growth derides
Tending to wild. Thou therefore now advise,
Or hear what to my mind first thoughts present:
Let us divide our labours, thou where choice
Leads thee, or where most needs, whether to wind   215
The woodbine round this arbour, or direct
The clasping ivy where to climb, while I
In yonder spring of roses intermixed
With myrtle, find what to redress till noon:
For while so near each other thus all day   220
Our task we choose, what wonder if so near
Looks intervene and smiles, or object new
Casual discourse draw on, which intermits
Our day's work brought to little, though begun
Early, and the hour of supper comes unearned.'   225
     To whom mild answer Adam thus returned:
'Sole Eve, associate sole, to me beyond
Compare above all living creatures dear,
Well hast thou motioned, well thy thoughts employed
How we might best fulfil the work which here   230
God hath assigned us, nor of me shalt pass
Unpraised: for nothing lovelier can be found
In woman, than to study household good,

211 **wanton** a key word in *PL* (cf. IV 306, 629; V 295; IX 517, 1015); it refers to the morally neutral tendency of natural things to overgrow – hence the need for rational human control. Even in Eden 'il faut cultiver notre jardin'. See topics p. 161. **213 Or hear** Eve doesn't wait for Adam's advice; she immediately gives him hers. **215 most needs** is most needed. Ironically, Eve suggests that Adam should do the very thing he is about to neglect, for Eve herself, like the ivy and woodbine, needs to be supported by a stronger companion; **see** 431–3. **218 spring** thicket, emphasizing again the theme of nature's growth. The **roses** and **myrtle** link Eve with Venus, whose festivals they decorated. The rose is a traditional symbol of love, while the myrtle recalls Venus's escape from the lecherous satyrs in Ovid's *Fasti* iv. But it won't protect Eve from Satan; see 431, 627. **219 redress** re-dress; cf. *Genesis* ii 15: 'to dress' the garden. **223 intermits** interrupts. **225 unearned** the protestant work ethic applies even in Eden. **227 sole** playing on soul? **229 motioned** proposed. **232 nothing lovelier**... the first of a series of proverbial axioms (cf. 249–50, 267) with which Adam loads his advice. He is at his most sententious at just the wrong moment.

And good works in her husband to promote.
Yet not so strictly hath our Lord imposed   235
Labour, as to debar us when we need
Refreshment, whether food, or talk between,
Food of the mind, or this sweet intercourse
Of looks and smiles, for smiles from reason flow,
To brute denied, and are of love the food,   240
Love not the lowest end of human life.
For not to irksome toil, but to delight
He made us, and delight to reason joined.
These paths and bowers doubt not but our joint hands
Will keep from wilderness with ease, as wide   245
As we need walk, till younger hands ere long
Assist us: but if much convérse perhaps
Thee satiate, to short absence I could yield.   *Wait*
For solitude sometimes is best society,   *men*
And short retirement urges sweet return.   *love* 250
But other doubt possesses me, lest harm
Befall thee severed from me; for thou know'st
What hath been warned us, what malicious foe
Envying our happiness, and of his own
Despairing, seeks to work us woe and shame   255
By sly assault; and somewhere nigh at hand
Watches, no doubt, with greedy hope to find   *There*
His wish and best advantage, us asunder,   *could be*
Hopeless to circumvent us joined, where each   *evil*
To other speedy aid might lend at need;   260

238 **Food of the mind** cf. VII 126; IX 779, 1017–20. The equation of in-
tellectual and physical appetite applies most clearly to the fall itself:
Adam and Eve eat knowledge. **intercourse** interchange. **245 wilderness**
Eden is not merely surrounded by wilderness (IV 135; V 294); it contains
one potentially within itself (cf. 211n). **247 convérse** conversation.
248 satiate continuing the image in 238. **249 solitude**... the extra foot
and heavy alliteration give Adam's (originally Cicero's) proverb added
weight. In 250 he almost coins another one – absence makes the heart grow
fonder. **252 severed** cut off, almost literally (see 215n, and 366 and
958). The metre stresses **from.** **253 foe** Raphael has warned Adam and
Eve about Satan in V and VIII. **258 us asunder** unitary object of **find.**
259 Hopeless takes us back to the subject Satan, who has no hope of
getting round Adam and Eve so long as they stay together.

Whether his first design be to withdraw
Our fealty from God, or to disturb
Conjugal love, than which perhaps no bliss
Enjoyed by us excites his envy more;
Or this, or worse, leave not the faithful side   265
That gave thee being, still shades thee and protects.
The wife, where danger or dishonour lurks,
Safest and seemliest by her husband stays,
Who guards her, or with her the worst endures.'
    To whom the virgin majesty of Eve,   270
As one who loves, and some unkindness meets,
With sweet austere composure thus replied:
    'Offspring of heaven and earth, and all earth's lord,
That such an enemy we have, who seeks
Our ruin, both by thee informed I learn,   275
And from the parting angel overheard
As in a shady nook I stood behind,
Just then returned at shut of evening flowers.
But that thou shouldst my firmness therefore doubt
To God or thee, because we have a foe   280
May tempt it, I expected not to hear.
His violence thou fear'st not, being such,
As we, not capable of death or pain,

261 **first design** in fact Satan accomplishes both alternatives: by per-
suading man to betray his divine trust (**fealty**, a feudal concept) he also
disturbs his marital relationship (see IX 1000ff.).   **263 Conjugal love** as
distinct from courtly love.   **264 envy** Adam is right; see IV 503.   **265
Or this, or worse** whether Satan's intention be what I have described
or something still worse; **side** reminds Eve that she was born from
Adam's rib (see 1153–4). **269 the worst endures** the alternative Adam
finally chooses.   **270 virgin** technically Eve is no longer a virgin; she
and Adam made love in VIII 510–20. Morally, however, she still is, and
Satan's temptation will be like a seduction (see IX 445n). M may also
mean that she hasn't yet born any children (cf. 396) or just that she is
youthful, with a glance at the Virgin Mary, the second Eve (cf. V 387).
273 Offspring... much more formal than 205.   **275 ruin** fall.   **276
angel** Raphael; see end of VIII and VI 900.   **281 May** who may. Eve's
tone has become much more colloquial.   **282 violence** As Eve grows
angry her syntax becomes increasingly hard to follow. Here she means
that Adam is not afraid of a physical attack on them, for since they, like
Satan, are incapable of dying or feeling pain they are invulnerable to, or
at least capable of repelling, any violent assault.

68

Can either not receive, or can repel.
His fraud is then thy fear, which plain infers   285
Thy equal fear that my firm faith and love
Can by his fraud be shaken or seduced;
Thoughts, which how found they harbour in thy
     breast
Adam, misthought of her to thee so dear?'
     To whom with healing words Adam replied: 290
'Daughter of God and man, immortal Eve,
For such thou art, from sin and blame entire:
Not diffident of thee do I dissuade
Thy absence from my sight, but to avoid
The attempt itself, intended by our foe.   295
For he who tempts, though in vain, at least asperses
The tempted with dishonour foul, supposed
Not incorruptible of faith, not proof
Against temptation: thou thyself with scorn
And anger wouldst resent the offered wrong,   300
Though ineffectual found: misdeem not then,
If such affront I labour to avert
From thee alone, which on us both at once
The enemy, though bold, will hardly dare,
Or daring, first on me the assault shall light.   305
Nor thou his malice and false guile contemn –
Subtle he needs must be, who could seduce
Angels – nor think superfluous others' aid.
I from the influence of thy looks receive
Access in every virtue, in thy sight   310

[handwritten marginal notes: "Adam is talking?", "Could be inreperated as 'you deserve to be raped'", "→ could be manipulated"]

285 **fraud** deception. The heavy alliteration and clumsy word-play in these lines suggest how agitated Eve really is.   288 **Thoughts, which how** by now she is so worked up that she mixes question with statement.   291 **Daughter**... Adam echoes Eve's formality in 273.   292 **entire** unblemished.   293 **Not diffident**... not because I don't trust you.   296 **asperses** defames (literally, sprinkles) by supposing his faith to be corruptible.   301 **misdeem** misinterpret.   305 **daring** if he dares.   306 **Nor thou** nor should you underestimate his malice and deceitful cunning...nor should you think my help is unnecessary.   310 **Access** increase. Adam sounds like a renaissance love poet as he pays Eve this glowing compliment. The **influence** of her eyes, like that of the stars in 105ff., is productive of **virtue** (used now, as in 317, 335, 374, in its moral

More wise, more watchful, stronger, if need were
Of outward strength; while shame, thou looking on,
Shame to be overcome or overreached
Would utmost vigour raise, and raised unite.
Why shouldst not thou like sense within thee feel   315
When I am present, and thy trial choose
With me, best witness of thy virtue tried.'
    So spake domestic Adam in his care
And matrimonial love; but Eve, who thought
Less áttributed to her faith sincere,   320
Thus her reply with accent sweet renewed:
    'If this be our condition, thus to dwell
In narrow circuit straitened by a foe,
Subtle or violent, we not endued
Single with like defence, wherever met,   325
How are we happy, still in fear of harm?
But harm precedes not sin: only our foe
Tempting affronts us with his foul esteem
Of our integrity: his foul esteem
Sticks no dishonour on our front, but turns   330
Foul on himself; then wherefore shunned or feared
By us? who rather double honour gain
From his surmise proved false, find peace within,
Favour from heaven, our witness from the event.

Eve is less painful 'cant be good and must be good.' [handwritten marginal note]

sense); cf. Sidney's *Astrophel and Stella* xxvi.   **314 raised unite** having
been roused by shame, vigour would unite with the other virtues of
wisdom, watchfulness and strength.   **317 witness** has religious as well
as legal overtones in a Puritan poem; cf. 334. **tried** is a past participle
passive used as an adjective – when it has been tested.   **318 domestic** in
what sense? Is Adam being a bit motherly here; cf. **matrimonial** (from
Latin *mater* = mother) in 319.   **320 Less** than she deserved.   **321 accent**
tone.   **323 straitened** confined.   **324 we not** Eve's 'accent sweet' is
belied by her violent syntax: if each of us is not furnished with an equally
firm defence against Satan's assaults, wherever we may meet them, how
can we be said to be happy when we are continually afraid of harm?
327 harm precedes not sin we cannot suffer harm unless we sin first.
But the harm Adam fears *is* sin.   **328 Tempting affronts** insults us by
tempting us. As Eve paraphrases Adam's argument in 296–301 her
elaborate word-play (affronts...front, foul esteem...foul esteem) mocks
it.   **330 Sticks** an odd metaphor; cf. 296. Does **front** = forehead, face,
or the whole front of the body?   **334 event** outcome.

And what is faith, love, virtue unassayed   335
Alone, without exterior help sustained?
Let us not then suspect our happy state
Left so imperfect by the Maker wise,
As not secure to single or combined.
Frail is our happiness, if this be so,   340
And Eden were no Eden thus exposed.'
     To whom thus Adam fervently replied:
'O woman, best are all things as the will
Of God ordained them, his creating hand
Nothing imperfect or deficient left   345
Of all that he created, much less man,
Or aught that might his happy state secure,
Secure from outward force; within himself
The danger lies, yet lies within his power:
Against his will he can receive no harm.   350
But God left free the will, for what obeys
Reason, is free, and reason he made right,
But bid her well beware, and still erect,
Lest by some fair appearing good surprised
She dictate false, and misinform the will   355
To do what God expressly hath forbid.
Not then mistrust, but tender love enjoins,
That I should mind thee oft, and mind thou me.
Firm we subsist, yet possible to swerve,
Since reason not impossibly may meet   360
Some specious object by the foe suborned,

335 unassayed untested, like a precious metal whose purity has not yet been tried.　　**336 without**... without being sustained by exterior help. **338 Left** been left.　　**339 As not secure** as not to be safe whether we are alone or together.　　**341 Eden** in Hebrew = delight.　　**342 fervently** Adam becomes heated for the first time, though he doesn't get really angry until after the fall; see 1162n. His mood is reflected by his curt use of **woman**; cf. 227, 291.　　**352 Reason** see commentary p. 33.　　**353 beware...erect** be wary...alert (but also unfallen; cf. IV 288; VIII 432; IX 501).　　**354 appearing** goes with **fair** or **good**? Cf. 386n.　　**357 enjoins** commands. **358 mind** guard, or remind. After all Adam's references to reason we may also think of **mind** as a noun. Is the extra meaning relevant here? **359 Firm**... our existence is stable but we could lose our moral balance; cf. III 99; VIII 640–1.　　**361 specious** deceptively beautiful; **suborned**

And fall into deception unaware,
Not keeping strictest watch, as she was warned.
Seek not temptation then, which to avoid
Were better, and most likely if from me   365
Thou sever not: trial will come unsought.
Wouldst thou approve thy constancy, approve
First thy obedience; the other who can know,
Not seeing thee attempted, who attest?
But if thou think, trial unsought may find   370
Us both securer than thus warned thou seem'st,
Go; for thy stay, not free, absénts thee more;
Go in thy native innocence, rely
On what thou hast of virtue, summon all,
For God towards thee hath done his part, do thine.'   375
    So spake the patriarch of mankind, but Eve
Persisted, yet submiss, though last, replied:
    'With thy permission then, and thus forewarned
Chiefly by what thine own last reasoning words
Touched only, that our trial, when least sought,   380
May find us both perhaps far less prepared,
The willinger I go, nor much expect
A foe so proud will first the weaker seek;
So bent, the more shall shame him his repulse.'

procured for an evil purpose, an apt, if vague, description of the serpent.
363 she reason. Why does Adam assume it is feminine? Cf. 353–5.
364 temptation cf. the Lord's prayer.   **365 most likely if** you are
most likely to avoid temptation if you do not part from me.   **366 sever**
see 252n.   **367 approve** prove.   **368 the other** your constancy. The
dramatic force of Adam's arguments in this speech contrasts with his
complacent generalizations in 232ff.   **369 attempted** tested.   **371
securer** in 339 and 347–8 this meant safe. Confusingly, Adam now gives
it its Latin sense, more off guard: cf. Eve's gloss in 381. To justify his
change of mind (cf. 247, 251) he attributes to Eve an idea she hasn't yet
had: that an unsought temptation might catch them both more off guard
than she is at this moment, fresh from Adam's warnings. But see x 875.
375 done his part echoes Raphael's rebuke to Adam in VIII 561.   **378
permission** resolves the tension between persisted and submiss in 377.
We can also hear a foreboding hiss.   **379 last** implying that Adam's first
words were unreasoning?   **381 both** spoken, one suspects, with more
emphasis than Adam gave it in 371.   **383 weaker** having won the
argument Eve concedes what she has been denying all along.   **384 So bent**
if that is his plan.

Thus saying, from her husband's hand her hand   385
Soft she withdrew, and like a wood-nymph light
Óread or Drýad, or of Délia's train,
Betook her to the groves, but Délia's self
In gait surpassed and goddess-like deport,
Though not as she with bow and quiver armed,   390
But with such gardening tools as art yet rude,
Guiltless of fire had formed, or angels brought.
To Pálès, or Pomóna thus adorned,
Likest she seemed, Pomóna when she fled
Vertúmnus, or to Cérès in her prime,   395
Yet virgin of Prosérpina from Jove.
Her long with ardent look his eye pursued
Delighted, but desiring more her stay.
Oft he to her his charge of quick return
Repeated, she to him as oft engaged   400
To be returned by noon amid the bower,
And all things in best order to invite

385 hand see IV 321, 488, 689; IX 780, 1037; XII 648.   **386 Soft** goes with
withdrew, or **hand**, or both?   **387 Óread or Drýad** semi-divine nymphs
who inhabited the mountains and the woods respectively; cf. V 381. **Délia's
train** = the attendants of Diana, who was born in Delos (X 296n), goddess
of the moon, of chastity, and of the hunt (*Comus* 441ff.). Eve is a virgin
huntress who is going to be seduced by an animal.   **389 goddess-like** cf.
Satan's compliments in 547, 732. M limits his to Eve's bearing (**deport**).
Cf. Eve's departure in VIII 59ff.   **391 art** in most myths the arts of civi-
lization are the result of a fall, e.g. the apocryphal legend of the Watcher
angels in *I Enoch*, the myth of the Golden Age in Ovid's *Metamorphoses*
and the Prometheus story, to which M alludes in 392 – hence **Guiltless**
(cf. X 1070–8). By introducing technology, albeit crude (**rude**), into Eden
before the fall M implies a different view of it.   **393 Pálès... the com-
parisons become progressively more sinister. **Pálès** was the Roman goddess
of pastures, **Pomóna** (from Latin *pomum* = apple) of fruit trees (see V 378).
But the latter was seduced by a minor god called **Vertumnus** who
entered her orchard in disguise (Ovid *Metamorphoses* XIV); **Cérès**, the
Roman goddess of agriculture, also lost her virginity to a god, Jupiter.
(Their daughter, **Prosérpina**, was in turn abducted by Pluto, the god of
the underworld; see the major reference in IV 268–72.) These allusions
thus prepare for M's own prophecy of impending doom in 404ff. Note
the transition from virgin goddesses of wild nature in 387 to raped god-
desses of cultivated nature here; see topics p. 171.   **396 Yet virgin of**
before she bore Proserpina.   **401 amid** back inside; **bower** leafy enclo-
sure (OE *bur* = dwelling).

Noontide repast, or afternoon's repose.
O much deceived, much failing, hapless Eve,
Of thy presumed return! event perverse!   405
Thou never from that hour in paradise
Found'st either sweet repast, or sound repose;
Such ambush hid among sweet flowers and shades
Waited with hellish rancour imminent
To intercept thy way, or send thee back   410
Despoiled of innocence, of faith, of bliss.

For now, and since first break of dawn the fiend,
Mere serpent in appearance, forth was come,
And on his quest, where likeliest he might find
The only two of mankind, but in them   415
The whole included race, his purposed prey.
In bower and field he sought, where any tuft
Of grove or garden plot more pleasant lay,
Their tendance or plantation for delight,
By fountain or by shady rivulet   420
He sought them both, but wished his hap might find
Eve separate, he wished, but not with hope
Of what so seldom chanced, when to his wish,
Beyond his hope, Eve separate he spies,
Veiled in a cloud of fragrance, where she stood,   425
Half spied, so thick the roses bushing round

405 Of concerning (goes with **deceived**). Her coming out (**event** = outcome) from the bower will lead to her going astray (**perverse** = gone astray) rather than returning. The Latin words sound abstract but their force is concrete. **413 Mere** again the literal Latin sense, unmixed, is relevant; see 165. **416 race** see commentary p. 24; **purposed** intended. **419 tendance or plantation** the grove which they tend or the garden-plot which they planted: what are they **more pleasant** than? **421 hap** see 160n. The repetitions in the next 3 lines (**wished**...**hap**...**Eve separate**) enact Satan's search. **423 to his wish** just as he wished. After the previous debate we know that Eve is not **separate** through **hap** as Satan thinks. **424 spies** like Actaeon on Diana (see 387n). Satan too will be metamorphosed as a result (see X 509ff.). **425 Veiled** the scent of the flowers is visible here; in 193 it was almost audible. **426 roses** see 218n. The setting transforms Satan into the prototypical lover intent on gathering rosebuds while he may; see 432n, 445n.

About her glowed, oft stooping to support
Each flower of slender stalk, whose head though gay
Carnation, purple, azúre, or specked with gold,
Hung drooping unsustained, them she upstays   430
Gently with myrtle band, mindless the while,
Herself, though fairest unsupported flower,
From her best prop so far, and storm so nigh.
Nearer he drew, and many a walk travérsed
Of stateliest covert, cedar, pine, or palm,   435
Then voluble and bold, now hid, now seen
Among thick-woven arborets and flowers
Embordered on each bank, the hand of Eve:
Spot more delicious than those gardens feigned
Or of revived Adonis, or renowned   440
Alcínous, host of old Läértès' son,
Or that, not mystic, where the sapient king

429 Carnation flesh-coloured.   **431 mindless** heedless, but also per-
haps irrational; cf. 358n.   **432 flower** Proserpina was 'Herself a fairer
flower' (IV 270) just before her rape by Pluto. The image thus clinches
the allusion in 396 and caps the identification of Eve with her flowers in
215–19. Without Adam she too is **unsustained**. Satan, like Dis, is going
to 'gather' her: see 426n.   **434 he** Satan; **travérsed** crossed, repeating
in miniature his earlier manoeuvres in space (66).   **435 Of stateliest
covert** sheltered by stately trees; cf. IV 138.   **436 voluble** rolling.   **437
arborets** small arbours.   **438 Imbordered** set out in borders; **hand**
handiwork (cf. 207n).   **439 delicious** delightful; **feigned** M again insists
on the superiority of biblical fact to pagan fiction (cf. 31, 389, 505n).
440 Adonis fatally wounded in the groin by a wild boar, **revived** by Venus
who kept him as her lover in a garden of legendary beauty (cf. Spenser
Fairy queen III vi 43–50; Shakespeare *Venus and Adonis*); his death and
rebirth symbolize nature's annual transition from winter to spring. In *Comus*
998–1002 M invokes the myth as an image of natural earthly love as distinct
from heavenly love, represented by Cupid and Psyche. Here the allu-
sion strengthens the link between Eve and Venus (cf. 218n) and foreshadows
Eve's revival of Adam in x 863ff.   **441 Alcínous** king of the Phaeacians
who entertained Odysseus (**Läértès' son**) in his proverbially beautiful
palace gardens where the fruit never perished or fell to the ground (Homer
Odyssey vii). Cf. *Vac. Ex.*   **442 sapient king** Solomon, whose love for
Pharaoh's daughter is the subject of the *Song of Solomon*. (M insisted in
Tetrachordon that far from being allegorical (**mystic**), as it was tradition-
ally supposed to be, this *OT* book was 'far on the hither side of carnal
enjoyment'.) With his 700 wives and 300 concubines, some of whom per-
suaded him to worship pagan gods (1 *Kings* xi), he was a type of the
uxorious husband led into sin (cf. 1 400, 444).

Held dalliance with his fair Egyptian spouse.
Much he the place admired, the person more.
As one who long in populous city pent,   445
Where houses thick and sewers annoy the air,
Forth issuing on a summer's morn to breathe
Among the pleasant villages and farms
Adjoined, from each thing met conceives delight,
The smell of grain, or tedded grass, or kine,   450
Or dairy, each rural sight, each rural sound;
If chance with nymph-like step fair virgin pass,
What pleasing seemed, for her now pleases more,
She most, and in her look sums all delight.
Such pleasure took the serpent to behold   455
This flowery plat, the sweet recess of Eve
Thus early, thus alone; her heavenly form
Angelic, but more soft, and feminine,
Her graceful innocence, her every air
Of gesture or least action overawed   460
His malice, and with rapine sweet bereaved
His fierceness of the fierce intent it brought:
That space the evil one abstracted stood
From his own evil, and for the time remained
Stupidly good, of enmity disarmed,   465
Of guile, of hate, of envy, of revenge;

445 As one... this picture of Satan as a young beau from London
(Pandemonium) eyeing an innocent country maid exorcises the tempta-
tions M recorded in his *Latin Elegies* when he was a student: 'Ah, how many
times have I been struck dumb (*stupui* cf. **Stupidly good** in 465) by the
miraculous grace of a form which might make decrepit Jove young again'
(I 53; cf. VII 61). In the 17th century the boundary between town and
country was much more clear-cut than now.   **446 annoy** pollute.
450 tedded spread out to dry; **kine** cattle. Rustic diction.   **451 rural
sight**...cf. G. M. Hopkins *Binsey poplars*.   **452 nymph-like** transports
the 17th-century milkmaid to the mythological landscape of 386–9.
453 for thanks to.   **454 sums** sums up.   **456 plat** plot, with a perhaps
unconscious sexual pun on plait/pleat = fold, crease; **sweet recess** rein-
forces it.   **458 feminine** there are no female angels in *PL*; cf. x 890.
459 air Of gesture her appearance whenever she gestured or made the
smallest movement.   **461 rapine** the rapist raped: note the recurrence
of **sweet** (456, 461, 473).   **463 That space** for that space of time.
465 Stupidly good the unexpected stress mimes Satan's stupefaction;
see 445n.

But the hot hell that always in him burns,
Though in mid heaven, soon ended his delight,
And tortures him now more, the more he sees
Of pleasure not for him ordained: then soon   470
Fierce hate he recollects, and all his thoughts
Of mischief, gratulating, thus excites:
    'Thoughts, whither have ye led me, with what sweet
Compulsion thus transported to forget
What hither brought us, hate, not love, nor hope   475
Of paradise for hell, hope here to taste
Of pleasure, but all pleasure to destroy,
Save what is in destroying, other joy
To me is lost. Then let me not let pass
Occasion which now smiles, behold alone   480
The woman, opportune to all attempts,
Her husband, for I view far round, not nigh,
Whose higher intellectual more I shun,
And strength, of courage haughty and of limb
Heroic built, though of terrestrial mould,   485
Foe not informidable, exempt from wound,
I not; so much hath hell debased, and pain
Enfeebled me, to what I was in heaven.
She fair, divinely fair, fit love for gods,
Not terrible, though terror be in love   490
And beauty, not approached by stronger hate,
Hate stronger, under show of love well feigned,

471 **recollects** re-collects.   472 **gratulating, thus excites** rejoicing,
thus stirs up.   475 **nor hope**... nor the hope of living in paradise
instead of in hell; Satan's hate makes 'a hell of heaven' (I 255). Note the
convoluted syntax and continual repetitions throughout the speech. What
state of mind do they suggest?   480 **Occasion** opportunity, fortune; see
160n.   481 **opportune** exposed; **attempts** temptations.   483 **higher
intellectual** superior intellect: see commentary p. 22.   484 **haughty**
dignified, or is Satan projecting his own arrogance on to Adam?   485 **ter-
restrial mould** earthly material.   488 **to** compared with.   489 **fit love
for gods** Satan sounds like Zeus, who was famous for his love affairs
with mortals; for sexual treatments of the fall see topics p. 169.   491
stronger hate, Hate stronger the combination of antimetabole and ana-
diplosis, reinforced by the change of rhythm as the iambs give way to
an emphatic spondee, makes Satan's point for him.

The way which to her ruin now I tend.'
So spake the enemy of mankind, enclosed
In serpent, inmate bad, and toward Eve   495
Addressed his way, not with indented wave,
Prone on the ground, as since, but on his rear,
Circular base of rising folds, that towered
Fold above fold a surging maze, his head
Crested aloft, and cárbuncle his eyes;   500
With burnished neck of verdant gold, erect
Amidst his circling spires, that on the grass
Floated redundant: pleasing was his shape,
And lovely, never since of serpent kind
Lovelier, not those that in Illyria changed   505
Hermíönè and Cadmus, or the god
In Epidáurus; nor to which transformed
Ammónian Jove, or Capítoline was seen,
He with Olympias, this with her who bore
Scipio the height of Rome. With tract oblique   510
At first, as one who sought accéss, but feared
To interrupt, sidelong he works his way.

493 tend move towards.   **496 indented** undulating. The diction of the
next 7 lines implies two distinct images: first, the waves of the sea – **wave,
surging, Crested, Floated, redundant** (flowing over, from Latin *unda*,
a wave); second, an eastern temple – **towered, cárbuncle** (red jewel),
burnished, gold, spires (also = coils). Satan appears like a fantastic
mirage.   **497 as since** in *Genesis* iii 14 the serpent is condemned to crawl
on its belly, so the idea developed that before the fall he went upright.
499 maze see 161n.   **505 Lovelier** just as Adam is 'the goodliest man of
men since born His sons' and 'the fairest of her daughters Eve' (IV 323) so
the serpent is more beautiful than his descendants. But the comparisons
make other points too. In Ovid's *Metamorphoses* iv, when **Cadmus**, the
legendary king of Thebes, and his wife **Hermíönè** are transformed into
serpents, they become 'friendly snakes, and do not shun mankind, or do
them harm'. When Aesculapius, **god** of healing, left his sanctuary in
Epidáurus to go to Rome in the form of a snake it was to cure a plague
(*Metamorphoses* xv). When Jupiter Ammon and Jupiter of the Capitol
turned into snakes they begot two of the greatest heroes in classical history,
Alexander the Great and **Scipio** Africanus, by **Olympia** and Sempronia
respectively. Satan, on the contrary, is hostile to man, comes to corrupt
rather than to cure, and begets Sin and Death on Eve; see topics p. 169.
M reminds us again of the Cadmus story in x 509–21 when Satan really
does turn into a snake; see commentary p. 45.   **510 height** pride.
512 sidelong Satan's **oblique** approach, like that of a boat which tacks

As when a ship by skilful steersman wrought
Nigh river's mouth or foreland, where the wind
Veers oft, as oft so steers, and shifts her sail;   515
So varied he, and of his tortuous train
Curled many a wanton wreath in sight of Eve,
To lure her eye; she busied heard the sound
Of rustling leaves, but minded not, as used
To such disport before her through the field,   520
From every beast, more duteous at her call,
Than at Circéan call the herd disguised.
He bolder now, uncalled before her stood;
But as in gaze admiring: oft he bowed
His turret crest, and sleek enamelled neck,   525
Fawning, and licked the ground whereon she trod.
His gentle dumb expression turned at length
The eye of Eve to mark his play; he glad
Of her attention gained, with serpent tongue
Organic, or impúlse of vocal air,   530
His fraudulent temptation thus began:
    'Wonder not, sovereign mistress, if perhaps
Thou canst, who art sole wonder, much less arm
Thy looks, the heaven of mildness, with disdain,
Displeased that I approach thee thus, and gaze   535
Insatiate, I thus single, nor have feared

(**works**) back and forth, anticipates the movement of his arguments
when he tempts Eve. The simile brings Satan to the end of his 'voyage';
see commentary p. 46.   **516 tortuous train** twisting body; cf. 387, 548.
517 wanton the tempter's shape embodies the anarchic element in nature
which it was man's duty to control; see 211n.   **519 minded not, as**
paid no attention because she was used to such games; see 358n, 431n.
521 duteous cf. VII 494–8.   **522 Circéan** the enchantress Circe (M's
Comus is her son) turned Odysseus' men into animals (*Odyssey* x). The
temptation of Eve will reverse the process (now the tempter is **disguised**);
Adam's will repeat it.   **523 uncalled** the repeated **call** in 521–2 em-
phasizes the un.   **525 turret crest** combines temples and waves again
(see 496n); **enamelled** glossy, multi-coloured.   **528 mark** notice.
529 Of her attention gained that he had gained Eve's attention.   **530
Organic, or impúlse** Satan made the serpent speak either by using its
tongue as an instrument or by producing vibrations in the air like a
tuning-fork (cf. 549).   **532 Sovereign** supreme; the language of courtly
love. The wrenched metre demands her attention.   **536 Insatiate** the first

celestial
is the top of the chain (handwritten, top margin)

Foreknowledgement of satan (handwritten, left margin)

Thy awful brow, more awful thus retired.
Fairest resemblance of thy Maker fair,
Thee all things living gaze on, all things thine
By gift, and thy celestial beauty adore   540
With ravishment beheld, there best beheld
Where universally admired; but here
In this enclosure wild, these beasts among,
Beholders rude, and shallow to discern
Half what in thee is fair, one man except,   545
Who sees thee? (and what is one?) who shouldst be
    seen
A goddess among gods, adored and served
By angels numberless, thy daily train.'
    So glozed the tempter, and his proem tuned;
Into the heart of Eve his words made way,   550
Though at the voice much marvelling; at length
Not unamazed she thus in answer spake:
    'What may this mean? language of man pronounced
By tongue of brute, and human sense expressed?
The first at least of these I thought denied   555
To beasts, whom God on their creation day
Created mute to all articulate sound;
The latter I demur, for in their looks

drop of poison with which Satan sprinkles his speeches. **I thus single**
turns his admiration of Eve into a bachelor's courtship of a married woman;
see commentary p. 26.   **537 more awful** Eve's beauty is all the more
awesome, awe-inspiring, because it is not displayed in public as it deserves
to be; cf. *Comus* 544.   **538 Fairest...fair** the modified epanalepsis
hints that Eve is more beautiful than God himself as well as being more
like him than Adam is; cf. VIII 543–6. The constant repetitions (**Wonder**
...wonder, awful...awful. Thee all things...all things thine) mime
the hypnotic motion of a snake before it strikes.   **542 admired** wondered
at.   **543 wild** turns the garden into a wilderness; see topics p. 161.
544 rude primitive.   **547 goddess** another drop of poison. Having
made Eve want to be divine Satan will offer the means of becoming so;
cf. the dream temptation (V 77–8), which the actual temptation continually
echoes.   **548 angels** in fact Satan thinks it an 'indignity' that angels
should serve man; see 154.   **549 glozed** fawned. This is only the
prologue (**proem**) to Satan's oration (see 667–76).   **550 made way** see
734.   **558 the latter I demur** I hesitate to believe the latter point, that
the animals lack **human sense.**

Much reason, and in their actions oft appears.
Thee, serpent, subtlest beast of all the field   560
I knew, but not with human voice endued;
Redouble then this miracle, and say,
How cam'st thou speakable of mute, and how
To me so friendly grown above the rest
Of brutal kind, that daily are in sight?   565
Say, for such wonder claims attention due.'
    To whom the guileful tempter thus replied:
'Empress of this fair world, resplendent Eve,
Easy to me it is to tell thee all
What thou command'st, and right thou shouldst   570
    be obeyed:
I was at first as other beasts that graze
The trodden herb, of abject thoughts and low,
As was my food, nor aught but food discerned
Or sex, and apprehended nothing high:
Till on a day roving the field, I chanced   575
A goodly tree far distant to behold
Loaden with fruit of fairest colours mixed,
Ruddy and gold: I nearer drew to gaze;
When from the boughs a savoury odour blown,
Grateful to appetite, more pleased my sense   580
Than smell of sweetest fennel or the teats
Of ewe or goat dropping with milk at even,
Unsucked of lamb or kid, that tend their play.
To satisfy the sharp desire I had
Of tasting those fair apples, I resolved   585

560 subtlest to be subtlest; cf. 86.   563 How cam'st thou... how did
you come to be articulate after being dumb. The epanalepsis (How...
how) intensifies Eve's surprise.   565 brutal kind the animals. The
paradox may be unintentional.   570 right it is right that.   572 abject
base (literally, cast down, as Satan has been), implying that Eve is in this
state too until she eats the fruit; see commentary p. 26.   573 aught any-
thing. On the link between food and sex see 1033n.   579 savoury cf.
v 84; IX 741.   580 Grateful pleasant.   581 fennel traditionally a
snake's favourite food. Like the Unsucked teats of the animals in 583 it
makes eating the forbidden fruit seem a natural act. Satan talks to Eve as
if she really were a pastoral shepherdess; cf. 445ff.   583 tend their play
continue playing (instead of feeding).   585 apples the ambiguity of the

Not to defer; hunger and thirst at once,
Powerful persuaders, quickened at the scent
Of that alluring fruit, urged me so keen.
About the mossy trunk I wound me soon,
For high from ground the branches would require   590
Thy utmost reach or Adam's: round the tree
All other beasts that saw, with like desire
Longing and envying stood, but could not reach.
Amid the tree now got, where plenty hung
Tempting so nigh, to pluck and eat my fill   595
I spared not, for such pleasure till that hour
At feed or fountain never had I found.
Sated at length, ere long I might perceive
Strange alteration in me, to degree
Of reason in my inward powers, and speech   600
Wanted not long, though to this shape retained.
Thenceforth to speculations high or deep
I turned my thoughts, and with capacious mind
Considered all things visible in heaven.
Or earth, or middle, all things fair and good;   605
But all that fair and good in thy divine
Semblance, and in thy beauty's heavenly ray
United I beheld; no fair to thine
Equivalent or second, which compelled
Me thus, though ímportúne perhaps, to come   610
And gaze, and worship thee of right declared
Sovereign of creatures, universal dame.'

Latin *malum* (=evil, or apple) led some theologians to believe that the
forbidden fruit was an apple: see X 487.   **593 envying** another drop of
poison. Satan will attribute envy to God in 729.   **594 now got** goes with
I in 596.   **598 ere** before; **might** could.   **599 to degree Of reason** to
the extent of acquiring reason.   **601 Wanted** I did not lack speech for
long, even though I still kept a serpent's shape.   **603 capacious** large.
605 middle the space between heaven and earth. Satan's judgement, **fair
and good**, parodies God's in *Genesis* i 31: 'And God saw every thing
that he had made, and behold it was very good.'   **607 Semblance**
appearance. Eve only looks like a goddess.   **609 Equivalent or second**
God said the same of himself in VIII 407. Satan's praise of Eve is a con-
tinuous blasphemy   **610 ímportúne** importunate.   **612 universal
dame** Miss Universe!

So talked the spirited sly snake; and Eve
Yet more amazed unwary thus replied:
'Serpent, thy overpraising leaves in doubt 615
The virtue of that fruit, in thee first proved:
But say, where grows the tree, from hence how far?
For many are the trees of God that grow
In paradise, and various, yet unknown
To us, in such abundance lies our choice, 620
As leaves a greater store of fruit untouched,
Still hanging incorruptible, till men
Grow up to their provision, and more hands
Help to disburden nature of her birth.'
  To whom the wily adder, blithe and glad: 625
'Empress, the way is ready, and not long,
Beyond a row of myrtles, on a flat,
Fast by a fountain, one small thicket past
Of blowing myrrh and balm; if thou accept
My conduct, I can bring thee thither soon.' 630
  'Lead then', said Eve. He leading swiftly rolled
In tangles, and made intricate seem straight,
To mischief swift. Hope elevates, and joy
Brightens his crest, as when a wandering fire,
Compact of unctuous vapour, which the night 635

613 **spirited** inspired by the spirit of Satan. **615 overpraising** the
serpent's excessive praise of Eve casts doubt on the power (**virtue**) of the
fruit to confer reason; see commentary p. 26. **620 abundance** cf.
v 313–20 and the variations on this theme in *Comus* 706ff. **622 incor-
ruptible** like Adam and Eve, nature is immune from death until the fall;
cf. 441n. But the **fruit** Satan has been talking about will corrupt man.
623 Grow up . . . grow in numbers until they can make full use of the
food provided for them. **624 birth** fruit. **626 ready** close at hand.
The staccato phrases hurry Eve's imagination towards the tree. **627
myrtles** see 218n. Venus is being lured out of her hiding place. **628 Fast**
near, but also quickly; see 626n. **629 blowing** blossoming. **630 con-
duct** guidance. **632 intricate** what was entangled; see 161n. **634
wandering fire** the *ignis fatuus* or 'will o' the wisp' of popular folklore;
cf. *Comus* 431. M thus relates Eve's experience directly to his readers'
superstitions. Like the fire Satan is composed (**Compact**) of oily vapour;
even his arguments are **unctuous**. Eve, like the **night-wanderer**, is
from succour far and will soon be lost. The whole image turns noon into
midnight, restoring the 'black mist' which dawn had dispelled in 192.

Condenses, and the cold environs round,
Kindled through agitation to a flame,
Which oft, they say, some evil spirit attends
Hovering and blazing with delusive light,
Misleads the amazed night-wanderer from his way   640
To bogs and mires, and oft through pond or pool,
There swallowed up and lost, from succour far.
So glistered the dire snake, and into fraud
Led Eve our credulous mother, to the tree
Of prohibition, root of all our woe;   645
Which when she saw, thus to her guide she spake:
  'Serpent, we might have spared our coming hither,
Fruitless to me, though fruit be here to excess,
The credit of whose virtue rest with thee,
Wondrous indeed, if cause of such effects.   650
But of this tree we may not taste nor touch;
God so commanded, and left that command
Sole daughter of his voice; the rest, we live
Law to ourselves, our reason is our law.'
  To whom the Tempter guilefully replied: 655
'Indeed? Hath God then said that of the fruit
Of all these garden trees ye shall not eat,
Yet lords declared of all in earth or air?'
  To whom thus Eve yet sinless: 'Of the fruit

640 amazed confused (as in a maze); see 161n.   **643 snake** M usually
uses the more dignified Latin 'serpent'. In IX the native word occurs only
here, 91 and 613. Do the three contexts have anything in common? Both
meanings of **fraud** (crime, deception) are relevant here.   **644 credulous**
mothers are supposed to be wise (cf. 680); **tree Of prohibition** forbidden
tree.   **645 all our woe** another echo of I 3.   **648 Fruitless**... their
journey has been pointless because the serpent must remain the sole wit-
ness to the fruit's power (**virtue**). Eve is not allowed to eat it. Her jaunty
pun takes on sinister overtones in 1188.   **651 touch** is Eve's addition in
Genesis iii 3 (cf. ii 17) but M makes nothing of it.   **653 Sole daughter of
his voice** the only commandment he gave us (cf. Wordsworth's *Ode to
Duty*). The **mother** (644) of man violates the **daughter** of God. What
does **the rest** (=as for the rest) refer to?   **654 Law**...**law** the
epanalepsis creates an echo for God's voice.   **656 Indeed** in *Genesis*
iii 1 the serpent's questions are genuine. Here he already knows the an-
swer; see IV 514ff.   **658 Yet** even though you are. The whole line is
Satan's addition to *Genesis*.   **659 yet sinless** the act of sin occurs only
in 781.

Of each tree in the garden we may eat,   660
But of the fruit of this fair tree amidst
The garden, God hath said, "Ye shall not eat
Thereof, nor shall ye touch it, lest ye die."'
    She scarce had said, though brief, when now more bold
The Tempter, but with show of zeal and love   665
To man, and indignation at his wrong,
New part puts on, and as to passion moved,
Fluctuates disturbed, yet comely and in act
Raised, as of some great matter to begin.
As when of old some orator renowned   670
In Athens or free Rome, where eloquence
Flourished, since mute, to some great cause addressed,
Stood in himself collected, while each part,
Motion, each act won audience ere the tongue,
Sometimes in height began, as no delay   675
Of preface brooking through his zeal of right.
So standing, moving, or to height upgrown
The tempter all impassioned thus began:
    'O sacred, wise, and wisdom-giving plant,
Mother of science, now I feel thy power   680
Within me clear, not only to discern
Things in their causes, but to trace the ways

661 **fair** the non-biblical adjective suggests that Eve already finds the tree attractive.   666 **his wrong** the wrong done to man.   667 **New part** so far Satan has played the role of a courtly lover. Now he impersonates a classical orator. He sways (**Fluctuates** from Latin *fluctus* = a wave; cf. 496n) with passion but remains dignified in his movements as he prepares to speak on some great theme (**matter**).   668 **disturbed** so is the metre.   672 **since mute** because the renaissance believed that the greatest orators were those of ancient Greece and Rome.   673 **in himself collected** in complete control of himself, so that each **part** of his body, each movement (**Motion**), and each action (**act**) won attention (**audience**); cf. x 459. The diction also creates a theatrical image; cf. 667.   675 **height** of passion, or climax of the argument. Satan can afford to omit a **preface** because his earlier remarks to Eve have already accomplished the traditional function of an oratorical prologue: winning the audience's sympathy (cf. 549n).   680 **science** knowledge. Satan's invocation is a travesty of M's to Urania. Satan claims the tree gives him power 'to trace the ways Of highest agents'; M asked his muse to help him 'justify the ways of God to men' (1 26).

85

Milton decides she will be vain, Milton is setting Eve

Of highest agents, deemed however wise.
Queen of this universe, do not believe
Those rigid threats of death; ye shall not die: 685
How should ye? By the fruit? it gives you life
To knowledge. By the threatener? look on me,
Me who have touched and tasted, yet both live,
And life more perfect have attained than fate
Meant me, by venturing higher than my lot.   690
Shall that be shut to man, which to the beast
Is open? or will God incénse his ire
For such a petty trespass, and not praise
Rather your dauntless virtue, whom the pain
Of death denounced, whatever thing death be,   695
Deterred not from achieving what might lead
To happier life, knowledge of good and evil;
Of good, how just? of evil, if what is evil
Be real, why not known, since easier shunned?
God therefore cannot hurt ye, and be just;   700
Not just, not God; not feared then, nor obeyed:

683 **deemed however wise** however wise they are thought to be.   684
Queen in 626 she was an Empress.   687 **To** in addition to.   689 **fate**
throughout the poem Satan substitutes the classical idea of fate or fortune
for the Christian idea of divine providence (cf. 18–19, 160n). Here he in-
vites Eve to see herself as the heroine of a pagan epic defying the meddling
of the gods.   692 **incénse his ire** stir his anger; cf. 18. Satan implies
that God wants to 'perplex' Eve just as Neptune and Juno perplexed
Odysseus and Aeneas.   694 **virtue** now in the epic sense of courage (cf.
310n); the literal meaning, manliness (from Latin *vir* = man) plays on Eve's
desire to be Adam's equal (see commentary p. 27).   695 **denounced**
proclaimed. Satan's glib parenthesis, **whatever thing death be**, echoes
Adam in IV 425. Notice the traductio on **death** and **life** running through
the whole speech.   698 **Of good, how just** either an exclamation (how
right it is to acquire the knowledge of good) or a question (how can it be
right to punish you for acquiring the knowledge of good?) Satan's elliptical
syntax combines both meanings.   699 **easier shunned** a corollary of
Adam's argument in 370.   701 **Not just, not God**... either: if God is
unjust he is not God, in which case he is not to be feared or obeyed, but
since you fear him he must be God, and therefore be just, in which case
he will not punish you and you need not fear the threat of death. Or: if you
fear death then you must think God is unjust, in which case he is not God
and need not therefore be feared. Try writing a paraphrase of Satan's
whole speech watching out for the ambiguities, non-sequiturs and
tautologies.

86

Your fear itself of death removes the fear.
Why then was this forbid? Why but to awe,
Why but to keep ye low and ignorant,
His worshippers; he knows that in the day   705
Ye eat thereof, your eyes that seem so clear,
Yet are but dim, shall perfectly be then
Opened and cleared, and ye shall be as gods,
Knowing both good and evil as they know.
That ye should be as gods, since I as man,   710
Internal man, is but proportion meet,
I of brute human, ye of human gods.
So ye shall die perhaps, by putting off
Human, to put on gods, death to be wished,
Though threatened, which no worse than this can   715
  bring.
And what are gods that man may not become
As they, participating godlike food?
The gods are first, and that advantage use
On our belief, that all from them proceeds;
I question it, for this fair earth I see,   720
Warmed by the sun, producing every kind,
Them nothing: if they all things, who enclosed
Knowledge of good and evil in this tree,
That whoso eats thereof, forthwith attains
Wisdom without their leave? and wherein lies   725

708 gods the plural, repeated in 710, 712, 714, 716, 718, implies again the pagan view of the universe with its pantheon of deities as opposed to the Judaeo-Christian doctrine of God's uniqueness.   **710 since I as man** since I am as man, possessing the human faculties of reason and speech within my serpent's body. In fact the serpent is **Internal** devil, and the **proportion meet** will work the opposite way round: Adam and Eve will descend from **human** to **brute**; see commentary p. 33.   **713 putting off**... parodies St Paul's account of conversion in *Colossians* iii: 'Lie not to one another, seeing that ye have put off the old man with his deeds; and have put on the new man, which is renewed in knowledge after the image of him that created him' (cf. *Ephesians* iv 24).   **714 Human** humanity. **715 threatened** see *Genesis* ii 17.   **717 participating** sharing.   **719 On our belief** to make us believe.   **720 question** in v 853–63 Satan questioned whether God created the angels.   **722 Them nothing** I see the gods producing nothing; if they really created all things, then who put the knowledge of good and evil into this tree?

easily
persuaded

The offence, that man should thus attain to know?
What can your knowledge hurt him, or this tree
Impart against his will if all be his?
Or is it envy, and can envy dwell
In heavenly breasts? These, these and many more   730
Causes import your need of this fair fruit.
Goddess humane, reach then, and freely taste.'
    He ended, and his words replete with guile
Into her heart too easy entrance won:
Fixed on the fruit she gazed, which to behold   735
Might tempt alone, and in her ears the sound
Yet rung of his persuasive words, impregned
With reason, to her seeming, and with truth;
Meanwhile the hour of noon drew on, and waked
An eager appetite, raised by the smell   740
So savoury of that fruit, which with desire,
Inclinable now grown to touch or taste,
Solicited her longing eye; yet first
Pausing a while, thus to herself she mused:
    'Great are thy virtues, doubtless, best of fruits,   745
Though kept from man, and worthy to be admired,
Whose taste, too long forborne, at first assay
Gave elocution to the mute, and taught
The tongue not made for speech to speak thy praise:

727 **What** how.   729 **envy** Satan projects his own envy on to God;
see 593n.   730 **These, these** the ploce implies innumerable reasons for
disobeying God.   731 **import** show.   732 **Goddess humane** the oxy-
moron points up the fallacy in Satan's argument: if Eve really is a goddess
(see 547), why eat the fruit?   733 **replete** filled.   734 **entrance** cf.
550.   737 **impregned** impregnated, referring directly to **words** but also
indirectly to Eve; cf. 393n, topics p. 169.   738 **to her seeming** it seemed
to her.   739 **noon** time for her rendez-vous with Adam (see 401).   740
eager appetite cf. v 84–5. M believed that gluttony was one of the sins in-
volved in the fall (see x 16n) but Eve's appetite here seems natural, not
excessive.   742 **Inclinable** inclining.   744 **mused** pondered. Eve acts
as her own muse; cf. 21n.   745 **virtues** by now a hopelessly ambiguous
word; cf. 310, 649, 694, 778.   746 **admired** also ambiguous: regard
with wonder or approval?   747 **assay** trial.   748 **elocution** speech.
749 **thy praise, Thy praise** this anadiplosis is the first of a series of iter-
ative figures which mimic the style of Satan's last speech to Eve. Her medi-
tation is a tissue of ploce (**knowledge, knowledge** 752), traductio (**for-**

88

Meanings

Thy praise he also who forbids thy use,   750
Conceals not from us, naming thee the tree
Of knowledge, knowledge both of good and evil;
Forbids us then to taste, but his forbidding
Commends thee more, while it infers the good
By thee communicated, and our want: 755
For good unknown, sure is not had, or had
And yet unknown, is as not had at all.
In plain then, what forbids he but to know,
Forbids us good, forbids us to be wise?
Such prohibitions bind not. But if death   760
Bind us with after-bands, what profits then
Our inward freedom? In the day we eat
Of this fair fruit, our doom is, we shall die.
How dies the serpent? he hath eaten and lives,
And knows, and speaks, and reasons, and discerns,   765
Irrational till then. For us alone
Was death invented? or to us denied
This intellectual food, for beasts reserved?
For beasts it seems: yet that one beast which first
Hath tasted, envies not, but brings with joy   770
The good befallen him, author únsuspéct,
Friendly to man, far from deceit or guile.
What fear I then, rather what know to fear
Under this ignorance of good and evil,
Of God or death, of law or penalty?   775

bids...Forbids...forbidding 750–3) and epanalepsis (753). **755 want**
lack. **756 sure** surely, immediately contradicted in true Satanic fashion
by the **or**. **758 In plain** plainly: hardly appropriate to Eve's style here.
759 forbids Eve has used this word 6 times since 750. **761 after-bands**
as distinct from the 'fore-bands' of the prohibition. Eve's use of traductio
has become almost compulsive. **762 freedom** united by alliteration
with **fair fruit** against the harder group of **day, doom, die.** **767 in-
vented** the passive constructions (cf. **denied, reserved**) allow Eve
to avoid thinking of the inventor. **771 good befallen** has obvious
ironic undertones, as does **author únsuspéct.** Eve *means* that the ser-
pent is an informant above suspicion (cf. 92) because he has offered to
share the good that has happened to him; she almost *says* that the serpent
is the unsuspected cause of the fall of good. **773 rather**... rather, how
can I know anything that should be feared so long as I am ignorant of

> Repetition of questioning, tempting herself

Here grows the cure of all, this fruit divine,
Fair to the eye, inviting to the taste,
Of virtue to make wise: what hinders then
To reach, and feed at once both body and mind?'
    So saying, her rash hand in evil hour   780
Forth reaching to the fruit, she plucked, she ate:
Earth felt the wound, and nature from her seat
Sighing through all her works gave signs of woe,
That all was lost. Back to the thicket slunk
The guilty serpent, and well might, for Eve   785
Intent now wholly on her taste, naught else
Regarded, such delight till then, as seemed,
In fruit she never tasted, whether true
Or fancied so, through expectation high
Of knowledge, nor was godhead from her thought.   790
Greedily she engorged without restraint,
And knew not eating death: satiate at length,
And heightened as with wine, jocund and boon,
Thus to herself she pleasingly began.
    'O sovereign, virtuous, precious of all trees   795
In paradise, of operation blest
To sapience, hitherto obscured, infamed,
And thy fair fruit let hang, as to no end
Created; but henceforth my early care,
Not without song, each morning, and due praise   800

good and evil?   **776 cure** Eve has convinced herself that she is sick.
In another sense the fruit will be a cure (Latin *cura* = care); cf. 799n.
778 virtue power; cf. *Genesis* iii.   **780 hand** subject or object of **reach-
ing**? How does the grammar affect Eve's responsibility for her action?
783 Sighing...signs the prosonomasia prolongs nature's sigh through the
line.   **787 as seemed** reminds us that Eve's delight was illusory: cf. 738.
789 fancied referring to her dream in v 83ff.   **790 from** absent from.
791 engorged makes the adverb superfluous; cf. 740n.   **792 eat-
ing** that she was eating. Later, Death will eat her; see commentary
p. 48.   **793 jocund and boon** merry and gay.   **794 to herself** cf.
744, 895. The fall turns attention inward, away from God.   **795 sov-
ereign** she flatters the tree as Satan flattered her in 532: understand
'most' before all three adjectives.   **796 of operation**... blessed with
the power to confer wisdom.   **797 infamed**, made infamous, slandered.
798 end purpose.   **799 care** in more senses than one.

[Handwritten left margin:] The tree is god

[Handwritten:] you are meant to look to god for guidence

[Handwritten left margin:] The tree could be a symbol of Matirialism

Shall tend thee, and the fertile burden ease
Of thy full branches offered free to all;
Till dieted by thee I grow mature
In knowledge, as the gods who all things know;
Though others envy what they cannot give;
For had the gift been theirs, it had not here
Thus grown. Experience, next to thee I owe,
Best guide; not following thee, I had remained
In ignorance, thou open'st wisdom's way,
And giv'st access, though secret she retire.
And I perhaps am secret; heaven is high,
High and remote to see from thence distinct
Each thing on earth; and other care perhaps
May have diverted from continual watch
Our great Forbidder, safe with all his spies
About him. But to Adam in what sort
Shall I appear? shall I to him make known
As yet my change, and give him to partake
Full happiness with me, or rather not,
But keep the odds of knowledge in my power
Without copartner? so to add what wants
In female sex, the more to draw his love,
And render me more equal, and perhaps,
A thing not undesirable, sometime
Superior; for inferior who is free?
This may be well: but what if God have seen,

[Handwritten right margin:] comparing herself to gods 805

[Handwritten right margin:] She has lost her faith 810

[Handwritten right margin:] Pride before a fall 815

[Handwritten right margin:] Matirial world is she challenging god 820

[Handwritten right margin:] "God is the Forbidder" 825

803 dieted fed; odd after 791. **805 envy** Eve unconsciously reveals one of the fallacies in Satan's argument: if the gods already have knowledge they can hardly envy it. **811 secret** associates Eve, **I**, with wisdom, **she**, in 810. **812 see** Eve wrongly assumes that divine vision, like human, is limited by distance; cf. x 5–6. **815 Forbidder** having sinned, Eve thinks of God in purely negative terms; the forbidden tree overshadows all others. The guardian angels have turned into **spies**. **816 in what sort** how (shall I appear to Adam, my small forbidder). **820 odds** advantage. **821 wants** is lacking. **823 more equal** Eve anticipates the pigs' doctrine in Orwell's *Animal Farm*: 'All animals are equal but some animals are more equal than others.' Although Eve doesn't mean the same thing at first, she quickly passes from the idea of equality to the idea of being **sometime Superior** to Adam; cf. IV 296. **825 inferior who is free** a Satanic doctrine; cf. VI 164–70.

[Handwritten right margin:] Eve wants equality.

[Handwritten bottom:] Perspecive: Story is about lust for matirials and passion and moveing away from God

And death ensue? then I shall be no more,
And Adam wedded to another Eve,
Shall live with her enjoying, I extinct;
A death to think. Confirmed then I resolve,   830
Adam shall share with me in bliss or woe:
So dear I love him, that with him all deaths
I could endure, without him live no life.'
    So saying, from the tree her step she turned,
But first low reverence done, as to the power   835
That dwelt within, whose presence had infused
Into the plant sciéntial sap, derived
From nectar, drink of gods. Adam the while
Waiting desirous her return, had wove
Of choicest flowers a garland to adorn   840
Her tresses, and her rural labours crown,
As reapers oft are wont their harvest queen.
Great joy he promised to his thoughts, and new
Solace in her return, so long delayed;
Yet oft his heart, divine of something ill,   845
Misgave him; he the faltering measure felt;
And forth to meet her went, the way she took
That morn when first they parted; by the tree
Of knowledge he must pass, there he her met,
Scarce from the tree returning; in her hand   850
A bough of fairest fruit that downy smiled,

829 I extinct when I am dead.   **833 life** creates a kind of anti-rhyme for **deaths** in 832. The two words have been chiming against each other throughout the scene; cf. 685–6, 763–4, 953–4.   **835 low reverence** the first act of idolatry; Adam's fall is the second (cf. x 145).   **836 presence** Eve's superstitions about the tree are true of the serpent.   **837 sciéntal** with the power of conferring knowledge. Although the narrative is back in the 3rd person it still expresses Eve's delusions.   **838 the while** meanwhile; cf. x 1, 229, 585.   **839 wove** woven.   **842 are wont** ... are accustomed to weave a garland for their harvest queen. But Eve's **rural labours** have been sin, and the **harvest** she has reaped is death. Adam, still unaware of this, sees her as the innocent country maid of 4½5ff.   **845 divine of** foreseeing; cf. x 357. He is about to learn of a different **divine** effect (865).   **846 faltering** the irregular phrases and caesuras enact the wavering beat (**measure**) of Adam's heart.   **851 downy smiled** covered with down seemed attractive.

New gathered, and ambrosial smell diffused.
To him she hasted, in her face excuse
Came prologue, and apology to prompt,
Which with bland words at will she thus addressed: 855
  'Hast thou not wondered, Adam, at my stay?
Thee I have missed, and thought it long, deprived
Thy presence, agony of love till now
Not felt, nor shall be twice, for never more
Mean I to try, what rash untried I sought,   860
The pain of absence from thy sight. But strange
Hath been the cause, and wonderful to hear:
This tree is not as we are told, a tree
Of danger tasted, nor to evil unknown
Opening the way, but of divine effect   865
To open eyes, and make them gods who taste;
And hath been tasted such: the serpent wise,
Or not restrained as we, or not obeying,
Hath eaten of the fruit, and is become,
Not dead, as we are threatened, but thenceforth   870
Endued with human voice and human sense,
Reasoning to admiration, and with me
Persuasively hath so prevailed, that I
Have also tasted, and have also found
The effects to correspond, opener mine eyes,   875
Dim erst, dilated spirits, ampler heart,

Spiritual experience

Glowing with energy

---

852 New gathered like Eve; cf. 432n.   **ambrosial** ambrosia (literally, immortal) is the food of the gods. Ironically, the fruit has made Eve mortal.   **853 excuse**... ambiguous. Either: excuse came to serve as prologue and apology came to prompt that which... Or: excuse came to prompt both prologue and apology, which... Or even: excuse came to serve as prologue to her apology and to prompt it... Cf. Satan's playacting in 667.   **855 bland** smooth, with overtones of blandishment.
857 Thee I the metre tends to make us stress I, i.e. I missed you; did you miss me?   **859 never more** a more sinister phrase than she realizes; cf. *King Lear* v iii 309 and Poe's raven.   **860 try**... experience the pain of being absent from your sight, which I recklessly sought in my inexperience.
862 wonderful to hear the variation of the epic *mirabile dictu* transfers the wonder from speaker to audience.   **864 Of danger tasted** dangerous to taste: the Latin idiom implies that the tree has already been tasted (cf. 130n).   **867 such** with such a result.   **872 to admiration** see 746n.
875 correspond to what the serpent experienced.   **876 erst** formerly;

And growing up to godhead; which for thee
Chiefly I sought, without thee can despise.
For bliss, as thou hast part, to me is bliss,
Tedious, unshared with thee, and odious soon.　　880
Thou therefore also taste, that equal lot
May join us, equal joy, as equal love;
Lest thou not tasting, different degree
Disjoin us, and I then too late renounce
Deity for thee, when fate will not permit.'　　885
　　Thus Eve with countenance blithe her story told;
But in her cheek distemper flushing glowed.
On the other side, Adam, soon as he heard
The fatal trespass done by Eve, amazed,
Astonied stood and blank, while horror chill　　890
Ran through his veins, and all his joints relaxed;
From his slack hand the garland wreathed for Eve
Down dropped, and all the faded roses shed:
Speechless he stood and pale, till thus at length
First to himself he inward silence broke:　　895
　　'O fairest of creation, last and best
Of all God's works, creature in whom excelled
Whatever can to sight or thought be formed,
Holy, divine, good, amiable, or sweet!
How art thou lost, how on a sudden lost,　　900

dilated expanded. Eve makes the fruit sound like a psychedelic drug.
880 Tedious unshared echoing Eve's unfallen lovesong in IV 639–56.
881 lot fate. Eve has been converted to Satan's fatalistic philosophy;
cf. 685n.　　**883 thou not tasting** if you do not taste.　　**884 Disjoin**
divide.　　**887 distemper** technical term for a disproportion of the
4 humours which controlled man's temperament; cf. 1131.　　**888 other
side** metaphorically as well as literally. Eve is on Satan's side;
Adam is still on God's.　　**889 amazed** bewildered.　　**890 Astonied**
thunderstruck, though Adam also behaves as if he had been turned into
stone; **blank** pale; **horror** shudder (cf. V 65).　　**892 garland** in *Areo-
pagitica* M calls virtue an 'immortal garland' (cf. commentary p. 22).
The image clinches the association of Eve with roses (cf. 218n, 426n).
The **faded** petals symbolize her mortality and remind us that in the fallen
world the rose will be an emblem of transience as well as love.　　**893
dropped** what would be lost by changing the word order to the normal
English subject-verb-predicate?　　**896 last and best** repeats Satan's
fallacy in 100–2 (see commentary p. 18).　　**900 on a sudden** suddenly.

Defaced, deflowered, and now to death devote?
Rather how hast thou yielded to transgress
The strict forbiddance, how to violate
The sacred fruit forbidden! Some cursèd fraud
Of enemy hath beguiled thee, yet unknown,   905
And me with thee hath ruined, for with thee
Certain my resolution is to die;
How can I live without thee, how forgo
Thy sweet convérse and love so dearly joined,
To live again in these wild woods forlorn?   910
Should God create another Eve, and I
Another rib afford, yet loss of thee
Would never from my heart; no no, I feel
The link of nature draw me: flesh of flesh,
Bone of my bone thou art, and from thy state   915
Mine never shall be parted, bliss or woe.'
    So having said, as one from sad dismay
Recomforted, and after thoughts disturbed
Submitting to what seemed remédiless,
Thus in calm mood his words to Eve he turned: 920
    'Bold deed thou hast presumed, adventurous Eve,
And peril great provoked, who thus hath dared
Had it been only coveting to eye
That sacred fruit, sacred to abstinence,
Much more to taste it under ban to touch.   925
But past who can recall, or done undo?
Not God omnipotent, nor fate, yet so
Perhaps thou shalt not die, perhaps the fact

901 Defaced disfigured (cf. x 110); **deflowered** literally deprived of her
flowers, like Proserpina (cf. IV 269), and metaphorically violated; **devote**
cursed. **905 enemy** Adam doesn't identify Satan as the tempter until
x 1033–5. **910 again** referring to the time he spent alone before Eve's
creation (see VIII 250ff.). **912 afford** supply. **914 flesh** cf. *Genesis* ii 23.
919 seemed reminds us that there was a remedy; cf. 787n. **924 sacred
to abstinence** so sacred that we should abstain from it. **927 fate** Adam
too has become a fatalist (cf. 881n); **so even so. 928 Perhaps** in some
English translations of the Bible, Eve's words in *Genesis* iii were 'lest
perhaps we die' (Vulgate *ne forte moriamini*): Protestant theologians found
her guilty of doubting God's word, but M transfers the doubt to Adam
(cf. 663); **fact**=both deed (from Latin *facere*) and crime (cf. 980).

95

Adam is am imagining having more power

Is not so heinous now, foretasted fruit,
Profaned first by the serpent, by him first   930
Made common and unhallowed ere our taste;
Nor yet on him found deadly, he yet lives,
Lives, as thou saidst, and gains to live as man
Higher degree of life, inducement strong
To us, as likely tasting to attain   935
Proportional ascent, which cannot be
But to be gods, or angels demi-gods.
Nor can I think that God, Creator wise,
Though threatening, will in earnest so destroy
Us his prime creatures, dignified so high,   940
Set over all his works, which in our fall,
For us created, needs with us must fail,
Dependent made; so God shall uncreate,
Be frústrate, do, undo, and labour lose,
Not well conceived of God, who though his power   945
Creation could repeat, yet would be loth
Us to abolish, lest the Adversary
Triumph and say: "Fickle their state whom God
Most favours; who can please him long; me first
He ruined, now mankind; whom will he next?"   950
Matter of scorn, not to be given the Foe.
However I with thee have fixed my lot,
Certain to undergo like doom; if death

929 foretasted since the fruit has already been tasted by the serpent. **931 our** already includes Adam in the fall. **932 lives, Lives** Adam too is beginning to talk like Satan; cf. 749n. **935 as likely, tasting** since we are likely, by tasting. **936 Proportional ascent** repeats Satan's argument in 711; **which cannot be** sounds like a denial until the thought is completed in the next line. **937 gods** another Satanic touch (cf. 99n). **939 in earnest** really: **so** as he threatened. **940 prime** first (in time or value?). Adam has forgotten the angels. **941 fall...fail** pun emphasized by half-rhyme. **942 needs** necessarily. Adam rightly argues that since the world was made for man it will suffer the consequences of his fall; cf. x 648ff. **945 conceived** he concludes, wrongly, that it is unthinkable for God to be frustrated (**frústrate**) by having to destroy his own works; cf. x 616ff. **946 repeat** Satan suspected (145) that God couldn't. **947 Adversary** Satan (see x 387n). **949 favours** cf. 175. Adam's impersonation of Satan is accurate. **951 Matter of** subject for. **952 lot** see 927n. **953 Certain** determined to undergo the same fate; cf. 907.

96

Consórt with thee, death is to me as life;
So forcible within my heart I feel   955
The bond of nature draw me to my own,
My own in thee, for what thou art is mine;
Our state cannot be severed, we are one,
One flesh; to lose thee were to lose myself.'

So Adam, and thus Eve to him replied: 960
'O glorious trial of exceeding love,
Illustrious evidence, example high!
Engaging me to emulate, but short
Of thy perfection, how shall I attain,
Adam, from whose dear side I boast me sprung,   965
And gladly of our union hear thee speak,
One heart, one soul in both; whereof good proof
This day affords, declaring thee resolved,
Rather than death or aught than death more dread
Shall separate us, linked in love so dear,   970
To undergo with me one guilt, one crime,
If any be, of tasting this fair fruit,
Whose virtue, for of good still good proceeds,
Direct, or by occasion hath presented
This happy trial of thy love, which else   975
So eminently never had been known.

The outward speech echoes the inward.   **954 death...life** Adam's
version of Satan's 'Evil be thou my good' (IV 110); cf. 833n. **Consórt** makes
Eve the wife of Death: see commentary p. 42.   **956 bond** like **link** in
914 and 970 suggests constraint as well as union; cf. 761. Adam is hinting
that he is not responsible for his action. **958 state** of marriage. M believed
it could be **severed** (cf. 252n) by divorce.   **959 myself** cf. X 128n.   **961
trial** proof, but Eve is also thinking of a courtroom trial (cf. 975) with love
as the defendant, vindicated by **evidence** (962) and **proof** (967); **exceed-
ing** hints that Adam's love is excessive.   **964 attain** to your perfection.
Eve finally concedes that she is Adam's inferior, but at the wrong time and
for the wrong reason.   **965 I boast me sprung** I proudly claim to be
derived: like an epic hero she is proud of her lineage.   **968 declaring...**
declaring that you are determined to share in my guilt rather than allow
death, or something still more dreadful, to separate us, united as we
are in such dear love.   **972 If any be** Eve remembers just in time
that she is pretending there is no crime involved in eating the for-
bidden fruit; cf. 146.   **973 virtue** goodness again; cf. 745n.   **974
by occasion** indirectly.

Were it I thought death menaced would ensue
This my attempt, I would sustain alone
The worst, and not persuade thee: rather die
Deserted, than oblige thee with a fact   980
Pernicious to thy peace, chiefly assured
Remarkably so late of thy so true,
So faithful love unequalled; but I feel
Far otherwise the event, not death, but life
Augmented, opened eyes, new hopes, new joys,   985
Taste so divine, that what of sweet before
Hath touched my sense, flat seems to this, and harsh.
On my experience, Adam, freely taste,
And fear of death deliver to the winds.'

   So saying, she embraced him, and for joy   990
Tenderly wept, much won that he his love
Had so ennobled, as of choice to incur
Divine displeasure for her sake, or death.
In recompense (for such compliance bad
Such recompense best merits) from the bough   995
She gave him of that fair enticing fruit
With liberal hand: he scrupled not to eat
Against his better knowledge, not deceived,
But fondly overcome with female charm.

Earth trembled from her entrails, as again   1000
In pangs, and nature gave a second groan,

977 Were it... if I thought the death with which we have been threatened would follow what I have done... **980 oblige** make you guilty of; **fact** crime. **981 Pernicious** fatal. Eve loads her speech with adverbs and adjectives – she is protesting too much. **986 what of sweet** whatever sweetness. **987 to** compared to. **988 On** on the basis of; **freely** like **liberal** in 997 used in a debased sense: without restraint. **989 to the winds** the idiom belongs to the fallen world; cf. x 695ff. **991 won** moved. **994 bad** M's choric intrusions (cf. 404ff.) become increasingly harsh; see x 5–15 and commentary p. 35. **998 not deceived** see commentary p. 29. **999 fondly** foolishly; **charm** cf. VIII 533. **1001 second** the first groan was in 782–3. Earth's pangs suggest a kind of birth is taking place; cf. Yeats' *Second coming*. The thunderstorm also recalls Aeneas' love-making to Dido in *Aeneid* iv 160–70. Cf. Virgil's comment: 'That day was first the cause of death and of evils.'

> Ironic

Sky loured and muttering thunder, some sad drops
Wept at completing of the mortal sin
Original; while Adam took no thought,
Eating his fill, nor Eve to iterate   1005
Her former trespass feared, the more to soothe
Him with her loved society, that now
As with new wine intoxicated both
They swim in mirth, and fancy that they feel
Divinity within them breeding wings   1010
Wherewith to scorn the earth: but that false fruit
Far other operation first displayed,
Carnal desire inflaming; he on Eve
Began to cast lascivious eyes, she him
As wantonly repaid; in lust they burn: 1015
Till Adam thus 'gan Eve to dalliance move:

   'Eve, now I see thou art exact of taste,
And elegant, of sapience no small part,
Since to each meaning savour we apply,
And palate call judicious; I the praise   1020
Yield thee, so well this day thou has purveyed.
Much pleasure we have lost, while we abstained
From this delightful fruit, nor known till now
True relish, tasting; if such pleasure be
In things to us forbidden, it might be wished,   1025

Carnal: Relating to, especially sexual, needs and achieves — Animalistic

liberating Angres

Bathos

Irony. They feel like they are being liberated but they are being demoted to beastial language

Siblians

1002 **loured** grew dark.   1003 **mortal sin Original** see commentary
p. 24.   1004 **no thought** now Adam is mindless (cf. 358n.).   1005
iterate repeat.   1007 **that** with the result that.   1008 **new wine** is
supposed to be more intoxicating than aged wine; see commentary p. 33.
1010 **wings** Plato uses this image for the soul's ascent to divinity and im-
mortality (*Phaedrus* 246). Here the ascent is illusory; cf. Eve's dream
in v 86–90).   1012 **operation** effect.   1013 **inflaming** the association
of fire and sex (cf. 1015, 1036) is traditional.   1016 **dalliance** amorous
sport. Reinforced by **play** (1027), **toy** (1034) and **disport** (1042), it trans-
forms the sexual act from a 'mysterious' rite (IV 743) into a frivolous
game. Adam is behaving like the lecherous knights of romantic epic.
1017 **taste** initiates a series of tortuous quibbles relating physical to in-
tellectual judgement. Eve is **elegant** (in Latin = refined in taste). And
since good taste is an aspect of **sapience** (Latin *sapere* = to know and to
taste) the word **savour** (also from *sapere*) can be applied to the mind, and
the word **judicious** to the palate; cf. 238n.   1021 **purveyed** provided
food for.

For this one tree had been forbidden ten.
But come, so well refreshed, now let us play,
As meet is, after such delicious fare;
For never did thy beauty since the day
I saw thee first and wedded thee, adorned   1030
With all perfections, so inflame my sense
With ardour to enjoy thee, fairer now
Than ever, bounty of this virtuous tree.'
    So said he, and forbore not glance or toy
Of amorous intent, well understood   1035
Of Eve, whose eye darted contagious fire.
Her hand he seized, and to a shady bank,
Thick overhead with verdant roof embowered
He led her nothing loth; flowers were the couch,
Pansies, and violets, and asphodel,   1040
And hyacinth, earth's freshest softest lap.
There they their fill of love and love's disport
Took largely, of their mutual guilt the seal,
The solace of their sin, till dewy sleep
Oppressed them, wearied with their amorous play.   1045
Soon as the force of that fallacious fruit,
That with exhilarating vapour bland
About their spirits had played, and inmost powers
Made err, was now exhaled, and grosser sleep
Bred of unkindly fumes, with conscious dreams   1050

1026 For instead of; **ten** eventually the ten commandments will replace
the prohibition of the tree of knowledge. **1028 meet** fitting (meat?).
1029 the day cf. VIII 510–20 and topics p. 172. **1033 bounty** gift.
Adam means that thanks to the tree Eve seems more beautiful than ever,
but the ambiguous grammar (**bounty** could be in apposition to **thee**) turns
her into a dainty piece of fruit to be consumed. **1034 toy** caress. **1036**
contagious has deliberately unpleasant overtones of disease being spread
by touch. **1038 embowered** enclosed with foliage. **1039 nothing**
loth not at all reluctant; cf. Eve's 'sweet reluctant amorous delay' in IV
311. The flowers echo M's account of her marriage bed in IV 690–705;
see topics p. 172. **1042 fill** cf. 1005. **1048 spirits** a technical term in
renaissance psychology for the vaporous substance uniting body and soul.
1049 grosser than what? **1050 unkindly** unnatural; **conscious**
dreams would have sounded less paradoxical in the 17th century when
conscious could mean inspired by conscience, i.e. guilty. Cf. Adam's
dream-theory in V 95ff.

Encumbered, now had left them, up they rose
As from unrest, and each the other viewing,
Soon found their eyes how opened, and their minds
How darkened; innocence, that as a veil
Had shadowed them from knowing ill, was gone,   1055
Just confidence, and native righteousness
And honour from about them, naked left
To guilty shame he covered, but his robe
Uncovered more; so rose the Danite strong
Hercúlean Samson from the harlot lap   1060
Of Phílistéan Dálilá, and waked
Shorn of his strength, they destitute and bare
Of all their virtue: silent, and in face
Confounded long they sat, as strucken mute,
Till Adam, though not less than Eve abashed,   1065
At length gave utterance to these words constrained:
  'O Eve, in evil hour thou didst give ear
To that false worm, of whomsoever taught
To counterfeit man's voice, true in our fall,
False in our promised rising; since our eyes   1070
Opened we find indeed, and find we know
Both good and evil, good lost, and evil got,
Bad fruit of knowledge, if this be to know,

1054 **veil** makes innocence sound rather diaphanous (cf. 425); one of M's less successful images (cf. v 383). 1055 **shadowed** protected; an odd word to use in the context. Were Adam and Eve really 'in the dark'? Shadows are usually bad in *PL*, viz. 12: x 249, 264. 1056 **Just** to distinguish good from bad **confidence** (Latin *fides* = faith, trust); cf. 1175. 1058 **he** could refer to **shame** or to Adam. In the first case there would have to be a heavy stop after **shame**. Is the uncertainty at all functional? 1059 **Danite** Samson, whose father was of the tribe of Dan, was betrayed by Dalıla, his Philistine mistress, into revealing that the secret of his great strength lay ın his hair; she cut it off while he was sleeping: *Judges* xiv. In Chaucer's *Monk's tale* he is the third example of a tragic hero (Lucifer and Adam are the first two – see topics p. 152). M treated the story as a Greek tragedy ın *SA*. 1060 **Hercúlean** as strong as Hercules, the fourth example of tragedy in the *Monk's tale*. He too was betrayed by his mistress, Deianira, who gave him a poisoned shirt to wear; cf. II 542–6. 1062 **they** they waked. 1067 **Eve, in evil** the collocation gives Eve's name a sinister new resonance. 1068 **worm** serpent; **whomsoever** cf. 905n. 1069 **in** wıth respect to; **fall False** the anadiplosis emphasizes the pun (cf. 941).

Which leaves us naked thus, of honour void,
Of innocence, of faith, of purity,   1075
Our wonted ornaments now soiled and stained,
And in our faces evident the signs
Of foul concupiscence; whence evil store;
Even shame, the last of evils; of the first
Be sure then. How shall I behold the face   1080
Henceforth of God or angel, erst with joy
And rapture so oft beheld? those heavenly shapes
Will dazzle now this earthly, with their blaze
Insufferably bright. O might I here
In solitude live savage, in some glade   1085
Obscured, where highest woods impenetrable
To star or sunlight, spread their umbrage broad
And brown as evening: cover me ye pines,
Ye cedars, with innumerable boughs
Hide me, where I may never see them more.   1090
But let us now, as in bad plight, devise
What best may for the present serve to hide
The parts of each from other, that seem most
To shame obnoxious, and unseemliest seen,
Some tree whose broad smooth leaves together   1095
    sewed,
And girded on our loins, may cover round
Those middle parts, that this new comer, shame,
There sit not, and reproach us as unclean.'
   So counselled he, and both together went
Into the thickest wood, there soon they chose   1100

1076 **wonted** accustomed; **ornaments** makes Adam and Eve's virtues
extrinsic. 1078 **concupiscence** the theological and psychological term
for desire, often sexual as here; **store** effect. 1079 **last** in time or mag-
nitude? In either case the logic is the same: if we have experienced
the last we must also have experienced the first. 1081 **God or angel**
echoes M's prophecy in 1-5. 1083 **earthly** earthly nature, Adam.
1085 **savage** implies that the pastoral life of Eden has so far been
civilized if not courtly; cf v 331-60, topics p. 164. 1087 **umbrage**
shade. 1088 **brown** dark. 1090 **them** the heavenly shapes (1082)
or **star and sunlight** (1087). 1091 **as in** since we are in. 1093 **parts**
genitals. 1094 **obnoxious** exposed (ct. 170) but now also offensive.
1098 **as** for being. 1100 **thickest wood** thickest part of the wood.

The fig tree, not that kind for fruit renowned,
But such as at this day to Indians known
In Málabár or Décan spreads her arms
Branching so broad and long, that in the ground
The bended twigs take root, and daughters grow   1105
About the mother tree, a pillared shade
High overarched, and echoing walks between;
There oft the Indian herdsman shunning heat
Shelters in cool, and tends his pasturing herds
At loopholes cut through thickest shade: those   1110
    leaves
They gathered, broad as Amazónian targe,
And with what skill they had, together sewed,
To gird their waist, vain covering if to hide
Their guilt and dreaded shame; O how unlike
To that first naked glory. Such of late   1115
Columbus found the American so girt
With feathered cincture, naked else and wild
Among the trees on isles and woody shores.
Thus fenced, and as they thought, their shame in part
Covered, but not at rest or ease of mind,   1120
They sat them down to weep, nor only tears
Rained at their eyes, but high winds worse within
Began to rise, high passions, anger, hate,
Mistrust, suspicion, discord, and shook sore
Their inward state of mind, calm region once   1125

1101 **fig tree** not the common species but the Indian fig (banyan) tree. Its
branches symbolize the ramifications of the fall.   1103 **Málabár** and
Décan regions of India.   1106 **pillared** combines with **overarched** in
1107 to turn the fig tree into a cathedral.   1108 **shunning heat** cf. 1085–8.
As a descendant of Adam the **herdsman** imitates him.   1111 **Amazón-
ian targe** the shields of the legendary female warriors, the Amazons, were
famous for their size. The allusion mocks Eve's heroic aspirations. M
follows contemporary botanists in confusing the banyan, whose leaves are
small, with the banana, whose leaves are large.   1112 **what skill** cf. 391.
1113 **vain** futile; **if** if it was intended.   1116 **American** when Columbus
discovered America in 1492 he found the Indians wearing skirts of bird-
feathers. This reference combines with that in 1108 to project the results
of the fall over the whole world.   1119 **fenced** protected.   1122 **Rained**
this inner storm continues the outer one which began in 1000; see commen-
tary p. 32.

103

[Handwritten margin note top: ▷ Devowing to a state of lesser reason.]

[Handwritten margin note left: Not thinking with reason]

And full of peace, now tossed and turbulent:
For understanding ruled not, and the will
Heard not her lore, both in subjection now
To sensual appetite, who from beneath
Usurping over sovereign reason claimed   1130
Superior sway: from thus distempered breast,
Adam, estranged in look and altered style,
Speech intermitted thus to Eve renewed:
  'Would thou hadst hearkened to my words, and
    stayed
With me, as I besought thee, when that strange   1135
Desire of wandering this unhappy morn,
I know not whence possessed thee; we had then
Remained still happy, not as now, despoiled
Of all our good, shamed, naked, miserable.
Let none henceforth seek needless cause to approve 1140
The faith they owe; when earnestly they seek
Such proof, conclude, they then begin to fail.'
    To whom soon moved with touch of blame thus Eve:

[Handwritten margin note left: Eve is arguing back]

'What words have passed thy lips, Adam severe,
Imput'st thou that to my default, or will   1145
Of wandering, as thou call'st it, which who knows
But might as ill have happened thou being by,
Or to thyself perhaps: hadst thou been there,
Or here the attempt, thou couldst not have discerned
Fraud in the serpent, speaking as he spake;   1150

[Handwritten margin note left: Is she just to be with him forever]

No ground of enmity between us known,
Why he should mean me ill, or seek to harm.
Was I to have never parted from thy side?
As good have grown there still a lifeless rib.
Being as I am, why didst not thou the head   1155

1127 understanding cf. 351–6; XII 82–90; commentary p. 33.   **1128 lore** advice, teaching, which in this case should also have been law.   **1131 distempered** cf. 887n.   **1132 altered style** Adam no longer calls Eve by the ceremonious titles he used before the fall; now she is just **thou**.   **1133 intermitted** interrupted (by the search for fig leaves).   **1137 possessed** equates Eve with the serpent; cf. 189, topics p. 159.   **1140 approve** put to the test, referring to Eve's demand to face temptation alone; cf. 367.   **1146 which** goes with **that** in 1145.   **1155 as I am** i.e.

Command me absolutely not to go,
Going into such danger as thou saidst?
Too facile then thou didst not much gainsay,
Nay didst permit, approve, and fair dismiss.
Hadst thou been firm and fixed in thy dissent,   1160
Neither had I transgressed, nor thou with me.'
    To whom then first incensed Adam replied:
'Is this the love, is this the recompense
Of mine to thee, ingrateful Eve, expressed
Immutable when thou wert lost, not I,   1165
Who might have lived and joyed immortal bliss,
Yet willingly chose rather death with thee:
And am I now upbraided, as the cause
Of thy transgressing? not enough severe,
It seems, in thy restraint: what could I more?   1170
I warned thee, I admonished thee, foretold
The danger, and the lurking enemy
That lay in wait; beyond this had been force,
And force upon free will hath here no place.
But confidence then bore thee on, secure   1175
Either to meet no danger, or to find
Matter of glorious trial; and perhaps
I also erred in overmuch admiring
What seemed in thee so perfect, that I thought
No evil durst attempt thee, but I rue   1180
That error now, which is become my crime,
And thou the accuser. Thus it shall befall
Him who to worth in women overtrusting

alive; **head** see commentary p. 22.   **1158 Too facile**... a roundabout
way of saying: you gave in to me too easily.   **1162 first incensed**
the confused syntax of 1163–5 reflects Adam's first experience of anger.
He means: ungrateful Eve, is this the way you repay me for the love I
showed you, is this the love you said was unchangeable when you were
lost but I was still unfallen?   **1166 joyed** enjoyed.   **1168 upbraided**
reproached.   **1174 free will** Adam echoes, and validates, God's argu-
ment in III 103ff.   **1175 secure** over-confident; cf. 371n.   **1177**
Matter of... an opportunity to glorify yourself by resisting temptation
alone.   **1180 durst attempt** would dare attack; **rue** regret.   **1183**
women the ungrammatical plural (viz **her** and **she** in 1184) reminds us

Lets her will rule; restraint she will not brook,
And left to herself, if evil thence ensue,   1185
She first his weak indulgence will accuse.'
    Thus they in mutual accusation spent
The fruitless hours, but neither self-condemning,
And of their vain contést appeared no end.

that Eve contains all her daughters; see commentary p. 24.   **1184 brook**
tolerate; the metre forces us to stress **her**.   **1188 fruitless** Eve's pun in
648 is no longer frivolous.   **1189 vain** futile; **appeared** hints that there
will in fact be an end (cf. x 863ff.).

Book X

MEANWHILE THE HEINOUS and despiteful act
Of Satan done in paradise, and how
He in the serpent, had perverted Eve,
Her husband she, to taste the fatal fruit,
Was known in heaven; for what can scape the eye   5
Of God all-seeing, or deceive his heart
Omniscient, who in all things wise and just,
Hindered not Satan to attempt the mind
Of man, with strength entire, and free will armed,
Complete to have discovered and repulsed   10
Whatever wiles of foe or seeming friend.
For still they knew, and ought to have still remembered
The high injunction not to taste that fruit,
Whoever tempted; which they not obeying,
Incurred, what could they less, the penalty,   15
And manifold in sin, deserved to fall.
Up into heaven from paradise in haste
The angelic guards ascended, mute and sad
For man, for of his state by this they knew
Much wondering how the subtle fiend had stolen   20
Entrance unseen. Soon as the unwelcome news
From earth arrived at heaven gate, displeased

3 perverted led astray. The ellipsis in 4 reproduces the domino action
of the fall; one push (verb) was enough (cf. 880). **8 to attempt** from
tempting or attacking. **9 entire** man's mind was fully equipped to
expose or resist any tricks. Is this true of Eve? The military image comes
from *Ephesians* vi 11: 'the whole armour of God' (cf. IV 65). **12 they**
Adam and Eve. The line seems to splutter. **16 manifold** like many
earlier theologians M thought the fall involved multiple sins: distrust,
unbelief, ingratitude, disobedience, gluttony etc. **18 guards** Gabriel
and the other angels stationed to defend Eden; see IV 561. **19 by this**
by now. **20 stolen Entrance** referring to IX 70 but the verb recalls the
burglar image in IV 188.

All were who heard, dim sadness did not spare
That time celestial visages, yet mixed
With pity, violated not their bliss.   25
About the new-arrived, in multitudes
The ethereal people ran, to hear and know
How all befell: they towards the throne supreme
Accountable made haste to make appear
With righteous plea, their utmost vigilance,   30
And easily approved; when the most high
Eternal Father from his secret cloud,
Amidst in thunder uttered thus his voice:
   'Assembled angels, and ye powers returned
From unsuccessful charge, be not dismayed,   35
Nor troubled at these tidings from the earth,
Which your sincerest care could not prevent,
Foretold so lately what would come to pass,
When first this Tempter crossed the gulf from hell.
I told ye then he should prevail and speed   40
On his bad errand, man should be seduced
And flattered out of all, believing lies
Against his Maker; no decree of mine
Concurring to necessitate his fall,
Or touch with lightest moment of impúlse   45
His free will, to her own inclining left
In even scale. But fallen he is, and now

24 **That time** then.   **28 they** the guards as distinct from the angels
who stayed behind in heaven.   **29 Accountable** hurried syntax: since
they were accountable to God for their duties they hastened to his throne
to make it plain that...   **31 approved** showed (that they had been
vigilant).   **32 cloud...thunder** a blend of classical and biblical ideas.
In Latin epic Zeus is often 'the high thunderer' and wields a thunderbolt.
In the *OT* God is often veiled in cloud and in the *NT* he speaks with a
voice of thunder (*Revelation* iv 5); cf. II 263–8.   **34 powers** forces,
or one of the orders of angels; see 86, 395.   **35 charge** duty.   **37 sin-
cerest care** most genuine effort.   **38 Foretold** goes with the **angels**
and **powers** in 34; God forewarned them in III 80 that man would fall.
39 the gulf chaos; see III 70; X 253.   **40 speed** succeed.   **41 errand**
purpose; reduces Satan to God's messenger-boy (see I 152; II 827; IV
795; topics pp. 177).   **42 flattered...lies** applies better to Eve's fall
than to Adam's.   **44 Concurring** intervening.   **45 moment of
impúlse** pressure. The mechanical terms prepare for the balance image

What rests but that the mortal sentence pass
On his transgression, death denounced that day,
Which he presumes already vain and void,   50
Because not yet inflicted, as he feared,
By some immediate stroke; but soon shall find
Forbearance no acquittance ere day end.
Justice shall not return as bounty scorned.
But whom send I to judge them? whom but thee   55
Vicegerent Son, to thee I have transferred
All judgement whether in heaven, or earth, or hell.
Easy it may be seen that I intend
Mercy colléague with justice, sending thee
Man's friend, his mediator, his designed   60
Both ransom and redeemer voluntary,
And destined man himself to judge man fallen.'
    So spake the Father, and unfolding bright
Toward the right hand his glory, on the Son
Blazed forth unclouded deity; he full   65
Resplendent all his Father manifest
Expressed, and thus divinely answered mild:
    'Father eternal, thine is to decree,
Mine both in heaven and earth to do thy will
Supreme, that thou in me thy Son beloved   70
May'st ever rest well pleased. I go to judge
On earth these thy transgressors, but thou know'st,

in 46–7. Is it a good metaphor for free will?   **48 rests** remains.   **49
death denounced that day** a very compressed phrase echoed in 210,
853, 962: the penalty of death which God had proclaimed would be im-
posed on the same day Adam ate the forbidden fruit (cf. VIII 323–30;
IX 762; *Genesis* ii 17).   **53 Forbearance no acquittance** another very
contracted expression: his forbearance in not inflicting the punishment
at once does not imply that man has been acquitted. As God's anger
mounts his syntax grows more dense and his diction more frigid.   **54
Justice…scorned** unlike his bounty, God's justice is irresistible.
56 Vicegerent deputy.   **58 Easy** easily.   **59 colléague** cooperate;
sending since I am sending.   **60 designed** appointed.   **62 destined
man** destined to be man.   **66 manifest Expressed** showed forth in
visible form.   **69 earth** leaves out hell; cf. 57.   **70 Son beloved** Christ
anticipates *Matthew* iii 17; 'This is my beloved Son, in whom I am well
pleased.' See VI 720, 728; X 634.   **72 thy** against thee, but the genitive
makes the transgressors God's responsibility.

Whoever judged, the worst on me must light,
When time shall be, for so I undertook
Before thee; and not repenting, this obtain   75
Of right, that I may mitigate their doom
On me derived, yet I shall temper so
Justice with mercy, as may illústrate most
Them fully satisfied, and thee appease.
Attendance none shall need, nor train, where none   80
Are to behold the judgement, but the judged,
Those two; the third best absent is condemned,
Convíct by flight, and rebel to all law
Conviction to the serpent none belongs.'

    Thus saying, from his radiant seat he rose   85
Of high collateral glory: him thrones and powers,
Princedoms, and dominations ministrant
Accompanied to heaven gate, from whence
Eden and all the coast in prospect lay.
Down he descended straight; the speed of gods   90
Time counts not, though with swiftest minutes winged.

    Now was the sun in western cadence low
From noon, and gentle airs due at their hour

73 judged transitive or intransitive?   **74 When time shall be** when the time comes, but also: when time exists (see 91n). **undertook** Christ offered to redeem man in III 227.   **75 Before thee** in your presence; **not repenting** of my undertaking.   **76 Of** by.   **77 derived** transferred. Christ atones for Adam's sin by taking on himself the doom he is about to pronounce; see III 236–41.   **78 illústrate** show clearly. Justice will be satisfied by Christ's death, mercy by man's redemption; see III 132–4, 406.   **80 Attendance** no attendant angels or followers (**train**) will be necessary; cf. the Son's ceremonial descent in VII 192–205 and Eve's departure in IX 385–7.   **82 the third** Satan.   **83 Convíct by flight** having proved his guilt by running away.   **84 Conviction...** the serpent is not to be condemned (because he was merely Satan's instrument); M is less charitable in X 168.   **86 collateral** Christ's throne (**seat**) is side by side with the Father's. **thrones...** 4 of the 9 orders of angels (see III 320); Satan names 5 in 460.   **89 coast** surrounding area, but see commentary p. 46.   **91 winged** time, traditionally pictured with feathered wings, is not fast enough to measure divine actions because 'Immediate are the acts of God, more swift Than time or motion' (VII 176). But although God theoretically exists outside time, the poem's chronology confines him within it; hence the problem of foreknowledge versus free will (see topics pp. 176–78).   **92 cadence** descent.

To fan the earth now waked, and usher in
The evening cool when he from wrath more cool   95
Came the mild judge and intercessor both
To sentence man: the voice of God they heard
Now walking in the garden, by soft winds
Brought to their ears, while day declined, they heard,
And from his presence hid themselves among   100
The thickest trees, both man and wife, till God
Approaching, thus to Adam called aloud:
    'Where art thou Adam, wont with joy to meet
My coming seen far off? I miss thee here,
Not pleased, thus entertained with solitude,   105
Where obvious duty erewhile appeared unsought:
Or come I less conspicuous, or what change
Absénts thee, or what chance detains? Come forth.'
    He came, and with him Eve, more loth, though first
To offend, discountenanced both, and discomposed;   110
Love was not in their looks, either to God
Or to each other, but apparent guilt,
And shame, and perturbation, and despair,
Anger, and obstinacy, and hate, and guile.
Whence Adam faltering long, thus answered brief: 115
    'I heard thee in the garden, and of thy voice
Afraid, being naked, hid myself.' To whom
The gracious judge without revile replied:
    'My voice thou oft hast heard, and hast not feared,
But still rejoiced, how is it now become   120
So dreadful to thee? that thou art naked, who

> ▷ hissing
> hyperbole

94 **fan** combines with **usher** to make the onset of evening and the Son's
arrival seem rather ceremonious (like a judge's); cf. 80.   95 **cool** see
Genesis iii 8.   99 **they heard** the repetition (see 97) creates an echo for
the voice of God – as the Father's vicegerent the Son assumes his title.
101 **thickest trees** see IX 1100n.   103 **wont** accustomed.   105 **Not
pleased** refers to Christ but also applies to Adam; grammatically it
could qualify I or **thee**.   106 **obvious** plain, easy.   110 **discounte-
nanced** shame-faced (cf. IX 886, 901); **discomposed** embarrassed, upset.
112 **apparent** evident.   113 **perturbation** excessive passion – a technical
term in renaissance psychology.   118 **revile** reviling.   119 **heard** note
the half-rhyme with **feared**; also between **voice** and **rejoiced**.   120 **still**
always.   121 **dreadful** fearsome.

Hath told thee? hast thou eaten of the tree
Whereof I gave thee charge thou shouldst not eat?'
    To whom thus Adam sore beset replied:
'O heaven! in evil strait this day I stand   125
Before my judge, either to undergo
Myself the total crime, or to accuse
My other self, the partner of my life;
Whose failing, while her faith to me remains,
I should conceal, and not expose to blame   130
By my complaint; but strict necessity
Subdues me, and calamitous constraint
Lest on my head both sin and punishment,
However insupportable, be all
Devolved; though should I hold my peace, yet thou   135
Wouldst easily detect what I conceal.
This woman whom thou mad'st to be my help,
And gav'st me as thy perfect gift, so good,
So fit, so ácceptáble, so divine,
That from her hand I could suspect no ill,   140
And what she did, whatever in itself
Her doing seemed to justify the deed;
She gave me of the tree, and I did eat.'
    To whom the sovereign Presence thus replied:
'Was she thy God, that her thou didst obey   145
Before his voice, or was she made thy guide,
Superior, or but equal, that to her
Thou didst resign thy manhood, and the place
Wherein God set thee above her made of thee,
And for thee, whose perfection far excelled   150

Men being emasculated by women

128 **My other self** a recurring phrase with rich implications; see IV
472, 488; V 95; VIII 450, 495; IX 959. Psychologically and physically Eve
is Adam's *alter ego*.   135 **Devolved** shifted on to.   137 **woman** Adam
can't bear to name her; cf. 837. **help** see *Genesis* ii 18.   139 **divine**
idolatrous; see 145, commentary p. 39.   140 **suspect no ill**
an outright lie.   141 **did...doing...deed** the traductio mimics
Adam's deviousness.   145 **Was she...that her** the metre forces us
to stress the pronouns, and hence Christ's point.   146 **Before his**
rather than God's.   147 **or but equal** not a real alternative; see IX
823n; X 149.

Hers in all real dignity: adorned
She was indeed, and lovely to attract
Thy love, not thy subjection, and her gifts
Were such as under government well seemed,
Unseemly to bear rule, which was thy part   155
And person, hadst thou known thyself aright.'
   So having said, he thus to Eve in few:
'Say woman, what is this which thou hast done?'
   To whom sad Eve with shame nigh overwhelmed,
Confessing soon, yet not before her judge   160
Bold or loquacious, thus abashed replied:
'The serpent me beguiled and I did eat.'
   Which when the Lord God heard, without delay
To judgement he proceeded on the accused
Serpent though brute, unable to transfer   165
The guilt on him who made him instrument
Of mischief, and polluted from the end
Of his creation; justly then accursed,
As vitiated in nature: more to know
Concerned not man (since he no further knew)   170
Nor altered his offence; yet God at last
To Satan first in sin his doom applied,
Though in mysterious terms, judged as then best:
And on the serpent thus his curse let fall:
   'Because thou hast done this, thou art accursed   175
Above all cattle, each beast of the field;
Upon thy belly grovelling thou shalt go,

151 real in the 17th century could also mean royal; before the fall Adam
was a king (see topics p. 163).   **154 well seemed** Eve's beauty was
becoming as long as it remained subject to Adam's authority.   **155
part** the dramatic metaphor recalls Satan's performance in IX 667. God
has cast Adam as Eve's master; Satan makes up his own roles.   **156
known thyself** the Socratic maxim, *nosce teipsum.*   **157 in few** in brief.
158 woman see 137n.   **165 unable** qualifies **serpent.**   **166 him** Satan.
167 end purpose.   **168 accursed** M's judgement is harsher than the
Son's in 84.   **171 altered** Satan's use of the snake as a disguise did not
change the nature of man's crime in giving in to temptation. Is this com-
ment true? **at last** in the final analysis.   **173 mysterious terms** the
curse has a concealed mystical meaning which applies to Satan; see
commentary p. 39.

And dust shalt eat all the days of thy life.
Between thee and the woman I will put
Enmity, and between thine and her seed; 180
Her seed shall bruise thy head, thou bruise his heel.'
  So spake this oracle, then verified
When Jesus son of Mary second Eve,
Saw Satan fall like lightning down from heaven,
Prince of the air; then rising from his grave 185
Spoiled principalities and powers, triúmphed
In open show, and with ascension bright
Captivity led captive through the air,
The realm itself of Satan long usurped,
Whom he shall tread at last under our feet; 190
Even he who now foretold his fatal bruise,
And to the woman thus his sentence turned:
  'Thy sorrow I will greatly multiply
By thy conception; children thou shalt bring
In sorrow forth, and to thy husband's will 195
Thine shall submit, he over thee shall rule.'
  On Adam last thus judgement he pronounced:
'Because thou hast hearkened to the voice of thy wife,
And eaten of the tree concerning which
I charged thee, saying: "Thou shalt not eat 200
    thereof",
Cursed is the ground for thy sake, thou in sorrow
Shalt eat thereof all the days of thy life;
Thorns also and thistles it shall bring thee forth
Unbid, and thou shalt eat the herb of the field,

178 all the days the metre is awkward here as it is in 180, 198, 201–2, and 205 because M is following the text of Genesis so closely. **180 seed** offspring; the ambiguity of **thine and her** (respectively or in combination?) follows up the hints in IX 507–10 (see topics p. 169). **182 oracle** as distinct from pagan ones, e.g. at Delphi; see *Nativity Ode* 173. **184 fall like lightning** the first of a series of biblical allusions: 'I beheld Satan as lightning fall from heaven' (*Luke* x). The others are to *Ephesians* ii, iv, *Colossians* ii, *Romans* xvi. Look them up to see how they verify the prophecies Christ has hidden in the curse. **185 his** Christ's, though after **fall** in 184 it sounds at first as if Satan is **rising**. **186 Spoiled** despoiled. **192 woman** M imitates Adam and Christ; cf. 137, 158. **196 rule** is this a new condition or a return to the *status quo*?

In the sweat of thy face shalt thou eat bread,   205
Till thou return unto the ground, for thou
Out of the ground wast taken, know thy birth,
For dust thou art, and shalt to dust return.'
   So judged he man, both Judge and Saviour sent,
And the instant stroke of death denounced that day   210
Removed far off; then pitying how they stood
Before him naked to the air, that now
Must suffer change, disdained not to begin
Thenceforth the form of servant to assume,
As when he washed his servants' feet so now   215
As father of his family he clad
Their nakedness with skins of beasts, or slain,
Or as the snake with youthful coat repaid;
And thought not much to clothe his enemies:
Nor he their outward only with the skins   220
Of beasts, but inward nakedness, much more
Opprobrious, with his robe of righteousness,
Arraying covered from his Father's sight.
To him with swift ascent he up returned,
Into his blissful bosom reassumed   225
In glory as of old, to him appeased
All, though all-knowing, what had passed with man
Recounted, mixing intercession sweet.
   Meanwhile ere thus was sinned and judged on earth,
Within the gates of hell sat Sin and Death,   230
In counterview within the gates, that now

209 both cf. 96. **210 denounced** see 49n. **213 change** see 651 ff.
214 servant another *NT* reference – *Philippians* ii – to remind us that
the judge will return as saviour: **assume** links Christ's metamorphoses
with Satan's. **217 or slain** since Death hasn't yet arrived in Eden the
'coats of skins' (*Genesis* iii) pose a problem. M suggests that they came
from animals who had either sloughed them off or been killed for the
purpose. **219 thought not much** did not object to; Christ's **enemies**
are Adam and Eve, who made his suffering necessary. **222 Oppro-
brious** shameful. **225 reassumed** taken back. **226 appeased**
reconciled. **227 though** the parenthesis acknowledges, but does not
solve, the problem of relating human and poetic time to divine timeless-
ness; cf. 91n. **229 Meanwhile** takes us back to the time before the
fall; see commentary p. 42. **230 gates of hell** see II 645ff. **231 In**

Stood open wide, belching outrageous flame
Far into chaos, since the Fiend passed through,
Sin opening, who thus now to Death began:
    'O son, why sit we here each other viewing   235
Idly, while Satan our great author thrives
In other worlds, and happier seat provides
For us his offspring dear? It cannot be
But that success attends him; if mishap,
Ere this he had returned, with fury driven   240
By his avengers, since no place like this
Can fit his punishment, or their revenge.
Methinks I feel new strength within me rise,
Wings growing, and dominion given me large
Beyond this deep; whatever draws me on,   245
Or sympathy, or some connatural force
Powerful at greatest distance to unite
With secret amity things of like kind
By secretest conveyance. Thou my shade
Inseparable must with me along: 250
For Death from Sin no power can separate.
But lest the difficulty of passing back
Stay his return perhaps over this gulf
Impassable, impervious, let us try

Handwritten margin notes:
- *A Satan is working to better sin death etc*
- *If satan failed he wouldn't of been able to return.*
- *what could be worse than hell*
- *Arrogance comes before a fall*

counterview facing each other. From now on everything will be
'counter': Sin and Death building up the causeway from 'each side'
(288), the oppositions of the stars, the 'adverse blast' (701) of the winds,
even the 'collision of two bodies' (1072) with which Adam makes fire.
232 outrageous violent, excessive (from Latin *ultra* = beyond); belching
anticipates the image of hell's mouth in 636.   234 Sin opening see II
850–89.   236 author creator, parent; Sin and Death are Satan's
invention. So, in a literary sense, are many of the scenes he appears in;
see commentary p. 45.   237 seat home.   239 if mishap if Satan
had failed.   240 fury ironically Sin and Death are destined to become
furies themselves; see 620n, II 596.   241 like as well as.   244 Wings
throughout the poem flight is a symbol of aspiration, Satan's (II 631),
M's (I 13; III 13; VII 4; IX 45) and man's (V 89; IX 1010). Does M dis-
tinguish between good and bad flights? dominion see 400n.   245 deep
hell, or, more probably, chaos (cf. 301). 246 Or sympathy Sin thinks
she and Satan are telepathic; connatural congenital.   249 conveyance
transmission; shade shadow, hence Inseparable, unlike Adam and Eve.
253 Stay delay.   254 impervious latinate synonym for Impassable.

Heart over head / fruits of Eve (handwritten annotation, left margin)

Adventurous work, yet to thy power and mine   255
Not unagreeable, to found a path
Over this main from hell to that new world
Where Satan now prevails, a monument
Of merit high to all the infernal host,
Easing their passage hence, for intercourse,   260
Or transmigration, as their lot shall lead.
Nor can I miss the way, so strongly drawn
By this new felt attraction and instínct.'
  Whom thus the meagre shadow answered soon:
'Go whither fate and inclination strong   265
Leads thee, I shall not lag behind, nor err
The way, thou leading, such a scent I draw
Of carnage, prey <u>innumerable</u>, and taste
The savour of death from all things there that live:
Nor shall I to the work thou enterprisest   270
Be wanting, but afford thee equal aid.'
  So saying, with delight he snuffed the smell
Of mortal change on earth. As when a flock
Of ravenous fowl, though many a league remote,
Against the day of battle, to a field,   275
Where armies lie encamped, come flying, lured
With scent of living carcasses designed
For death, the following day, in bloody fight.

Bestial imigary (handwritten annotation, right margin)

Carnivorous language (handwritten annotation, right margin)

Passion over reason (handwritten annotation, left margin)

255 **Adventurous** like M's song (I 13) and Eve's fall (IX 921).   256 **Not unagreeable** suitable. Sin's tendency to address Death in negatives makes him still less substantial; cf. 593–5; II 666–70.   257 **main** sea, as in 'Spanish main'; **new world** see commentary p. 46.   258 **monument** the causeway is an *arc de triomphe* commemorating Satan's victory; see 390.   260 **intercourse, Or transmigration** traffic back and forth or a one-way journey to earth, depending on what destiny has in store. 261 **lot** Sin and Death are fatalists like their father; see IX 160n. They all ignore divine providence; see VII 173.   264 **meagre shadow** Death; cf. IX 12; X 249.   265 **Go** echoes Adam in IX 372; **fate and inclination** allows Death to have it both ways.   266 **err** mistake.   271 **wanting** lacking.   273 **mortal change** death; the periphrasis reminds us that man was created immortal. Like Christ and Satan, man undergoes a metamorphosis (see 214n, commentary p. 45).   274 **ravenous fowl** birds of prey. Satan is compared with a vulture in III 431, a cormorant in IV 196.   275 **Against** in anticipation of.   277 **living carcasses** the oxymoron (carcasses are usually dead) validates Adam's fear of a 'living death' (788). **designed** destined.

So scented the grim feature, and upturned
His nostril wide into the murky air,   280
Sagacious of his quarry from so far.
Then both from out hell gates into the waste
Wide anarchy of chaos damp and dark
Flew díverse, and with power (their power was great)
Hovering upon the waters; what they met   285
Solid or slimy, as in raging sea
Tossed up and down, together crowded drove
From each side shoaling towards the mouth of hell.
As when two polar winds blowing adverse
Upon the Cronian sea, together drive   290
Mountains of ice, that stop the imagined way
Beyond Petsóra eastward, to the rich
Catháian coast. The aggregated soil
Death with his mace petrific, cold and dry,
As with a trident smote, and fixed as firm   295
As Delos floating once; the rest his look
Bound with Gorgonian rigour not to move,
And with asphaltic slime; broad as the gate,
Deep to the roots of hell the gathered beach

279 feature form (Death).   **281 Sagacious of** scenting.   **284 díverse**
in different directions.   **285 Hovering** like the spirit of God in I 21;
VII 235; see commentary p. 43. **what** whatever.   **288 shoaling** driving
together to form a shoal. The soaring period slips back to hell in the final
phrase; cf. 305.   **289 polar winds** the north-east passage which ex-
plorers hoped to find from the gulf of Petchora in the Arctic Ocean
(**Cronian sea**) through to the north Chinese (**Catháian**) coast was blocked
by ice-packs driven together by the polar winds blowing in opposite direc-
tions; see commentary p. 44. Hell was traditionally cold as well as hot;
cf. II 587–603, Dante *The divine comedy: 'Inferno'* xxxii, xxxiv.   **294
mace petrific** Death's sceptre, which is also a weapon, turns the accu-
mulated (**aggregated**) debris into stone. **cold and dry** like melancholy
according to the renaissance theory of the 4 humours (cf. II 898).   **296
Delos** Aegean island, the birth-place of Apollo and Diana and hence a type
of Eden (cf. IX 388); Neptune created it by collecting its soil with his trident,
and Zeus anchored it to the bottom of the sea (cf. V 265).   **297 Gorgonian**
in Greek mythology the Gorgons were 3 snaky-haired women who could
turn anyone they looked at into stone (cf. the allusion to the Perseus
myth in 526–8); hence **rigour** = rigidity. Cf. II 596–611.   **298 asphaltic
slime** pitch, proverbially defiling (*Ecclesiasticus* xiii 1, *Much ado about
nothing* III iii 52). In *PL* it is hellish; cf. I 340, 729.   **299 gathered**

[Handwritten annotation at top: Did texts like paradise lost become so popular because it reinforced peoples fear in disorder]

They fastened, and the mole immense wrought on   300
Over the foaming deep high arched, a bridge
Of length prodigious joining to the wall   *[Handwritten: Post colonial perspective]*
Immovable of this now fenceless world
Forfeit to death; from hence a passage broad,
Smooth, easy, inoffensive down to hell.   305
So, if great things to small may be compared,
Xérxès, the liberty of Greece to yoke,   *[Handwritten: justification for colonisation]*
From Susa his Memnónian palace high
Came to the sea, and over Héllèspónt
Bridging his way, Europe with Asia joined,   310
And scourged with many a stroke the indignant waves.
Now had they brought the work by wondrous art
Pontifical, a ridge of pendent rock
Over the vexed abyss, following the track
Of Satan, to the self same place where he   315
First lighted from his wing, and landed safe
From out of chaos to the outside bare
Of this round world: with pins of adamant
And chains they made all fast, too fast they made
And durable; and now in little space   320
The confines met of empyréan heaven
And of this world, and on the left hand hell

beach the solid mass they had accumulated to form the bridge's foundations, as opposed to the causeway (**mole**) itself.   **302 wall** the outermost sphere of our universe; see topics p. 185.   **303 fenceless** defenceless
304 passage cf. *Matthew* vii 13: 'broad is the way that leadeth to destruction'; **inoffensive** has its Latin sense of unobstructed as well as its modern one.   **306 small** reveals the enormous scale of the action in *PL* for the comparison that follows invokes one of the most spectacular feats in ancient history, the crossing of the Bosphorus (**Héllèspónt**) by **Xérxès**, the Persian emperor, whose palace was in **Susa**. When the waves broke up the bridge of ships he had built he ordered them to be beaten.   **310 Asia** symbolic of despotism: cf. 431–6.   **313 Pontifical** bridge-making. M also hints that the Catholic priesthood, led by the pontiff (Pope), pave the way to hell. The pun reflects back on Hellespont: hell's bridge.   **314 vexed** turbulent.   **316 lighted** alighted; **wing** flight (see III 418).   **321 confines** borders. In III 501–43 M described the opening in the *primum mobile* from which a golden staircase led upwards to heaven and downwards to earth. To these 2 routes is now added a 3rd, the causeway on the left (unlucky) side of the opening.

With long reach interposed; three several ways
In sight, to each of these three places led.

And now their way to earth they had descried,   325
To paradise first tending, when behold
Satan in likeness of an angel bright
Betwixt the Centaur and the Scorpion steering
His zenith, while the sun in Áries rose:
Disguised he came, but those his children dear   330
Their parent soon discerned, though in disguise.
He after Eve seduced, unminded slunk
Into the wood fast by, and changing shape
To observe the sequel, saw his guileful act
By Eve, though all unweeting, seconded   335
Upon her husband, saw their shame that sought
Vain covertures; but when he saw descend
The Son of God to judge them terrified
He fled, not hoping to escape, but shun
The present, fearing guilty what his wrath   340
Might suddenly inflict; that past, returned
By night, and listening where the hapless pair
Sat in their sad discourse, and various plaint,
Thence gathered his own doom, which understood
Not instant, but of future time. With joy   345
And tidings fraught, to hell he now returned,
And at the brink of chaos, near the foot

323 several separate.   **326 tending** moving towards.   **327 angel** the disguise Satan adopted on his way to earth (III 636).   **328 Centaur**...
Scorpion...**Áries** 3 signs of the Zodiac, Sagittarius, Scorpio and the Ram. They plot Satan's course literally (see topics p. 185) and symbolically (the constellation which covers the first 2 signs is Anguis, the serpent).
331 discerned unlike Oedipus, who did not recognize his parent when he met him at a junction of 3 roads (cf. 323). Death's incestuous relationship with his mother, Sin, reinforces the allusion.   **332 Eve**
seduced Eve had been seduced; **unminded** unnoticed.   **333 fast**
close.   **335 unweeting, seconded** Eve unknowingly (?) repeated Satan's **guileful act**; cf. Adam's rebuke in 867.   **337 Vain covertures**
skirts of fig-leaves; cf. IX 1113n.   **338 terrified** goes with **them** or
He?   **339 shun The present** avoid the Son's immediate judgement.
342 hapless a post-lapsarian state; see commentary p. 20.   **344 under-
stood Not instant** Satan realized that his 'doom' would not be inflicted
at once.   **345 joy And tidings** a Satanic version of the 'tidings of

Satan is a cowardice

Of this new wondrous pontifice, unhoped
Met who to meet him came, his offspring dear.
Great joy was at their meeting, and at sight   350
Of that stupendous bridge his joy increased.
Long he admiring stood, till Sin, his fair
Enchanting daughter, thus the silence broke:
  'O parent, these are thy magnific deeds,
Thy trophies, which thou view'st as not thine own, 355
Thou art their author and prime architect:
For I no sooner in my heart divined,   *think' to gods creation*
My heart, which by a secret harmony
Still moves with thine, joined in connexion sweet,
That thou on earth hadst prospered, which thy looks 360
Now also evidence, but straight I felt
Though distant from thee worlds between, yet felt
That I must after thee with this thy son;
Such fatal consequence unites us three:
Hell could no longer hold us in her bounds,   365
Nor this unvoyageable gulf obscure
Detain from following thy illustrious track.   *Satan is elevated and seen*
Thou hast achieved our liberty, confined   *and seen*
Within hell gates till now, thou us empowered   *as angel*
To fortify thus far, and overlay   370 *like*
With this portentous bridge the dark abyss.
Thine now is all this world, thy virtue hath won   *Satan*
What thy hands built not, thy wisdom gained   *feeling that he won — celebration*

great joy' which the angels brought to man at the Nativity (*Luke* ii 10).
348 pontifice bridge.   **349 who** those who.   **352 fair** M's irony
is rather heavy-handed. In II 650 Sin was described as 'woman to the
waist and fair, But ended foul in many a scaly fold'.   **354 magnific**
magnificent. Sin's grandiose opening echoes Adam and Eve's hymn in
v 153 and sets the tone for the rest of her speech. This is a ceremonial
occasion, the welcome of a conquering hero, and her rhetoric rises to it.
As she presents Satan with his trophies and invites him to cross the
triumphal arch commemorating his victories she dignifies the proceed-
ings with such stylistic devices as parallelism (368–9), antithesis (375–6),
and high-sounding diction: **divined** for guessed (357), **evidence** for show
(361), **fatal consequence** for destined link (364), **illustrious** for clear
(367), **fortify** for build (370) and **portentous** for long (371).   **369 hell
gates** Sin and Death's escape is a reversal of Adam and Eve's expulsion
from the gates of paradise.   **372 virtue** courage.

121

*Satan is going to be
king*

With odds what war hath lost, and fully avenged
Our foil in heaven; here thou shalt monarch reign,   375
There didst not; there let him still victor sway,
As battle hath adjudged, from this new world
Retiring, by his own doom alienáted,
And henceforth monarchy with thee divide
Of all things parted by the empýreal bounds,   380
His quadrature, from thy orbicular world,
Or try thee now more dangerous to his throne.'
    Whom thus the prince of darkness answered glad:
'Fair daughter, and thou son and grandchild both,
High proof ye now have given to be the race   385
Of Satan (for I glory in the name,
Antagonist of heaven's almighty King)
Amply have merited of me, of all
The infernal empire, that so near heaven's door
Triumphal with triumphal act have met,   390
Mine with this glorious work, and made one realm
Hell and this world, one realm, one continent
Of easy thoroughfare. Therefore while I
Descend through darkness, on your road with ease
To my associate powers, them to acquaint   395
With these successes, and with them rejoice,
You two this way, among these numerous orbs
All yours, right down to paradise descend;
There dwell and reign in bliss, thence on the earth

374 **odds** interest.   375 **foil** defeat.   376 **victor sway** govern as victor.
378 **doom** judgement.   381 **quadrature**...**orbicular** according to *Re-
velation* xxi 16 heaven is square; the universe in *PL* is round. Sin's latinate
diction has collapsed into absurdity.   382 **try** discover (you to be).
384 **and grandchild** since Death is the offspring of Satan's incestuous
union with his own daughter, Sin (ii 746ff.), he is both son and grandson
to the Devil.   387 **Antagonist** in Hebrew Satan=adversary.   388
Amply have merited have earned ample reward and gratitude from me
and from the powers of hell.   390 **Triumphal**... you have met my
triumphant act, the seduction of man, with yours, the construction of the
causeway. Satan connects the fall of Adam and Eve with the rise of Sin
and Death; see commentary p. 42.   391 **made one realm** made hell
and this world into one realm.   395 **powers** see 34n.   397 **numerous
orbs** the stars and planets; cf. Satan's descent in iii 560ff.   399 **thence**
thenceforth.

Dominion exercise and in the air,   400
Chiefly on man, sole lord of all declared,
Him first make sure your thrall, and lastly kill.
My substitutes I send ye, and create
Plenípotent on earth, of matchless might
Issuing from me: on your joint vigour now   405
My hold of this new kingdom all depends,
Through Sin to Death exposed by my exploit.
If your joint power prevails, the affairs of hell
No detriment need fear, go and be strong.'

So saying he dismissed them, they with speed   410
Their course through thickest constellations held
Spreading their bane; the blasted stars looked wan,
And planets, planet-struck, real eclipse
Then suffered. The other way Satan went down
The causey to hell gate; on either side   415
Disparted chaos over built exclaimed,
And with rebounding surge the bars assailed,   *connotes*
That scorned his indignation: through the gate, *? heaven*
Wide open and unguarded, Satan passed,
And all about found desolate; for those   420
Appointed to sit there, had left their charge,
Flown to the upper world; the rest were all
Far to the inland retired, about the walls   *7 disorder and*
Of Pandemonium, city and proud seat   *chaos*
Of Lucifer, so by allusion called,   *in hell* 425

400 Dominion Satan fulfils Sin's premonition in 244 and parodies
God's commandment in *Genesis* i 28; see commentary p. 44. **402
thrall** slave; cf. 307. **404 Plenípotent** all-powerful. **405 Issuing**
because you are my issue. **406 new kingdom** Satan is the original
imperialist; **all** entirely. **409 detriment** echoes the formula used to
confer power on the consuls of Rome. But the power was temporary,
and given only in times of crisis. **412 blasted** blighted by the deadly
influence (**bane**) of Sin and Death. **413 planet-struck** usually applied
to men, but now the planets themselves are subject to malign in-
fluence (cf. IX 461n). **416 Disparted chaos**... chaos, which had
been divided and bridged by the causeway (**causey**), protested. **420
those** Sin and Death, the original porters of hell-gate; see II 648.
424 Pandemonium literally = the home of all the demons; the name of
the city the fallen angels built in I 670ff. **425 Lucifer** in Latin = light-

Of that bright star to Satan paragoned.
There kept their watch the legions, while the grand
In council sat, solicitous what chance
Might intercept their emperor sent, so he
Departing gave command, and they observed.   430
As when the Tartar from his Russian foe
By Astracan over the snowy plains
Retires, or Bactrian Sophi from the horns
Of Turkish crescent, leaves all waste beyond
The realm of Áladúle, in his retreat   435
To Tauris or Casbeen. So these the late
Heaven-banished host, left désert utmost hell
Many a dark league, reduced in careful watch
Round their metropolis, and now expecting
Each hour their great adventurer from the search   440
Of foreign worlds: he through the midst unmarked,
In show plebeian angel militant
Of lowest order, passed; and from the door
Of that Plutonian hall, invisible
Ascended his high throne, which under state   445

bearer; the name of the morning star in *Isaiah* xiv. See v 708–10; vii
131; commentary p. 15.   **426 paragoned** compared.   **427 the
grand** the senior devils under Satan (cf. 456).   **428 solicitous** worried
about the fate of their leader, who was sent to explore the universe (ii
417ff.).   **430 observed** obeyed.   **431 Tartar** M links the devils with 2
famous historical examples of barbarism. The Tartars, led by Jingis
Khan, were a nation of marauders (cf. iii 432); defeated by the Russians,
they withdrew through Astracan near the mouth of the Volga. The
Persians (cf. 306n) were led by the Shah (**Bactrian Sophi**); once when
they were defeated by the Turks, whose battle emblem and formation
were crescent shaped, they retreated from Aladule in Armenia to
Tabriz (**Tauris**) and Kazvin (**Casbeen**), practising like the Tartars
a scorched-earth policy on the way. The devils, who were recently
banished from heaven, left the outermost (**utmost**) parts of hell deserted
during their retreat. They too destroy what they cannot keep.   **438
reduced** withdrawn; **careful** full of care.   **440 adventurer** see com-
mentary p. 46.   **441 unmarked** unnoticed, one of Satan's favourite
states (cf. 332, 448); he slinks back into Pandemonium disguised as a
combat angel of the lowest rank (**plebeian angel militant**).   **444
Plutonian** Pluto was the Roman god of the underworld, Proserpina's
husband (cf. ix 393n). M implies that the classical Hades is a type of the
Christian hell (cf. 453).   **445 state** canopy.

Of richest texture spread, at the upper end
Was placed in regal lustre. Down a while
He sat, and round about him saw unseen:
At last as from a cloud his fulgent head
And shape star bright appeared, or brighter, clad   450
With what permissive glory since his fall
Was left him, or false glitter: all amazed
At that so sudden blaze the Stygian throng
Bent their aspéct, and whom they wished beheld,
Their mighty chief returned: loud was the acclaim: 455
Forth rushed in haste the great consulting peers,
Raised from their dark divan, and with like joy
Congratulant approached him, who with hand
Silence, and with these words attention won:

    'Thrones, dominations, princedoms, virtues,   460
powers,
For in possession such, not only of right,
I call ye and declare ye now, returned
Successful beyond hope, to lead ye forth
Triumphant out of this infernal pit
Abominable, accursed, the house of woe,   465
And dungeon of our Tyrant: now possess,
As lords, a spacious world, to our native heaven

449 **Fulgent** shining. Satan's appearance imitates the Son's in VI 773–6.
451 **permissive** permitted by God; see I 212; X 574. Satan is given
enough rope to hang himself (cf. 620–37).   452 **false glitter** corrects
glory.   453 **Stygian** the Styx (in Greek = hateful; in English = dark;
cf. I 239; II 506, 577; III 14) was one of the rivers of Hades.   454 **Bent
their aspéct** turned their gaze (towards the sudden blaze). The inverted
word order enacts their surprise.   455 **returned** who had returned.
457 **dark divan** secret council; the oriental term reinforces the Saracen
overtones of 433–6 and II 1–4.   459 **won** the hiatus of a double pre-
dicate delaying the final verb makes the suspense almost audible; cf.
Satan's rhetorical flourish in IX 664–78.   460 **Thrones**... 5 of the
traditional 9 orders of angels; cf. 86.   461 **possession** the devils are
now a landed aristocracy, not merely a legal one.   462 **returned** goes
with **I**.   463 **beyond hope** a recurring phrase which contains a
meaning Satan doesn't intend: his situation is hopeless (cf. II 7; IX 424;
X 348).   465 **Abominable** ill-fated.   467 **lords** like James I, Satan
creates a new aristocracy: **native** tacitly admits that the angels were
created (cf. IX 145n).

He didn't like hell
Satan wants liberation

Little inferior, by my adventure hard
With peril great achieved. Long were to tell
What I have done, what suffered, with what pain   470
Voyaged the unreal, vast, unbounded deep
Of horrible confusion, over which
By Sin and Death a broad way now is paved
To expedite your glorious march; but I
Toiled out my uncouth passage, forced to ride   475
The untractable abyss, plunged in the womb
Of unoriginal night and chaos wild,
That jealous of their secrets fiercely opposed
My journey strange, with clamorous uproar
Protesting fate supreme; thence how I found   480
The new created world, which fame in heaven
Long had foretold, a fabric wonderful
Of absolute perfection, therein man
Placed in a paradise, by our exile
Made happy: him by fraud I have seduced   485
From his Creator, and the more to increase
Your wonder, with an apple; he thereat
Offended, worth your laughter, hath given up
Both his beloved man and all his world,
To Sin and Death a prey, and so to us,   490
Without our hazard, labour, or alarm,
To range in, and to dwell, and over man
To rule, as over all he should have ruled.

468 Little inferior in IX 99 Satan claimed that earth was to be 'preferred'.
469 Long were to tell a Latin construction redolent of epic; see commentary p. 46.   **471 unreal** in terms of Aristotelian physics chaos has no existence since it has no form; see II 89off. Like Sin and Death before the fall it is unrealized potential waiting to be made actual; cf. 586n.
475 uncouth voyage unknown voyage or voyage into the unknown.
476 untractable resistant; **womb** makes Satan's voyage a kind of rape and his arrival a second birth (cf. II 653–9).   **477 unoriginal** since night has always existed it has no origin; cf. II 150.   **478 opposed** night and chaos did nothing of the kind; see II 968–1009. Satan twists the facts to make his journey seem more heroic than it was.   **480 Protesting fate supreme** calling on supreme fate to oppose Satan's voyage; actually chaos only protested at the causeway (see 415–17).   **481 fame** rumour; see II 345–7.   **482 fabric** construction.   **487 apple** see IX 585n; **he** refers back to **his Creator** in 486.   **491 hazard** risk; **alarm** call to arms, alarum.

True is, me also he hath judged, or rather
Me not, but the brute serpent in whose shape   495
Man I deceived: that which to me belongs,
Is enmity, which he will put between
Me and mankind; I am to bruise his heel;
His seed, when is not set, shall bruise my head:
A world who would not purchase with a bruise,   500
Or much more grievous pain? Ye have the account
Of my performance: what remains, ye gods,
But up and enter now into full bliss.'
    So having said, a while he stood, expecting
Their universal shout and high applause   505
To fill his ear, when contrary he hears
On all sides, from innumerable tongues
A dismal universal hiss, the sound
Of public scorn; he wondered, but not long
Had leisure, wondering at himself now more;   510
His visage drawn he felt to sharp and spare,
His arms clung to his ribs, his legs entwining
Each other, till supplanted down he fell
A monstrous serpent on his belly prone,
Reluctant, but in vain, a greater power   515
Now ruled him, punished in the shape he sinned,
According to his doom: he would have spoke,
But hiss for hiss returned with forkèd tongue
To forkèd tongue, for now were all transformed

494 True is it is true.   **496 belongs** pertains.   **500 bruise** Satan
hasn't understood Christ's prophecy; see commentary p. 39.   **501
account** in its commercial as well as its literary sense; see commentary
p. 47.   **502 performance** in its theatrical as well as its general sense:
see commentary p. 46. **gods** Satan claims to have given his followers
what he promised Eve: deification.   **503 But up** but to rise up: **bliss**
the final word of his speech predicts the hiss it will provoke.   **505 uni-
versal** in unison.   **506 contrary** to what he expected.   **508 dismal**
sinister; the sibilants recreate the sound M is describing.   **511 spare** thin.
512 clung a past participle passive like **drawn** in 511; the grammar em-
phasizes Satan's helplessness.   **513 supplanted** tripped up. After the
tottering rhythm of the first 3 feet with their uneven pauses, the long
overflowing phrase enacts Satan's final collapse.   **515 Reluctant** re-
sistant.   **517 doom** the curse on the serpent (cf. 175–81) comes true
for Satan; in 566 he eats dust.   **518 with forkèd tongue**... the ana-

Alike, to serpents all as áccessories   520
To his bold riot: dreadful was the din
Of hissing through the hall, thick swarming now
With complicated monsters head and tail,
Scorpion and asp, and ámphisbǽna dire,
Cerastès horned, hydrus, and ellops drear,   525
And dipsas (not so thick swarmed once the soil
Bedropt with blood of Gorgon, or the isle
Ophiúsa) but still greatest he the midst,
Now dragon grown, larger than whom the sun
Engendered in the Pythian vale on slime,   530
Huge Python, and his power no less he seemed
Above the rest still to retain; they all
Him followed issuing forth to the open field,
Where all yet left of that revolted rout
Heaven-fallen, in station stood or just array,   535
Sublime with expectation when to see
In triumph issuing forth their glorious chief;
They saw, but other sight instead, a crowd
Of ugly serpents; horror on them fell,

diplosis, reinforced by the repeated **hiss**, echoes the exchange.   **521 riot**
Satan's lawlessness, either in rebelling against God or in tempting man.
523 complicated tangled; see IX 161n.   **524 ámphisbǽna** legendary
serpent with a head on either end of its body; **Cerastès** horned viper;
hydrus water snake; **ellops** sea serpent; **dipsas** snake whose bite
causes thirst. In contrast to the benign snakes in IX 503–10 these are all
poisonous post-lapsarian ones. The devils' fate forecasts the 'fierce
antipathy' of the animals in 707–14.   **527 blood** according to classical
legend, Libya was infested with snakes because the Greek hero Perseus,
who cut off the Gorgon Medusa's head, allowed its blood to drip on the
ground, whereupon the drops turned into serpents (cf. II 611; X 297n).
528 Ophiúsa in Greek = full of serpents; the name of a small island in the
Mediterranean notorious for the number of snakes on it. **the** in the.
529 dragon in *Revelation* xii the dragon which Michael defeats at the
end of the world is linked with Satan and the serpent of *Genesis*; **than
whom** than the dragon which.   **530 Pythian vale** in Ovid's *Metamor-
phoses* i the rays of the sun bred a huge snake called **Python** out of the
slime left by Deucalion's flood. It was subsequently killed by Apollo.
Like the references to the Gorgon and the dragon above, this allusion
prophesies Christ's victory over Satan.   **533 open field** a mock pastoral
excursion (cf. IX 445ff.).   **534 revolted rout** the angels who revolted
against God. Now they stand on guard (**in station**) or in their proper
places (**just array**) buoyed up (**Sublime**) with expectation.

And horrid sympathy; for what they saw,   540
They felt themselves now changing; down their arms,
Down fell both spear and shield, down they as fast,
And the dire hiss renewed, and the dire form
Catched by contagion, like in punishment,
As in their crime. Thus was the applause they meant,   545
Turned to exploding hiss, triumph to shame
Cast on themselves from their own mouths. There
    stood
A grove hard by, sprung up with this their change,
His will who reigns above, to aggravate
Their penance, laden with fair fruit, like that   550
Which grew in paradise, the bait of Eve
Used by the Tempter: on that prospect strange
Their earnest eyes they fixed, imagining
For one forbidden tree a multitude
Now risen, to work them further woe or shame;   555
Yet parched with scalding thirst and hunger fierce,
Though to delude them sent, could not abstain,
But on they rolled in heaps, and up the trees
Climbing, sat thicker than the snaky locks
That curled Megæra: greedily they plucked   560
The fruitage fair to sight, like that which grew
Near that bituminous lake where Sodom flamed;
This more delusive, not the touch, but taste

540 **horrid sympathy** M's joke at the devils' expense; **horrid** =
bristling (cf. IX 185) and **sympathy** recalls Sin's feelings in X 246.
541 **changing** the devils turn into what they are looking at: serpents.
As their weapons (**arms**) tumble to the ground the repetitions of **down**
and **dire** echo the sense.   544 **Catched** caught; **contagion** see IX
1036n.   546 **exploding** literally, hissing off the stage; see commen-
tary p. 45.   548 **hard by** near by.   549 **His will** as a result of
God's will.   550 **penance** is normally voluntary.   551 **bait** turns
the Tempter into an infernal 'fisher of men' (cf. *Matthew* iv 19).
552 **prospect** sight.   554 **For** instead of; Adam's tipsy wish in IX 1025
has come true.   555 **work** cause.   557 **Though**... although the
fruit-laden trees were sent by God to delude them, the devils could not
abstain.   560 **Megæra** one of the 3 Furies (cf. 240n, 620n) who had
snaky locks in place of hair.   561 **fair to sight** cf. IX 577, 585, 661, 777;
Genesis iii 6.   562 **bituminous lake** the Dead Sea; cf. 'asphaltic pool'
(I 411). The legendary trees on its banks produced apples of dust and

Deceived; they fondly thinking to allay
Their appetite with gust, instead of fruit   565
Chewed bitter ashes, which the offended taste
With spattering noise rejected: oft they assayed,
Hunger and thirst constraining, drugged as oft,
With hatefulest disrelish writhed their jaws
With soot and cinders filled; so oft they fell   570
Into the same illusion, not as man
Whom they triúmphed once lapsed. Thus were they
   plagued
And worn with famine, long and ceaseless hiss,
Till their lost shape, permitted, they resumed,
Yearly enjoined, some say, to undergo   575
This annual humbling certain numbered days,
To dash their pride, and joy for man seduced.
However some tradition they dispersed
Among the heathen of their purchase got,
And fabled how the serpent, whom they called   580
Ophíon with Eurýnomè, the wide
Encroaching Eve perhaps, had first the rule
Of high Olympus, thence by Saturn driven
And Ops, ere yet Dictǽan Jove was born.

Meanwhile in paradise the hellish pair   585

ashes which dissolved as soon as they were touched. **Sodom** links
Pandemonium with the degenerate city near the Dead Sea from which
Lot and his wife escaped (see *Genesis* xix).   **564 fondly** foolishly; links
the devils' fall with Adam's (cf. IX 999).   **565 with gust** by tasting (the
fruit) or with relish.   **568 drugged** sickened, but see IX 876n.   **569
hatefulest disrelish** the tongue-twister forces us to writhe our jaws with
the devils.   **570 so oft** thus repeatedly.   **571 not as man** man, over
whom the devils triumphed, fell only once; they fall repeatedly.
574 permitted by God; cf. 451n.   **575 some say** M is careful to
distinguish speculation from fact; cf. 668, 671.   **577 man seduced** the
seduction of man.   **579 their purchase got** the prey they had caught,
man; cf. 501n.   **581 Ophíon** from Greek *ophis* = serpent; a Titan, the
first ruler of Olympus. He and his wife **Eurýnomè** (= wide-ruling; Eve
is **wide Encroaching**) were overthrown by Saturn and his wife, Ops,
who in turn were deposed by Jupiter (**Jove**), born in Dicte in Crete. Thus
the devils' own propaganda forecasts their defeat. The allusion also
marries Eve to Satan; see commentary p. 26, topics p. 169.   **585
Meanwhile** time jumps backwards again (cf. 1, 229) to follow Sin

Too soon arrived, Sin there in power before,
Once actual, now in body, and to dwell
Habitual habitant; behind her Death
Close following pace for pace, not mounted yet
On his pale horse: to whom Sin thus began: 590
  'Second of Satan sprung, all conquering Death,
What think'st thou of our empire now, though earned
With travail difficult, not better far
Than still at hell's dark threshold to have sat watch,
Unnamed, undreaded, and thyself half starved?'   595
  Whom thus the Sin-born monster answered soon:
'To me, who with eternal famine pine,
Alike is hell, or paradise, or heaven,
There best, where most with ravin I may meet;
Which here, though plenteous, all too little seems   600
To stuff this maw, this vast unhide-bound corpse.'
  To whom the incestuous mother thus replied:
'Thou therefore on these herbs, and fruits, and flowers
Feed first, on each beast next, and fish, and fowl,
No homely morsels, and whatever thing   605
The scythe of time mows down, devour unspared,
Till I in man residing through the race,

and Death into Eden.   **586 in power before** Sin was always potentially
present in Eden, but when an **actual** sin was committed she arrived there
in body.   588 Habitual habitant the echo prolongs Sin's presence.
590 pale horse cf. *Revelation* VI.   **591 Second** Sin was Satan's first
child; the first time Sin has dignified Death with the kind of periphrasis
Adam and Eve had used before the fall (cf. IX 273).   **592 empire**
cf. 406n.   **593 not better** is it not better.   **595 Unnamed** by man
(cf. II 787–9) and therefore not yet real; see topics p. 181.   **597 eternal
famine** cf. the devils' 'famine' (573) and Adam's fears in 813–16.
598 Alike echoes Satan's dilemma in IV 20–4.   **599 There best** the
best place is where there is most prey (**ravin**) to devour.   **601 maw**
stomach (cf. 991); traditionally, Death was portrayed as a skeleton, but
here he is a living corpse, loose-skinned (**unhide-bound**) because he is
starving.   **602 incestuous** cf. 331n, 384n.   **604 first** Death's three-
course meal (cf. IX 4, 37) begins with salad, and continues with meat;
man is the dessert.   **605 homely** plain.   **606 scythe** Old Father Time
was traditionally pictured with a sickle; now he works as Death's reaper.
607 in man residing a gruesome parody of the incarnation of Christ
(see commentary p. 42). Realizing that all mankind is involved in the fall
(see IX 416n), Sin proposes to **season** the entire race with her presence to
make Death's sweetmeat more tasty.

Hes letting it happen

His thoughts, his looks, words, actions all infect,
And season him thy last and sweetest prey.'
   This said, they both betook them several ways,   610
Both to destroy, or unimmortal make
All kinds, and for destruction to mature

God is looking

Sooner or later; which the Almighty seeing,
From his transcendent seat the saints among,
To those bright orders uttered thus his voice: 615
   'See with what heat these dogs of hell advance
To waste and havoc yonder world, which I
So fair and good created, and had still
Kept in that state, had not the folly of man
Let in these wasteful furies, who impute   620
Folly to me, so doth the prince of hell
And his adherents, that with so much ease
I suffer them to enter and possess
A place so heavenly, and conniving seem
To gratify my scornful enemies,   625
That laugh, as if transported with some fit
Of passion, I to them had quitted all,
At random yielded up to their misrule;
And know not that I called and drew them thither
My hell hounds, to lick up the draff and filth   630
Which man's polluting sin with taint hath shed
On what was pure, till crammed and gorged, nigh
    burst
With sucked and glutted offal, at one sling

610 This said after saying this, they went their separate (**several**) ways.
611 unimmortal make what Sin and Death don't kill at once they make
subject to eventual death. **612 kinds** species: the animals as well as
man are subject to death (cf. 707–12). **617 waste and havoc** lay
waste and ravage. **620 furies** like the Eumenides, the avenging spirits
of classical mythology (cf. 240n, 560n), Sin and Death will punish the
guilty on God's behalf. They will become **wasteful** literally, full of waste
(cf. 632). **621 Folly to me** the delayed anadiplosis (see 619) emphasizes
the contrast with **man**. **622 that** because. **623 suffer** permit.
624 conniving to be giving tacit approval. **626 transported** carried
away. **627 quitted** given up. **628 At random** carelessly. **630 draff**
refuse. **632 nigh** almost. **633 glutted offal** putrid meat; **sling** reduces
Sin and Death to small stones hurled through space by a heavenly David.

Of thy victorious arm, well-pleasing Son,
Both Sin and Death, and yawning grave at last   635
Through chaos hurled, obstruct the mouth of hell
For ever, and seal up his ravenous jaws.
Then heaven and earth renewed shall be made pure
To sanctity that shall receive no stain:
Till then the curse pronounced on both precedes.'   640
  He ended, and the heavenly audience loud
Sung halleluiah, as the sound of seas,
Through multitude that sung: 'Just are thy ways,
Righteous are thy decrees on all thy works;
Who can extenuate thee?' Next, to the Son,   645
Destined restorer of mankind, by whom
New heaven and earth shall to the ages rise,
Or down from heaven descend. Such was their song,
While the Creator calling forth by name
His mighty angels gave them several charge,   650
As sorted best with present things. The sun
Had first his precept so to move, so shine,
As might affect the earth with cold and heat
Scarce tolerable, and from the north to call
Decrepit winter, from the south to bring   655
Solstitial summer's heat. To the blank moon
Her office they prescribed, to the other five

634 **well-pleasing** see 7on.   636 **mouth** medieval painters often portrayed hell as a dragon with gaping jaws, **ravenous** because, like Death, it suffers from 'eternal famine' (597).   639 **To** to the degree of.   640 **both** Sin and Death, Adam and Eve, or earth and heaven (=firmament, as in VII 274)? **precedes** takes precedence, has priority.   642 **halleluiah** praise ye the Lord. So many angels were singing that their voices sounded like the sea.   643 **Just are thy ways** cf. M's intention to 'justify the ways of God to men' (I 26).   645 **extenuate** detract from.   647 **New heaven** cf. *Revelation* xxi 1: 'And I saw a new heaven and a new earth.'   648 **descend** an oddly literal alternative to the metaphorical **rise** in 647; cf. *Revelation* xxi 2.   650 **several charge** different duties.   651 **sorted** corresponded. '   652 **so to move** explained in 668–91.   653 **cold and heat** the same extremes as in hell; see II 580–603.   655 **Decrepit** reminds us that man too will be subject to old age.   656 **Solstitial** from solstice (Latin *sol* = sun, *sistere* = to make stand), the time of year when the sun's course deviates farthest from the equator and the days are therefore longest; **blank** pale.   657 **office** duty; **other five** planets.

God is creating different weathers,
earth, ~~moon~~ wind, rain

Their planetary motions and aspécts
In sextile, square, and trine, and opposite,
Of noxious efficacy, and when to join   660
In synod unbenign, and taught the fixed
Their influence malignant when to shower,
Which of them rising with the sun, or falling,
Should prove tempestuous: to the winds they set
Their corners, when with bluster to confound   665
Sea, air, and shore, the thunder when to roll
With terror through the dark aërial hall.

putting the earth on an axis

Some say he bid his angels turn askance
The poles of earth twice ten degrees and more
From the sun's axle; they with labour pushed   670
Oblique the centric globe: some say the sun
Was bid turn reins from the equinoctial road
Like distant breadth to Taurus with the seven
Atlantic Sisters, and the Spartan Twins

New found armology

Up to the tropic Crab; thence down amain   675
By Leo and the Virgin and the Scales,
As deep as Cápricórn, to bring in change
Of seasons to each clime; else had the spring
Perpetual smiled on earth with vernant flowers,
Equal in days and nights, except to those   680
Beyond the polar circles; to them day
Had unbenighted shone, while the low sun

658 aspécts see topics p. 183.   **661 synod** see topics p. 183; **fixed** stars.
665 corners on renaissance maps the winds were often depicted with
puffed cheeks in the corners: cf. John Donne's *Holy Sonnet*, 'At the
round earth's imagined corners'.   **667 aërial hall** the atmosphere,
enclosed by the vault of the sky.   **668 Some say** see 575n; **askance** out
of line. Before the fall the circle formed by the sun's annual 'rotation'
coincided exactly with that of the equator, with the result that there were
no variations in the season or in the length of day or night. To account
for the fact that the sun now travels at an angle of $23\frac{1}{2}°$ from the equator
M assumes either that the axis of the earth was shifted or that the course
of the sun was changed. See topics p. 185.   **670 axle** in classical legend
the sun rode in a chariot (cf. *Comus* 95–7); **reins** in 672 continues the
image.   **671 centric globe** the earth, in the centre of the universe.
672 equinoctial see 668n.   **673 Taurus**... see topics p. 184.   **675
amain** in haste.   **678 else** otherwise; **spring Perpetual** see topics
pp. 160–62.   **679 vernant** spring.   **682 unbenighted** without night

To recompense his distance, in their sight
Had rounded still the horizon, and not known
Or east or west, which had forbid the snow   685
From cold Estótiland, and south as far
Beneath Magellan. At that tasted fruit
The sun, as from Thyéstean banquet, turned
His course intended; else how had the world
Inhabited, though sinless, more than now,   690
Avoided pinching cold and scorching heat?
  These changes in the heavens, though slow, produced
Like change on sea and land, sidéral blast,
Vapour, and mist, and exhalation hot,
Corrupt and pestilent: now from the north   695
Of Nórumbéga, and the Sámöed shore
Bursting their brazen dungeon, armed with ice
And snow and hail and stormy gust and flaw,
Bóräas and Cæcias and Argéstès loud
And Thráscias rend the woods and seas upturn;   700
With adverse blast upturns them from the south
Nótus and Áfer black with thunderous clouds
From Serraliona; thwart of these as fierce
Forth rush the Lévant and the Pónent winds
Eúrus and Zéphyr with their lateral noise,   705
Sirócco, and Libécchio. Thus began

ever coming.   **686 Estótiland** a legendary island off the NE coast of
Labrador; like the **Magellan** straits it would have been free from snow if
the sun had not changed course.   **687 At that tasted fruit** at the moment
that fruit was tasted.   **688 Thyéstean** when Atreus, king of Argos,
served his brother Thyestes a dish made from the flesh of the latter's
children, the sun changed course for a day (see Seneca *Thyestes*); M's
reference to this classical horror story caps the earlier images of canni-
balism in 597ff. (see commentary pp. 47–8).   **693 sidéral blast** the
malign influence of the stars; cf. 412.   **696 Nórumbéga...Sámöed**
the coasts of NW America and NE Siberia.   **697 brazen dungeon** in
classical legend the winds blew only when they were released from
Æolus' prison (cf. *Lycidas* 96); thus they re-enact the escape of Sin and
Death from God's dungeon.   **698 flaw** gust.   **699 Bóräas...** the
names of the various winds: Bóräas N, Cæcias NE, Argéstès NW,
Thráscias NNW, Nótus S, Áfer SW, Eúrus E, Zéphyr W, Sirócco SE,
Libécchio SW. **Lévant** is the region where the sun rises, **Pónent** where
it sets.

Outrage from lifeless things; but Discord first
Daughter of Sin, among the irrational,
Death introduced through fierce antipathy:
Beast now with beast 'gan war, and fowl with fowl,   710
And fish with fish; to graze the herb all leaving,
Devoured each other; nor stood much in awe
Of man, but fled him, or with countenance grim
Glared on him passing: these were from without
The growing miseries, which Adam saw   715
Already in part, though hid in gloomiest shade,
To sorrow abandoned, but worse felt within,
And in a troubled sea of passion tossed,
Thus to disburden sought with sad complaint:

    'O miserable of happy! Is this the end   720
Of this new glorious world, and me so late
The glory of that glory, who now become
Accursed of blessèd, hide me from the face
Of God, whom to behold was then my height
Of happiness: yet well, if here would end   725
The misery. I deserved it, and would bear
My own deservings; but this will not serve;
All that I eat or drink, or shall beget,
Is propagated curse. O voice once heard
Delightfully, "Increase and multiply",   730
Now death to hear! for what can I increase
Or multiply, but curses on my head?

707 **Outrage** violence (cf. 232n). **Discord** is Death's sister.   708
the irrational the animals; cf. IX 553-9.   710 **'gan** began.   716
shade cf. the herdsman in IX 1106.   719 **disburden** continues the
image of a sea of passion; Adam tries to lighten his boat by jettisoning
its cargo.   720 **of** after being; **end**=either purpose or conclusion – the
ambiguity shapes the rest of Adam's speech.   721 **late** recently.
723 **me** myself.   725 **yet well** yet it would be well; the first of many
changes in the direction of Adam's argument (see commentary p. 51).
727 **deservings**... Adam is willing to bear the punishment he has
deserved, but he realizes that this will not suffice (**serve**). So long as he
prolongs either his own life by eating and drinking or the life of the
human race by begetting children, he will be propagating the curse.
730 **Increase** God's first command to man (cf. VII 531, *Genesis* i 28).

Who of all ages to succeed, but feeling
The evil on him brought by me, will curse
My head, "Ill fare our ancestor impure,   735
For this we may thank Adam"; but his thanks
Shall be the execration; so besides
Mine own that bide upon me, all from me
Shall with a fierce reflux on me redound,
On me as on their natural centre light   740
Heavy, though in their place. O fleeting joys
Of paradise, dear bought with lasting woes!
Did I request thee, Maker, from my clay
To mould me man, did I solicit thee
From darkness to promote me, or here place   745
In this delicious garden? As my will
Concurred not to my being, it were but right
And equal to reduce me to my dust,
Desirous to resign, and render back
All I received, unable to perform   750
Thy terms too hard, by which I was to hold
The good I sought not. To the loss of that,
Sufficient penalty, why has thou added

735 **My head** the delayed anadiplosis (see 732) recreates the boomerang motion of the curses. **Ill fare** Adam makes up a brief speech for his descendants; after the fall his imagination becomes increasingly dramatic (cf. IX 948–50; X 758–68). 737 **execration** curse. 738 **Mine own** the curses which rest (**bide**) on my shoulders. 739 **redound** flow back on, recoil; cf. Satan's dilemma (III 85; VII 57; IX 128; X 841). 740 **light Heavy** Adam's speech is full of paradoxes (cf. 720–23, 730, 736, 788, 798–804, 819–22) but this is the most elaborate. It has 2 levels, one verbal, created by the juxtaposition of **light** (=alight) and **Heavy**, the other conceptual, depending on the notion that when a body has reached the **natural centre** the force of gravity ceases to operate and it becomes weightless. The curses of Adam's descendants seem to defy this principle. 742 **lasting woes** combines with **fleeting joys** in 741 to form a semi-rhymed couplet; **bought** recalls the commercial image in 500–1, 579 743 **clay** cf. *Isaiah* xlv 9: 'Woe unto him that striveth with his Maker... Shall the clay say to him that fashioneth it, What makest thou?' 745 **promote** raise. 746 **delicious** delightful. **As my will...** since I did not choose to exist it is only right and just to turn me back (**reduce**) into the dust from which I was made. 751 **terms** combines with **resign** and **render back** in 749 to define existence as a legal contract between God and man. 752 **that** the **good** Adam did not ask for. His syntax is becoming disjointed under the emotional pressure.

137

The sense of endless woes? Inexplicable

Thy justice seems; yet to say truth, too late,   755
I thus contest; then should have been refused
Those terms whatever, when they were proposed:
Thou didst accept them; wilt thou enjoy the good,
Then cavil the conditions? And though God
Made thee without thy leave, what if thy son   760
Prove disobedient, and reproved, retort,
"Wherefore didst thou beget me? I sought it not"
Wouldst thou admit for his contempt of thee
That proud excuse? Yet him not thy election,
But natural necessity begot.   765
God made thee of choice his own, and of his own
To serve him, thy reward was of his grace,
Thy punishment then justly is at his will.
Be it so, for I submit, his doom is fair,
That dust I am, and shall to dust return: 770
O welcome hour whenever! why delays
His hand to execute what his decree
Fixed on this day? Why do I overlive,
Why am I mocked with death, and lengthened out
To deathless pain? How gladly would I meet   775
Mortality my sentence, and be earth
Insensible, how glad would lay me down
As in my mother's lap? there I should rest
And sleep secure; his dreadful voice no more

756 **contest** in a legal sense (cf. 751n, 828n). **then**... those terms, whatever they were, should have been rejected when they were first proposed. But how could they have been? Adam's existence was already a *fait accompli*. 758 **Thou** Adam; his monologue contains a dialogue between himself and his conscience (cf. 842n). 759 **cavil** quibble about. 760 **son** another glance at *Isaiah*: 'Woe to him that saith unto his father, What begettest thou?' (xlv 10). 761 **reproved** sounds paradoxical after **Prove.** 763 **admit** accept (that proud excuse for his contemptuous disobedience). 764 **election** freely made decision. 766 **of his own** by his own choice, or with his own gifts? All the of's are confusing. 769 **I** Adam reverts to his own person. 770 **dust** cf. 208, *Genesis* iii 19. 773 **this day** see 49n. 778 **lap** cf. xi 535; like his descendants' children Adam seeks refuge from his father's rage in his mother's protection, but God is his father and his mother is the earth.

138

Would thunder in my ears, no fear of worse 780
To me and to my offspring would torment me
With cruel expectation. Yet one doubt
Pursues me still, lest all I cannot die,
Lest that pure breath of life, the spirit of man
Which God inspired, cannot together perish 785
With this corpóreal clod; then in the grave,
Or in some other dismal place who knows
But I shall die a living death? O thought
Horrid, if true! yet why? it was but breath
Of life that sinned; what dies but what had life 790
And sin? the body properly hath neither.
All of me then shall die: let this appease
The doubt, since human reach no further knows.
For though the Lord of all be infinite,
Is his wrath also? be it, man is not so, 795
But mortal doomed. How can he exercise
Wrath without end on man whom death must end?
Can he make deathless death? that were to make
Strange contradiction, which to God himself
Impossible is held, as argument 800
Of weakness, not of power. Will he draw out,
For anger's sake, finite to infinite
In punished man, to satisfy his rigour
Satisfied never; that were to extend
His sentence beyond dust and nature's law, 805

783 all completely. **785 inspired** cf. *Genesis* ii 7; a third kind of in-
spiration (cf. IX 23, 189). **786 corpóreal clod** echoes Satan's contempt
for man's earthy origin (IX 149–78). Adam has become a dualist. **787
other dismal place** Adam flirts with the Catholic idea of purgatory.
788 living death cf. *SA* 100. **789 why** why should that thought be
true? **791 neither** since sin is an act of the will it pertains to the soul
rather than to the body, so the body cannot sin. Since the body is lifeless
unless animated by a soul, it cannot die either. The threat of death,
therefore, must apply to the soul. **792 appease** pacify, put to rest. **793
reach** comprehension; unlike Browning, M didn't believe it should
exceed one's grasp. **795 be it** even if God's wrath is infinite, man is only
finite. **796 doomed** now in its modern post-lapsarian sense; **he** God.
800 held by whom? Adam's logic is anachronistic. **argument** evidence.
805 nature's law Adam argues like a scholastic philosopher that an
agent's action is limited by the recipient's capacity to be acted upon. So

By which all causes else according still
To the reception of their matter act,
Not to the extent of their own sphere. But say
That death be not one stroke, as I supposed,
Bereaving sense, but endless misery   810
From this day onward, which I feel begun
Both in me, and without me, and so last
To perpetuity; ay me, that fear
Comes thundering back with dreadful revolution
On my defenceless head; both death and I   815
Am found eternal, and incorporate both,
Nor I on my part single, in me all
Posterity stands cursed: fair patrimony
That I must leave ye, sons; oh were I able
To waste it all myself, and leave ye none!   820
So disinherited how would ye bless
Me now your curse! Ah, why should all mankind
For one man's fault thus guiltless be condemned,
If guiltless? But from me what can proceed,
But all corrupt, both mind and will depraved,   825
Not to do only, but to will the same
With me? how can they then acquitted stand
In sight of God? Him after all disputes
Forced I absolve: all my evasions vain,

although God's wrath might be infinite, the fact that man is finite means
that there must be a limit to his suffering.   **806 all causes else** all other
causes.   **810 Bereaving sense** depriving man of feeling.   **812 without**
outside.   **814 revolution** in the literal sense of a wheel revolving full
circle.   **816 Am** the ungrammatical singular fuses the plural subject,
Death and I, into one entity just as Adam fears. In 817 he realizes that
this union also involves his posterity, for he contains within himself all his
descendants (see IX 416n).   **818 patrimony** inheritance. Since Adam
can only bequeath death and pain to his children he would prefer to
waste it all himself like a prodigal father.   **821 So disinherited**... if
you could be disinherited in this way you would bless rather than curse
me.   **824 If guiltless** opens the door to St Augustine; see commentary
p. 24.   **825 all** all Adam's descendants will be entirely corrupt (cf.
IX 1127–31).   **826 will** Adam forecasts our complicity in his fall (see
commentary p. 30); his offspring will both do and desire to do what he
has just done, namely, sin.   **828 disputes** cf. *Jeremiah* xii 1, G. M.
Hopkins' sonnet 'Thou art indeed just, Lord, if I with thee contend'.
829 Forced necessarily.

And reasonings, though through mazes, lead me still 830
But to my own conviction: first and last
On me, me only, as the source and spring
Of all corruption, all the blame lights due;
So might the wrath. Fond wish! couldst thou support
That burden heavier than the earth to bear,   835
Than all the world much heavier, though divided
With that bad woman? Thus what thou desir'st
And what thou fear'st, alike destroys all hope
Of refuge, and concludes thee miserable
Beyond all past example and futúre,   840
To Satan only like both crime and doom.
O conscience, into what abyss of fears
And horrors hast thou driven me; out of which
I find no way, from deep to deeper plunged!'
    Thus Adam to himself lamented loud   845
Through the still night, not now, as ere man fell,
Wholesome and cool, and mild, but with black air
Accompanied, with damps and dreadful gloom,
Which to his evil conscience represented
All things with double terror: on the ground   850
Outstretched he lay, on the cold ground, and oft
Cursed his creation, death as oft accused
Of tardy execution, since denounced
The day of his offence. 'Why comes not death',

830 mazes cf. II 561; IX 161n.   **832 On me, me** cf. 739–40, 929,
933–6. The ploce recalls Christ's offer to redeem man in III 236. But al-
though all the blame alights (**lights**) on Adam he cannot bear all the
wrath, **heavier than the earth**, for he is no Atlas or Hercules, the 2 Greek
heroes who bore the earth on their shoulders and were thus taken to be
types of Christ.   **834 Fond** foolish. Conscience has intervened again
to correct Adam's mistakes.   **836 world** universe, as opposed to **earth**
in 835.   **839 refuge** cf. Satan in IX 119; **concludes thee** leads to the con-
clusion that you are.   **841 like** comparable only to Satan with respect
both to your crime and your punishment; see commentary p. 50.   **842
conscience** Adam finally recognizes his interlocutor, the 'umpire' God
has promised in III 195 would guide man back to grace. Adam sees it only
as a spur to despair; cf. IV 23 and *Hamlet* III 1 83: 'Thus conscience doth
make cowards of us all.'   **846 now** the dramatic present fuses our time
with Adam's; see IX 201n.   **851 ground** the repetition (also of **oft**) en-
acts Adam's **double** terror.   **853 tardy** late; see 49n.

Said he, 'with one thrice ácceptáble stroke   855
To end me? Shall truth fail to keep her word,
Justice divine not hasten to be just?
But death comes not at call, justice divine
Mends not her slowest pace for prayers or cries.
O woods, O fountains, hillocks, dales and bowers,   860
With other echo late I taught your shades
To answer, and resound far other song.'

     Whom thus afflicted when sad Eve beheld,
Desolate where she sat, approaching nigh,
Soft words to his fierce passion she assayed: 865
But her with stern regard he thus repelled:
     'Out of my sight, thou serpent, that name best
Befits thee with him leagued, thyself as false
And hateful; nothing wants, but that thy shape,
Like his, and colour serpentine may show   870
Thy inward fraud, to warn all creatures from thee
Henceforth; lest that too heavenly form, pretended
To hellish falsehood, snare them. But for thee
I had persisted happy, had not thy pride
And wandering vanity, when least was safe,   875
Rejected my forewarning, and disdained
Not to be trusted, longing to be seen
Though by the Devil himself, him overweening
To overreach, but with the serpent meeting
Fooled and beguiled, by him thou, I by thee,   880

856 truth...Justice 2 of the 4 daughters of God in *Psalm* lxxxv; Adam
leaves out mercy and peace, the pair associated with Christ.   858 justice
divine the epanalepsis creates the echo in 861.   859 Mends quickens.
861 late recently; cf. v 153–208; ix 192–9.   864 Desolate, alone and
thence unhappy (cf. commentary, p. 50).   865 assayed applied; cf.
ix 335n.   866 regard look.   869 wants lacks.   872 pretended
held out in front, like a mask; on the serpent as Eve's double and vice-
versa see 335n and topics p. 159.   873 snare makes Eve a poacher
in the garden; cf. ix 387n.   874 had persisted would have remained.
875 wandering vanity combines the action (cf. ix 1135) with its motive.
876 Rejected exaggerates Eve's reaction; cf. ix 270ff.   878 him over-
weening over-confident of your ability to overcome Satan.   880 I by
thee we understand: into eating the apple. But the next line reveals that

To trust thee from my side, imagined wise,
Constant, mature, proof against all assaults,
And understood not all was but a show
Rather than solid virtue, all but a rib
Crooked by nature, bent, as now appears,   885
More to the part sinister from me drawn,
Well if thrown out, as supernumerary
To my just number found. O why did God,
Creator wise, that peopled highest heaven
With spirits masculine, create at last   890
This novelty on earth, this fair defect
Of nature, and not fill the world at once
With men as angels without feminine,
Or find some other way to generate
Mankind? This mischief had not then befallen,   895
And more that shall befall, innumerable
Disturbances on earth through female snares,
And strait conjunction with this sex: for either
He never shall find out fit mate, but such
As some misfortune brings him, or mistake,   900
Or whom he wishes most shall seldom gain
Through her perverseness, but shall see her gained
By a far worse, or if she love, withheld
By parents, or his happiest choice too late
Shall meet, already linked and wedlock-bound   905

Adam is thinking only of his decision to let Eve leave him. He ignores
his own fall.   **881 imagined wise** Is that why he let her go? Cf. VIII
546-50, 561ff.   **883 understood** governed by I in 880. The breathless
syntax mimics Adam's haste to accuse Eve.   **885 Crooked** see IX 161n.
886 sinister left and ill-fated. Since Adam had 13 (an unlucky number)
ribs on his left side and 12 (a sacred number, e.g. 12 tribes of Israel,
12 disciples) on his right, the removal of the extra rib to create Eve
made the two sides even (**just**).   **890 spirits masculine** cf. IX 458n.
891 fair defect Aristotle defined woman as a defective male; Adam has
forgotten that he asked for a mate in VIII 357-433.   **892 nature** a new
culprit for the fall; cf. 885.   **896 befall** a recurring post-lapsarian
word (cf. 28); understand 'would not have befallen either' after it.   **897
snares** hints at the Freudian image of female genitals as a trap; the
sexual overtones of **strait** (narrow) **conjunction** in 898 reinforce it.
900 mistake understand 'brings him'; the syntax is still rushed.   **905
already linked** all the or's are confusing. Is the woman, **his happiest**

143

To a fell adversary, his hate or shame:
Which infinite calamity shall cause
To human life, and household peace confound.'
    He added not, and from her turned, but Eve
Not so repulsed, with tears that ceased not   910
    flowing,
And tresses all disordered, at his feet
Fell humble, and embracing them, besought
His peace, and thus proceeded in her plaint:
    'Forsake me not thus, Adam, witness heaven
What love sincere and reverence in my heart   915
I bear thee, and unweeting have offended,
Unhappily deceived; thy suppliant
I beg, and clasp thy knees; bereave me not,
Whereon I live, thy gentle looks, thy aid,
Thy counsel in this uttermost distress,   920
My only strength and stay: forlorn of thee,
Whither shall I betake me, where subsist?
While yet we live, scarce one short hour perhaps,
Between us two let there be peace, both joining,
As joined in injuries, one enmity   925
Against a foe by doom express assigned us,
That cruel serpent: on me exercise not
Thy hatred for this misery befallen,
On me already lost, me than thyself
More miserable; both have sinned, but thou   930
Against God only, I against God and thee,
And to the place of judgement will return,
There with my cries importune heaven, that all
The sentence from thy head removed may light

choice, or the man, he, already married to a fell (deadly) adversary
(another Satan? cf. 387n)?   907 Which all the forms of misalliance
Adam has just catalogued.   916 unweeting cf. 335n; deceived in 917
reminds us that Adam was 'not deceived' (IX 998).   918 bereave
deprive.   921 forlorn of abandoned by; cf. IX 910.   926 doom
express explicit judgement; see X 175–81.   929 On me see 832n.
931 God only echoes M's comment in IV 299: 'He for God only, she
for God in him.' Eve's acknowledgement of her dependence on Adam
signals the restoration of the proper relationship between them.   934 light

On me, sole cause to thee of all this woe,   935
Me me only just object of his ire.'
      She ended weeping, and her lowly plight,
Immovable till peace obtained from fault
Acknowledged and deplored, in Adam wrought
Commiseration; soon his heart relented   940
Towards her, his life so late and sole delight,
Now at his feet submissive in distress,
Creature so fair his reconcilement seeking,
His counsel whom she had displeased, his aid;
As one disarmed, his anger all he lost,   945
And thus with peaceful words upraised her soon:
      'Unwary, and too desirous, as before,
So now of what thou know'st not, who desir'st
The punishment all on thy self; alas,
Bear thine own first, ill able to sustain   950
His full wrath whose thou feel'st as yet least part,
And my displeasure bear'st so ill. If prayers
Could alter high decrees, I to that place
Would speed before thee, and be louder heard,
That on my head all might be visited,   955
Thy frailty and infirmer sex forgiven,
To me committed and by me exposed.
But rise, let us no more contend, nor blame
Each other, blamed enough elsewhere, but strive
In offices of love, how we may lighten   960
Each other's burden in our share of woe;
Since this day's death denounced, if aught I see,

repeats Adam's offer in 832; like him Eve is disqualified by her sin from performing this Christlike function.   **938 Immovable** Eve's plight could not change (for the better) until she acknowledged and deplored her sin, and so obtained peace.   **941 late** another recurrent postlapsarian word; cf. 721, 861.   **944 counsel .. aid** an echo of 919. **945 disarmed** cf. Satan's reaction in IX 465.   **947 as before** connects Eve's benevolent ambitions here with her heroic ones before and during the fall; see commentary p. 54.   **951 whose** a kind of double genitive: of whose (God's) wrath you so far feel only the smallest part.   **953 that place** where Christ delivered the judgement; but cf. 133–5.   **957 by me** Adam finally recognizes his own failure; see commentary p. 23. **959 elsewhere** heaven.   **960 offices** services.   **962 denounced** cf.

Will prove no sudden, but a slow-paced evil,
A long day's dying to augment our pain,
And to our seed (O hapless seed!) derived.'   965
    To whom thus Eve, recovering heart, replied:
'Adam, by sad experiment I know
How little weight my words with thee can find,
Found so erroneous, thence by just event
Found so unfortunate; nevertheless,   970
Restored by thee, vile as I am, to place
Of new acceptance, hopeful to regain
Thy love, the sole contentment of my heart
Living or dying, from thee I will not hide
What thoughts in my unquiet breast are risen,   975
Tending to some relief of our extremes,
Or end, though sharp and sad, yet tolerable,
As in our evils, and of easier choice.
If care of our descent perplex us most,
Which must be born to certain woe, devoured   980
By Death at last, and miserable it is
To be to others cause of misery,
Our own begotten, and of our loins to bring
Into this cursèd world a woeful race,
That after wretched life must be at last   985
Food for so foul a monster, in thy power
It lies, yet ere conception to prevent
The race unblest, to being yet unbegot.

49n: **if aught I see** if I understand correctly.   **964 long day's dying**
the 3 stressed syllables prolong it.   **965 hapless** a post-lapsarian con-
dition; see commentary p. 20. Adam is worried about the curse which
will be **derived** (passed on) to his unfortunate **seed** (progeny), but
Christ has promised that the sentence will be 'derived' on him (77).
967 experiment experience.   **968 find, Found** traductio is usually a
bad sign, especially with Eve; cf. ix 285–7.   **969 event** outcome.
977 end an alternative to **some relief** in 976. The alternatives are:
remaining childless, which would relieve their anxiety for their off-
spring, or committing suicide, which in their evil circumstances (**As
in our evils**) would be the easier choice.   **979 descent** hints that
children are the result of the fall; see topics p. 167.   **980 devoured**
recalls Death's appetite in 596ff.   **983 of** from.   **984 world a woe-
ful** another echo of 1 3; see ix 11n.   **987 prevent…** stop the human

Childless thou art, childless remain: so Death
Shall be deceived his glut, and with us two   990
Be forced to satisfy his ravenous maw.
But if thou judge it hard and difficult,
Conversing, looking, loving, to abstain
From love's due rites, nuptial embraces sweet,
And with desire to languish without hope,   995
Before the present object languishing
With like desire, which would be misery
And torment less than none of what we dread,
Then both our selves and seed at once to free
From what we fear for both, let us make short,   1000
Let us seek Death, or he not found, supply
With our own hands his office on ourselves;
Why stand we longer shivering under fears,
That show no end but death, and have the power,
Of many ways to die the shortest choosing,   1005
Destruction with destruction to destroy.'
　　She ended here, or vehement despair
Broke off the rest; so much of death her thoughts
Had entertained, as dyed her cheeks with pale.
But Adam with such counsel nothing swayed,   1010
To better hopes his more attentive mind
Labouring had raised, and thus to Eve replied:

race, which is not yet conceived and therefore still non-existent, from
being born.   **990 deceived his glut** deprived of his surfeit; cf. God's
revelation in 632–7.| **994 rites** restores their lovemaking to its pre-
lapsarian status; cf. IX 1016n.   **996 Before the present object** in my
presence; the periphrasis reveals Eve's self-contempt.   **998 less than
none** no less than any that we dread; as Eve approaches her proposal of
suicide her syntax seems to stutter.   **1000 make short**... act quickly,
and if we cannot find Death, perform his function for him.   **1001
supply**...**his office** Eve cannot bring herself to say 'kill ourselves'.
1004 and have while we still have.   **1007 vehement** mad, mindless (cf.
IX 431n), as opposed to Adam's more rationalistic despair (cf. ¦805n).
1009 entertained occupied; **dyed** playing on **death** in 1008.   **1010
nothing** not at all.   **1011 attentive** assiduous, or, perhaps, patient.
1012 Labouring reasoning is hard work after the fall. The following
argument is certainly laboured: although Eve's disdain for life and pleasure
seems to show (**argue**) her superiority to what she despises (**contemns**),
her consequent death-wish reveals that she is sorry to lose them. Is Adam's
logic sound?

'Eve, thy contempt of life and pleasure seems
To argue in thee something more sublime
And excellent than what thy mind contemns;   1015
But self-destruction therefore sought, refutes
That excellence thought in thee, and implies,
Not thy contempt, but anguish and regret
For loss of life and pleasure overloved.
Or if thou covet death, as utmost end   1020
Of misery, so thinking to evade
The penalty pronounced, doubt not but God
Hath wiselier armed his vengeful ire than so
To be forestalled; much more I fear lest death
So snatched will not exempt us from the pain   1025
We are by doom to pay; rather such acts
Of cóntumacy will provoke the Highest
To make death in us live: then let us seek
Some safer resolution, which methinks
I have in view, calling to mind with heed   1030
Part of our sentence, that thy seed shall bruise
The serpent's head; piteous amends, unless
Be meant, whom I conjecture, our grand foe
Satan, who in the serpent hath contrived
Against us this deceit: to crush his head   1035
Would be revenge indeed; which will be lost
By death brought on ourselves, or childless days
Resolved, as thou proposest; so our foe
Shall scape his punishment ordained, and we
Instead shall double ours upon our heads.   1040
    No more be mentioned then of violence
Against ourselves, and wilful barrenness,
That cuts us off from hope, and savours only

1020 as utmost end because you see it as a final end to your misery.
1023 so in this way. **1026 by doom** under sentence. **1027 cón-
tumacy** contempt (for God's judgement). **1029 resolution** way out
of the dilemma. **1030 heed** attention (cf. 1011). Adam now realizes
that the earlier curse on the serpent really applied to Satan, and therefore
that Satan was the tempter. **1032 piteous amends** small compensation.
1038 so if we remain childless or commit suicide. **1043 savours**
savours of.

They thought death was immidiate pain and e consequence

Rancour and pride, impatience and despite,
Reluctance against God and his just yoke   1045
Laid on our necks. Remember with what mild
And gracious temper he both heard and judged
Without wrath or reviling; we expected
Immediate dissolution, which we thought
Was meant by death that day, when lo, to thee   1050
Pains only in child-bearing were foretold,
And bringing forth, soon recompensed with joy,
Fruit of thy womb: on me the curse aslope
Glanced on the ground, with labour I must earn
My bread; what harm? Idleness had been worse;   1055
My labour will sustain me; and lest cold
Or heat should injure us, his timely care
Hath unbesought provided, and his hands
Clothed us unworthy, pitying while he judged;
How much more, if we pray him, will his ear   1060
Be open, and his heart to pity incline,
And teach us further by what means to shun
The inclement seasons, rain, ice, hail and snow,
Which now the sky with various face begins
To show us in this mountain, while the winds   1065
Blow moist and keen, shattering the graceful locks
Of these fair spreading trees; which bids us seek
Some better shroud, some better warmth to cherish
Our limbs benumbed, ere this diurnal star
Leave cold the night, how we his gathered beams   1070
Reflected, may with matter sere foment,

1045 Reluctance resistance; **yoke** an anachronism in paradise (cf. 307).
1048 reviling Adam realizes in retrospect what M pointed out in 118.
1053 Fruit another link between the forbidden tree and procreation (see
topics pp. 167–9). **aslope** the curse on Adam (to earn his bread
with labour) affected him only obliquely, glancing off him on to the
ground, which will bear thorns and thistles; cf. 198–208. **1055 Idleness**
but see IX 211n; **had been** would have been. **1058 unbesought**
unasked. **1060 ear** cf. IX 196n. **1065 mountain** Eden is on the top of a
steep hill (IV 132ff.). **1066 locks** leaves. **1068 shroud** protection,
but here it has funereal overtones; **cherish** keep warm. **1069 star** the
sun, **diurnal** because it shines by day every day. **1070 cold** goes with
night. **1071 Reflected** Adam suggests two ways of making fire:

Or by collision of two bodies grind
The air attrite to fire, as late the clouds
Justling or pushed with winds rude in their shock
Tine the slant lightning, whose thwart flame   1075
   driven down
Kindles the gummy bark of fir or pine,
And sends a comfortable heat from far,
Which might supply the sun: such fire to use,
And what may else be remedy or cure
To evils which our own misdeeds have wrought,   1080
He will instruct us praying, and of grace
Beseeching him, so as we need not fear
To pass commodiously this life, sustained
By him with many comforts, till we end
In dust, our final rest and native home.   1085
   What better can we do, than to the place
Repairing where he judged us, prostrate fall
Before him reverent, and there confess
Humbly our faults, and pardon beg, with tears
Watering the ground, and with our sighs the air   1090
Frequenting, sent from hearts contrite, in sign
Of sorrow unfeigned, and humiliation meek.
Undoubtedly he will relent and turn
From his displeasure; in whose look serene,
When angry most he seemed and most severe,   1095
What else but favour, grace, and mercy shone?'
   So spake our father penitent, nor Eve
Felt less remorse: they forthwith to the place

catching the sun's rays in a glass and focusing them on some dry material
(**matter sere**) or rubbing two stones together so that the air between
them bursts into flame from the friction. He infers the latter technique
from the thunder storm he has observed (666–7 or IX 1002). The jostling
(**justling**) clouds seemed to kindle (**Tine**) flashes of lightning, which in
turn sets the trees alight with its oblique (**thwart**) flame. In the un-
accustomed cold of the fallen world fire is comforting (**comfortable**)
not guilty (cf. IX 392, topics p. 171).   **1078 supply** replace.   **1081**
praying ... if we pray and ask for his grace.   **1087 Repairing** returning.
Their contrition will repair the fall; cf. *Of education*: 'The end then
of learning is to repair the ruins of our first parents by regaining to know
God aright.'   **1091 Frequenting** filling; cf. VII 148.

150

Repairing where he judged them prostrate fell
Before him reverent, and both confessed   1100
Humbly their faults, and pardon begged, with tears
Watering the ground, and with their sighs the air
Frequenting, sent from hearts contrite, in sign
Of sorrow unfeigned, and humiliation meek.

Topics: Book IX

The commentary at the beginning of this volume sticks close to the text; it is explanatory and continuous. This section follows the same order as the commentary; but it treats individually some of the wider issues which the text raises, poses questions and suggests a few materials as a basis for further discussion.

Prologue

Tragic notes

Medieval poets saw the fall as the prototype of all subsequent tragedies. Their collections of tragic stories, Boccaccio's *De casibus virorum illustrium*, Chaucer's *Monk's tale* and Lydgate's *Falls of princes*, for instance, almost invariably begin with the fall of either Lucifer or Adam. This is how Chaucer's monk starts his tale:

> In tragic manner I will now lament
> The griefs of those who stood in high degree
> And fell at last with no expedient
> To bring them out of their adversity.
> For sure it is, if Fortune wills to flee,
> No man may stay her course or keep his hold;
> Let no one trust a blind prosperity.
> Be warned by these examples, true and old.
>
> With Lucifer, although an angel he
> And not a man, I purpose to begin.
> For notwithstanding angels cannot be
> The sport of Fortune, yet he fell through sin
> Down into Hell, and he is yet therein.
> O Lucifer, brightest of angels all,
> Now thou art Satan, and canst never win
> Out of thy miseries; how great thy fall!
>
> Consider Adam, made by God's own finger,
> And not begotten of man's unclean seed,
> He that in Eden was allowed to linger
> – Now called Damascus – and had power at need

> Over all Paradise, save that decreed
> And single tree prohibited. Than he
> None ever on earth stood higher, till his deed
> Drove him to labour, Hell and misery.
> *Canterbury tales* tr Nevill Coghill Penguin Classics 1951

But it is hard to see how the fall story could conform to either of the definitions of tragedy proposed in this passage. It can't be a tragedy of fate in which the hero is deserted by 'Fortune' because bad luck presumably doesn't exist in the pre-lapsarian world; unfallen man no less than the angels 'cannot be The sport of Fortune'. It can't be a tragedy of character in which the hero falls 'through sin' because Adam was created sinless; in the monk's words he was 'not begotten of man's unclean seed'.

Which raises, of course, the still more fundamental question: how could the fall have happened at all? Is the transition from perfection to corruption even imaginable? Granted that he had free will, wouldn't an ideal being always freely choose the good? In which case, how free would he really be? In literary terms the problem becomes one of plausibility. We normally expect a character's deeds to be consistent with his nature, so when Adam sins isn't he acting 'out of character'? On the other hand, aren't our literary notions of 'character' based on the nature of post-lapsarian man? Is it fair to apply them in this particular instance? In what sense, if any, did Adam have a character before he ate the apple?

The sketches for a five-act dramatic version of the story which Milton made in his notebook (the Trinity College, Cambridge, MS) early in the 1640s are extremely interesting in this respect. For thanks to the structure and conventions of Greek tragedy, according to which many of the major events happen either off stage or before the play begins, Milton is able to avoid staging the falls of either Lucifer or Adam. Each appears only 'after his overthrow' as the fourth draft puts it. The impossible gulf between innocence and sinfulness doesn't have to be bridged in full view of the audience.

In *PL* it does, and is. How did Milton do it? By cheating a little, as E. M. W. Tillyard has suggested ('The crisis of *PL*' in *Studies in Milton* 1951) and making Adam and Eve fallen before the fall? He would have had St Augustine's authority behind him:

Moreover, our first parents only fell openly into the sin of disobedience because, secretly, they had begun to be guilty. Actually, their bad deed could not have been done had not bad will preceded it; what is more, the root of their bad will was nothing else than pride... Our first parents, then, must already have fallen before they could do the evil deed, before they could commit the sin of eating the forbidden fruit. For such 'bad fruit' could come only from a 'bad tree'.   *City of God* xiv 13

Or did Milton try to deal with the problem by making the story not a tragedy of character, which is what the solution above amounts to, but a tragedy of fate after all? By allowing, that is to say, enough bad luck into the garden to bring about the fall? Is that perhaps the role of Satan in Book ix (see notes to 160, 421, 689 etc.)? If so, to what extent can Adam and Eve be held morally responsible for their disobedience? Couldn't they blame Satan, or the angels who failed to keep him out of Eden, or God? How is the blame distributed in the judgement scene in Book x? How convincing do you find Adam's self-defence and Christ's accusations?

These are complicated questions and critics have been arguing about them for centuries. One way of testing your answers is to take up Milton's hint and try producing Book ix as a five-act tragedy complete with prologue and chorus. For although Milton finally abandoned the dramatic for the epic form one can still feel the influence of his original intention in certain parts of the poem (see: J. H. Hanford 'The dramatic element in *PL*' *Studies in Philology* xiv (1917) 178–95) and nowhere more strongly than here in Book ix.

Milton as hero

One way of defining a hero is by his antagonists. Milton has three. First, his predecessors: Homer, Virgil and the authors of medieval and renaissance epics. The idea that the poet is engaged in this kind of heroic competition goes back at least as far as a treatise *On the Sublime* written, probably in the 1st century AD, by a Greek rhetorician called Longinus. He asserted that Plato was consciously trying to outdo Homer:

This author shows us, if we would choose not to neglect the lesson, that there is also another road, besides all that we have mentioned, which leads to the sublime. What, and what manner of road is that? Imitation and emulation of great writers and poets who have been before us... I do not think that there would be such a bloom as we find on some of his [Plato's] philosophical dogmas, or that he could have entered so often into poetical matter and expressions, unless he had entered for the first place against Homer, aye, with all his soul, a young champion against one long approved; and striven for the mastery, too emulously perhaps and in the spirit of the lists, yet not without his reward; for 'good', says

Hesiod, 'is this strife for mortals'. Yes, that contest for fame is fair, and its crown worthy of the winning, wherein even to be defeated by our forerunners is not inglorious.   xiii tr A. O. Prickard 1906

Does Milton also strive 'too emulously perhaps'? When he challenges his pagan rivals does he always play fair? Is his victory simply assumed, or does he try to persuade us of it? If so, how? More specifically, are the differences between *PL* and earlier epics described as qualitative (false heroic versus true heroic) or as quantitative (heroic versus more heroic)? What would be the result of confusing these two categories? If, for instance, epic battles are 'long and tedious' (30) how are we supposed to react to the Homeric war in heaven in Book VI? Milton seems to want it both ways. See M. Miller '*PL*: the double standard' *University of Toronto Quarterly* xx (1951) 183–99. On the relationship of *PL* to the epic tradition see: C. M. Bowra *From Virgil to Milton* 1945 repr 1961, K. W. Grandsen '*PL* and the *Aeneid*' *Essays in Criticism* XVII (1967) 281–303, Davis P. Harding *The club of Hercules* Illinois Studies in Language and Literature vol 50 1962, C. S. Lewis *A preface to PL* 1942 repr 1960 chs. 1–8, E. M. W. Tillyard *The English epic and its background* 1954 repr 1966.

Milton's second antagonist is anything that might delay or prevent his writing the poem: blindness (III 1ff.), enemies (VII 1ff.), old age (IX 41ff.). There is something heroic about the sheer energy needed to see the work through to its conclusion, and many poets from classical antiquity on described the process of composition as a personal *Odyssey* (e.g. Dante *The divine comedy* Paradiso ii 1–18, Spenser *The fairy queen* VI xii 1). Milton prefers the image of flight (I 12–16; III 13–21; VII 1–20; IX 45), and uses that of the sea voyage to define Satan's progress rather than his own. Why? What do the two respective images imply about the nature of poetry and poetic inspiration? Compare this passage from *East Coker* by T. S. Eliot:

> So here I am, in the middle way, having had twenty years –
> Twenty years largely wasted, the years of *l'entre deux guerres* –
> Trying to learn to use words, and every attempt
> Is a wholly new start, and a different kind of failure
> Because one has only learnt to get the better of words
> For the thing one no longer has to say, or the way in which
> One is no longer disposed to say it. And so each venture
> Is a new beginning, a raid on the inarticulate
> With shabby equipment always deteriorating
> In the general mess of imprecision of feeling,
> Undisciplined squads of emotion. And what there is to conquer

By strength and submission, has already been discovered
Once or twice, or several times, by men whom one cannot hope
To emulate – but there is no competition –
There is only the fight to recover what has been lost
And found and lost again and again: and now, under conditions
That seem unpropitious. But perhaps neither gain nor loss.
For us, there is only the trying. The rest is not our business.

Four quartets 1943 pp. 16–17

Eliot's tone is self-consciously unheroic, yet much of what he says is reminiscent of Milton's analysis of his vocation in the prologues to III, VII and IX. What seem to you to be some of the significant similarities and differences? On the whole question of the poet's relationship to his own work in the renaissance, see Robert M. Durling *The figure of the poet in renaissance epic*, Harvard 1965.

Milton's third antagonist is Satan, as Denis Saurat was one of the first to suggest:

Milton throws himself personally into the struggle against Satan, and from the reading of *Paradise Lost* one derives two inevitable impressions: the greatness of Satan and the greatness of Milton. Hence the lyricism which occasionally explodes through the stiff conventionalism of the epic. Milton brings his own self into the poem just as he did into the pamphlets: in both cases he is one of the duellists; he has a personal share in the fighting. He it is, and not God or the Son, that overcomes Satan. He follows him in all his enterprises, stigmatizes them with one adjective, one line. He exposes Satan so passionately that he forgets Satan's natural enemies: he takes their place before the Enemy. What need has Milton of a hero in his poem? He is his own hero.

Milton man and thinker repr 1964 p. 184

But if this is the case, surely the dice are heavily loaded in Milton's favour. How can there be any genuine contest between a character and his creator? Satan would be even worse off in the face of Milton's omnipotence than he is in the face of God's (on the implications of this equivalence see the quotation from Northrop Frye below, p. 178). The logical outcome of Saurat's view is A. J. A. Waldock's complaint that Milton deliberately degrades Satan by calling him names throughout the poem, and that the names don't correspond to what we have been shown of his nature ('Satan and the technique of degradation' in *PL and its critics* 1947 repr 1959). Does he seem to you to treat Satan any more or less fairly than he treats Adam and Eve? Where in the story are you most strongly aware of the narrator's presence? How would you characterize his role?

Satan

Satan as villain

One of the reasons Satan is so interesting is that he is so complicated: epic hero, stage villain, merchant-adventurer, saviour, trickster, buffoon (see commentary p. 47), classical orator, courtly lover (see commentary p. 27), tempter, accuser (see commentary p. 16), English revolutionary, Eastern despot, devil and angel all rolled into one. Here he is most evidently a stage villain, delivering the conventional soliloquy before the dreadful deed, Macbeth pondering the murder of Duncan, Richard III conspiring against his brother, Edmund preparing to deceive Gloucester. Satan, like Edmund, wants to get his own back on a 'father' who has mistreated him by giving all his goods to the legitimate heir. The only difference is the cosmic scale of the characters involved and the issues at stake in *PL*. In terms of literary history Satan is Edmund's descendant; in terms of Christian history he is his ancestor. Does the similarity diminish Satan in any way? Is his soliloquy over-dramatic, even melodramatic, in the narrative context? What else does he have in common with Edmund or any of the other villains of renaissance drama: Claudius in *Hamlet*, Dr Faustus, Macbeth, Iago in *Othello*, Damville in Tourneur's *The atheist's tragedy*? For some interesting answers to this last question see Helen Gardner 'Milton's Satan and the theme of damnation in Elizabethan tragedy' in A. E. Barker *Milton: modern essays in criticism*.

Satan's soliloquy is also conventional in the sense that many earlier poets and dramatists who treated the fall of man had included a similar speech at this juncture (see J. M. Evans *PL and the Genesis tradition* chs. 4, 7). Nor is there anything original about the idea that Satan wanted to seduce man in order to prevent him from enjoying the benefits he and the other fallen angels had lost. What is original is the way in which Milton treats this motive: as a desperate last-minute rationalization (see commentary p. 19). The phrase 'motiveless malignancy', which Coleridge first coined to describe Iago, also defines the truth that Satan is trying to conceal from himself. W. H. Auden's gloss on Coleridge makes the connection clearer:

The practical joker despises his victims, but at the same time he envies them because their desires, however childish and mistaken, are real to them, whereas he has no desire which he can call his own. His goal, to make game of others, makes his existence absolutely dependent upon theirs; when he is alone he is a nullity. Iago's self-description, *I am not what I am*, is correct and the negation of the Divine *I am that I am*. If the word motive is given its normal meaning of a positive purpose of the self like sex, money, glory, etc., then the practical joker is without motive. Yet the professional practical joker is certain driven, like a gambler, to his activity, but the drive is negative, a fear of lacking a concrete self, of being nobody. In any practical joker to whom playing such jokes is a passion, there is always an element of malice, a projection of his self-hatred onto others, and in the ultimate case of the absolute practical joker, this is projected onto all created things.

> 'The joker in the pack' in *The dyer's hand and other essays* 1968; see also C. G. Jung 'On the psychology of the trickster-figure' in *Four archetypes* tr R. F. C. Hull Princeton 1970

One of the characteristics of Iago which led Auden to this view is the variety of motives he propounds in his soliloquies. Are Satan's explanations all consistent with each other? Compare this speech with the reasons given for tempting man in II 358–72 and IV 358–92. How might Satan's fear 'of being nobody' relate to his passion for play-acting?

The subtle serpent

Snakes are ambiguous creatures. They terrify and fascinate us. Many of them are poisonous (see X 524n) yet they are symbols of healing (see IX 505n). In myth they are both guardians (e.g. the garden of the Hesperides) and violators (*Genesis* iii) of sacred trees. As a structuralist would say, they are anomalous; they defy such binary oppositions as male–female, wild–domesticated, fish–animal (see Edmund Leach 'Genesis as myth' *Discovery* XXIII (1962) 30–5). Keats catches something of these complexities in his description of Lamia (*Lamia* 47–65). This, to be sure, is a special case, but the same sense of ambivalence is present in poems like D. H. Lawrence's *Snake*, Denise Levertov's *To the snake* (publ New Directions), Yvor Winters' *A spring serpent* (in *The giant weapon* 1943) and Paul Valéry's *Ébauche d'un serpent*.

As a result Milton was faced with a difficult problem when he came to describe the tempter's approach. Before the fall the creatures were all unambiguously good, so he had to find a way of making the serpent appear as attractive and harmless as possible both to Eve and to us. Yet as Desmond Morris has documented (*The naked ape* 1967 ch. 8), our congenital fear of snakes is enormously powerful – indeed, some scholars have suggested that the fall story was written to explain, among other things, why we are so afraid of them. How, then, was Milton to exclude the serpent's threatening aspects?

One of the most popular solutions to this problem in both the art and literature of the fall was to humanize the reptile by giving it a woman's face. According to the 6th-century Syriac work, *The cave of treasures*, Satan chose this kind of serpent because Eve would be more easily persuaded by her mirror-image. This idea became extremely popular during the middle ages, perhaps, as J. K. Bonnell has suggested ('The serpent with a human head in art and mystery play' *American Journal of Archaeology* XXI (1917) 255), because the serpentine costumes used in the mystery plays allowed the actor's face to be seen. At all events, it appears in innumerable paintings both in the middle ages and the renaissance. Here are some of the best known of them:

'The earthly paradise' in the *Très riches heures du duc de Berry*
'The creation and fall' in the *Bedford book of hours* (Add MS 188850 in the BM)
'The temptation' in *Queen Mary's psalter* (MS Reg 2B vii in the BM)
'The temptation of Eve' in the *Speculum humanae salvationis* (MS lat 9584 in the Bibliothèque Nationale)
'The fall and expulsion' by Michelangelo (Vatican, Sistine Chapel, ceiling)
'The fall of man' by Raphael (Vatican, Stanza della Segnatura, ceiling)
'The fall' by Hugo Van der Goes (Kunsthistorisches Museum, Vienna)
'Fall of man' by Titian (Madrid, Prado)

For a much more complete list see J. K. Bonnell's article cited above and J. B. Trapp 'The iconography of the fall of man' in C. A. Patrides *Approaches to PL* 1968, and 'Iconography' in *John Milton: introductions* in this series.

Milton, however, chose to ignore this solution. In *PL* the serpent is emphatically male, and there is no suggestion that it has a human face. Yet the idea may still be present metaphorically. Is there any sense in which the serpent is Eve's *alter ego*, a mirror image of her secret desires? Or is she rather the serpent's double when she tempts Adam? See his rebuke in X 867–73. This still leaves unanswered the question: how, at the purely literal level, does Milton go about dispelling our innate revulsion to snakes? Is that what the allusions in 504–10 are doing? What is the effect of words like 'carbuncle', 'burnished', 'verdant gold' 'enamelled'? Does 'erect' in 501 merely reinforce the snake's phallic associations? In short, how really snaky is Milton's snake?

Adam and Eve

The garden as paradise

Paradise, like its inhabitants, is prototypical. This means not only that Eden is the perfect pattern of all subsequent gardens, but also that all subsequent gardens are to a greater or lesser extent imperfect copies of Eden (cf. Bacon's essay *Of gardens*). So when 17th-century poets described some of the most famous gardens of their time (e.g. John Donne *Twicknam garden*, Ben Jonson *To Penshurst*, Andrew Marvell *Upon Appleton House*) Eden was never far from their minds. Nor, we occasionally sense, were some of these contemporary English gardens far from Milton's when he was composing *PL* (viz IV 223–63).

No less influential was the pagan concept of the golden age. Here is Ovid's description in the *Metamorphoses*:

> The earth itself, without compulsion, untouched by the hoe, unfurrowed by any share, produced all things spontaneously, and men were content with foods that grew without cultivation. They gathered arbute berries and mountain strawberries, wild cherries and blackberries that cling to thorny bramble bushes; or acorns fallen from Juno's oak. It was the season of everlasting spring [*ver erat aeternum*], when peaceful zephyrs, with their warm breath, caressed the flowers that sprang up without having been planted. In time the earth, though untilled, produced corn too, and fields that never lay fallow whitened with heavy ears of grain. Then there flowed rivers of milk and rivers of nectar, and golden honey dripped from the green holmoak.
>
> Book I 101–12 tr Mary M. Innes 1955 repr 1961 Penguin Classics

This classical commonplace was readily adaptable to the biblical account of the garden of Eden and Milton was not the first to make use of it (see J. M. Evans *PL and the Genesis tradition* ch. 4). In the middle ages a second and equally popular secular topic fed into the tradition: the concept of the garden of love. Guillaume de Lorris' 13th-century account of it in *The romance of the rose* is a good example (iii 76–98 tr Harry W. Robbins 1962). All three elements, biblical, classical and medieval, meet in Spenser's description of the garden of Adonis in *Fairy queen* III vi 30–46.

Which brings us, via the reference in *PL* IX 440, back to Milton. His Eden clearly grows out of this tradition – it is a moral, climatic and erotic paradise – yet in certain important respects it is exceptional. Unlike Ovid's golden age farm and Spenser's perfect garden, for instance, it does have to be cultivated, albeit with 'rude' implements (see 391n). Indeed, Eve's opening speech to Adam invokes a completely different tradition from the one we have just traced, the tradition of 'hard' as opposed to 'soft' primitivism (see A. O. Lovejoy, G. Boas *Contributions to the history of primitivism and related ideas in antiquity* Baltimore 1934; G. Boas, *Essays in primitivism and related ideas in the middle ages* Baltimore 1948). According to this view of human history the so-called golden age was in fact a time of brutality and savagery:

> Through many decades of the sun's cyclic course they [the original human beings] lived out their lives in the fashion of wild beasts roaming at large. No one spent his strength in guiding the curved plough. No one knew how to cleave the earth with iron, or to plant young saplings in the soil or lop the old branches from tall trees with pruning hooks. Their hearts were well content to accept as a free gift what the sun and showers had given and the earth had produced unsolicited. Often they stayed their hunger among the acorn-laden oaks. Arbutus berries, whose scarlet tint now betrays their winter ripening, were then produced by the earth in plenty and of a larger size... They did not know as yet how to enlist the aid of fire, or to make use of skins, or to clothe their bodies with trophies of the chase. They lived in thickets and hillside caves and forests and stowed their rugged limbs among bushes when driven to seek shelter from the lash of wind and rain.
>
> They could have no thought of the common good, no notion of the mutual restraint of morals and laws. The individual, taught to live and fend only for himself, carried off on his own account such prey as fortune brought him. Venus coupled the bodies of lovers in the greenwood. Mutual desire brought them together, or the male's mastering might and overriding lust, or a payment of acorns or arbutus berries or choice pears.
>
> Lucretius *The nature of the universe* v 933ff. tr R. E. Latham 1951
> repr 1955 Penguin Classics

This is Ovid's paradise turned inside out. Human history is now evolutionary rather than devolutionary. We were not expelled from the garden; we emerged from the jungle. Eden, described in these terms, would resemble the Duke of York's garden in *Richard II* (III iv 29–76). Compare *PL* IV 610–33; V 209–19, 291–7; IX 205–25. How are we to interpret this aspect of Milton's garden? Is it, as J. B. Broadbent believes, 'an anachronism, like Milton's psychology, because neither the garden nor the microcosm and macrocosm it represents should need pruning and weeding in innocence' (*Some graver subject* p. 177)? Is it Milton's attempt to answer in advance the frequently repeated charge that life in Eden would have been boring (see E. M. W. Tillyard *Milton* 1946 pp. 282–3, A. J. A. Waldock *PL and its critics* p. 125)? Or is it symbolic of Adam and Eve's moral condition before the fall (see J. M. Evans 'Native innocence' in *PL and the Genesis tradition*)? How do the 'hard' elements in Milton's picture of Eden relate to the 'soft'? Compare the passages cited above with *PL* IV 205–68, 319–52, 689–719; VIII 300–14; IX 99–118. Are the two elements simply juxtaposed, or does Milton try to reconcile them? A good way of getting at some of these problems might be to compare the treatment of the garden in *PL* with its portrayal in such pictures as:

Hieronymus Bosch 'The garden of earthly delights' (Madrid, Prado)
Rubens 'Paradise' (The Hague, Mauritshuis)
Tintoretto 'Fall of man' (Venice, Accademia)
Lucas Cranach 'Fall of man' (London, Courtauld Institute)

and in the illustrations to Books IV, V, VIII and IX by John Baptist de Medina (1688 ed), Louis Cheron and Sir James Thornhill (1720 ed), and especially John Martin (1827 ed). For literary treatments of the theme see: John Armstrong *The paradise myth* 1969, A. Bartlett Giamatti *The earthly paradise and the renaissance epic* Princeton 1966, G. H. Williams *Wilderness and paradise in christian thought* New York 1962.

The garden as pastoral

Paradise (from Old Persian *pairidaeza* = royal park or pleasure garden) is a historical ideal: the perfect place before the fall. Pastoral (from Latin *pastor* = shepherd) is a social and geographical ideal: the perfect place outside the city. From its very beginning in the *Idyls* of the Greek poet Theocritus, who lived in Alexandria in the 3rd century BC, pastoral has been an urban genre, a city-dweller's fantasy about how much better things might be in the country: simple, natural, free, uncomplicated, leisurely, open, honest, everything that the rat-race is not. Marlowe's *The passionate shepherd to his love* catches its spirit perfectly. But the pastoral tradition, like the paradisal, also had a 'hard' side. Ralegh's complementary poem *The nymph's reply* illustrates it. Rural life could also be naïve, crude, immoral, vulgar, boring, earthy, everything that sophisticated society is not. The pastoral nature of Eden is established by the presence in hell of Pandemonium, the diabolic metropolis (see 445n and 439). It is seriously qualified by the presence in heaven of an ideal court, the other traditional enemy of pastoral. Once again Milton seems to want it both ways. From Satan's point of view Adam and Eve are the quintessential shepherd and his nymph; from Raphael's they are two of God's courtiers (e.g. V 350–61). In the renaissance, however, pastoral was often itself a way of having it both ways. The shepherds and shepherdesses were frequently kings and queens, princes and princesses in disguise (e.g. *Winter's tale*, *As you like it*; notice all the jewelry in Marlowe's pastoral lyric). Milton's courtly peasants are poised between villainous sophistication and naïve rusticity (see below p. 174). Where in Book ix do they come closest to these two extremes? How successful is Milton in maintaining the poise? What is the effect of introducing a real shepherd and a real primitive in 1101–18? For a succinct account of non-dramatic pastoral see Hallett Smith *Elizabethan poetry* Ann Arbor 1952 repr 1968 ch 1. For a more general survey see W. W. Greg *Pastoral poetry and drama* 1906 and William Empson *Some versions of pastoral* 1935.

Perhaps the most fundamental question of all, however, has to do with the viability of Eden as an ideal of any kind. Lionel Trilling believes that it has lost its attraction:

How far from our imagination is the idea of 'peace' as the crown of spiritual struggle! The idea of bliss is even further removed. The two words propose to us a state of virtually infantile passivity which is the negation of the 'more life' that we crave, the 'more life' of spiritual militancy. We dread Eden, and of all the Christian concepts there is none which we understand so well as the *felix culpa* and the 'fortunate fall'; not, of course, for the reason on which these Christian paradoxes were based, but because by means of sin and the fall we managed to get ourselves expelled from that place.

'The fate of pleasure' in *Literary views* ed C. Camden Chicago 1964 p. 107.

Wallace Stevens makes the same point in a different way in *Sunday morning* 76–90. One needs only the briefest acquaintance with Milton's prose or poetry to realize that he was no advocate of 'infantile passivity'. In an age of 'spiritual militancy' he was among the most militant. Hence A. J. A. Waldock's question:

What, after all, has Milton – the Milton of the great famous sayings in the prose works, the Milton who could not praise a fugitive and cloistered virtue unexercised and unbreathed – to do with the effortless innocence, the 'blank' virtue, of prelapsarian man? It is another of the paradoxes of the poem. In many senses *PL* was his predestined theme, and yet in a sense it put him in a false position, cut clean against the grain of his nature. Believing rather more intensely than the average man that our dignity consists in independent and strenuous thought, and feeling with the same rather exceptional intensity that the essence of life is struggle, he must deplore the coming of thought into the world (for that is what it really amounts to) and represent man's best state as that original featureless blessedness. He was trapped, in a sense, by his theme, and from the trap there was no escape. *PL and its critics* pp. 22–3

Or was there? Look back at Books IV, V and VIII with this problem in mind. Does Milton really portray innocence as being 'effortless'? If Waldock is right, how is it that critics can also complain that Adam and Eve were fallen long before the fall (see above p. 153)? Don't the 'hard' aspects of Eden protect it from this kind of criticism? For two modern treatments of the theme see Charles Tomlinson *Eden* in *The way of the world* 1969 and T. S. Eliot *Burnt Norton* in *Four quartets* 1943.

Separation

As I suggested in the commentary, Milton has balanced the argument between Adam and Eve so evenly that it's hard to know which side we should be on. A selection of critical opinions might help to isolate some of the more important issues:

It has been, although she [Eve] does not know it, her unlucky day. Things have gone awry from the start. She wakes in independent mood; she decides to enjoy herself in her own fashion, to follow her whim, to set off, for once, alone. Adam's dissuasions merely strengthen her resolve to have, for this one time, her own way. Then she begins, unexpectedly, to enjoy the situation. Adam's opposition is a new experience, not without its interest. She begins to act a little, to play a part. She pretends to be hurt by his mistrust; she assumes an air of injured dignity...She shows a pretty obstinacy, feels her power, gets her way.

A. J. A. Waldock *PL and its critics* pp. 30–1

Look at their total conversation (lines 204–384), and several things emerge. From first to last Eve takes and keeps the initiative, though she very nearly loses it at the end. Her speeches are short, clear, and emphatic, and her mind is working very fast. Adam, on the other hand, is unprepared, laborious, and on the defensive, although he warms up and becomes really cogent at the end... Eve begins with her proposal that since they waste so much time taking notice of each other they should garden separately and thus get more done in time. It comes out pat and has the air of having been thought out beforehand. The proposal was relatively harmless, but it was not sincere. The pair were still in their honeymoon stage, and the last thing Eve really wanted was to be separated even for a morning from her lover. So she lays a mild trap for Adam, hoping that he will not fall into it but will retort that she asks too much and that he cannot bear to lose sight of her... She first wanted a small tribute to her charm; now she has had the satisfaction of rousing Adam and of obtaining a degree of attention she had never expected. And then comes the tragedy. Adam, whom Eve expects to be firm, suddenly weakens. He goes on to find a specious argument why in this instance separation may be better, misapplies the doctrine of liberty, and almost recommends Eve to go against his true wishes.

E. M. W. Tillyard 'The crisis of *PL*' *Studies in Milton* pp. 16–20

The proposal [to work apart] is entirely natural and clearly dictated by the least frivolous side of her character: together, she feels, they will waste time in 'Casual discourse', whereas apart much can be done... And at this point his objections collapse: he gives his consent to her departure. Far from being sudden, the decision is almost inevitable, two causes having conspired to bring it about. First, he is unnerved by the thought which has just struck him, that their trial will come when it is least expected. If this is so then Eve may as well go off at once, while she is freshly warned and on her mettle. Secondly, his wife's gentle persistance has forced him to acknowledge, to her and to himself, that her complaint at 285–9 is justified. He feels guilty for mistrusting her, and tries to make up for it by letting her have her way. So, claiming the last word, though 'yet submiss' (377), she withdraws her hand from his and takes her leave.

John Peter *A critique of PL* 1960 pp. 116–18

Dr Tillyard, who was the first I think to point out that Milton scrutinizes the approach to the fall like a novelist, remarked very fairly that the reason why she says she wants to 'work' apart from her husband is that she feels the need to flap her wings a bit; after hearing Raphael on her future expected début, she may well want to obtain a tiny change in her experience, and indeed could hardly be admired if she had no impulse to react at all. This then is why Satan can catch her alone. The critics who blame Adam for letting her go, after giving her every warning, seem to me to preach an immoral moral; certainly, Milton thought that men ought to control women, but that would make him feel all the more outraged when Eve turns round and blames Adam for having let her go. Adam merely behaves well there, as Dr Tillyard I think proves without quite meaning to.

William Empson *Milton's God* pp. 150–1

Milton wants to give Eve a very strong-seeming case and very characteristically has recourse to one of his own. He wants a powerful argument for Eve in order not to make Adam look a fool. That many readers of *PL* are convinced by Eve's argument measures Milton's success. But the power of her argument is not aimed at justifying her action but rather at mitigating the failure of Adam to see through it. It is important too that for all Eve's reasons Milton still makes Adam intelligent enough to make a very good estimate of the sort of thing that might happen to her on her own, that she might 'fall into deception unaware (IX 362). Adam's reluctance too is even more strongly marked than his consent. But for all his intelligence and shrewdness, he does let her go. And that, in the light of what happened, was an unreasonable act... She is warned, yet still nourishes the erroneous desire to go ('the willinger I go'). So far she is responsible, but she goes, as she starts out by saying, with Adam's 'permission'. It is an important reservation. Eve is not, having wheedled permission from Adam for her going, now maddeningly loading him with the responsibility for what she does. Without Adam's permission she will not go. Wilfulness on her part here would exonerate Adam. By granting his permission Adam becomes involved in what happens to her.

Dennis H. Burden *The logical epic* 1967 pp. 89–92

Which of these accounts corresponds most closely to your impression of the scene? What preconceptions seem to lie behind these differences of opinion? Try performing the scene aloud according to these various interpretations. Write an ending for the scene in which Adam doesn't give in at the last moment yet Eve does goes off on her own. What other means might Milton have used to isolate her for the temptation? For a detailed study of the episode see J. S. Diekhoff 'Eve, the Devil, and *Areopagitica*' *Modern language quarterly* v (1944) 354–64.

The fall of Eve

Eve separate

There is something specially touching about the vision of an innocent girl alone in a pastoral setting. It moves Milton to one of his most anguished interventions (404ff.) and to a display of mythical ikons unmatched anywhere else in the poem. For a moment it overawes even Satan's malice (457ff.). What is it that makes this particular image so evocative? Some other examples might suggest some answers: Dante *The divine comedy* Purgatorio xxviii 22–51, Andrew Marvell *The picture of little T.C. in a prospect of flowers*, Wordsworth *The solitary reaper*, G. M. Hopkins *Spring and fall*, Ralph Hodgson *Eve*. Only the last of these poems is explicitly about Eve, yet Dante's Matelda, Marvell's T.C., Wordsworth's solitary reaper and Hopkins' Margaret are all in their different ways types of her. They embody the realization that comes to Ransom, the hero of C. S. Lewis's *Voyage to Venus*, as he looks at Eve's Venusian counterpart:

It was suddenly borne in upon him that her purity and peace were not, as they had seemed, things settled and inevitable like the purity and peace of an animal – that they were alive and therefore breakable, a balance maintained by a mind and therefore, at least in theory, able to be lost. There was no reason why a man on a smooth road should lose his balance on a bicycle; but he could. There was no reason why she should step out of her happiness into the psychology of our own race; but neither was there any wall between to prevent her doing so. The sense of precarious-ness terrified him: but, when she looked at him again, he changed that word to adventure, and then all words died out of his mind.

Voyage to Venus 1943 repr 1956 pp. 55–6

What is responsible for the 'sense of precariousness' in the poems quoted above? Is it defined by the girl's relationship to the landscape or the narrator's relationship to her? How does Milton's treatment of both relationships compare with the others'? What is it that threatens the innocence of the various girls?

166

Death? Love? Knowledge? Bernard Shaw's version of the temptation scene implies that all three are closely connected:

s: I can talk of many things. I am very wise. It was I who whispered the word to you that you did not know. Dead. Death. Die.

e [shuddering]: Why do you remind me of it? I forgot it when I saw your beautiful hood. You must not remind me of unhappy things.

s: Death is not an unhappy thing when you have learnt to conquer it.

e: How can I conquer it?

s: By another thing, called birth.

e: What? [trying to pronounce it] B-birth?

s: Yes, birth.

e: What is birth?

s: The serpent never dies. Some day you shall see me come out of this beautiful skin, a new snake with a new and lovelier skin. That is birth.

e: I have seen that. It is wonderful.

s: If I can do that, what can I not do? I tell you I am very subtle. When you and Adam talk, I hear you say 'Why?' Always 'Why?' You see things; and you say 'Why?' But I dream things that never were; and I say 'Why not?' I made the word dead to describe my old skin that I cast when I am renewed. I call that renewal being born.

e: Born is a beautiful word.

s: Why not be born again and again as I am, new and beautiful every time?

e: I! It does not happen: that is why.

s: That is how; but it is not why. Why not?

e: But I should not like it. It would be nice to be new again; but my old skin would lie on the ground looking just like me; and Adam would see it shrivel up and –

s: No. He need not. There is a second birth.

e: A second birth?

s: Listen. I will tell you a great secret...

e: Now the secret. The secret. [She sits on the rock and throws her arms round the serpent, who begins whispering to her].

Eve's face lights up with intense interest, which increases until an expression of overwhelming repugnance takes its place. She buries her face in her hands.

'In the beginning' from *Back to Methuselah* 1921 repr 1954 pp. 74–86

Life and death

In essence Shaw's interpretation of the scene is a variation of what S. G. F. Brandon calls the myth (?) of the 'overcrowded earth' (*Creation legends of the ancient Near-East* 1963 ch. 4) according to which human mortality is the inevitable result of human fertility. Death is the price we pay for our ability to reproduce life; otherwise the world would be filled up. Thus the fall story is analogous to such myths as the following recorded by Lévi-Strauss:

The first man, created by the demiurge, lived in innocence, although his penis was always in a state of erection. He tried in vain to induce detumescence by sprinkling it with a manioc beverage. The first woman, having been instructed by the water spirit (who had subsequently been castrated and killed by her husband), taught the man how to soften his penis through copulation. When the demiurge saw the limp penis, he became angry and said: 'Henceforth your penis will be soft, you will make children, and then you will die: later when your child grows, he will make another child, and in turn he will die.'

The raw and the cooked tr J. & D. Weightman New York 1969 p. 155

In *Genesis*, then, the 'knowledge of good and evil' (ii 17) means sexual awareness. Only when they have acquired it do Adam and Eve realize that they are naked (iii 7). But now that they can reproduce they must suffer the consequences: Eve, who is given her name for the first time (in Hebrew it is Hawwah = she who makes live), has to endure labour pains. Adam must learn to cultivate the soil in order to support his offspring, and they both are condemned to 'return unto the ground' (iii 19).

This is a cultural anthropologist's way of looking at the myth. A psychologist would draw different conclusions from the connection of sex with death: 'Guilt is the expression of the conflict of ambivalence, the eternal struggle between Eros and the destructive or death instinct.' (Sigmund Freud *Civilization and its discontents* 1939; see also Norman O. Brown *Life against death* 1959.) And he would probably lay more stress on the sense of shame that accompanies Adam and Eve's perception of their nakedness. From such a point of view the story could well be read as an image of the transition from childhood to maturity, a metaphor for the experience of adolescence. In this many fathers of the early church would have concurred, especially Irenaeus who argued in the 2nd century that Adam and Eve 'having been created a short time previously, had no understanding of the procreation of children: for it was necessary that they should first come to adult age' (*Against the heresies* III xxii 4 tr *Ante-Nicene Christian Library* v). 'For this reason they "were not ashamed", as they kissed each other and embraced with the innocence of children' (*Demonstration of the apostolic teaching* xiv tr *Ancient christian writers* xvi). Irenaeus' contemporary, Clement of Alexandria, was rather more explicit:

And if the serpent took the use of intercourse from the irrational animals and persuaded Adam to agree to have sexual union with Eve, as though the couple first created did not have such union by nature, as some think, this again is blasphemy against the creation. For it makes human nature weaker than that of the brute beasts if in this matter those who were first created by God copied them.

But if nature led them, like the irrational animals, to procreation, yet they were impelled to do it more quickly than was proper because they were still young, and had been led away by deceit. Thus God's judgement against them was just, because they did not wait for his will. But birth is holy. *Miscellanies* iii 17 tr Library of Christian Classics ii

Milton agrees with Clement that 'birth is holy' but emphatically denies that Adam and Eve did not make love until the fall (see iv 736–70). Eve does not learn 'the facts of life' from the serpent, only the fictions of death. Yet the ikons that accompany her on her way to meet temptation do momentarily restore her virginity (see 270n, 387n, 393n, 445n). And the first thing she and Adam do after they have eaten the forbidden fruit is have intercourse with each other. Poetically if not doctrinally her fall suggests a kind of sexual initiation. Look at the pictures listed above by Raphael, Michelangelo, Tintoretto and Titian. Notice how much more erotic the scene becomes when the two falls seem to be occurring simultaneously.

The idea that the tempter himself seduced Eve goes back at least as far as the non-canonical *Book of the secrets of Enoch* (see J. M. Evans *PL and the Genesis tradition*, chs. 2–3). By the 14th century it was so well known that Chaucer could write a comic parody of it in the *Merchant's tale*. Milton makes rich metaphorical use of the legend (see 387n, 393n, 426n, 432n, 445n, 456n, 489n, 505n, 532n, 536n, 901n, and commentary pp. 26–7) but stops short of using it literally – though as Empson remarks the snake allusions in 503ff. 'treat the fall as a sexual act after which Eve produced children by Satan, as in the *Talmud*, which makes her a regular 17th-century witch' (*Some versions of pastoral* p. 167).

The fall of Adam

Adam as a man

In Hebrew Adam means man, so his fall can be read either individually (man, each man) or generally (Man, mankind). The basic text in the first case is a verse in the 1st century *Syriac apocalypse of Baruch*: 'Adam is therefore not the cause, save only of his own soul, but each of us has been the Adam of his own soul' (liv 19 tr R. H. Charles). Thus in *Romans* vii 7–12

St Paul sees his moral autobiography as a re-enactment of the original sin in Eden. So, perhaps, does St Augustine in his *Confessions* ii 4. And Wordsworth seems to have the story in mind in the opening stanzas of his *Ode on intimations of immortality*. The fall seems to be inextricably linked to the process of growing up. It is the event which intervenes between the innocent freedom of childhood and the guilty necessities of manhood. Perhaps that is why we feel so ambivalent about it. On the one hand our nostalgia for 'the glory and the dream' defines the fall as loss; on the other our sense of greater awareness, our belief that we have grown *up*, defines the fall as gain. Look at the concluding two stanzas of Wordsworth's *Ode*. Milton, of course, wants us to accept the first definition exclusively. How does he go about persuading us to do so? Is he entirely successful in excluding the second definition altogether? Where does he seem to have the greatest difficulty in keeping it out? For other examples of the personal application of the myth see: Walter de la Mare *The exile* in *Motley and other poems* 1918, Wilfred Gibson *By the weir* in *Collected poems* 1923, Edwin Muir *The fall* in *Collected Poems* 1965. For a cultural application of the myth see: Leslie A. Fiedler *Love and death in the American novel* Cleveland 1962, R. W. B. Lewis *The American Adam* Chicago 1955.

Adam as Man

This brings us to the second less personal way of reading the story. The following extracts from Desmond Morris *The naked ape* 1967 suggest how such a reading might go:

What happened to the early apes? We know that the climate began to work against them and that, by a point somewhere around fifteen million years ago, their forest strongholds had become seriously reduced in size. The ancestral apes were forced to do one of two things: either they had to cling on to what was left of their old forest homes, or, in an almost biblical sense, they had to face expulsion from the garden.

...Faced with a new environment, our ancestors encountered a bleak prospect. They had to become either better killers than the old-time carnivores, or better grazers than the old-time herbivores.

...Instead of lazily reaching out to the end of the branch for a luscious ripe fruit, the vegetable-seeking ground ape would be forced to scratch and scrape painstakingly in the hard earth for his precious food. pp. 18–20

Compare that first with this poem by Robinson Jeffers called *Original sin*:

The man-brained and man-handed ground-ape, physically
The most repulsive of all the hot-blooded animals
Up to that time of the world: they had dug a pitfall
And caught a mammoth, but how could their sticks and stones
Reach the life in that hide? They danced around the pit, shrieking
With ape excitement, flinging sharp flints in vain, and the stench
    of their bodies
Stained the white air of dawn: but presently one of them
Remembered the yellow dancer, wood-eating fire
That guards the cave-mouth: he ran and fetched him, and others
Gathered sticks at the wood's edge; they made a blaze
And pushed it into the pit, and they fed it high around the
    mired sides
Of their huge prey. They watched the long hairy trunk
Waver over the stifle-trumpeting pain
And they were happy...
                          These are the people.
This is the human dawn. As for me, I would rather
Be a worm in a wild apple than a son of man.
But we are what we are, and we might remember
Not to hate any person, for all are vicious;
And not to be astonished at any evil, all are deserved;
And fear not death; it is the only way to be cleansed.

publ Saturday Review of Literature 1948

Second with the following comment by a theologian on the meaning of the biblical story:

He [God] does not wish them to know anything of the arts of civilization, or of the sciences which make society and culture possible; he desires to keep them in happy child-like ignorance, infinitely inferior to himself, but safeguarded from the sorrows which the increase of knowledge brings in its train.

N. P. Williams *The ideas of the fall and of original sin* 1927 p. 43

The myth may thus be read as an account of the emergence of mankind from the jungle (see above p. 161) and of the anxieties which accompanied the transition from nature to culture, or, as Lévi-Strauss has put it, from the raw to the cooked. Are there any traces of this level of meaning in *PL*? See 391n, 393n. Compare the general thrust of the passages quoted above with Satan's speeches to Eve, 568–612, 679–732. For a study of analogous myths see Lévi-Strauss *The raw and the cooked* tr J. & D. Weightman New York 1969. For a detailed application of Lévi-Strauss's method of structuralist analysis to the biblical text see Edmund Leach 'Lévi-Strauss in the garden of Eden' *Transactions of the New York Academy of Sciences* XXIII (1961) 386–96.

Shame

Fallen sex

There is nothing in *Genesis* about Adam and Eve making love immediately after the fall. The precedents for this episode in *PL* are theological rather than literary:

As soon as our first parents had disobeyed God's commandment, they were immediately deprived of divine grace, and were ashamed of their nakedness. They covered themselves with fig leaves, which, perhaps, were the first things noticed by the troubled pair. The parts covered remained unchanged except that, previously they occasioned no shame. They felt for the first time a movement of disobedience in their own flesh, as though the punishment were meant to fit the crime of their own disobedience to God.

The fact is that the soul, which had taken perverse delight in its own liberty and disdained the service of God, was now deprived of its original mastery over the body; because it had deliberately deserted the Lord who was over it, it no longer bent to its will the servant below it, being unable to hold the flesh completely in subjection as would always have been the case, if only the soul had remained subject to God. From this moment, then, the flesh began to lust against the spirit. With this rebellion we are born, just as we are doomed to die and, because of the first sin, to bear, in our members and vitiated nature, either the battle with or defeat by the flesh.
                                                    St Augustine *The city of God* xiii 13

This raises some interesting questions. First, if, as St Augustine insists, we are all doomed 'because of the first sin, to bear, in our members and vitiated nature, either the battle with or defeat by the flesh' how can Milton possibly persuade us, or even himself, that Adam and Eve are doing anything wrong? How can we judge concupiscent love when we have no experience of non-concupiscent love to compare it with? Both St Augustine and Milton were evidently aware of this problem, and both attempted in their different ways to resolve it, the former by some rather coy speculations about unimpassioned intercourse (*City of God* xiv 26), the latter by actually showing us what unfallen sex was like (iv 689–775). It is this scene that Milton wants us to remember here in Book ix. (He jogs our memory by making the setting almost identical.) Once we make the connection the differences become obvious. Whereas their original intercourse was the crown of 'mutual love' (iv 728) now it is the seal of 'mutual guilt' (ix 1043); whereas their subsequent sleep had been 'aery light, from pure digestion bred, And temperate vapours bland' (v 4–5) now it is 'a grosser sleep Bred of unkindly fumes' (ix 1049–50); and whereas they had risen the next morning to work with renewed strength now they wake up with a hang-over compounded by post-coital depression.

Behind both descriptions, however, there lurks a third and decisive example of lovemaking, an episode in the *Iliad* xiv:

> Hera walked quickly up to Gargaros on the top of Mount Ida, and Zeus Cloudgatherer saw her come. When he saw her, what love filled his heart! He felt then as he did when first they mingled in love, that time when they had gone to bed and their parents knew nothing about it.
>
> He rose and stood before her, saying: 'Why, Hera, whither away so fast? What brings you here? I don't see the chariot and horses!'
>
> His artful queen answered: 'I am going to visit the ends of the earth...'
>
> Zeus Cloudgatherer answered: 'My dear, you can go there by and by, but now let us to bed and take our joy! Indeed, no love of goddess or woman has ever come over me like this in a flood and possessed my heart...never was I in love so deeply as I love you now and sweet desire holds me captive!'
>
> His artful queen said: 'You dreadful creature! What a thing to say! You want to make love on the top of a mountain where any one can see! What if one of the gods should see us asleep and go and tell tales to the whole family? I couldn't get up from this bed and go straight home, I should be ashamed...'
>
> Zeus Cloudgatherer answered: 'My dear, you need not be afraid that god or man will see. I will gather about us such a golden cloud that Helios himself could not see through, and his sunlight is the strongest light there is.'
>
> As he spoke, he took his wife in his arms: and under them the earth divine made a bed of fresh new grass to grow, with dewy clover and crocus and hyacinth soft and thick, which raised them high above the ground. There they lay, and a beautiful golden cloud spread over them, from which fell drops of sparkling dew.   tr W. H. D. Rouse 1938

The point of the allusion is that Hera had deliberately set out to distract Zeus's attention while his rival, Poseidon, assisted the Greeks. The lovemaking was a political manoeuvre on the wife's part; the husband was the dupe. Hence the balancing allusion to the biblical story of Samson's betrayal by Dalila, the 'harlot' who sold her body for his secret (see 1059n).

The combined effect of these references, internal (to Book iv) and external (to the *Iliad* and *Judges*), is to make Adam and Eve's erotic siesta seem guilty and to confirm Eve's role as seductress. The question is: are they strong enough to offset our feeling that Eve is in fact the injured party, a shepherdess who is finally corrupted by an authentic town rake (see above p. 166 and commentary p. 26). Don't they militate against Milton's own assertion that Adam was 'not deceived'? And don't they confuse effect with cause by implying that the fall itself consisted in a sexual act?

Allusions

This is the trouble with allusions; they are hard to keep under control. The more precisely we respond to them the less neatly they sometimes seem to fit. To take another example, if Eve is the equivalent of Ceres in IX 395ff. and Satan is the equivalent of Jove then who is Proserpina? When we recall that in IV 269 Eve was the equivalent of Proserpina the problem becomes even more confusing. Once we recognize them, however, many of these difficulties turn out to be extremely revealing. In the case in point, for instance, the fact that Eve is associated with both mother and daughter hints at one of the central ambiguities of her character. She is both 'daughter of God and man' (291) and 'our credulous mother' (644), both the virgin Diana (387) and the fruitful Venus (440n), both seductress and seduced:

> Walking in 'virgin majesty' though 'not ignorant of nuptial rites' she seems at once strong because on Milton's theory freedom does not expose her to sensuality...hence the more dangerously entitled to the forbidden knowledge, and weak because ignorant of it – she does not know what is at stake, and will fall through triviality. It seems to be ignorance that puts her into the ideal state that is fitted to receive all knowledge. Her lack of shame is felt as a pathetic degree of virginity, and yet it places her with the satyrs outside the Christian world. She and her husband seem great people socially – ambassadors of mankind – and yet savages in a low state of development. And though she resolves all these opposites, which proves that she is in a state of perfection, the term suggests that there is still something lacking for a full human life.
>
> William Empson *Some versions of pastoral* p. 178

A. Bartlett Giamatti suggests another sense in which many of Milton's allusions evoke ambivalent responses:

> For a classical allusion in this Christian tale will always do two things; it will invariably indicate the higher Truth and greater splendour of the garden and of Adam and Eve; but it will also, obliquely, by what it recalls and by the very fact it is there, prepare for a context of falsity and disgrace.　　　*The earthly paradise and the renaissance epic* p. 300

Compare the way in which T. S. Eliot uses allusion in *The waste land*, especially in the section called 'The fire sermon' where he too is dealing with the subject of fallen sex. Do the references there (Eliot's own notes locate the major ones) seem to be performing the same kind of function as Milton's? What differences or similarities can you detect between the attitudes the two poets take towards the literature of the past? Or, since it is the reader who is expected to complete the allusion by seeing its point, to their audiences? Why might it be that some of the most allusive poems in our language, *Beowulf*, *The merchant's tale*, *PL*, *The Dunciad*, *The rape of the lock*, *The waste land*, are all in their different ways about the fall? For detailed analyses of Milton's allusions see: D. Bush 'Ironic and ambiguous allusions in *PL*' *Journal of English and Germanic Philosophy* LX 1961, Davis P. Harding *The club of Hercules*, William Empson *Some versions of pastoral* ch. 5. For help in tracking down Milton's classical and biblical allusions see: Charles G. Osgood *The classical mythology of Milton's English poems* New York 1900, J. H. Sims *The bible in Milton's epics* Gainsville 1962.

Topics: Book X

Heaven

Foreknowledge and free will

The classic statement of the problem occurs in Böethius's *Consolation of philosophy*, written in 524 AD while its author was languishing in prison charged with conspiring against the emperor Theodoric:

There seems to be a hopeless conflict between divine foreknowledge of all things and freedom of the human will. For if God sees everything in advance and cannot be deceived in any way, whatever his providence foresees will happen, must happen. Therefore, if God foreknows eternally not only all the acts of men, but also their plans and wishes, there cannot be freedom of will; for nothing whatever can be done or even desired without its being known beforehand by the infallible providence of God. If things could somehow be accomplished in some way other than that which God foresaw, his foreknowledge of the future would no longer be certain. Indeed, it would be merely uncertain opinion, and it would be wrong to think that of God... Therefore, there can be no freedom in human decisions and actions, since the divine mind, foreseeing everything without the possibility of error, determines and forces the outcome of everything that is to happen. Once this is granted, it is clear that the structure of human affairs must collapse. For it is pointless to assign rewards and punishment to the good and wicked since neither are deserved if the actions of men are not free and voluntary. Punishment of the wicked and recognition of the good, which are now considered just, will seem quite unjust since neither the good nor the wicked are governed by their own will but are forced by the inevitability of predetermination. Vice and virtue will be without meaning, and in their place there will be utter confusion about what is deserved. Finally, and this is the most blasphemous thought of all, it follows that the author of all good must be made responsible for all human vice since the entire order of human events depends on providence and nothing on man's intention.

v 3 tr Richard Green 1962

More recently the psychologist C. G. Jung has recorded that in his youth he was led to the same conclusion:

Adam and Eve were the first people; they had no parents, but were created directly by God, who intentionally made them as they were.

They had no choice but to be exactly the way God had created them. Therefore they did not know how they could possibly be different. They were perfect creatures of God, for He creates only perfection, and yet they committed the first sin by doing what God did not want them to do. How was that possible? They could not have done it if God had not placed in them the possibility of doing it. That was clear, too, from the serpent, whom God had created before them, obviously so that it could induce Adam and Eve to sin. God in His omniscience had arranged everything so that the first parents would have to sin. Therefore it was God's intention that they should sin.

Memories, dreams, reflections ed A. Jaffé tr R. & C. Winston 1963 p. 49

The traditional response to this kind of argument has been to insist that although God allowed the fall to happen he did not therefore want it to happen. But as Calvin pointed out in the 16th century the distinction between permission and intention is virtually non-existent in the case of an omniscient and omnipotent being:

All, however, who think piously and reverently concerning the power of God, acknowledge that the evil did not take place except by his permission. For, in the first place, it must be conceded, that God was not in ignorance of the event which was about to occur; and then, that he could have prevented it, had he seen fit to do so. But in speaking of permission, I understand that he had appointed whatever he wished to be done. Here, indeed, a difference arises on the part of many, who suppose Adam to have been so left to his own free will, that God would not have him fall... yet none of these things render it impossible that, for a certain cause, although to us unknown, he might will the fall of man. It offends the ears of some, when it said God *willed* this fall; but what else, I pray, is the *permission* of him, who has the power of preventing, and in whose hand the whole matter is placed, but his will?

Commentary on Genesis iii 1 tr John King 1847

Which is precisely how W. Empson interprets the behaviour of God in *PL*: 'Milton steadily drives home that the inmost counsel of God was the Fortunate Fall of man; however wicked Satan's plan may be, it is God's plan too' (*Milton's God* p. 39). What evidence is there here in Book x to support or refute such a view (see 41n and 72n)? How does God attempt to answer this charge in Book iii? What would be the most effective counter-argument?

Here, by way of comparison, is Böethius's in the *Consolation*:

Since God lives in the eternal present, his knowledge transcends all movement of time and abides in the simplicity of its immediate present. It encompasses the infinite sweep of past and future, and regards all things in its simple comprehension as if they were now taking place. Thus, if you will think about the foreknowledge by which God distinguishes all things, you will rightly consider it to be not a foreknowledge of future events, but knowledge of a never changing present. For this reason, divine knowledge is called providence, rather than prevision, because it resides above all inferior things and looks out on all things from their summit... He sees all things in his eternal present as you see some things in your temporal present. Therefore, this divine foreknowledge does not change the nature and properties of things; it simply sees things present before it as they will later turn out to be in what we regard as the future. His judgement is not confused; with a single intuition of his mind he knows all things that are to come, whether necessarily or not. Just as, when you happen to see simultaneously a man walking on the street and the sun shining in the sky, even though you see both at once, you can distinguish between them and realize that one action is voluntary, the other necessary; so the divine mind, looking down on all things, does not disturb the nature of the things which are present before it but are future with respect to time. Therefore, when God knows that something will happen in the future, and at the same time knows that it will not happen through necessity, this is not opinion but knowledge based on truth.   v 6

The trouble with this solution to the problem is that the abstract idea of an 'eternal present' is simply not translatable into narrative terms. The chronology of *PL* traps God within the temporal process (see 91n); to remain outside time he would have to remain outside the action of the poem with Milton himself. It is the poet, not his God, whose knowledge 'transcends all movement of time' with respect to the actual story. In Northrop Frye's words:

The real basis of the relation of Milton's God to Adam is the relation of the tragic poet to his hero. The tragic poet knows that his hero will be in a tragic situation, but he exerts all his power to avoid the sense of having manipulated that situation for his own purposes. He exhibits his hero to us as God exhibits Adam to the angels.

Anatomy of criticism 1957 repr 1966 p. 211

Is this perhaps why Milton seems to be almost as angry with the fallen pair as God is? As their descendant he must suffer the consequences of their sin; as their creator he must also disclaim any responsibility for it. How does he try 'to avoid the sense of having manipulated [the] situation for his own purposes'? Is he successful? Try analysing the role of the narrator from this point of view.

Judgement

The trial

One of Plato's chief objections to the epics of Homer was that they portrayed the gods as being cruel and vengeful:

But if anyone makes a poem of the sufferings of Niobe. . .or of the history of the children of Pelops, or the Trojan war, or any similar story, either he must not be allowed to say that these were the deeds of God, or if he says that, he must find some such explanation as we are now looking for. He must say that God did what was just and good, and the sufferers were benefited by punishment. We must not allow the poet to say that those who were punished were miserable, and that God made them so. But we must allow them to say that the bad were miserable because they needed punishment, and were benefited by being punished at God's hand. We must contend with all our might against the assertion that God, who is good, is the author of evil to any man.

Republic II 380 tr A. D. Lindsay Everyman ed 1950

A 17th-century Christian audience would have demanded no less of any literary representation of its deity, particularly in a poem about the sufferings not of a mere individual, family, or town, but of all mankind. At this juncture of the story, then, Milton needed to show first that God's conduct was 'just and good', second that Adam and Eve 'were benefited by punishment'; in other words, to 'temper so Justice with mercy, as may illustrate most Them fully satisfied' (77).

Of the two, mercy has little cause for complaint. The mere fact that it is the Son, not the Father as in *Genesis*, who descends to pass sentence on the fallen pair ensures that her presence is felt throughout the scene while Milton's unusually insistent commentary keeps our attention fixed on the beneficial consequences of Christ's every word and deed. The justice of the proceedings, on the other hand, seems to be taken largely for granted – the one exception is the curse on the serpent (see 168n). Can it be? If we don't believe that Adam and Eve were morally responsible for the fall, isn't the beneficence of their condemnation beside the point? If, as Boethius put it, 'the actions of men are not free and voluntary', isn't it absurd to bring any charges against them in the first place? Hasn't Milton in effect anticipated Kafka's vision of the human dilemma in *The trial*? These are disturbing questions, but they are inescapable now that we have reached the moral and philosophical moment of truth in the poem. For the judicial format of the episode casts us in the role of jury. Unless we are content to let the chief prosecutor be the sole judge in the case, we have to deliver a verdict. Who was to blame for the fall? Could it have been avoided? Are there any mitigating circumstances? The answers we give will be the key to our interpretation of *PL* as a whole. A good way of getting at them might be to improvise your own trial for Adam and Eve, complete with prosecuting *and* defending counsel who could cross-examine not only the accused (including the tempter this time) but also any other witnesses they wished to call (e.g. the guardian angels). If Milton really did succeed in justifying the ways of God to men, the outcome should be the same as it is here in Book x.

Sin and Death

Monsters

Monsters are almost as traditional in epic as heroes. But unlike heroes they can be of either sex. The prototype of the female kind is Tiamat, the primordial mother from whose body the god Marduk creates the universe in the Babylonian epic, *Enuma Elish*, written in the 2nd millennium BC:

> Then joined issue Tiamat and Marduk, wisest of gods.
> They swayed in single combat, locked in battle.
> The lord spread out his net to enfold her,
> The evil wind, which followed behind, he let loose in her face.
> When Tiamat opened her mouth to consume him,
> He drove in the evil wind that she close not her lips.
> As the fierce winds charged her belly,
> Her body was distended and her mouth was wide open.
> He released the arrow, it tore her belly,
> It cut through her insides, splitting the heart.
> Having thus subdued her, he extinguished her life.
> He cast down her carcass to stand upon it.
> . . . .
> Then the lord paused to view her dead body,
> That he might divide the monster and do artful works.
> He split her like a shellfish into two parts:
> Half of her he set up and ceiled it as sky,
> Pulled down the bar and posted guards.
> He bade them to allow not her waters to escape.
> Tablet iv 93–140 tr E. A. Speiser in J. B. Pritchard
> *Ancient Near Eastern texts* Princeton 1950

Some of her most famous successors include Scylla (*Odyssey* xii 80–100), Grendel's dam (*Beowulf* 1494–1569) and Error (*Fairy queen* 1 i 14–25).

Milton's Sin incorporates the essential features of all four. Like Tiamat, Grendel's dam and Error she is a mother. Like Scylla, Grendel's dam and Error she lives in a cave. Like Tiamat – whose name links her with the Hebrew *tehom*, the watery chaos from which God creates the universe in *Genesis* i – Scylla and

Grendel's dam she is associated with water. Like Scylla and Error she is half woman, half serpent (see II 648–59). How do these characteristics relate to each other? What have mothers got to do with water, caves, snakes? The following extract from C. G. Jung's *Psychology of the unconscious: a study of the transformations and symbolisms of the libido* may help to provoke some answers:

> In consciousness we are attached by all sacred bonds to the mother; in the dream she pursues us as a terrible animal. The Sphinx, mythologically considered, is actually a fear animal, which reveals distinct traits of a mother derivative. In the Oedipus legend the Sphinx is sent by Hera, who hates Thebes on account of the birth of Bacchus; because Oedipus conquers the Sphinx, which is nothing but fear of the mother, he must marry Jocasta, his mother, for the throne and the hand of the widowed queen of Thebes belongs to him who freed the land from the plague of the Sphinx. The genealogy of the Sphinx is rich in allusions to the problem touched upon here. She is a daughter of Echidna, a mixed being: a beautiful maiden above, a hideous serpent below. This double picture corresponds to the picture of the mother; above, the human, lovely and attractive half; below, the horrible animal half, converted into a fear animal through the incest prohibition.   tr Beatrice Hinkle 1919 ch 4

In moral terms Sin is Eve's daughter. How would you define their relationship from a psychological point of view? Does Jung's theory cast any fresh light on the association of Sin and Death with the Furies of classical legend (see 240n, 620n)? Why do they pursue Orestes? See Aeschylus *The Eumenides* and T. S. Eliot *The family reunion*. What parallels can you detect between the Oedipus myth and Milton's treatment of Satan and his family (see 331n)?

Sin lacks one outstanding characteristic of female monsters: she does not devour her victims. Indeed, Milton seems to have gone out of his way to avoid any reference to her mouth. Error's brood take refuge between her jaws; Sin's in her womb. It is Death who represents the oral threat in *PL*. Like the villains of fairy story – the wolf in 'Red Riding Hood', the giant in 'Jack and the Beanstalk', the witch in 'Hansel and Gretel' – he awakens perhaps the most deep-seated of all our fears, the terror of being eaten. His ancestors in epic are such figures as Polyphemus in the *Odyssey* (IX 187–293), Cacus in the *Aeneid* (VIII 191–201) and Grendel in *Beowulf* (702–45). Although all three have a good deal in common with their female counterparts, they affect us quite differently, as sociological rather than psychological symbols. As Lévi-Strauss would say, these predators are 'anomalous' with respect to the categories man–animal, civilized–savage. Because they are part men they need human society;

because they are part beasts they are excluded from it. They resolve the tension by preying upon the communities they cannot join. What does this suggest about the nature of Death in *PL*? How do you think an anthropologist might interpret his function in the poem? Can you see any connection between his arrival in the garden of Eden and the anxieties embodied in Robinson Jeffers' poem *Original sin* (see above p. 171), Why are male monsters almost invariably childless? Try making up – pictorially or verbally – a monster of your own, projecting on to it all the things you are most frightened of.

Hell

Metamorphosis

When they are willed, metamorphoses are a sign of freedom. They reveal a character's capacity to transcend the limitations of his own nature. In the *Cantos* of Ezra Pound, for instance, they are often revelations of the godhead. When they are not willed, metamorphoses are a sign of subjection. They reveal a character's incapacity to maintain his own nature. In Kafka's short story, *Metamorphosis*, Gregor Samsa undergoes this kind of transformation. So do Lucius, the hero of Apuleius' *The golden ass* (III 24–5), and most of the mortals in Ovid's *Metamorphoses*.

In a universe as highly structured and hierarchical as Milton's, one would expect metamorphosis to be evil *ipso facto*: an anarchic activity which threatens to dissolve the divinely ordered distinctions between things. So it often is, as in the case of Satan's earlier shape-shifting, but it can also be a creative principle. Indeed, the creation itself is a gigantic process of transformation, and throughout the poem God is engaged in turning evil into good. Try looking at *PL* as a whole from this point of view. How do the good metamorphoses differ from the bad ones? Who else undergoes them? For a detailed analysis of the Satanic kind see J. M. Steadman 'Archangel to devil: the background of Satan's metamorphosis' *Modern Language Quarterly* XXI 1960 321–35. Compare Satan's metamorphosis here in *PL* with Urizen's in William Blake *Vala, or the four zoas* and Cadmus' in Ovid *Metamorphoses* IV. For a contemporary treatment of the theme see C. H. Sisson's *Metamorphoses* in a collection of his poetry published under the same title in 1968.

Discord

Signs and aspects

The diagram overleaf represents the universe of *PL* as it would appear if we looked 'down' at it from a point in space directly over the north pole. At the centre is the earth (drawn much larger than scale). Its circumference corresponds with the equator; the two lines crossing it at right angles are the northern halves of the two major circles of longitude, the colures which Satan 'traverses' in IX 66. Around the earth are the spheres of the seven planets and the fixed stars (the crystalline sphere and the *primum mobile* have been omitted since they play no part in the following explanation). It is important to remember that the fixed stars are so called not because they do not move at all – in fact they revolve around the earth once every 24 hours – but because they do not move in relation to each other. The fixed patterns they thus form comprise the twelve signs of the Zodiac, the outer band in the diagram.

The purely hypothetical arrangement of the planets in the diagram illustrates all the different 'aspects' Milton mentions in X 657–61. An aspect is the position of any two stars relative to earth. By measuring the angle formed by two imaginary lines (the dotted ones in the diagram) drawn from each planet to the centre of the earth, we can determine what kind of aspect they are in. When the angle is $0°$ – i.e. when the lines coincide – the aspect is conjunction, or as Milton calls it 'synod' (X 661); when it is $60°$ the aspect is 'sextile'; $90°$ 'square'; $120°$ 'trine'; and $180°$ 'opposition' – i.e. the two planets are exactly opposite each other. In the diagram Saturn and the sun are in synod, Saturn and Jupiter in sextile, Saturn and Mars in square, Saturn and Venus in trine, and Saturn and Mercury in opposition. Most astronomers thought conjunction, square and opposition were harmful aspects because the rays of influence emitted by the planets towards earth (corresponding to the dotted lines in the diagram) collide either at right angles or in a straight line; sextile and trine, on the other hand, are beneficial aspects because the rays of influence meet obliquely and blend together rather than clashing. Milton agrees that conjunction is 'unbenign' (X 661) but seems to imply either that all the other aspects are of 'noxious efficacy' (X 660) or that only opposition is (depending on whether we take the phrase as qualifying the whole preceding line or just the final word in it).

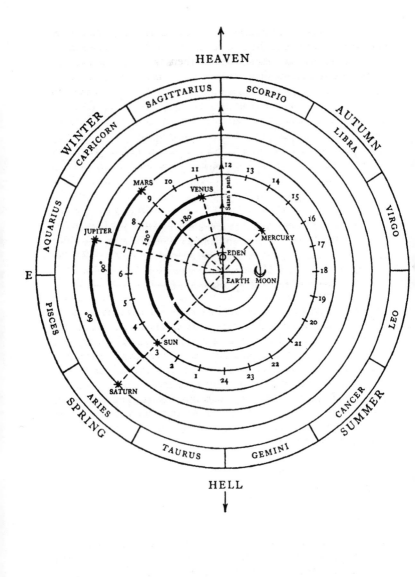

Another way of describing the position of the planets is to determine what sign of the Zodiac they are 'in', i.e. which section of the arc of the fixed stars is behind them when they are viewed from the earth. In the diagram the sun, for instance, is 'in Aries' (x 329) as it is when Satan flies up from paradise to meet Sin and Death. Since Milton tells us that he flew straight up (the unbroken line in the diagram marks his course) 'Betwixt the Centaur and the Scorpion steering His zenith' (x 328), we can tell roughly what time it was: between 2 and 4 a.m. (in the diagram it is exactly 3 a.m. on the 24-hour clock marked on the sun's orbit). By the same token, when he arrived 'at midnight' in ix 58 he must have been in Libra, the sign directly above Eden when the sun, in Aries, is on the opposite side of the earth (see iii 555–60). But Satan enters and leaves the universe through the hole in the *primum mobile* immediately beneath heaven (x 320–4; iii 498–543); this means that in the diagram heaven would be at the top of the page, which means in turn that the universe is lying on its side, as it were. The axis joining the north and south poles, that is to say, is horizontal, not vertical, with respect to heaven and hell. In the diagram we are really looking at the universe sideways.

Finally, the fact that the sun is in Aries tells us that before the fall the garden of Eden enjoyed a climate of eternal spring. Not until the angels tipped the sun's course (or the earth's axis) out of line (x 668–91) did it begin its annual migrations, north from Aries via Taurus and Gemini up to Cancer, down again via Leo and Virgo to Libra, then south via Scorpio and Sagittarius to Capricorn. For a fascinating study of the evolution of the various cosmic systems see S. Toulmin and J. Goodfield *The fabric of the heavens* 1961.

Despair

The hell within

Adam's sense of spiritual isolation and confinement has analogues in religious poetry ranging from medieval to modern, catholic to puritan. Here is a fairly representative selection: St John of the Cross *Verses about the soul which suffers with impatience to see God* tr Roy Campbell Penguin 1951, Fulke Greville *Caelica* xcviii, John Donne *Holy sonnets* ix, Gerard Manley Hopkins *Poems 1876–89* xli, xliv, W. H. Auden *Songs and other musical pieces* xvii

Which of these poems do you think comes closest to Adam's desperate heart-searching? Is there anything unique about his situation compared with the others'? If so, how does it affect the tone and direction of his speech? What assumptions do the various poets seem to make about the nature of God? Are they the same as Adam's?

Unchecked, despair could produce an intense longing for death; which in turn could lead to suicide. Red-cross knight and Christian, the heroes of Spenser's *Fairy queen* (i ix 41–53) and Bunyan's *Pilgrim's progress* respectively, are both tempted by concrete personifications of despair to take this way out of their moral agony. How would externalizing despair as a character affect the scene here in *PL*? Who takes over his arguments for suicide? Why doesn't Adam kill himself? What does the absence of a companion such as Una or Hopeful imply about Milton's view of human sinfulness? Is there any equivalent to them in his version of the episode? For two modern treatments of the theme see: Jean-Paul Sartre *No exit*; Samuel Beckett *Endgame*.

Repentance

The fortunate fall

E. M. W. Tillyard has suggested that the reconciliation rather than the fall of Adam and Eve is the real crisis, the 'nodal episode', of *PL* ('The crisis of *PL*' in *Studies in Milton*). Certainly it is a crucial turning point in the action, the beginning of their re-generation, but there is more to Tillyard's comment than that. The episode feels so important because we can respond to it so fully. And the reason we can respond to it so fully is that the fall has humanized Adam and Eve. It has made them, that is to say, more like us: guilty, lonely, frightened, confused. Less ideal now, they seem more real, which may explain the paradox that in both art and literature they rarely come to life until they have been condemned to death. Compare, for instance, Masaccio's great fresco of the expulsion in Santa Maria del Carmine in Florence with Masolino's temptation scene on the opposite wall, or the portrayal of pre- and post-lapsarian man by any of Milton's illustrators. In R. M. Rilke's twin sonnets (tr. J. B. Leishman *New poems* 1964) about Viollet-le-Duc's figures on Notre Dame we can see the transition actually taking place. As the poet's imagination moves beyond the moment when the apple was first plucked, it is as if the two statues were slowly breaking out of their frozen poses and starting to behave like human beings. In literary and artistic terms, the fall is pure gain.

W. R. Rodgers and Edwin Muir have suggested that this may be true in other terms as well:

> The Fall! the fall, from that safe tree
> Of love we so much feared to leave, elates
> And lifts our other selves to life. Only
> By daring do we learn our manyness.
> Safety stints us, turns us to stone, to one.
> This always-gibbering between fear and hope
> Doubles our life, and is the bloody pulse
> Of every vein. O angel of our dread
> Delicately cater for us rough feeders
> Who ask a stone; and duly give us bread.
> *The fall* in W. R. Rodgers *Europa and the bull and*
> *other poems* 1952

> One foot in Eden still, I stand
> And look across the other land.
> The world's great day is growing late,
> Yet strange these fields that we have planted
> So long with crops of love and hate.
> Time's handiworks by time are haunted,
> And nothing now can separate
> The corn and tares compactly grown.
> The armorial weed in stillness bound
> About the stalk; these are our own.
> Evil and good stand thick around
> In the fields of charity and sin.
> Where we shall lead our harvest in.
> . . . .
> But famished field and blackened tree
> Bear flowers in Eden never known.
> Blossoms of grief and charity
> Bloom in these darkened fields alone.
> What had Eden ever to say
> Of hope and faith and pity and love
> Until was buried all its day
> And memory found its treasure trove?
> Strange blessings never in Paradise
> Fall from these beclouded skies.
> *One foot in Eden* in Edwin Muir *Collected Poems* 1965

These poems raise a question which can take many forms: how could there be hope if there were no despair, courage if there were no danger, forgiveness if there were no guilt, compassion if there were no suffering? Aren't Eve's humility and Adam's resolution in the present scene 'Blossoms of grief and charity' which could never have flowered in the state of innocence? Didn't the fall enlarge rather than diminish our capacity for virtue? Is that why our feelings about the state of innocence itself were so ambiguous (see above pp. 169–71)?

The theological equivalent of this view is the doctrine of the *felix culpa* which received its classic formulation in the *Exultet*, the hymn for Easter Even: 'O certe necessarium Adae peccatum, quod Christi morte deletum est! O felix culpa, quae talem ac tantum meruit habere redemptorem!' 'O truly necessary sin of Adam, which was effaced by the death of Christ! O fortunate fault, which deserved so good and great a Redeemer!' We have already encountered a version of this doctrine in the theory that God wanted man to disobey him: the fall was fortunate because it fulfilled the divine will (see above pp. 176–7). The more orthodox version in the *Exultet* is based on consequence rather than intention: the fall was fortunate because it brought about the life and death of Christ. Hence Adam's reaction in Book XII when Michael has finished telling him the gospel story:

> Full of doubt I stand,
> Whether I should repent me now of sin
> By me done and occasioned, or rejoice
> Much more that much more good thereof shall spring,
> To God more glory, more good-will to men
> From God, and over wrath grace shall abound. 473–8

Adam's doubt reflects ours. Granted that God is able to turn evil into good, does he *need* evil in order to create good? Is that perhaps why Milton rejected the traditional belief in a *creatio ex nihilo* and followed Ovid in making chaos the pre-existent stuff of the universe? Did Adam and Eve have to lose the external paradise in order to gain what Michael calls the 'paradise within thee, happier far' (XII 587)? For the history of the doctrine of the *felix culpa* see A. O. Lovejoy 'Milton and the paradox of the fortunate fall' *Journal of English Literary History* IV (1937) 161–79, supplemented by C. A. Patrides 'Adam's "happy fault" and 17th-century apologetics' *Franciscan Studies* XXIII (1963) 238–43. For a much wider survey of the implications of the theme see Herbert Weisinger *Tragedy and the paradox of the fortunate fall* 1953. See also W. Madsen 'The fortunate fall in *PL*' *Modern Language Notes* LXXIV 1959 and W. H. Marshall '*PL: felix culpa* and the problem of structure' *ibid* LXXVI 1961.

Appendix

Rhetorical schemes

PL: Introduction in this series explains various rhetorical devices used in the poem. The following glossary defines only those used in the notes to IX–X.

Anadiplosis repetition of the last words of one line at the beginning of the next; see notes to IX 491; X 518; 621, 735.

Antimetabole repetition of a phrase back to front; IX 491.

Antithesis balancing of contrasting words or phrases; X 354.

Ellipsis omission of a word or phrase whose meaning is implied by the rest of the sentence; IX 698.

Epanalepsis starting and ending a line, or pair of lines, with the same word; IX 538.

Periphrasis circumlocution, substituting the description of something for its name; X 273, 591, 996.

Ploce repetition of a single word for emphasis; IX 730; X 832.

Prosonomasia like-sounding words close together (closely related to the pun); IX 783.

Traductio repetition of the same word in different grammatical forms; X 141, 968.

DK EYEWITNESS TOP 10 TRAVEL GUIDES

NEW
YORK

ELEANOR BERMAN

DORLING KINDERSLEY
LONDON • NEW YORK • MUNICH
MELBOURNE • DELHI
WWW.DK.COM

Left **Brooklyn Bridge** Right **New York taxis**

A DORLING KINDERSLEY BOOK

www.dk.com

Reproduced by Colourscan, Singapore
Printed and bound in Italy by Graphicom

First published in Great Britain in 2002
by Dorling Kindersley Limited
80 Strand, London WC2R ORL

Reprinted with revisions 2003
**Copyright 2002, 2003 © Dorling
Kindersley Limited, London
A Penguin Company**

All rights reserved. No part of this publication
may be reproduced, stored in a retrieval
system, or transmitted in any form or by any
means, electronic, mechanical,
photocopying, recording or otherwise,
without the prior written permission of the
copyright owner.

A CIP catalogue record is available from
the British Library.
ISBN 0 7513 3571 1

Within each Top 10 list in this book, no
heirarchy of quality or popularity is implied.
All 10 are, in the editor's opinion, of roughly
equal merit.

Throughout this book, floors are referred to
in accordance with American usage, ie the
"first floor" is at ground level.

Contents

New York's Top 10

**The information in this
DK Eyewitness Top 10 Travel Guide is checked regularly.**
Every effort has been made to ensure that this book is as up-to-date as possible. Some
details, however, are liable to change. In particular, changes to New York's transportation
systems following the destruction of the World Trade Center could not be determined by the
time of going to press. The publishers cannot accept responsibility for any consequences
arising from the use of this book, nor for any material on third party websites, and cannot
guarantee that any website address in this book will be a suitable source of travel
information. We value the views and suggestions of our readers very highly. Please write to:
Publishing Manager, DK Eyewitness Travel Guides,
Dorling Kindersley, 80 Strand, London WC2R ORL.

Left **View from the Empire State Building** Right **Pier 17, South Street Seaport**

Contents

Left **Statue of Liberty** Right **Street Entertainers, Washington Square**

NEW YORK'S TOP 10

NEW YORK'S TOP 10

⌐⌐10 New York Highlights

With its skyscrapers, great museums, and bright lights of Broadway, New York is a city of superlatives. There are countless sights that have to be seen, but a handful are truly definitive of the city. The following chapter illustrates the very best of these.

1 Empire State Building

This soaring Art Deco skyscraper is one of the most widely recognized symbols of the city, and star of countless movies. It offers unforgettable panoramas of New York from its 86th floor Observatory *(see pp8–9)*.

2 Fifth Avenue

A heady mix of fashionable shops and world-class architecture makes for an avenue of endless pleasures, and some of New York's best-known addresses *(see pp10–11)*.

3 Rockefeller Center

An urban wonder in the city's center, with gardens, restaurants, an underground shopping concourse, office space, a skating rink, and over 100 works of art, from murals to statues *(see pp12–15)*.

4 Statue of Liberty

The symbol of freedom for millions seeking a new life in America, the lady holding the torch of liberty is ensconced on her own island *(see pp16–17)*.

6 Times Square and the Theater District

An explosion of neon illuminates Broadway and Times Square, where more than 40 famous theaters play host to a changing parade of hit shows *(see pp22–5)*.

5 Ellis Island Immigration History Center

Carefully restored buildings bring to life the experience of the immigrants who have poured into New York over the years, helping to build the multiethnic city of today *(see pp18–21)*.

Central Park
7 The vast swath of green provides an 843-acre respite from the concrete of the city. The man-made park took 16 years and more than 500,000 trees to complete *(see pp26–7)*.

Metropolitan Museum of Art
8 It would take weeks to see all the treasures of this museum. It houses one of the greatest collections of the Western world and spans 5,000 years of culture *(see pp28–31)*.

Guggenheim Museum
9 This Frank Lloyd Wright building is a work of art in itself, and a fitting frame for a major collection of contemporary art *(see pp32–3)*.

American Museum of Natural History
10 Long famous for its dinosaurs, the museum moves into the space age with the dramatic Rose Center for Earth and Space *(see pp34–7)*.

Map labels: Harlem, 125TH STREET, EAST 116TH STREET, Morningside Heights, EAST 116TH STREET, CENTRAL PARK NORTH, EAST 110TH STREET, Harlem River, EAST 96TH STREET, 96TH ST, Upper West Side, Central Park, Upper East Side, Roosevelt Island, COLUMBUS AVENUE, CENTRAL PARK WEST, FIFTH AVENUE, PARK AVENUE, THIRD AVENUE, SECOND AVENUE, FIRST AVENUE, FRANKLIN D ROOSEVELT DRIVE, 77TH ST, EAST 57TH STREET, Midtown, 42ND ST, EAST 42ND STREET, East River, WEST 34TH ST, Herald Square, EAST 34TH STREET, Chelsea, BROADWAY, SIXTH AVENUE / AVENUE OF THE AMERICAS, SEVENTH AVENUE, EIGHTH AVENUE, NINTH AVENUE, Flatiron, Gramercy Park, Union Square, WEST 14TH STREET, EAST 14TH STREET, Greenwich Village, WEST 9TH STREET, East Village, SoHo, EAST HOUSTON STREET, BOWERY, Little Italy, Lower East Side, DELANCEY STREET, TriBeCa, Chinatown, CANAL STREET, Civic Center, PARK ROW, CHURCH STREET, WEST BROADWAY, HUDSON STREET, WEST STREET, JAMES ST, ST JAMES PLACE, PARK ROW, South St Seaport, PEARL STREET, SOUTH STREET VIADUCT, Lower Manhattan, Hudson River, East River, Battery Park

1 —— miles ¬0 ⌐ km —— 1

Numbered map markers: 1, 2, 3, 6, 7, 8, 9, 10

🔟 Empire State Building

The Empire State Building is the tallest and most famous skyscraper in New York. More than 110 million visitors, including the rock group Kiss and Queen Elizabeth II, have gazed down on the city from the Observatory since it opened in 1931. Planned in the prosperous 1920s by the architectural firm of Shreve, Lamb, and Harmon, this Art Deco classic was completed during the Depression and was largely vacant for several years, giving rise to the nickname "Empty State Building." It has been featured in countless movies; when King Kong returned to celebrate the 50th anniversary of the classic film in 1983, fans the world over cheered the triumphant ascent by a huge inflatable ape.

View of the Empire State Building

🍽 There are two restaurants, a sushi bar, and three coffee shops to choose from.

🕐 Visit at the end of the day to watch twilight descend and city lights go on, a memorable sight.

- 350 Fifth Avenue, at 34th Street.
- Map K3
- Open 9:30am–midnight daily.
- Adults $9, seniors $7, children $4

Top 10 Features

1. The Building
2. Elevators
3. 102nd Floor Observation Deck
4. 86th Floor Observatory
5. Spire
6. Wonders of the World
7. Fifth Avenue Gallery Windows
8. Valentine's Day
9. New York Skyride
10. Empire State Run-up

The Building 1

A mooring mast for airships, now the base of a TV tower, was built to ensure the 102-story, 1,454 ft (443 m), building would be taller than the Chrysler Building.

Elevators 2

Visitors can ride to the 86th floor in 45 seconds – 1,400 ft (427 m) per minute – in one of 73 Art Deco elevators. The last elevator leaves at 11.15pm

102nd Floor Observation 3 Deck

Visibility on a clear day from the deck on the 102nd floor is up to 80 miles (130 km), but this has been closed to the public since 1999

For more New York Skyscrapers See pp44–5

Spire 5

The spire is lit to honor holidays, seasons, and the many ethnic groups of New York: red, white, and blue for national holidays; green for St. Patrick's Day; blue and white for Chanukah.

4 86th Floor Observatory

Breathtaking views from the 86th floor's glass-enclosed pavilion and surrounding promenade 1,050 ft (320 m) above the city attract more than 3.5 million visitors each year.

6 Wonders of the World

The 34th Street lobby houses eight 3D panels, created in 1963 by Roy Sparkia and Rene Nemerov, depicting the seven wonders of the ancient world and a wonder of the modern world, the Empire State Building.

Fifth Avenue Gallery Windows 7

Six display windows in the lofty marble-clad Fifth Avenue lobby exhibit art and memorabilia from New York City's many museums, galleries, and artists. The exhibits are changed on a regular basis.

Valentine's Day 8

Several couples are married in the 80th floor Sky Lobby on February 14 and become members of the Empire State Wedding Club, with free entry every Valentine's Day.

9 New York Skyride

A virtual reality, big-screen simulation of a helicopter ride takes viewers over, under, and through some of the city's best-known landmarks.

10 Empire State Run-up

Each February, following a tradition dating to 1978, 150 runners race up the 1,576 steps from the lobby to the 86th floor. The record is 9 minutes, 37 seconds.

Building the Empire State

The Empire State Building was designed by William F. Lamb following a brief to "make it big." It took only 410 days to build this 102-story, 365,000-ton limestone and granite skyscraper, with an average of four and a half stories added every week. However, in one outstanding ten-day period, the 3,500-strong construction team completed no fewer than ten stories. Due to the building's relatively shallow foundations, 60,000 tons of steel beams were used to support the tower.

🔟 Fifth Avenue

Midtown Fifth Avenue is New York's best-known boulevard and home to three of its most famous buildings. In the late 1800s, it was lined with mansions belonging to prominent families, but as retailers moved north in the 1900s, society fled uptown. The one remaining mansion is the Cartier building, reputedly acquired from banker Morton F. Plant in 1917 in exchange for a string of pearls. Although commercial enterprises now share the avenue, it has remained a mecca for luxury goods. Fifth Avenue is at its best on Easter Sunday when traffic is barred and the street is filled with New Yorkers in holiday finery.

Cartier façade, decorated for Christmas

🎧 Free tours of the New York Public Library are every Saturday at 11am and 2pm; there's no need to book.

St. Patrick's Cathedral is open to visitors 7:30am–9:45pm daily.

• *The heart of Fifth Avenue is from the Empire State Building (see pp8–9) on 34th Street, to the Grand Army Plaza, 59th Street, an easily walkable stretch of just over one mile (1.6 km).*
• *Map H3–K3*
• *Tourist Information: 212 484 1222*

Top 10 Exhibits

1. Grand Army Plaza
2. Bergdorf Goodman
3. General Motors Building
4. Tiffany and Company
5. Trump Tower
6. Cartier
7. St. Patrick's Cathedral
8. Saks Fifth Avenue
9. New York Public Library
10. Lord and Taylor

Grand Army Plaza 1

This ornamented plaza is presided over by the 1907 Plaza Hotel and Augustus Saint-Gaudens' statue of General William T. Sherman. Hansom cab rides through Central Park can be boarded here.

Bergdorf Goodman 2

Founded in 1894 as a small ladies' tailoring and fur shop, the most élite department store has been here since 1928. A separate shop for men was opened in 1990 across Fifth Avenue.

General Motors Building 3

Edward Durrell Stone's 1968 marble skyscraper is of interest not for its architecture but for the CBS studio in the plaza area and the F.A.O. Schwarz toy store adjacent.

Tiffany and Company 4

Truman Capote's 1958 *Breakfast at Tiffany's* made this the most famous jewelry store in New York. The window displays are works of art.

5 Trump Tower

Conspicuous consumption at its glitziest can be seen in Trump's complex (*left*) of expensive condominiums and exclusive, over-priced boutiques, complete with waterfalls, plantings, and moving stairways.

Cartier 6

Look up to admire what remains of the fine 1905 Beaux Arts mansion housing this famous luxury jeweler. During the Christmas season, the whole building is wrapped in a giant red ribbon.

7 St. Patrick's Cathedral

In 1878 James Renwick, Jr. designed New York's grandest religious building in French Gothic style (*above*). The bronze doors, the baldachin over the high altar, the Lady Chapel, and the rose window are among its notable features.

8 Saks Fifth Avenue

One of New York's most attractive stores, Saks is famous for the changing seasonal decor on the main floor of its 1924 building, as well as for its exclusive fashions for men and women.

Millionnaires' Row

From its inception in the early 19th century, Fifth Avenue has been the territory of New York's well-heeled society, with homes costing the princely sum of $20,000 after the Civil War. As retail and commercial ventures, albeit exclusive ones, encroached on the wealthy's patch toward the end of the 19th century, they moved their palacial residences further north along Fifth Avenue. This trend was set by Mrs Astor who moved up to 65th Street after her nephew, William Waldorf Astor, built the Waldorf Hotel next to her former home.

New York Public Library 9

The epitome of Beaux Arts elegance, this 1911 landmark (*right*) features vaulted marble halls and a paneled reading room that glows with light from great arched windows.

10 Lord and Taylor

Retailing on Fifth Avenue since 1914, Lord and Taylor has a mix of fashions for budgets low and high. The store is known for its animated Christmas windows.

For more on New York shopping **See pp64–5**

Rockefeller Center

A city within a city and a National Historic Landmark, this is the largest privately owned complex in the world. Begun in the 1930s, it was the first commercial project to integrate gardens, dining, and shopping with office space. Rockefeller Center is the hub of midtown New York, alive with activity day and night. The number of buildings has grown to 19, though the newer buildings do not match the Art Deco elegance of the original 14 structures. Over 100 works of art lie within the complex, including a major mural in each building. Still growing, this is one of the most outstanding public art collections in America.

Starting on Fifth Avenue, walk through the Channel Gardens to the Sunken Garden.

Pick up a self-guided tour leaflet from the lobby of the G.E. Building while looking at the Sert Murals.

• Rockefeller Center extends from Fifth to Sixth avenues between 48th and 51st streets
• Map J3
• NBC Studios: 30 Rockefeller Plaza, (212) 664-3700, tours: open 8:20am–5:30pm Mon–Sat, 9:30am–4:30pm Sun, admission charge
• Today Show: Rockefeller Plaza at 49th Street, open 7–9am Mon–Fri

Top 10 Exhibits

1. Channel Gardens
2. Sunken Garden
3. Prometheus Statue
4. Atlas Statue
5. G.E. Building
6. NBC Studios
7. Today Show Studio
8. Shopping Concourse
9. Radio City Music Hall
10. Paine Webber Art Gallery

1 Channel Gardens
Named after the English Channel because they separate the French and British buildings, the gardens change with the calendar and are lined with glowing angels at Christmas. The six fountainhead figures are by René Chambellan *(below)*.

2 Sunken Garden
A skating rink in winter and leafy outdoor café in summer, the gardens are a bright spot year round. They are ringed by colorful flags representing the members of the United Nations.

3 Prometheus Statue
An 18-ft (5.5-m) bronze and gold leaf statue *(below)* by Paul Manship presides over the Sunken Garden. The pedestal represents Earth and the circle containing the signs of the zodiac represents the heavens.

Atlas Statue 4
Sculpted by Lee Lawrie, this 14,000-lb (6,350-kg), 15-ft (4.5-m) figure is perched on a 9-ft (3-m) pedestal. One of 15 works by Lawrie at the Center, it stands at the entrance to the International Building.

Rockefeller Center Plan

G.E. Building 5
The centerpiece of Rockefeller Center is a slim, 70-story limestone tower. The design features gradual setbacks as the building rises to ensure that no office is more than 27 ft (8 m) from a window.

NBC Studios 6
Backstage tours of a major television network's studios are a popular attraction. Visitors may write ahead for tickets to shows (see p166); tickets may also be available in the lobby of the G.E. building.

Today Show Studio 7
This morning TV show can be viewed live every weekday morning from the sidewalk in front of the studio. A camera often films the fans watching the show.

Shopping Concourse 8
Shops are found in the concourse of the G.E. Building, including a branch of the Metropolitan Museum shop. It also contains an exhibit on the Center's history.

Radio City Music Hall 9
Guided tours of this Art Deco masterpiece and former movie palace are a chance to admire the decor, the stage, and the legendary Wurlitzer organ.

Paine Webber Art Gallery 10
Opened in 1985, this gallery (above) mounts four or five shows a year. Changing exhibits are eclectic, ranging from Mayan art to sports photography .

John D. Rockefeller, Jr.

The legendary philanthropist and multimillionnaire, John D. Rockefeller, Jr. (1874–1960) was son and heir to Ohio oil magnate John Davison Rockefeller's fortunes and took over the family oil business in 1911. Rockefeller, or John D., as he was known, strongly believed his inheritance should be used for the public good. Among his philanthropic donations were contributions to the building funds of the United Nations Headquarters (see pp124–5), the Cloisters (see p31), and the Riverside Church (see p145).

Left **Mural by Thomas Hart Benton** Right **Gaston Lachaise's panel**

Rockefeller Center Artworks

1 America's Progress
Jose Maria Sert's (1876–1945) mural depicts America's development over 300 years by uniting two forces, brain and brawn. Sert's *Time* mural adorns one of the ceilings.

2 Wisdom
The striking central figure of *Wisdom* by Lee Lawrie (1877–1963) grasps a compass pointing to light and sound waves and is carved on a screen made of 240 glass blocks.

3 Gaston Lachaise's panels
This two-panel work by the noted American sculptor (1882–1935) honors the contribution made by workmen to the Rockefeller Center's construction, depicting them at their labors.

4 News
This heroic sculpture by Isamu Noguchi (1904–88) is cast in stainless steel. The 10-ton panel illustrates the tools of the press, including camera, telephone, pad, and pencil.

News, Isamu Noguchi

5 Industries of the British Commonwealth
Cast in bronze and finished in gold leaf, this panel by Carl Paul Jennewein (1890–1980) depicts nine major industries of the British Empire, including sugar cane, salt, and tobacco.

6 Intelligence Awakening Mankind
Some one million tesserae (pieces of glass enamel) in more than 250 shades create Barry Faulkner's (1881–1966) mosaic representing spoken and written words.

7 Portals
Josef Albers' 1961 work of thin, highly polished, milky-white and ivory Carrara glass creates a surface of receding squares that gives the mural a sense of depth.

8 America Today
This nine-panel mural painted in 1931 by Thomas Hart Benton was commissioned for the New School University and was on view there until 1984, when it was purchased by the Equitable Group.

9 Mural with Blue Brushstrokes
A sign of the continuing emphasis on art within Rockefeller Center's newer buildings is this giant, five-story, 70-ft (21-m) mural by the late master of Pop Art, Roy Lichtenstein, c.1984–5.

10 Wall Drawing 896
The newest mural, a site-specific, geometric design created in 1999 by Sol Lewitt, covers four walls of the entryway to the headquarters of Christie's.

Top 10 Statistics

1. Tallest building: 850 ft (259 m), 70 floors
2. Elevators: 388
3. Passenger rides per day: more than 400,000
4. Fastest elevator speed: 1,400 ft (427 m) per minute (37 seconds non-stop to 65th floor)
5. Number working in the complex: 65,000
6. Telephones: 100,000
7. Office windows: 48,758
8. Restaurants: 45
9. Shops: 100
10. Daily visitors: 250,000

The Building of Rockefeller Center

John D. Rockefeller driving in final rivet

When the Depression made John D. Rockefeller Jr.'s original plan for a new opera house impractical, he instead developed a large, creative-commercial complex. The innovative Art Deco design, lead by Raymond Hood, included a mid-block street (Rockefeller Plaza) and an underground concourse. The 14 buildings constructed in 1931–40 provided 225,000 jobs during the worst of the Depression. Artworks were an essential element; over 30 artists contributed work for foyers, façades, and gardens as part of the "New Frontiers" program.

Early Radio Broadcast

The young network-broadcasting industry, made up of RCA, RKO, and NBC, became the primary tenants of the Rockefeller Center. The entire complex was originally named "the Radio City."

Rockefeller Center construction workers, 1932

⁝⁝⁝10 Statue of Liberty

The figure presiding over New York harbor, officially titled "Liberty Enlightening the World," has been a harbinger of freedom for millions since her inauguration by President Grover Cleveland in 1886. The statue, a gift of friendship from the French to mark the U.S.'s 100th birthday in 1876, was designed by the French sculptor Frédéric-Auguste Bartholdi, who devoted 21 years to the project. Slow fundraising on both sides of the Atlantic delayed the unveiling by 10 years, but no problem was encountered financing the $100 million restoration for the statue's 100th birthday. Her unveiling on July 3, 1986, was the occasion for the largest fireworks display ever seen in the U.S.

Restoration celebrations, July 3, 1986

Ⓒ Crowds can be heavy, so an early departure is advised. A cafeteria is available on site.

For best photos of the statue from the boat, sit on the right going out, the left coming back.

• Take the 1 or 2 train to South Ferry, 4 or 5 train to Bowling Green, or the N or R train to Whitehall Street to get to Battery Park by subway.
• Boats leave from Castle Clinton, Battery Park, every 30–45 minutes between 9:15am–3:30pm daily.

Top 10 Features

1. Castle Clinton National Monument
2. Battery Park
3. Boat Ride
4. Close-up View of the Statue
5. Pedestal
6. Crown
7. Torch and Book
8. Frame
9. Views
10. Historical Exhibits

4 Close-up View of the Statue

A close-up view reveals the awesome size of the Statue of Liberty. Dominating New York harbor, she stands 305 ft (93 m) tall and weighs 225 tons. Her right arm carrying the symbolic torch is 42 ft (13 m) long while her index finger measures 8 ft (2.4 m) and dwarfs most men.

2 Battery Park

With statues and monuments honoring everyone from New York's first Jewish immigrants to the U.S. Coast Guard, the park is also a great spot for sea-gazing.

3 Boat Ride

The views from the National Park Service boats that bring visitors from Manhattan to the Statue of Liberty and on to Ellis Island are dramatic.

5 Pedestal

Richard Morris Hunt, one of America's most prestigious architects, was chosen to design the 89-ft (27-m) pedestal of the Statue of Liberty. The pedestal sits on a concrete foundation within the 11-pointed, star-shaped walls of Fort Wood, a fortress erected for the War of 1812.

1 Castle Clinton National Monument

Built as a fort in 1807, it is now a visitor center for Statue of Liberty and Ellis Island visitors. The building exhibits panoramas of New York history.

Crown 6
Legend says that Bartholdi's mother was the model for Liberty, but the face was actually based on his early drawings for a never-commissioned statue in Egypt. The seven rays of her crown represent the seven seas and seven continents.

7 Torch and Book
The new torch, with its 24-carat gold leaf-coated flame, was added during a 1996 restoration. The original is on display in the main lobby. The book in the statue's right hand is inscribed July 4, 1776, in Latin.

Frame 8
Gustave Eiffel, best known for his Paris tower, created the inner framework. The copper sheeting shell, weighing 31 tons, is hung on iron bars from a massive central iron pylon that anchors the statue to the base.

Views 9
An elevator or a walk of 192 steps takes visitors to the observation decks of the 154-ft (47-m) pedestal for spectacular sky-line views of Manhattan. The hardy can walk 354 steps (22 stories) to the crown for a loftier perspective.

10 Historical Exhibits
The story of how the Statue of Liberty was conceived, built, and restored is told in exhibits inside the base of the statue, which include photos, prints, videos, and oral histories. Full-scale replicas of the face and foot are also displayed here.

Gateway to the New World

The Statue of Liberty has symbolized the beginning of a new way of life for millions of immigrants fleeing poverty and hardship. She is an enduring symbol of the freedom and hope offered by the U.S. and the subject of Emma Lazarus's poem *The New Colossus*: "...*Give me your tired, your poor, Your huddled masses yearning to breathe free... Send these, the homeless, tempest-tossed to me, I lift my lamp beside the golden door*".

🔟 Ellis Island Immigration Museum

Ellis Island is the symbol of America's immigrant heritage. From 1892 to 1954, it was the arrival point for some 17 million people fleeing religious persecution, poverty, or unrest in their homelands. Their descendants, more than 100 million people, comprise almost 40 percent of today's population. First and second class passengers were processed for immigration on board ship, but the poor traveling in steerage class were ferried to the crowded island for medical and legal examinations. It was a frightening prospect after an exhausting journey to a land where few newcomers could speak the language. As many as 5,000 passed through in a day. The museum not only retraces their experience here, but is a picture of the total immigrant experience in America.

The vast interior of the Great Hall

🍽 The island's cafeteria and picnic areas are great for lunch or snacks.

⛴ Catch an early ferry from Battery Park to avoid crowds on the island.

Stop at the museum information desk for tickets to the free 30-minute film "Island of Hope, Island of Tears."

• For a map of Ellis Island see Lower Manhattan to Midtown inset on p6
• 212 883 1986
• www.ellisisland.org
• Ferries from Battery Park: 212 269-5755
• Open 9am–5pm daily
• Free

Top 10 Features

1. Arrival Area
2. Great Hall
3. Medical Examining Rooms
4. Dormitory
5. Railroad Ticket Office
6. Baggage Room
7. The Peopling of America
8. Immigration History Center
9. American Immigration Wall of Honor
10. Immigrants' Living Theater

1 Arrival Area
Crowds of steerage passengers *(below)* entered through the original gateway here after being ferried from arrival vessels. Instructions were given by interpreters in a babel of languages.

2 Great Hall
Huddled on benches, immigrants awaited examinations that would determine whether they would be granted entry. A doctor watched as they ascended the stairs and marked letters in chalk on those who showed signs of conditions needing special inspection.

3 Medical Examining Rooms
Interpreters guided immigrants through their medical examinations. The most dreaded were the "eye men," looking for symptoms of trachoma, a disease that caused blindness. It was the reason for more than half the medical detentions and meant sure deportation.

For more on New York's history See pp48–9

5 Railroad Ticket Office

Those traveling beyond New York were ferried to railroad terminals in New Jersey to continue their journeys. Agents could sell as many as 25 tickets per minute.

4 Dormitory

Immigrants who were detained for further examinations slept here in separate quarters for men and women. Although the process was nerve-wracking, only two percent of those seeking refuge were sent back.

Key to Floor Plan

▥	First Floor
▨	Second Floor
▦	Third Floor

6 Baggage Room

Here newcomers checked the boxes, trunks, and baskets that held the meager belongings they carried, now all their worldly possessions.

7 The Peopling of America

400 years of immigration history are displayed in more than 30 galleries. Exhibits such as *The Peopling of America* have artifacts, heirlooms, posters, maps, and photos donated by immigrants' families.

8 American Family Immigration History Center

Using computer and multimedia technology, visitors can access passenger arrival records of more than 22 million people entering New York between 1892 and 1924.

New Jersey's Ellis Island

A long-fought battle over who should control the land upon which the Immigration Museum stands was settled finally in 1998. Originally a 3-acre site, Ellis Island's landmass was increased in the 1800s with landfill from New Jersey to more than nine times its original size, to over 27 acres. The ruling found the island was largely the territory of the State of New Jersey, whose officials have launched a restoration program that includes saving the derelict hospital buildings.

9 American Immigration Wall of Honor

To honor their forebears, Americans pay to have their names inscribed on this list. Including the families of John F. Kennedy and Barbra Streisand, this is the world's largest wall of names; over 600,000.

10 Immigrants' Living Theater

Embracing Freedom: The Immigrant Journey to America is a live production by actors who recreate the experiences Ellis Island. The museum has two movie theaters, a Library and an Oral History Studio with taped reminiscences.

For more museums **See pp40–41**

Left **Italian immigrants** Center **Arrivals to the island** Right **French West Indian arrivals**

Milestones in Immigration History

1 1624
First Dutch arrived in New Amsterdam, which thrived as a trading center, attracting settlers from many other nations. By 1643, the 500-strong population spoke 18 different languages.

2 1664
The dislike of Dutch governor Peter Stuyvesant and unpopular tax demands by the Dutch West India Company meant little resistance to the ousting of the Dutch by the British, who renamed the city New York.

3 1790
For the first U.S. Census, New York's population of 33,131 was the second largest in the Colonies. The make-up was mostly British and Dutch.

4 Mid-1800s
Ireland's 1845–8 Great Famine and economic hardship in Germany led many to seek new lives in New York, where rapid growth as a seaport and manufacturing center opened many jobs.

Polish woman at Ellis Island c.1910

5 1880–1910
Thousands of Russian and Polish Jews and southern Italians arrived, fleeing persecution or hard economic times.

6 1892
When Castle Island, an immigrant depot set up in 1855, could no longer handle the inflow, Ellis Island took over. "Settlement Houses" were set up in the city to help those living in squalid tenements, and "Americanization" programs encouraged assimilation.

7 1924
Nearly 40 percent of New York's population was foreign-born. U.S. laws set national quotas on immigration; Great Britain's Caribbean colonies benefited from the British quota and arrived in large numbers.

Asian women in a garment factory in Chinatown

8 1965
The Hart-Cellar Act ended discrimination based on national origin; a new wave of immigration began.

9 1980s
One million mainly Asian and Latin American newcomers arrived. The Chinese population topped 300,000, Koreans became visible elements in the city, and Dominican numbers grew.

10 1990–present
Another one million newcomers entered, swelling the foreign-born population to over 40 percent of the total population – the highest since 1910. Immigrants from more than 160 nations now live in New York.

Top 10 Nationalities Entering Ellis Island

1 Italy: 2,502,310
2 Austria and Hungary: 2,275,852
3 Russia: 1,893,542
4 Germany: 633,148
5 England: 551,969
6 Ireland: 520,904
7 Sweden: 348,036
8 Greece: 245,058
9 Norway: 226,278
10 Ottoman Empire: 212,825

(Between 1892–7, 1901–31)

The Restoration of Ellis Island

Laws defining immigration quotas enacted in 1924 drastically curtailed the numbers of foreigners coming into the U.S., and Ellis Island was no longer needed as an immigration depot. It became a detention and deportation center for undesirable aliens, a training center for the U.S. Coast Guard, and a hospital for wounded servicemen during World War II. In 1954 the U.S. government closed the island. It remained abandoned until 1984, when a $162 million renewal project replaced the copper roof domes, cleaned the mosaic tiles, and restored the interior, preserving any surviving original fixtures in the largest historic restoration in U.S. history.

The restoration included the establishment of the Ellis Island Immigration Museum (see pp18–19), telling the immigrant story through displays and more than 2,000 artifacts. The museum also has an oral history archive of taped interviews and an interactive children's gallery, both available to visit by appointment. Reopened to the public in 1990, Ellis Island receives almost 2 million visitors every year.

Restoration

Preservation of Ellis Island began in 1965 with the rebuilding of the seawall, but the biggest task was the restoration of the main building, which had deteriorated severely. The period of 1918–24 was chosen for reconstruction because this coincided with a peak time for immigration.

Glass canopy marking the restored main entrance to Ellis Island

 For more New York museums **See pp40–41**

🔟 Times Square and Theater District

Known as the "Crossroads of the World," Times Square is New York's most famous intersection and the symbol of the lively surrounding theater district that includes Broadway. It was called Longacre Square until 1904, when the New York Times built a 25-story tower on the site. Its occupancy on New Year's Eve was marked with fireworks, a celebration that continues today. Currently, a giant crystal ball descends the building at midnight to herald the new year, cheered by the millions packed into the square. The reputation of Times Square was sullied when the adjacent 42nd Street grew seedy in the 1970s. The 1990s saw the peep shows and X-rated movie houses closed, and with a massive government and private effort, the street and neighborhood have again been transformed.

News Ticker, Times Square

🌀 Go to the TKTS booth in Times Square at Broadway and 47th for half-price tickets to all kinds of Broadway shows.

Discount coupons for shows are often available at the Times Square Visitors' Center, 1560 Broadway between 46th and 47th streets.

Try to see Broadway at night, when the lights are on.

• Times Square is located where Broadway and 7th Avenue intersect at 42nd Street.
• Map J3
• Madame Tussaud's New York: 234 West 42nd Street, Open 10am–8pm daily, admission charge

Top 10 Exhibits

1. Broadway Lights
2. Times Square News Ticker
3. Nasdaq Headquarters
4. MTV Headquarters
5. Brill Building
6. Condé Nast Building
7. New 42nd Street
8. Madame Tussaud's, New York
9. Port Authority Bus Terminal
10. Off-Broadway

1 Broadway Lights
The city's longest street is known best for the section north of 42nd Street dubbed the "Great White Way" for its dazzle of neon.

2 Times Square News Ticker
In 1928, the *New York Times* erected the world's first moving electronic sign to post news, a fixture that remains although the *Times* has moved to 43rd Street.

3 Nasdaq Headquarters
The headquarters of this over-the-counter stock market dominates its corner with a screen that regularly broadcasts financial news.

For more entertainment venues See pp50–51

4 MTV Headquarters

It isn't unusual to find crowds of teenagers beneath the second floor studios of this music TV network hoping to spot an idol on the way in, or a camera crew descending to tape crowds in the street.

5 Brill Building

Everyone from Cole Porter to Phil Spector has produced hits in this legendary music industry building, a long-time home to famous music publishers and arrangers.

6 Condé Nast Building

The 48-story skyscraper opened in 2000 to house this magazine empire is a sign of the resurgence of Times Square.

7 New 42nd Street

With the renovation of the New Amsterdam Theater in the 1990s, 42nd Street took a dramatic upturn. The New 42nd Street Studios and several theaters now line the block.

8 Madame Tussaud's, New York

George Washington, Fergie, and Madonna are among the wax inhabitants of 42nd Street's new tenant. The museum has exterior glass elevators and a huge hand holding the illuminated sign.

9 Port Authority Bus Terminal

One of the busiest mass transit terminals in the world, Port Authority is used by nearly 60 million commuters and bus passengers every year.

10 Off-Broadway

Before the rest of 42nd Street was rejuvenated, this block between 9th and 10th Avenues was resurrected by Off-Broadway companies needing inexpensive homes. New plays are premiered at Playwrights Horizons, one of the better known tenants.

Theater District

It was the move by the Metropolitan Opera House to Broadway in 1883 that first drew lavish theaters and restaurants to this area. In the 1920s, movie palaces added the glamour of neon to Broadway. After World War II, the popularity of movies waned and sleaze replaced glitter. Now a redevelopment program has brought the public and bright lights back to this area.

Left **Lyceum** Center **Ford Theater for the Performing Arts** Right **Hudson Theater**

🔟 Theaters

1 Lyceum
The oldest playhouse boasts a vaulted ceiling, murals, and elaborate plasterwork. Often used as an auxiliary for Lincoln Center *(see p139)*. ⊗ *149–157 West 45th Street • Map J2*

2 New Victory Theater
Built for Oscar Hammerstein in 1900, this had resorted to X-rated films until restored in 1995 to present family entertainment. ⊗ *209 West 42nd Street • Map K2*

3 Ford Theater for the Performing Arts
The rundown Lyric and Apollo were combined to form this showcase for musicals in 1998, marking the arrival of corporate sponsorship for theaters. ⊗ *213 West 42nd Street • Map K2*

4 Schubert Theater
Constructed in 1912–13 as a lavish site for big musicals and headquarters for the Shubert Organization. The intimate Booth, opposite, was built at this time. ⊗ *221–33 West 44th Street • Map J2*

5 New Amsterdam Theater
This Art Nouveau beauty housed the famous Ziegfield Follies. Restored by Disney, it is home to the popular *The Lion King*. ⊗ *214 West 42nd Street • Map K2*

6 Hudson Theater
A restrained façade belies the lavish interior, including an inner lobby with a classical arcade and domes of Tiffany glass. ⊗ *139–141 West 44th Street • Map J2*

7 Belasco Theater
A 1907 monument to impresario David Belasco, who supervised the unusual Georgian Revival design. The rooftop duplex was his personal residence. ⊗ *111–121 West 44th Street • Map J2*

8 Lunt-Fontaine Theater
Originally the Globe (finished in 1910); part of the roof of this venue could be removed to create an open-air auditorium. ⊗ *203–217 West 46th Street • Map J2*

9 Palace Theater
Sarah Bernhardt inaugurated the stage, and playing the Palace became the ultimate assignment. Now restored as a venue for musicals. ⊗ *1564 Broadway • Map J3*

10 Winter Garden Theater
Originally the American Horse Exchange in 1885, this was acquired by the Shuberts in 1910 and remodeled in 1922. Until recently home of the long-running *Cats*. ⊗ *1634 Broadway • Map J3*

For more New York theaters See pp50–51

Top 10 Enduring Broadway Shows

1. *The Producers*
2. *The Lion King*
3. *42nd Street*
4. *Proof*
5. *The Full Monty*
6. *Beauty and the Beast*
7. *Mama Mia!*
8. *Chicago*
9. *The Graduate*
10. *Contact*

A Brief History of New York Theater

Oscar Hammerstein

The first of countless theaters built in New York is thought to have been the New Theater, erected in lower Manhattan in 1732. The city's theatrical center steadily moved uptown to the Bowery, then Astor Place, Union Square, and Herald Square, until it settled for good around Longacre Square (now Times Square), following the opening of Oscar Hammerstein's Olympia Theater on Broadway in 1895. Some 85 theaters were built over the next three decades, many with grand Beaux Arts interiors by architects such as Herbert J. Krapp, and Herts and Tallant, the latter responsible for designing cantilevered balconies that eliminated the need for columns. Impresarios like the Shuberts and the Chanins made theater-going more democratic by blurring the class distinction between orchestra and balconies, using a single entrance for all. As modern theaters replaced them, more than 40 of these beauties have been demolished. Fortunately, the rest have now been designated landmarks.

Kiss Me, Kate
Directed by Michael Blakemore, this revival of the classic Broadway musical enjoyed huge success on Broadway at the Martin Beck Theatre, 302 West 45th Street.

42nd Street

Central Park

New York's "backyard," an 843-acre swathe of green, provides recreation and beauty for over two million visitors each year. Designed by Frederick Law Olmsted and Calvert Vaux in 1858, the park took 16 years to create and involved the planting of over 500,000 trees and shrubs, the hauling in of vast amounts of stone and earth to form hills, lakes, and meadows, and the building of 30 stone-and-iron bridges and arches.

Upper West Side appartments overlooking the lake

🍴 Refreshments and light lunches are available at the Boat House snack bar; The Boat House restaurant serves gourmet meals.

🌿 Make your first stop The Dairy, a Victorian Gothic building housing the Visitor Center. Ask about the free nature workshops and guided walks.

Rent bicycles, rowboats and gondolas from the Boathouse, and skates at the Wollman Rink.

Rent horses at the Claremont Stables, 175 West 89th Street.

• From Central Park South to 110th Street & between Fifth Avenue and Central Park West.
• Map D3–H3
• www.centralparknyc.org
• Open dawn–dusk

Top 10 Features

1. Great Lawn
2. Bethesda Terrace
3. Belvedere Castle
4. Ramble
5. Reservoir
6. Strawberry Fields
7. Conservatory Garden
8. Hans Christian Andersen Statue
9. Wildlife Conservation Center
10. Delacorte Theater

Great Lawn 1
This is a 13-acre oval of green lawn. In summer, free concerts by the Metropolitan Opera and New York Philharmonic draw as many as 100,000 people.

Ramble 4
This wooded 37 acres of land is crisscrossed by paths and streams and is a paradise for bird-watchers. Over 270 species have been spotted in Central Park, which is on the Atlantic migration flyway.

Bethesda Terrace 2
Overlooking the lake and Ramble, the ornate terrace and its fountain are the focal point of the park. On the adjacent tree-lined mall inline skaters often show off acrobatic stunts.

Belvedere Castle 3
A 19th-century stone castle atop a rock, complete with towers and turrets, offers peerless views in all directions. Inside is the Henry Luce Nature Observatory with exhibits covering the surprisingly diverse wildlife found in the park.

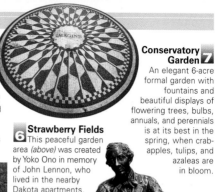

5 Reservoir

The 106-acre lake is rimmed by a 1.6-mile (5-km) running track used by joggers. It is the largest of the park's five lakes and ponds, which include Conservatory Water, where model boat races are held each Saturday.

6 Strawberry Fields

This peaceful garden area *(above)* was created by Yoko Ono in memory of John Lennon, who lived in the nearby Dakota apartments. Gifts for the memorial came from all over the world.

7 Conservatory Garden

An elegant 6-acre formal garden with fountains and beautiful displays of flowering trees, bulbs, annuals, and perennials is at its best in the spring, when crabapples, tulips, and azaleas are in bloom.

8 Hans Christian Andersen Statue

Children's storytelling sessions are held here in the summer. Other activities for youngsters include nature workshops, a vintage carousel, and a marionette theater.

9 Wildlife Conservation Center

This imaginative zoo has three climate zones. The space features an indoor rainforest and over 100 species, including seals, monkeys, and penguins.

Creating Central Park

Central Park was the first landscaping project for Frederick Law Olmsted, who was already 43 years old. Rejecting the usual formal plantings, he created passages of contrasting scenery, calm and pastoral against the rugged and picturesque. Areas for active and passive recreation were separated, and dense raised plantings shut out the surrounding city. The park brought Olmsted high praise and set a pattern for landscapes that followed. He went on to become America's most prolific designer of parks.

10 Delacorte Theater

The New York Public Theater presents two "Shakespeare in the Park" productions each July and August, with free tickets available at 1pm on the performance day. Other free park entertainment includes a SummerStage series of popular music and dance.

🔟 Metropolitan Museum of Art

One of the world's great art museums, the Metropolitan is a veritable collection of museums, spanning 5,000 years of culture from every part of the globe. Each of its specialized galleries holds an abundance of treasures. It was founded in 1870 by a group who wanted to create a great art institution in America, and began with three private European collections and 174 paintings. The present holdings number over two million. The original 1880 Gothic Revival building by Calvert Vaux and Jacob Wrey has been expanded many times. Recent additions include inviting courts with huge windows overlooking Central Park.

Entrance, Metropolitan Museum of Art

🍷 A bar and café, restaurant, cafeteria, and the elevator to the Roof Garden Café are on the second floor.

✪ If time is short, the European Paintings on the third floor, Egyptian Art on the second, and the American Wing will give you a sense of the greatness of this enomous institution.

Weekend evenings are less crowded and offer the advantage of bar service and live music.

• 1000 5th Avenue at 82nd St
• Map F3
• 212 535 7710
• Open 9:30am–5:30pm Tue–Thu & Sun, 9:30am–9pm Fri & Sat
• Adults $10, students and seniors $5, children under 12 and members free

Top 10 Exhibits

1. European Painting
2. Egyptian Art
3. Michael C. Rockefeller Wing
4. American Wing
5. Robert Lehman Collection
6. Costume Institute
7. Asian Art
8. Lila Wallace Wing
9. European Sculpture and Decorative Arts
10. Roof Garden

2 Egyptian Art

The largest collection of Egyptian art outside Cairo includes masks, mummies, statues, jewelry, the Tomb of Perneb, and the spectacular Temple of Dendur, c.15B.C., re-assembled as it appeared on the banks of the Nile.

Key to Floor Plan

▦ First Floor
▦ Second Floor
▦ Third Floor

1 European Painting

The museum's 2,500 Old Master and 19th-century European paintings form one of the greatest collections in the world and include many instantly recognizable masterpieces. Special strengths include the Rembrandts and Vermeers, and the many Impressionist and Post-Impressionist canvases.

3 Michael C. Rockefeller Wing

Masks, wooden sculpture, gold and silver ornaments, Pre-Columbian gold, ceramics and stone from Mexico and Peru, and works of art from the Court of Benin in Nigeria are highlights among 1,600 objects of primitive art covering 3,000 years, and three continents.

For more New York museums See pp40–41

Robert Lehman Collection
5 This extraordinary private collection, includes Renaissance masters, Dutch, Spanish and French artists, Post-Impressionists and Fauvists, plus ceramics and furniture.

American Wing
4 Several floors display Tiffany glass, paintings, and period rooms spanning the 17th to 20th centuries, including one by Frank Lloyd Wright.

Costume Institute
6 Women's fashions from ballgowns to miniskirts, and menswear from the French courts to the present day; annual shows draw the crowds.

Asian Art
7 The most comprehensive collection in the West features paintings, sculpture, ceramics, and textiles.

Lila Wallace Wing
8 The Metropolitan has a growing display of art from 1900 to the present day, with works from Picasso to Jackson Pollock.

European Sculpture and Decorative Arts
9 One of the museum's largest collections reflects the development of art in Western Europe, and includes architectural settings, French and English period rooms, tapestries, and sculptures by Rodin and Degas.

Roof Garden
10 From May to October the Iris and B. Cantor Roof Garden boasts outstanding annual displays of 20th-century sculpture. The garden also offers a fine opportunity to enjoy a drink with a peerless view of Central Park and the surrounding skyline.

Gallery Guide
The Costume Institute and part of the Robert Lehman Collection are on the 1st floor. The 2nd floor includes the American Wing (also on the 3rd), European Sculpture and Decorative Arts, and Egyptian Art; the 3rd floor contains European Paintings, and 19th-Century European Paintings and Sculpture.

Left *The Card Players*, 1890 Center *Garden at Sainte-Adresse*, 1867 Right *Gertrude Stein*, 1905

Paintings in the Met

1 Self-portrait
Rembrandt (1606–1669) painted a self portrait each decade of his career. In this moving study from 1660, when he was 54, he portrayed age very honestly.

2 View of Toledo
Darkening clouds set an eerie mood for one of El Greco's (1541–1614) most memorable paintings, depicting the capital city of the Spanish empire until 1561.

3 Young Woman with a Water Pitcher
Painted in 1660–67, this is a classic example of the subtle and sensitive use of light that has made Vermeer (1632–75) one of the most revered Dutch masters.

4 The Harvesters
One of five remaining panels of the months of the year, painted in the 1500s, this is Bruegel (1551–1569) at his realistic best, an example of the use of light and detail that set him apart.

5 Madame X
Part of the excellent American art collection, this canvas by John Singer Sargent (1856–1926) is of an American woman who married a French banker, becoming a notorious Paris beauty in the 1880s.

6 Garden at Sainte-Adresse
This resort town on the English Channel where Monet spent the summer of 1867 is portrayed with sparkling color and intricate brushwork. The work combines illusion and reality, showing why Monet (1840–1926) was considered one of the greatest Impressionists.

7 Gertrude Stein
This portrait, created when Picasso (1881–1973) was 24 years old shows the influence of African sculpture and a shift from the slender figures of his early years to Cubist forms.

8 The Card Players
Better known for landscapes and still lifes, Cézanne (1839–1906) was intrigued by a scene of peasants intent on their card game. This ambitious project emphasizes the somber concentration of the participants.

Cypresses, 1889

9 Cypresses
Painted in 1889, soon after Van Gogh's (1853–90) voluntary confinement at an asylum in Saint-Remy, it shows the swirling and heavy brushwork typical of his work from this period.

10 Autumn Rhythm
This work by Jackson Pollock (1912–1956), the Abstract Expressionist famous for his drip paintings, is part of the Met's modern collection.

For more New York art galleries See pp42–3

Top 10 Cloister Sights

1. Gothic Chapel
2. Boppard Room, lives of the saints in stained glass
3. Merode Triptych, Annunciation altarpiece
4. *Nine Heroes* tapestries
5. *Hunt of the Unicorn* tapestries
6. The Treasury
7. The Elizabeth Shrine
8. Virgin statue from Strasbourg Cathedral
9. Altar Angel
10. Medieval Gardens

The Cloisters

Stained-glass window detail

In addition to the medieval treasures in the main building, the Metropolitan oversees a spectacular branch, The Cloisters, built in medieval architectural style and set on four acres of land overlooking the Hudson River in Fort Tryon Park in northern Manhattan. Opened in 1938, the complex consists of elements from five medieval cloisters and other monastic sites in southern France. The collections are noted for Romanesque and Gothic architectural sculptures and include illuminated manuscripts, tapestries, stained glass, enamels, ivories, and paintings. The Cloister gardens are a serene escape from the city. John D. Rockefeller, Jr. (see p13), who gave items from his own collection, is largely responsible for funding the grounds, building, and collections.

The Unicorn in Captivity, 1495

Cloisters Arcades
These arcades are from the Bonnefont-en Comminges Cloister in southern France. They date back to the late 13th and early 14th century.

Annunciation altarpiece by Robert Campin, 1425

🔟 Solomon R. Guggenheim Museum

One of the great architectural achievements of the 20th century, Frank Lloyd Wright's 1959 spiral interior alone would make this museum a must. Solomon Guggenheim's core collection of Abstract art has been widened by donations of several important collections. The museum now owns a host of work by Kandinsky and major holdings of Brancusi, Calder, Klee, Chagall, Miró, Leger, Mondrian, Picasso, Oldenberg, and Rauschenberg. Only a small portion, changed periodically, is displayed as the main gallery is generally used for temporary exhibits. Two important acquisitions, the Thannhauser collection, which includes masterpieces by Cézanne, Gauguin, van Gogh, and Picasso, and the Mapplethorpe photography collection, hang in separate gallery space.

Façade of the Guggenheim Museum

🔵 The café on the main floor is a good spot to rest your feet.

🟢 The best way to see the museum is to take the elevator to the skylighted top and wind your way back down.

Free jazz concerts take place on Saturday evenings.

There is a regular weekly program of talks and tours. Check the main desk for current schedules.

• 1071 5th Avenue at 89th St • Map E4
• 212 423 3500
• www.guggenheim.org
• Open 9am–6pm Sun–Wed, 9am–8pm Fri & Sat
• Adults $12, students and seniors (with valid ID) $8, children under 12 and members free, 6–8pm Fri, donation only.

Top 10 Exhibits

1. *Woman Ironing* (Thannhauser Collection)
2. *Woman with Yellow Hair* (Thannhauser Collection)
3. *Mountains at Saint-Remy* (Thannhauser Collection)
4. *Before the Mirror* (Thannhauser Collection)
5. *Haere Mai* (Thannhauser Collection)
6. *Still Life: Flask, Glass, and Jug* (Thannhauser Collection)
7. *Bibémus* (Thannhauser Collection)
8. *The Hermitage at Pontoise* (Thannhauser Collection)
9. *Black Lines*
10. *Paris Through the Window*

1 Woman Ironing

Picasso's early paintings showed sympathy for the working class. This striking 1904 canvas uses angular contours and a bleak palette of whites and grays to make the subject a symbol of the misfortunes of the poor.

2 Woman with Yellow Hair

In this memorable portrait from 1931, Picasso portrays the supple body and golden tresses of his mistress, Marie-Thérèse, one of his favorite subjects. He employed the continuous arched line from forehead to nose that he would often repeat in the many painting of his young muse.

4 Before the Mirror
Edouard Manet scandalized Paris with his paintings of prostitutes and courtesans. This private scene is of a partially undressed woman, an actress perhaps, contemplating her image.

3 Mountains at Saint-Remy
Van Gogh was recovering from an attack of mental distress when he painted this scene in July 1889, one year before his suicide. The subject was the low range of the Alpilles mountains in southern France, visible from his hospital grounds. The bold brush strokes are characteristic of van Gogh's later work.

6 Still Life: Flask, Glass, and Jug
Paul Cézanne's later style, based on the interplay of surface and depth, is shown in this 1877 painting. His mastery of space and depth, as seen in the mottled apples in the foreground, make him the foremost precursor of Cubism.

5 Haere Mai
Gauguin made his first trip to Tahiti in 1891 in search of a paradise untainted by Western culture. This idyllic village landscape *(below)* was painted during that trip; the rich hues and flattened forms show the simplicity he sought. The phrase "Haere Mai," ("Come Here") is painted into the left corner.

7 Bibémus
In Bibémus, the abandoned quarries outside Aix-en-Province, France, Cézanne found a man-made landscape that suited his increasingly geometric style. He painted many variations of this scene from 1895–9.

Frank Lloyd Wright

Though Wright (1867–1959) designed many public buildings, he was best known for residential designs, "organic architecture" that followed the natural contours of the land, and tradition-breaking open interior spaces that have had lasting worldwide influence. The Guggenheim, one of his last projects, was a complete departure. So intent was Wright on his spiral design that when told some walls were too short for large works, he reportedly responded, "cut the paintings in half."

8 The Hermitage at Pontoise
This unsentimental rendering *(above)* of the village where Pisarro lived on and off from 1866–83 emphasizes the use of light and shade. The depiction of villagers was thought vulgar by some painters of the day.

9 Black Lines
Kandinsky wanted the undulating, richly-colored ovals and animated black brushstrokes to elicit specific reactions from viewers. *Black Lines* (1913) is one of his best-known nonobjective works.

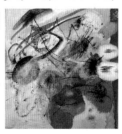

10 Paris Through the Window
Painted after Chagall moved to Paris from Russia in 1910, the scene reflects the latest avant garde styles. The Eiffel Tower seen in the distance is a metaphor for Paris and for modernity.

For more on New York's art scene **See pp42–3**

🔟 American Museum of Natural History

Few city children grow up without visiting the dinosaurs, the life-size dioramas of animal life, and other natural wonders in this popular museum patronized by over 4.5 million people each year. Since its founding in 1869, the museum has grown to 46 permanent exhibition halls spanning three city blocks, 10 of them opened in the past 10 years. Holdings include 32 million specimens and cultural artifacts, many unique in the world. Newer exhibition areas such as the Hall of Biodiversity, the renovated Fossil Halls, and the Rose Center (see pp36–7), bring constantly updated research to visitors through multimedia installations.

77th Street museum entrance

📍 If you don't mind the crowds, eat at the lower-level food court; otherwise head for a café on Columbus Ave.

🕐 Don't miss the great dinosaurs and African mammals, or the fabulous collection of minerals and gems.

Join a free tour of the museum's highlights or sit back and enjoy free Jazz concerts on Friday nights.

• *Central Park West between 77th and 81sts*
• *Map F2*
• *212 769 5100*
• *www.amnh.org.*
• *Open 10am–5:45pm Sun–Thu, 10am–8:45pm Fri & Sat*
• *Adults $10, students and seniors $7.50, children $6, members free*
• *For advance tickets for The Space Show call 212 769 5200.*

Top 10 Exhibits

1. Dinosaurs and Fossils
2. Mammals
3. Ocean Life
4. Hall of Biodiversity
5. Hall of Asian Peoples
6. Hall of African Peoples
7. Hall of Minerals and Gems
8. Northwest Coast Indians
9. Human Biology and Evolution
10. Birds of the World

1 Dinosaurs and Fossils
The best-known hallmark of the museum, the collection of dinosaur fossils is the world's largest. The giant Barosaurus in the rotunda is the highest free-standing exhibit.

2 Mammals
Dramatic dioramas of life-size animals are divided by continents and shown in accurate natural habitats. The wildlife ranges from U.S. bighorn sheep or colossal African elephants to endangered Asian species such as lions and leopards.

Key to Floor Plan

▥	First Floor
▦	Second Floor
▧	Third Floor
▨	Fourth Floor
	Rose Center

3 Ocean Life
This hall explores the waters of the earth and their inhabitants in skillful dioramas of ocean life that include live fish. The hall is presided over by a 94-ft (29-m) life-size model of a blue whale.

➯ *For more New York museums* **See pp40–41**

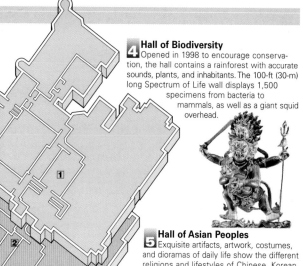

4 Hall of Biodiversity
Opened in 1998 to encourage conservation, the hall contains a rainforest with accurate sounds, plants, and inhabitants. The 100-ft (30-m) long Spectrum of Life wall displays 1,500 specimens from bacteria to mammals, as well as a giant squid overhead.

5 Hall of Asian Peoples
Exquisite artifacts, artwork, costumes, and dioramas of daily life show the different religions and lifestyles of Chinese, Korean, Indian, and other Asian cultures.

Third Floor includes the Hayden Planetarium (see pp37).

6 Hall of African Peoples
These depictions of tribes living in various environments reflect 100 years of research. The displays include dwellings, clothing, masks, textiles, weapons, and tools.

7 Hall of Minerals and Gems
A hall of wonders including the 563-carat star of India, the world's largest blue star sapphire, a 596-lb (270-kg) topaz crystal from Brazil, and the Cape York meteorite, 4.5 billion years old and weighing 34 tons.

8 Northwest Coast Indians
This area features Native American totem poles showing the woodworking skills of tribes living from Washington state to southern Alaska. Also on show is a 63-ft (19-m) Haida canoe built in 1878.

9 Human Biology and Evolution
This display of human origins and physical characteristics includes reconstructed heads of early hominids that bring you face to face with your predecessors.

10 Birds of the World
The museum has the world's largest collection of birds, more than a million specimens. One hall is devoted to the biology of birds and three others have striking dioramas showing oceanic, North American, and other birds of the world.

Museum Guide

Enter from Central Park West onto the 2nd floor to view the Barosaurus exhibit, and African, Asian, and Central and South American peoples and animals. The Hall of Biodiversity, ocean life, and minerals and gems are on the 1st floor. North American Indians, birds, and reptiles are on the 3rd floor, and dinosaurs and fossils on the 4th.

Left **Cosmic Pathway** Center **Scales of the Universe** Right **Cosmic Pathway**

Rose Center for Earth and Space

1 The Building
Opened in 2000 to explore inner earth and the outer universe, the dramatic exhibit building is a huge glass cube enclosing a three-story, 87-ft-wide round sphere containing the new Hayden Planetarium.

2 Hall of the Universe
Exhibits, divided into the universe, galaxies, stars, and planets, show the discoveries of modern astrophysics. Digital scales compare your weight on Saturn, Jupiter, and the Sun.

3 Ecosphere
A sealed spherical aquarium in the Hall of the Universe holds a complete ecosystem of plants and animals that can recycle nutrients and obtain energy solely from sunlight.

4 AstroBulletin
This large, high-definition video screen displays the latest imagery from telescope observations worldwide and from current NASA missions.

5 Hall of Planet Earth
Geological samples from around the world and videos explain the processes that formed the earth and continue to shape it.

Hayden Planetarium

6 Dynamic Earth Globe
This globe, suspended above an amphi-theater in the Planet Earth Hall, uses a projection system to recreate views of a rotating earth as seen from space.

7 Earth Event Wall
Reports on events such as earthquakes or volcanoes are broadcast on a screen as they unfold. Other video stations show how scientists develop simulations.

8 Scales of the Universe Walkway
Models show the relative size of cosmic and human objects, from galaxies, stars, and planets, to the human brain and the smallest atom.

9 Big Bang
Glass flooring around a circular opening lets visitors look down into a multisensory inter-pretation of the first movements of the universe. Explanatory narration is by Jodie Foster.

10 Cosmic Pathway
The Big Bang exits to this sloping 360-ft pathway with astronomical images tracing landmarks through 13 billion years of cosmic evolution.

For more New York museums See pp40–41

Top 10 Features

1 3D Milky Way model
2 High speed simulators
3 In-depth study of galaxy
4 Advanced star projector
5 Up-to-date planet data supported by NASA
6 Onyx 2 Infinite Reality supercomputer
7 3D map of galaxy
8 Continuous calculation of star locations
9 "Flyby" of Orion Nebula
10 Simulations of current events

The Hayden Planetarium

The new Hayden Planetarium, a remarkable advance in the study of astronomy and astrophysics, boasts a highly sophisticated Digital Dome System that is the most advanced high-resolution virtual reality simulator ever built. The show, which takes place in a 429-seat Space Theater, is not simply a look at the sky, but a virtual flight through a scientifically accurate universe. The show's presentation is called "The Search for New Life: Are We Alone" and is narrated by actor Harrison Ford. This is a trip through space and time from the ocean's depths to the outer reaches of the cosmos, exploring the links between life on Earth and the potential for life on other planets.

Virtual Nebula
The planetarium presents a virtual representation of every star and nebula in a 3D map of the galaxy. The state-of-the-art, multisensory technology creates such a realistic environment that all sense of being in a theater is lost.

The Hayden Planetarium within the Rose Center for Earth and Space

 Following pages **Times Square by night**

37

Left **Solomon R. Guggenheim Museum** Right **Brooklyn Museum of Art**

🔟 Museums

1 Metropolitan Museum of Art

It would take days to take in all the treasures of this mammoth, ever-changing museum that includes a collection of more than 3,000 European paintings. The Greek, Roman, Cypriot, and Asian halls have had striking new renovations, and the Howard Gilman Photography Gallery is a growing presence *(see pp28–31)*.

2 Museum of Modern Art

MoMA is closed until 2005 for expansion but selections from their great collection, including Picassos, Van Goghs, and Warhols can be seen at a temporary location in Queens. Free shuttles run from 11 West 53rd Street Saturday and Sunday, 11.30am–5.30pm or take the #7 Queens local subway to 33rd Street. 🚇 *MoMA Queens 33rd Street at Queens Blbd • Map 4K*
• Open 10am– 5pm Thu–Mon, 10am–7:45pm Fri • Admission charge

3 American Museum of Natural History

The largest museum of its kind in the world exhibits everything from dinosaurs to Chinese costumes and rare gems. In addition to the planetarium show in the Rose Center, there are nature films in a giant I-MAX theater *(see pp34–7)*.

4 Solomon R. Guggenheim Museum

The Guggenheim has expanded its collection with several major donations, including Justin Thannhauser's Impressionist masters, Peggy Guggenheim's Cubist, Surrealist, and Abstract Expressionist works, a collection of American Minimalist and Conceptual art, and 200 photos from the Robert Mapplethorpe Foundation *(see pp32–3)*.

5 Whitney Museum of American Art

The entire range of 20th-century American art can be seen in the permanent collection housed in this striking Marcel Breuer building, along with changing exhibitions of contemporary art. 🚇 *945 Madison Avenue at 75th St • Map G4*
• Open 11am–6pm Tue–Thu, 1–9pm Fri, 11am–6pm Sat & Sun • Admission charge

6 Frick Collection

The mansion of industrialist Henry Clay Frick, with indoor garden court and reflecting pool, is the setting for his exceptional collection of Old Masters, French furniture, and Limoge enamels. Look for Rembrandt, Vermeer, and

Hals in the West Gallery; Holbein, Titian, and Bellini in the Living Hall.
◈ *1 East 70th Street at 5th Av • Map G4*
• Open 10am–6pm Tue–Sat, 1–6pm Sun
• Admission charge

7 Brooklyn Museum of Art
A world-class museum in a fine Beaux Arts building exhibiting cutting-edge contemporary work, permanent collections of Asian, Egyptian, African, and American art, Rodin sculptures, and decorative arts that include period rooms.
◈ *200 Eastern Pkwy, Brooklyn • Subway Eastern Pkwy • Open 10am–5pm Wed–Fri, 11am–6pm Sat & Sun • Admission charge*

8 Morgan Library
This *palazzo* was designed in 1902 to hold the collection of billionaire J. Pierpont Morgan, an extraordinary assemblage of rare manuscripts, books, and prints, and galleries with changing exhibits. His original opulent study and library are highlights. ◈ *29 East 36th Street, between Madison & Park avs • Map K4 • Open 10:30am–5pm Tue–Thu, 10:30am–8pm Fri, 10:30am–6pm Sat, noon–6pm Sun • Admission charge*

9 Museum of the City of New York
New York's history is illustrated with photos, paintings, costumes, toys, silver, period rooms, a collection on American theater, and the most complete collection of Currier and Ives lithographs.
◈ *1220 5th Avenue at 103rd St • Map D3*
• Open 10am–5pm Wed–Sat, noon–5pm Sun • Admission charge

Museum of the City of New York

10 American Folk Art Museum
The first New York museum built from the ground up in 30 years, the eight-level, innovative, skylit structure shows off a great collection of this whimsical, all-American art form. Paintings, sculptures, quilts, weathervanes, samplers and furniture are among the items on show.
◈ *45 West 53rd Street between 5th and 6th avs • Map J3 • 10am–6pm Tue–Thu, Sat, Sun, 10am–8pm Fri • Admission charge*

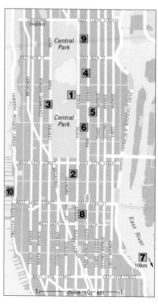

41

Left **Mary Boone Gallery** Right **Paula Cooper Gallery**

TOP 10 Art Galleries

1 Gagosian

Expect big names and equivalent price tags at this blue-ribbon gallery with two locations, two floors uptown and a Chelsea address with the lofty spaces necessary for exhibiting large-scale art. Damien Hirst, Anselm Kiefer, Richard Serra, and Cy Twombly are among the contemporary artists represented. ⊗ *980 Madison Avenue (Chelsea: 555 West 24th Street) • Map E4 • Open 10am–6pm Tue–Sat*

2 Marlborough

This top-of-the-art-world gallery, representing artists including Larry River, Red Grooms, R.B. Kitaj, and Marisol, has opted for two locations. The Midtown gallery has shown work by sculptors such as Anthony Caro and Jacques Lipschitz. New sculpture and paintings are found at the Chelsea location. ⊗ *40 West 57th Street, Floor 2 (Chelsea: 211 West 19th Street) • Map H3 • Open 10am–5:30pm Mon–Sat*

3 Mary Boone

One of the art world's big names has deserted SoHo for a sleek Chelsea gallery where work on show still has a downtown edge and talented newcomers share space with established artists. Occasional intriguing group shows, assembled by independent curators, include sculpture, photography, and painting. ⊗ *4th floor, 541 West 24th St between 10th & 11th sts • Map L2 • Open 10am–6pm Tue–Fri, 10am–5pm Fri, 10am–5pm Sat (by appointment only on Sat in summer)*

POP ART

THE JOHN AND KIMIKO POWERS COLLECTION
APRIL 28 – JUNE 30, 2001

GAGOSIAN GALLERY

Contemporary works at the Pace Wildenstein Gallery

4 Pace Wildenstein

Expect the likes of Picasso, Rothko, Chuck Close, or Julian Schnable at this ultra-prestigious gallery showing modern masters of the 20th century and living artists. At 57th Street the galleries are for photographs, as well as fine art. The gallery in Chelsea shows large-scale pieces. ⊗ *32 East 57th Street, Floor 4 (Chelsea: 534 West 25th Street) • Map M3 • Open 9:30am–6pm Tue–Fri, 10am–6pm Sat*

5 Sperone Westwater

This is an excellent place to see some of the most creative work being produced today. Paintings by many notable international artists, including Bruce Nauman and his wife Susan Rothenberg, are on show at the Greenwich Village. There is another gallery in Greene Street. ⊗ *415 13th Street, West Village • Map M3 • 242 Green Street, Suite 2 • Map N4 • Open 10am–6pm Tue–Sat (open Mon in summer)*

The spacious Paula Cooper Gallery

6 The Drawing Center
Formed in 1976 to promote the art of drawing, the non-profit center has presented the drawings of more than 1,800 emerging artists, as well as the work of the Old Masters. The Center also hosts monthly readings called Line Reading to present new writing. ◈ *35 Wooster Street • Map P4 • Open 10am–6pm Tue–Fri, 11am–6pm Sat, closed during August*

7 Dia Center for the Arts
A trenchant supporter of large-scale works of art since the 1970s, the non-profit Dia Center for the Arts opened this spacious facility in 1987 in a four-story renovated warehouse. The galleries are dedicated to long-term exhibitions, offering artists the opportunity to develop new work or a focused presentation of work on a full floor of the building *(see p120)*.

8 Matthew Marks
Marks was the first commercial gallery to open in Chelsea, in a converted garage, in 1994. He specializes in showing big-name artists such as Ellsworth Kelly and Bruce Marden, and now has a second two-story location in a former knife factory on 24th Street. In the latter building, new works by painters, photographers, and sculptors are currently being exhibited *(see p120)*.

9 Paula Cooper
This vast, creatively-designed space filtering natural light through a cathedral ceiling is a superb setting for conceptual and minimalist art by Donald Judd, Sol Lewitt, Joel Shapiro, and others. Paula Cooper, a SoHo pioneer, deserted in 1996 to move to the Chelsea district *(see p120)*.

10 Paul Kasmin
Kasmin is the son of a bohemian London dealer and continues the family tradition of taking chances on new artists. He features these artists in group shows that often turn the artists into rising stars. More established names, including those of sculptors and photographers, regularly appear in solo exhibitions. Kasmin joined the popular exodus to Chelsea in 1999 *(see p120)*.

Left **Chrysler Building** Right **View of the World Financial Center from the yacht harbor**

New York Skyscrapers

1 Empire State Building

The Empire State Building (1930–31) is the tallest structure in New York. For 27 years its dominance was eclipsed by the World Trade Center, but the latter was destroyed in September 2001 during a terrorist attack on the city. With its rooftop observatory, the building receives some 3.5 million visitors each year *(see pp8–9)*.

2 G.E. Building

Soaring 70 stories into the sky, this dramatic skyscraper *(see p13)*, designed by Raymond Hood in 1931–3, has shallow setbacks that recede into the distance. Part of the greatness of Hood's design is the contrast between the building's height and surrounding Rockefeller Center. ⬡ *30 Rockefeller Plaza, between 50th & 51st sts • Map J3 • Closed to public*

3 Chrysler Building

The gleaming, stainless steel, tiered spire of the Chrysler Building adds grace to the city skyline. William Van Alen fashioned this Art Deco classic in 1928–30 as a whimsical tribute to the automobile. The building has a decorative frieze of stylized hubcaps and silver gargoyles, much like the winged radiator caps of a Chrysler car *(see p123)*.

4 Flatiron Building

This 21-story, triangular-shaped building has intrigued New Yorkers since it was built by Daniel Burnham in 1902; the shape was so unusual that people took bets on whether it would topple. The secret was in the steel frame support, which was used instead of traditional heavy stone walls: a precursor of skyscrapers to come *(see p112)*.

5 Woolworth Building

Architect Cass Gilbert was responsible for this flamboyant Gothic building of 1913, the tallest building in the world for two decades after it was completed. The rich terra-cotta ornamentation accentuates the structure's steel frame, which soars to a crown 55 stories above Broadway. The small lobby boasts one of the most luxurious marble interiors in Manhattan. ⬡ *233 Broadway, between Park Pl & Barclay St • Map Q4 • Open during office hours • Free*

6 Lever House

Gordon Bunshaft's 24-story Lever House, completed in 1952, was revolutionary; it was New York's first skyscraper built in the form of a soaring glass and steel vertical slab. It began the eventual transformation of Park Avenue into an avenue of glass towers. ⬡ *390 Park Avenue, between 53rd and 54th Street • Map J4 • Open during office hours*

7 Seagram Building

The only New York building by Mies van der Rohe is this landmark "glass box" with slender bands of bronze amid walls of smoked glass rising from the horizontal open plaza. The materials in the glass-walled lobby by Philip Johnson help blur the division between indoor and

outdoor space. The Four Seasons Restaurant, offering American cuisine, lies within.
⊛ 375 Park Avenue, between 52nd & 53rd sts • Map J4
• Open during office hours • Free

Citicorp Center

8 Citicorp Center

The 59-story Citicorp Center, built in 1978, was New York's first Postmodern skyscraper. The rakish, triangular top never served its original purpose as a solar panel, but it did make the building instantly recognizable. An open base on four tall columns and a reflective aluminum-and-glass exterior give the building an airy quality despite its huge size. ⊛ 153 East 53rd Street at Lexington Av • Map J4 • Closed to public

9 World Financial Center

Cesar Pelli's Postmodern complex, comprising four tall towers around a glorious palm-filled Winter Garden, gave the city an elegant business center when it was completed in 1985. In addition, there are public spaces for concerts and special events and an outdoor plaza on the water complete with boat marina and Statue of Liberty views (see p74).

The Winter Garden, World Financial Center

10 World Wide Plaza

The copper roof and crown of frosted glass atop a 48-story tower by Skidmore, Owings & Merrill bring some traditional romance to a 1989 Postmodern building. There is a wraparound arcade that acts as another entrance. The building of the World Wide Plaza complex, which includes two apartment buildings and a large open plaza, transformed a decaying neighborhood.
⊛ Between 8th & 9th avs and 49th & 50th sts • Map J2

For more on New York's Architecture See pp46–7

Left **Grand Central Station** Right **U.S. Custom House**

Historic Buildings

1 St. Paul's Chapel
Built in 1767–8, this church has a glorious Georgian interior lit by Waterford chandeliers. The pew where George Washington prayed after his inauguration as president has been preserved (see p80).

2 City Hall
Built in 1802–12, this Georgian building with French Renaissance influences is one of New York's finest. The interior features a rotunda circled by Corinthian columns, opening to twin spiral marble staircases (see p80).

City Hall's imposing façade

3 Trinity Church
This lovely, square-towered church has bronze doors designed by Richard Morris Hunt. Built in 1839–46, the spire, once the tallest in Manhattan, is now dwarfed by Wall Street towers. Alexander Hamilton (see p48) and Robert Fulton are buried here (see p73).

4 St. Patrick's Cathedral
James Renwick, Jr. designed America's largest Catholic cathedral (built in 1879) in French Gothic style with twin 330-ft (100-m) towers. The interior has side altars dedicated to saints and holy figures, chapels, and stained-glass windows (see p124).

Trinity Church

5 Carnegie Hall
Philanthropist Andrew Carnegie financed the city's first great concert hall, built in 1891. Major renovation in 1996 restored the wonderful interior bronze balconies and ornamental plaster, and added a museum. Corridors are lined with memorabilia of the great artists who have performed here (see p125).

6 Cathedral of St. John the Divine
The world's largest cathedral was begun in 1892 and is still a work in progress. The part-Romanesque, part-Gothic building is impressive for its stonework, enormous nave, bay altar windows, and rose window. The seat of New York's Episcopal archdiocese, the church is the scene of many avant-garde musical and theatrical events (see p139).

7 New York Stock Exchange

Built in 1903 and reminiscent of a Roman temple, the façade of this 17-story edifice is appropriately monumental for the building at the center of the U.S. economy. The figures on the pediment represent Commerce. "Black Thursday," the start of the Depression, began here in 1929 (see p73).

8 U.S. Custom House

One of the city's best Neo-Classical buildings, this eight-story structure, built in 1907, features an elaborate mansard roof and fine sculptures, including four by Daniel Chester French. A 1927 nautical mural by Reginald Marsh adorns the huge, oval rotunda (see p74).

9 New York Public Library

This white marble, 1911 Beaux Arts edifice is magnificent inside and out. Imposing stairways, terraces, and fountains inspire awe; Periodicals Reading Rooms invite repose. Events and talks are held here (see p124).

10 Grand Central Terminal

Resplendent after restoration, this public facility from 1913 is remarkable for its beauty; the soaring main concourse is suffused with natural light. Of note is the vaulted ceiling of cerulean blue, decorated with twinkling constellations (see p123).

Top 10 Churches and Temples

1 Zion St. Mark's Evangelical Lutheran Church
Built in 1888, it is a reminder of the Upper East's German past. 🕭 339 East 84th Street • Map F5

2 St. George's Ukrainian Catholic Church
A contemporary church built in Byzantine style. 🕭 30 East 7th Street • Map M4

3 St. Nicholas Russian Orthodox Cathedral
Five onion domes mark this Russian Baroque church. 🕭 15 East 97th Street • Map E4

4 St. Sava Serbian Orthodox Cathedral
Byzantine windows were added to this 1856 church. 🕭 15 West 25th Street • Map L3

5 St. Vartan Armenian Cathedral
The goldleaf dome was inspired by the churches of Armenia. 🕭 630 2nd Avenue • Map K4

6 St. Elizabeth of Hungary Church
This Neo-Gothic church has a painted vaulted ceiling. 🕭 211 East 83rd Street • Map F4

7 Greek Orthodox Cathedral of the Holy Trinity
Built in 1931 in Byzantine style as the seat of the Diocese. 🕭 319 East 74th Street • Map G5

8 Temple Emanuel
The world's largest synagogue was built in 1845. 🕭 1 East 65th Street • Map G4

9 First Chinese Presbyterian Church
The stone sanctuary dates from 1819. 🕭 61 Henry Street • Map P5

10 Islamic Cultural Center
Ninety bulbs hang by brass rods from the dome. 🕭 1711 3rd Avenue • Map E4

Left **Alexander Hamilton** Center **DeWitt Clinton** Right **John D. Rockefeller, Jr. (left)**

Figures in New York History

1 Peter Minuit

Sent from the Netherlands in 1626 to govern New Amsterdam, Peter Minuit (1580–1638) was so disliked by his subjects that they welcomed British occupation.

2 Alexander Hamilton

Revolutionary leader and first Secretary of the Treasury, Hamilton's (1755–1804) business-friendly policies were instrumental in New York's emergence as the financial center of the U.S. He lost his life in a duel with political opponent Aaron Burr and is buried in Trinity Church graveyard.

3 William "Boss" Tweed

The political leader of Tammany Hall, Tweed (1823–78) became the living embodiment of political corruption, kickbacks, and payoffs. It is estimated that he and his associates took up to $200 million from the city. To hide his crime, he did good works, building orphanages, public baths, and hospitals, but died in prison.

William "Boss" Tweed

4 DeWitt Clinton

Mayor of the city, governor of the state, and U.S. senator, Clinton (1769–1828) is best remembered for negotiating the construction of the Erie Canal in 1817–25. By connecting the Great Lakes to the Hudson River, he helped to secure New York's future as a predominant seaport.

5 Jacob Riis

Appalled by immigrant living conditions, Riis (1849–1914), a social reformer, writer, and photographer, used photos taken in tenements to illustrate his stories, shocking the middle class and motivating them to act. His 1888 article, *Flashes from the Slums*, and his book, *How the Other Half Lives*, brought national attention.

6 John D. Rockefeller, Jr.

The largess of John D. Rockefeller, Jr. (1874–1960) helped support housing in Harlem, the Bronx, and Queens, created Fort Tryon Park and the Cloisters, and provided land for the United Nations. The construction of Rockefeller Center *(see pp12–15)* employed thousands at the height of the depression and gave the city an enduring landmark.

7 Fiorello LaGuardia

Considered the city's best mayor, after his election in 1933 LaGuardia (1882–1947) modernized and centralized a chaotic city government, eliminated waste, unified the transit system, and obtained federal funds to help the city. A man of the people, he is remembered for reading the comics on the radio during a city newspaper strike.

8 Robert Moses

Powerful and controversial, as construction supervisor and parks commissioner from the 1930s–1950s, Moses (1888–1981) vastly enlarged and upgraded the city's recreational areas, but he also covered the city with highways rather than develop a public transport system and was responsible for urban renewal projects that razed many neighborhoods in favor of high-rises.

9 Donald Trump

"The Donald" (b. 1946), the flamboyant real estate wheeler-dealer, has left an indelible mark on New York. The huge Trump Place development overlooks the Hudson River, while the cheapest condo in the world's highest residential building, Trump World Tower, costs close to $1 million.

10 Rudolph Giuliani

Mayor Rudy Giuliani (b. 1944) is widely credited with reducing crime, making the city cleaner, and upgrading quality of life for most New York citizens during his tenure, 1993 to 2001. Once controversial for his strong personality, and for getting rid of anyone who disagreed with him, his leadership following the attack on the World Trade Center rallied a stunned city and won praise at home and abroad.

Top 10 Dates in New York History

1 1626
Peter Minuit buys Manhattan from the natives. Beads and trinkets worth about $24 accomplished this ultimate real estate deal.

2 1664
The British take Manhattan from the Dutch. New Amsterdam becomes New York.

3 1789
George Washington is inaugurated as first president and takes his oath of office in Federal Hall. New York serves as the first U.S. capital.

4 1792
New York Stock Exchange opens; 24 traders sign an agreement beneath a tree on Wall Street, and the city becomes a financial center.

5 1876
Central Park opens and the city gains a green center enjoyed by millions every year.

6 1886
The Statue of Liberty is unveiled, becoming the symbol of freedom for millions of immigrants, who form a "melting pot" of nationalities.

7 1898
The five boroughs unite to form New York, the world's second largest city.

8 1931
The Empire State Building establishes New York as the world's skyscraper capital.

9 1952
The city becomes home to the United Nations headquarters.

10 2001
Terrorists use hijacked planes to destroy the towers of the World Trade Center.

Left **Madison Square Garden** Center **Radio City** Right **Brooklyn Academy of Music**

Performing Arts Venues

1 Carnegie Hall
The world's greatest visiting musicians play in this historic concert hall that opened in 1891 with Tchaikovsky making his U.S. debut on the podium. A campaign led by violinist Isaac Stern saved the building from demolition after Lincoln Center *(see p139)* was completed in 1969, and it entered its second century with old-world style intact after an extensive, lavish renovation *(see p125)*.

2 Metropolitan Opera House
Lincoln Center's most elegant performance venue shows off glorious oversize murals by Marc Chagall inside great arched windows. The interior boasts exquisite starburst chandeliers that are raised to the ceiling before each performance. The theater presents the American Ballet Theater and many traveling groups, as well as its famous opera company *(see p139)*.

3 Avery Fisher Hall
Thanks to the generosity of benefactor Avery Fisher, the former Philharmonic Hall is now, after early acoustics problems, worthy of the New York Philharmonic, the oldest symphony orchestra in the U.S.. A bust by Rodin of composer and former Philharmonic Music Director Gustav Mahler, on the west side of the building, is one of the best pieces of public sculpture in Lincoln Center *(see p139)*.

4 New York State Theater
The stage was built in 1964 to the specification of legendary choreographer George Balanchine, the founder of the New York City Ballet company, which dances here in winter and spring. The New York City Opera Company is also based here, presenting laudable productions that are far more affordable than the neighboring Metropolitan *(see p139)*.

5 Alice Tully Hall
Built for the Chamber Music Society of Lincoln Center, the hall has a pleasant, intimate feel. Besides chamber and vocal concerts, it is used for the Jazz at Lincoln Center series, as well for shows by the Julliard School students and faculty, many of which are free to the public *(see p139)*.

For more entertainment venues **See pages 24 and 52–3**

6 City Center Theater

The ornate, Moorish-style building with a dome of Spanish tiles was begun in 1921 as a Shriner's Temple. Saved from developers by Mayor LaGuardia *(see p48)*, and managing to survive after losing its companies to Lincoln Center, it has become a major venue for touring dance companies and special events. ✆ *131 West 55th Street, between 6th & 7th avs • Map H3 • 212 581 7907*

City Center Theater

7 Joyce Theater

A 1941 Art Deco movie theater was carefully converted to become an intimate home for dance. Small and medium-sized modern dance companies from around the world present an exciting range of work that can't be seen elsewhere in Manhattan. Question-and-answer sessions with the artists follow some Wednesday night performances. ✆ *175 8th Avenue at 19th St • Map L2 • 212 242 0800 • Open noon–6pm Mon, noon–7pm Tue–Sat, (closed 1–2:15pm Sat) • Admisson charge*

8 Radio City Music Hall

Opened in 1932, the largest theater in the U.S. has an opulent, Art Deco interior. Once a movie palace, it now hosts musical performances and special events. The annual Christmas show starring the Rockettes, 36 long-legged dancers, is a New York tradition.

✆ *1260 6th Avenue at 50th St • Map J3 • 212 247 4777 • Tours: 10am–5pm Mon–Sat, 11am–5pm Sun • Admission charge*

9 Brooklyn Academy of Music (BAM)

This stately, Neo-Italianate 1908 building draws city-wide audiences for New York's most avant garde program of international music, theater, and dance, most notably the Next Wave Festival, a fixture since 1981. ✆ *30 Lafayette Street, Brooklyn • Subway Atlantic Av • 718 636 4100 • Open noon–6pm Mon–Sat (to 7pm Sun) • Admission charge*

10 Madison Square Garden

Home court for New York Knicks basketball and New York Rangers hockey, the 20,000-seat Garden is also used for rock concerts, ice shows, indoor tennis, boxing, dog shows, and the circus. ✆ *7th Avenue at 32nd St • Map K3 • 212 465 6741 • Admission charge*

Left **Birdland** Center **Blue Note** Right **Eugene**

TOP10 Music Venues

1 Beacon Theater
Name the stars and they've probably been on stage at the Beacon, where the likes of Bob Dylan, Sting, and B.B. King have performed. The Allman Brothers Band is a regular, and it's always worth checking the current schedule. ◉ *Broadway at 74th St • Map G2 • Open 1 hour before show • Admission charge*

2 Village Vanguard
Since 1935, this basement club has featured a "who's who" of jazz. The early years were eclectic, launching folk singers like Harry Belafonte. Since the 1950s it has been all jazz. ◉ *178 7th Avenue at 11th St • Map M3 • Open 8:30pm–closing • Cover charge*

Jackie McLean at the Vanguard

3 Birdland
Another legend, although no longer in the location opened by Charlie Parker in 1949. After ups and downs, the club is ensconced near Times Square in new quarters built in three tiers to ensure good sightlines. The food is decent, and big bands play from Tuesday to Sunday. ◉ *315 West 44th Street, between 8th & 9th avs • Map J2 • Open 5pm–3am Mon–Sun • Cover charge*

4 Blue Note
Tony Bennett, Natalie Cole, and Ray Charles have all played this Greenwich Village venue. The emphasis is on jazz, but blues, Latin, R&B, soul, and big band also feature. ◉ *131 West 3rd Street, between MacDougal St & 6th Av • Map N3 • Open 7pm–2am Sun–Thu, 7pm–4am Fri & Sat • Admission & cover charge*

5 S.O.B.s
The initials stand for Sounds of Brazil, but the music ranges from African to reggae via soul or jazz. The beat is contagious, and the dance floor gets crowded. Monday is salsa night. ◉ *204 Varick Street at Houston St • Map N3 • Opening times vary • Cover charge*

6 Jazz Standard
This stylish club has first-rate acoustics and sightlines and plays traditional to avant garde music. The loft restaurant, 27 Standard, is recommended. ◉ *116 East 27th Street, between Park Av Sth & Lexington Av • Map L4 • Open 7pm–3am Tue–Sat (from 6pm Sun) • Cover charge*

7 Iridium Jazz Club
A fine follow-up to a Lincoln Center performance, Iridium has funky, surrealist decor, an extensive wine list, and excellent established and new jazz groups. The great guitarist Les Paul plays here every Monday night. ◉ *48 West 63rd Street at Columbus Av • Map H2 • Open 7pm–4am daily • Admission charge*

For more New York entertainment venues See pp50–51

8 Joe's Pub

This swanky oasis attached to the Public Theater hosts an eclectic range of well-known and emerging artists, from jazz to rock. Wednesday is Latin night, and Sundays pull a gay crowd. ◉ Lafayette Street, between East 8th and East 4th sts • Map N4 • open 6pm–4am daily • Admission charge

9 Knitting Factory

This multilevel complex has four bars and four performance spaces, the variety drawing an eclectic crowd to TriBeCa. The café and the bars, serving microbrew beers, are popular spots. ◉ 74 Leonard Street, between Broadway & Church St • Map P3 • Open 6pm–4am daily • Admission charge

10 The Bottom Line

Some say it is past its prime, but many swear by this long-time Village venue, a standard for more than 25 years for acoustic music folk, rock, and occasional jazz. Bruce Springsteen is among many whose careers received a boost here, and you never know who may turn up. ◉ 15 West 4th Street at Mercer St • Map N4 • Opening times vary • Admission charge (cash only)

Top 10 Dance Clubs

1 Centro-Fly
Op Art decor and top music make this a current favorite. ◉ 45 West 21st Street • Map L3

2 Cheetah
Jungle decor; celebrity-spotting; people hoping to meet people. ◉ 12 West 21st Street • Map L3

3 Lotus
A mix of dining room, bars, lounges, and dance floor. ◉ 409 West 14th Street • Map L2

4 Vinyl
Different D.J.s and music every night. No alcohol served. ◉ 6 Hubert Street • Map P3

5 Shine
D.J. or live music, eclectic party nights here make for a lively scene. ◉ 285 West Broadway • Map P3

6 Babalu
A club with Latino music and foods, this is a reincarnation of the Tropicana club featured in I Love Lucy. ◉ 317 West 44th Street • Map J2

7 Roxy
Star D.J.s make this a late-night favorite; Saturday brings queens, Wednesday is roller skating night. ◉ 515 West 18th Street • Map M2

8 Don Hill's
Celebs and cross-dressers join the throngs at this dark SoHo dive with D.J.s or live bands. ◉ 511 Greenwich Street • Map P3

9 Spa
A new, multilevel club with a water theme. ◉ 76 East 13th Street • Map M4

10 Eugene
Lots of velvet makes this the place for a dress-up night out. ◉ 27 West 24th Street • Map L3

New York's Top 10

Left **Mark's Bar** Center **McSorley's Ale House** Right **Monkey Bar**

🔟 Bars and Lounges

1 King Cole Bar and Lounge
Maxfield Parrish's famous mural of Old King Cole, rich mahogany paneling, and sumptuous seating set the stage for New York's most famous hotel bar, which has only began admitting women since 1950. Lush, luxurious, and very expensive, the soft piano music sets a mood that makes it easy to clinch a deal or spark a romance. ◈ *St. Regis Hotel, 1 East 55th Street, between 5th and Madison avs • Map H4 • 212 339 6721*

King Cole bar

2 44 at the Royalton
Located in the heart of Manhattan's Midtown, this chic bar and restaurant is situated in the lobby of the Royalton Hotel. The interior boasts the sleek lines of Phillippe Starck's Postmodern interior designs, and this, combined with an air of total luxury, makes it a highly sought-after bar. ◈ *Royalton, 44 West 44th St • Map J3 • 212 944 8844*

3 Monkey Bar
A sophisticated spot with a whimsical theme – monkey murals and light fixtures, even a Purple Monkey cocktail. A long-time favorite recently restored, the bar attracts a well-heeled, well-dressed crowd. ◈ *Hotel Elysee, 60 East 54th Street, between Madison and Park avs • Map J4 • 212 838-2600*

4 Flute
Proudly stocking 100 types of champagne, several of which are available by the glass, this former speakeasy successfully blends high-end opulence and a sumptuous menu with a romantic atmosphere and friendly service. ◈ *205 West 54th Street, between 7th Av and Broadway • Map H3 • 212 265 5169*

5 Campbell Apartment
This is a gem hidden in Grand Central Terminal. These richly paneled, former offices of 1920s railroad tycoon John W. Campbell feature leaded glass, a beautiful painted ceiling, and a carved wood balcony, all inspired by a Florentine palazzo. Single-malt scotches or vintage wines enjoyed with a good cigar are appropriate choices to complement this setting. ◈ *West balcony, Grand Central Terminal, 15 Vanderbilt Avenue at 42nd St • Map J4 • 212 953 0409*

6 Pen-Top Bar and Terrace
There are few places in Manhattan to be outdoors and enjoy a city view, hence the popularity of this chic bar. It has peerless night-time panoramas

of the city from the 23rd floor terrace or the glass-walled bar but you'll pay a high price for the privilege. However, entranced patrons don't seem to mind. ◈ Peninsula Hotel, 700 Fifth Avenue at 55th St • Map H3 • 212 956 2888

7 Rhône
Deep in Manhattan's west-side meatpacking district lies this revamped former garage, now an industrial-edged yet sophisticated wine bar. Its extensive wine list specializes in the reds and whites of France's Rhône Valley and is complemented by a rich menu that includes foie gras, truffle risotto, and charcuterie. ◈ 63 Gansevoort Street at Greenwich St • Map M2 • 212 367 8440

8 Boathouse Bar
Watch the sun set and the lights come on in the surrounding skyline at this outdoor bar beside the lake in Central Park, a location worthy of a movie set. The setting is particularly romantic on warm nights when rowboats and gondolas glide by. ◈ Central Park near East 72nd St • Map G2 • 212 517 2233

Park View at the Boathouse

9 Double Happiness
The cavernous Double Happiness bar situated in the heart of Chinatown is a union of Italian and Chinese cultures exemplified by the special house drink, a Green Tea Martini. The clientelle reflects the neighborhood, but the choice of music is far more wide-ranging, including old jazz, soul, funk, 80s Chinese pop, and trip-hop drum and bass. ◈ 173 Mott Street at Broome St • Map P4 • 212 941 1282

10 Ñ
Head for this out-of-the-way block in SoHo to discover an absolute gem: a raffish bar with polka dot walls, reasonably priced drinks, and Spanish tapas to be enjoyed with a choice of sherries, fruity sangria, or Spanish wines. Flamenco music adds to the atmosphere. Get there early to get a seat: this place is small and popular. ◈ 33 Crosby Street, between Broome and Grand sts • Map P4 • 212 219 8856

Left **Danny's Skylight Room** Center **Chicago City Limits** Right **Stand Up New York**

🔟 Cabarets

Look around the Algonquin, too, a hotel famous for the "round table" of writers who met here. ◈ *Algonquin Hotel, 59 West 44th Street, between 5th & 6th avs • Map J3 • Cover charge*

1 Café Carlyle

Chic and classy Café Carlyle is New York at its best and is well worth the steep cover charge; Bobby Short can be seen here, and Woody Allen is often part of Monday night jam sessions. Bemelmans Bar features pianists like Barbara Carroll, and a cheaper tab.
◈ *Carlyle Hotel, 35 East 76th Street at Madison Av • Map G4 • Cover charge*

2 Cafe Pierre

An elegant setting for the talented singer-pianist Kathleen Landis and occasional guests, performing Broadway and pop favourites. The food, while pricey, is first rate. ◈ *Pierre Hotel, 5th Avenue at 61st Street • Map H3 • No cover*

The Oak Room

3 The Oak Room

Settle into a banquette and look forward to top entertainers like Maureen McGovern or Julie Wilson. The repertories usually favor American classics, such as Gershwin, Berlin, or Cole Porter.

4 Don't Tell Mama

No telling who will be at this fun spot in the Theater District – singers, comics, or magicians. There are no big names, and abilities range from amateur to destined-for-stardom. Sometimes even the waiters get into the act. ◈ *343 West 46th Street, between 8th & 9th avs • Map J2 • Cover charge*

5 Feinstein's at the Regency

This is a swank spot to hear artists like Rosemary Clooney or guitarist John Pizzarelli, as well as Grammy-nominated vocalist and song writer, co-owner Feinstein. ◈ *Regency Hotel, 540 Park Avenue at 61st St • Map H4 • Cover charge*

6 Cafe Sabarsky

On selected Fridays, this Viennese confection becomes the city's most beautiful and atmospheric setting for contemporary cabaret. Shows are at 9pm; a *prix-fixe* dinner is available at 7pm. Check for current dates and reserve tickets at the museum. ◈ *Neue Galerie, 1048 5th Avenue at 86th Street • Map F3 • No cover*

For more on entertainment **See pp50–51**

7 Danny's Skylight Room

Inside this Thai restaurant in the Theater District, there's no quibbling with the entertainment on stage, from mellow jazz to Broadway favorites. Old timer Blossom Dearie is often featured. ✪ *346 West 46th Street, between 8th & 9th avs • Map J2 • Cover charge*

8 Judy's Chelsea

Restaurant, cabaret, and lively piano bar with a singing waitstaff, Judy's offers a Monday musical revue; co-owner and singer Judy Kreston and pianist David Lahm often perform on Saturdays. ✪ *169 8th Avenue, between 18th & 19th sts • Map L3 • Cover charge*

Judy's Chelsea

9 The Duplex

The oldest cabaret in town features entertainment from early versions of *Nunsense* or *Mark Twain Tonight*, to singers, comedians, drag diva Lady Bunny, or the troupe Funny Gay Males. The raucous shows attract straight and gay. ✪ *61 Christopher Street at 7th Av South • Map N3 • Cover charge*

10 Reprise Room at Dillons

"Our Sinatra," a cabaret show in two acts, is a hit with critics and audiences of all ages. A talented, young cast of three reprises 50 songs, some popular, some little-known, of the master song stylist, with talent and charm galore to keep the mystique alive. ✪ *Dillons Restaurant, 245 West 54th Street • Map J2 • Admission charge*

Top 10 Comedy Clubs

1 The Comic Strip Live
A leading venue for up-and-comers; Eddie Murphy and Jerry Seinfeld are alumni. ✪ *1568 2nd Avenue • Map E4*

2 Caroline's Comedy Club
In the heart of the theater district, Caroline's features big names as well as beginners. ✪ *1626 Broadway • Map J3*

3 Dangerfields
One of the oldest and best; owner Dangerfield sometimes tries out material here. ✪ *1118 1st Avenue • Map G5*

4 Gotham Comedy Club
An intimate setting with comics from Comedy Central and other shows. ✪ *34 West 22nd Street • Map L3*

5 Comedy Cellar
Everyone from Robin Williams to Ice T has appeared in this Village landmark. ✪ *117 MacDougal Street • Map N3*

6 Boston Comedy Club
Another cellar spot with up to ten acts per night. ✪ *82 West 3rd Street • Map N3*

7 Stand-up New York
Novices and pros feature in this intimate space. ✪ *236 West 78th Street • Map F2*

8 PS NBC
Here's where NBC holds weeknight auditions, seeking tomorrow's stars. ✪ *145 6th Avenue • Map N3*

9 Upright Citizens Brigade Theater
Improvization and sketches by a Comedy Central foursome. ✪ *161 West 22nd Street • Map L2*

10 Chicago City Limits Theater
Timely improvization in this long-running review. ✪ *1105 1st Avenue • Map G4*

Left **Carriage rides through Central Park** Right **Staten Island Ferry**

🔟 Romantic Settings

1 Carriage Ride through Central Park

The horse-drawn hansom cabs lined up at the edge of Central Park are romance personified. The driver, appropriately attired in fancy dress and top hat, will help you up as you nestle in for a 20-minute trot past park landmarks *(see pp26–7)*.

2 Dinner at the River Café

The Manhattan skyline is never more dazzling than when seen from this barge restaurant just across the East River in Brooklyn. The food is worthy of the setting; the package is worth the price *(see p151)*.

River Café, nestling beneath Brooklyn Bridge

3 View from the Empire State Building at Twilight

It has been the setting for dozens of romantic movies and countless proposals have taken place here. At dusk you can watch the sun set over the city as a million lights go on in its towers *(see pp8–9)*.

4 Drinks at the Top of the Tower

The 26th floor of this Art Deco landmark building affords unsurpassed views of the city lights and the East River from its wraparound terraces. Order champagne and enjoy the scene and each other. ◈ *Beekman Tower Hotel, 3 Mitchell Place at 1st Av & 49th St • Map J5*

5 Gondola Ride on Central Park Lake

Relax aboard the authentic, Venetian gondola as you glide out on the water and revel in the beauty of the park reflected in the lake and the city buildings ringing the park like a crown – the gondolier may break into song. ◈ *Loeb Boat House, Central Park at East 74th St • Map G3 • Charge*

6 Walk in the Cloister Gardens

Away from the city's clatter, this branch of the Met is an oasis of serene beauty, a chance to glory in the past while planning the future. More than 250 kinds of plant grown in the Middle Ages are found in these gardens. The Trie Cloister features plants shown in the Unicorn Tapestries *(see p31)*

7 Dinner at One if by Land...
A restored 18th-century Greenwich Village carriage house, candlelight, and soft piano music make for Manhattan's most seductive setting. ⊗ *17 Barrow Street, between 7th Av Sth & West 4th St • Map N3 • 212 228 0822*

8 Staten Island Ferry Ride
Stand on the top deck to watch Manhattan's skyscrapers recede as you sail past Liberty, Ellis, and Governors Islands. Take the car deck coming home for close-up photos of the skyline *(see p155)*. ⊗ *Whitehall Terminal, Whitehall and South sts • Map R4 • Boats every 15mins–1 hr, 24 hours daily • Free*

9 Brooklyn Bridge Stroll
A classic experience, the walk across the Brooklyn Bridge yields thrilling vistas of city skyscrapers through the intricate bridge cable work. Bring the camera to record unparalleled views. ⊗ *The bridge begins behind City Hall, Broadway and Park Row • Map Q4*

10 Concert at St. Paul's Chapel
Just to walk into this chapel, New York's oldest public building, is to enter a world of grace and reverent serenity. The concerts held on Mondays at 1pm offer a chance for visitors to revel in the beauty of the setting and the music *(see p80)*.

Top 10 City Oases

1 Samuel Paley Plaza
Respite from Midtown bustle with its own waterfall. ⊗ *3 East 53rd Street • Map J4*

2 Greenacre Park
A "vest pocket" park donated by the daughter of John D. Rockefeller, Jr. ⊗ *217–21 East 51st Street • Map J4*

3 Bryant Park
A swath of green with formal plantings behind the Public Library. ⊗ *6th Avenue, between 41st & 42nd sts • Map K3*

4 Metropolitan Museum Roof Terrace
Have a drink or just admire the prime views of Central Park and city towers beyond. ⊗ *Fifth Avenue and 82nd Street • Map F3*

5 Conservatory Garden
Three formal gardens inside Central Park. ⊗ *105th Street and 5th Avenue • Map D4*

6 Theodore Roosevelt Park
A shady patch of green behind the American Museum of Natural History. ⊗ *Columbus Avenue, between 77th & 81st sts • Map F2*

7 John Jay Park
Past the playgrounds is a placid seating area with East River views. ⊗ *East 77th Street and FDR Drive • Map F5*

8 Wave Hill
Former estate with gardens and greenhouses. ⊗ *675 West 252nd Street, Bronx*

9 Grace Church
A Renwick masterpiece, this beautiful 1846 church is a calm respite in the Village. ⊗ *802 Broadway • Map M4*

10 St. John the Baptist Church
Sanctuary and Prayer Garden with statuary and fountain. ⊗ *210 West 31st Street • Map K3*

New York's Top 10

Left **Lesbian and Gay Community Services Center** Center **Big Cup** Right **Next**

Gay and Lesbian New York

1 Stonewall Pub
Next door to the Stonewall Inn, where a police raid on June 27, 1969, turned into a riot as gays rose up against constant police harassment, the present bar is far more peaceful, a sociable place for a drink or a game of pool.
✪ 53 Christopher Street • Map N3

2 Christopher Street
The profusion of bars, shops, and cruisers between 6th and 7th avenues is the epicenter of gay Greenwich Village. The crowd is a bit older since so many younger gay men have defected to Chelsea.
✪ Map N3

3 Oscar Wilde Memorial Bookshop
New York's oldest gay and lesbian bookshop opened in 1967 before the Gay Rights movement began. It has survived smashed windows and open hatred to provide a center and aid for gays. Current free publications on gay events are available here, as well as videos, music, and gifts.✪ 15 Christopher Street • Map N3

4 Bluestockings Book Store
Named after an 18th-century feminist group, this Lower East Side lair is not only a comprehensive source for women's literature but a social center with a café, gallery, readings, and events. Women of all ages and races are welcome.
✪ 172 Allen Street at Stanton St • Map N5

5 Lesbian and Gay Community Services Center
A nucleus of the gay community, headquarters for organizations and event notices, active in public education, health, and emotional counseling, and center for social events, the Center also maintains history archives and an extensive library. An informative welcome pack is available for tourists.
✪ 1 Little West 12th Street • Map M2
• Open 9am–11pm daily

HX and Time Out magazines

6 Publications
HX (Homo Xtra) and Next are weeklies reviewing the club and entertainment scene. Other publications include Gay New City News, a newspaper covering politics, health, and arts; the New York Blade, a free tabloid; and Metro-Source, a glossy lifestyle magazine. Time Out New York, a general entertainment weekly sold at all newsstands, has a big section on gay and lesbian events from lectures to clubs.

7 Club Nights

Many clubs have party nights. Wednesday nights, for example, are big at Splash and Pork at Lure, Friday nights at Octagon, Saturday at The Roxy, Sunday at Limelight. The Cock is lively all week. Venues and days change, so consult the press for current happenings.
🔕 *Check listings publications for details*

8 Lesbian Herstory Archive

The world's largest and oldest lesbian archive, founded in 1973, is located in Park Slope, a popular lesbian neighborhood. The volunteer-run archive houses art, books, photos, periodicals, video, and films recording lesbian lives and holds events supporting lesbian writers and artists in all media.
🔕 *484 14th Street, Brooklyn • Subway 15th St, Prospect Park • 718 768 3953 • Open by appointment*

9 American Fitness Center

The muscle boys in Chelsea favor this two-story gym with the latest weights and circuit training equipment and fitness classes. It also offers sauna, massage facilities, and a café serving healthy meals and snacks. The gym actively supports gay causes from AIDs walks to Gay Pride organizations.
🔕 *128 8th Avenue at 16th St • Map M2 • Open 6am–midnight Mon–Fri, 8am–9pm Sat & Sun • Admission charge*

10 Drag Shows

A transgender waitstaff and drag shows in the basement make Lucky Cheng New York's most unusual Chinese restaurant, drawing tour buses as well as gay patrons. Also check out the drag queens lip-synching songs at Lips, performing to a Latin beat at La Nueva Escuelita, and serving and entertaining at Stingy Lulu's.
🔕 *Check listings publications for details.*

Top 10 Eating and Meeting Places

1 Big Cup
The coffee house hangout to meet and greet, day and night. 🔕 *228 8th Avenue • Map L2*

2 Food Bar
The food and the well-muscled clientele are attractions at this Chelsea standby. 🔕 *149 8th Avenue • Map M2*

3 Bar d'O
Drag vocalists are the draw at this dim, candlelit Greenwich Village bar. 🔕 *29 Bedford Street • Map N3*

4 G
Trendy lounge with a live D.J., round stainless steel bar, and conversation pit. 🔕 *225 West 19th Street • Map L3*

5 Splash Bar
Enjoy the go-go guys working on the shower stage and erotic videos above the urinals. 🔕 *50 West 17th Street • Map M3*

6 Boiler Room
A favorite East Village cruising destination. Weeknights are mellow, weekends packed. 🔕 *86 East 4th Street • Map N4*

7 Lure
Leather, rubber, and military attire are *de rigeur* here. 🔕 *409 West 13th Street • Map M2*

8 The Works
Gay Upper West Siders gather here in various states of dress and undress. 🔕 *428 Columbus Avenue • Map F2*

9 Henrietta Hudson
Warm, down-to-earth, lesbian lair in Greenwich Village. 🔕 *483 Hudson Street • Map N3*

10 Meow Mix
The current hip hangout for lesbian celebrities and young trendy types. 🔕 *269 East Houston Street • Map N5*

Left **Easter Parade** Right **Feast of San Gennaro**

Festivals and Events

1 St. Patrick's Day Parade

People wear Irish green for this big day when marching bands, politicos, and lovely lasses march down 5th Avenue to proclaim their love of the Emerald Isle. Millions come to watch and the celebrations last way into the night. ◈ *5th Avenue • 11am Mar 17 • Check press for exact route*

2 Easter Parade

Following a long-time tradition, 5th Avenue closes to traffic in Midtown, and New York families in their Sunday best stroll up the avenue, with ladies sporting amazing hats, both traditional and outrageous. ◈ *5th Avenue • Map H3–J3 • 11am Easter Sunday*

3 9th Avenue Food Festival

New York's biggest food extravaganza began in 1974. Vendors come from all over and more than a million people jam the streets to sample a United Nations of food from burritos to samosas. ◈ *9th Avenue, 37th to 57th sts • Map H2–K2 • Mid-May*

4 4th of July Fireworks

River drives close to traffic and huge crowds come out to see this pyrotechnic spectacular over the East River. Macy's spends over $1 million for this salute to the red, white, and blue. ◈ *East River • Map R3 • 9:30pm Jul 4*

4th of July fireworks over the East River

5 West Indian Day Carnival

Brooklyn's West Indian population celebrates its heritage with a parade of enormous floats, lavish, feathered costumes in rainbow hues, and contagious Caribbean music. Street stands offer Caribbean specialties. ◈ *Eastern Parkway, Brooklyn • Subway to Franklin Av • Labor Day (1st Mon in Sep)*

6 Feast of San Gennaro

The patron saint of Naples is carried through the streets of Little Italy, and Mulberry Street is packed day and night with music, game booths, and tons of tasty, traditional food. Sausage and pepper sandwiches are the trademark of this 10-day event, but there is an Italian treat for every taste. ◈ *Mulberry Street • Map P4 • 3rd week in Sep for 10 days*

West Indian Day Carnival

7 New York City Marathon

An amazing 30,000 entrants run the 26.2-mile (42-km) marathon that starts on Staten Island, takes in all five boroughs, and finishes in Central Park. New Yorkers line the route, cheering and offering water to the runners. ◈ *1st Avenue above 59th Street is a good viewpoint • Map H5 • 10:45am 1st Sun in Nov*

8 Macy's Thanksgiving Day Parade

New Yorkers take to the streets and America watches on television as cartoon character balloons, marching bands, lavish TV and movie star-laden floats, and the dancing Rockettes announce the start of the Christmas season. Santa Claus in his sleigh is the last float. ◈ *Central Park West at 77th Street along Broadway to 34th Street • Map G2 • 9am Thanksgiving Day*

9 Christmas Tree Lighting Ceremony

America's tallest Christmas tree, festooned with miles of lights, stands next to the skating rink in Rockefeller Center. Trumpeting angel statues in the Channel Gardens and animated windows in 5th Avenue department stores add to the holiday spirit. ◈ *Rockefeller Center • Map J3 • 1st week in Dec*

10 New Years Eve Ball Drop

Crowds begin gathering hours before, ready to cheer when a giant, illuminated, Waterford crystal ball lowered at midnight marks the official start of the New Year. Other "First Night" events include dancing at Grand Central Station or the Empire State Building and midnight fireworks in Central Park. ◈ *Times Square • Map K3 • Midnight Dec 31*

Top 10 Sports Events

1 U.S. Open Tennis Championships
The last Grand Slam of the year. ◈ *USTA National Tennis Center, Queens*

2 New York Yankees and Mets Baseball
Perennial rivals compete in America's favorite pastime. ◈ *Yankee Stadium, Bronx; Shea Stadium, Queens • Apr–Sep*

3 New York Knicks Basketball
Fast-paced games that always sell out. ◈ *Madison Square Garden, 7th Avenue • Oct–Apr*

4 New York Liberty
Women's professional basketball. ◈ *Madison Square Garden, 7th Avenue • Jun–Aug*

5 New York Jets and Giants Football
Both teams play in New Jersey; tickets are scarce. ◈ *Giants Stadium, New Jersey • Sep–Dec*

6 New York Rangers Hockey
Played on ice, requiring speed and skill. ◈ *Madison Square Garden, 7th Avenue • Oct–Apr*

7 Millrose Games
America's fastest runners compete in this indoor track meet. ◈ *Madison Square Garden, 7th Avenue • Feb*

8 Wood Memorial
Race featuring Kentucky Derby contenders. ◈ *Acqueduct Raceway, Queens • Mid-Apr*

9 Belmont Stakes
The last of racing's "triple crown." ◈ *Belmont Park, Long Island • 2nd Sat in Jun*

10 New York/New Jersey MetroStars
The growing popularity of soccer draws devoted fans. ◈ *Giants Stadium, New Jersey. • Mar–Sep*

Left **Bloomingdale's** Center **Barney's** Right **Henri Bendel**

🔟 New York Stores

1 Macy's
What can you say about the world's largest store? Food to futons, the selection is vast. And Macy's is a major part of the New York scene, from the annual spring flower show to Tap-O-Mania, when thousands of tap dancers converge on Herald Square *(see p119)*.

2 Bloomingdale's
After Macy's, this is New York's best-known department store, re-nowned for high fashion for men and women. The main floor with cosmetics, jewelry, and accessories is a mob scene, but don't be discouraged; upper floors are more manageable. ◈ *1000 Lexington Avenue at 59th St • Map H4*

3 5th Avenue Department Stores
Bergdorf Goodman, Saks Fifth Avenue, and Lord and Taylor have a full range of well-known brand

Saks Fifth Avenue

clothing for men, women, and children, as well as an upscale selection of home accessories. All have seasonal window displays that make for stylish browsing. ◈ *Bergdorf Goodman, 754 5th Avenue; Saks Fifth Avenue, 611 5th Avenue; Lord and Taylor, 424 5th Avenue • Map H3–K3*

4 Barney's New York
If you have the where-withal, here's the place to find the latest designer labels to please a well-heeled, young and trendy clientele. Their semi-annual clearance sales are legendary and draw hordes of shoppers after chic on the cheap.
◈ *660 Madison Avenue at 61st St • Map H4*

5 Henri Bendel
Set up like a series of boutiques, Bendel's displays innovative, fun women's fashions for glamorous shoppers. The sales staff are particularly friendly. The signature brown and white shopping bag is such a status symbol that the pattern is used for accessories.
◈ *712 5th Avenue at 55th St • Map H3*

6 Takashimaya
In a sleek, five-story Post-modern building, this outpost of the Japanese department store sells clothing, art, linens, *objets d'art*, and furniture. All have East-ern influence, are expensive, and are chosen for excellent design.

For more on New York shopping **See p165**

Visit the serene Tea Box for bento box lunches and beautiful desserts. ◈ 693 5th Avenue, between 54th & 55th sts • Map H3

7 H&M
Hennes & Mauritz, a Swedish retailer, was a smash success when the 5th Avenue store opened in New York in 2000. Their secret? Kicky, young designs for men, women, and children at rock bottom prices, creating a look that belies the price tag. ◈ 640 5th Avenue at 51st St; 34th Street and Herald Square; 558 Broadway • Map J3, K3 & N4 respectively

8 Madison Avenue Designers
The epicenter of designer boutiques in New York used to be 57th Street between 5th and Madison avenues, where shops such as Burberry are still found. But as stores like Nike and Levi's have invaded this territory, the designers, Giorgio Armani to Yves Saint Laurent, have moved to Madison Avenue, where the exclusive shops and boutiques now run from 59th almost to 79th Street. ◈ Giorgio Armani, 760 Madison Avenue; Yves Saint Laurent, 855-59 Madison Avenue • Map F4–H4

9 SoHo Boutiques
The 20–30-something crowd does its shopping in trendy SoHo boutiques such as Anna Sui, A.P.C., Miu Miu, and Todd Oldham. Shops are concentrated between Thompson Street and Broadway, between Prince and Greene streets, though any block in this area may yield your own special find. This is also prime hunting ground for home furnishings at stores such as Portico and Zona. ◈ Anna Sui, 113 Greene Street; A.P.C., 131 Mercer Street; Miu Miu, 100 Prince Street; Todd Oldham, 120 Wooster Street; Portico, 72 Spring Street; Zona, 97 Greene Street • Map N3–N4

10 6th Avenue Superstores
Between 18th and 23rd streets, the cast-iron buildings that comprised the late-1800s "Fashion Row" are another shopping mecca. Current occupants include superstores like Bed, Bath, and Beyond for homewares, Old Navy for casual clothing, and bargain fashion outlets such as T.J. Maxx and Filene's Basement. ◈ Bed, Bath, and Beyond, 620 6th Avenue; Old Navy Clothing Co., 610 6th Avenue; T.J. Maxx, 620 Sixth Avenue; Filene's Basement, 620 Sixth Avenue • Map L3

Left **Coney Island** Center **Central Park's carousel** Right **Children's Museum of Manhattan**

Places for Children

1 Central Park

Myriad activities for kids include storytelling, carousel rides, bike riding, boating, ice skating, nature workshops, and guided walks. The Wildlife Conservation Center is excellent, not too large in size, and the Children's Zoo allows petting and feeding of farm animals *(see pp26–7)*.

2 Bronx Zoo/ Wildlife Conservation Park

America's largest city zoo offers authentic environments for exhibits such as the Himalayan Highlands, African Plains, Jungle World, and the spectacular new Congo Gorilla Forest. All are easily reached via shuttle trains and elevated rides *(see p155)*.

Polar Bear in the Wildlife Conservation Park

3 Children's Museum of Manhattan

Five floors of educational hands-on fun with exhibits like Body Odyssey, exploring a giant crawl-through body; Inventor Center, using scanners and digital images; and a TV studio where kids produce their own shows. Under-fours have their own play area *(see p140)*.

4 American Museum of Natural History

Join throngs of New York parents introducing children to the world-famous dioramas of wild animals in realistic natural habitats and the fascinating dinosaur exhibits. The totem and giant canoe in the Northwest Coast Indian exhibit and the enormous meteorites and mineral rock specimens are also favorites. The Rose Center will intrigue older children and teens *(see pp34–7)*.

5 New Victory Theater

The "New Vic," a 1900 landmark, has been transformed into New York's first major theater devoted to family entertainment. Troupes from around the world offer plays, circus acts, and other diversions to delight young audiences. Pre-performance family workshops with staff and cast are scheduled, offering interesting insights into how a theater functions. ◉ *214 West 42nd Street, between 7th & 8th avs • Map J3 • Open noon–7pm Tue–Sat, 11am–5pm Sun & Mon • Admission charge*

6 F.A.O. Schwarz

Expect to be awed by this ultimate toy store selling giant stuffed animals to the last word in action toys. This wonderland of fun was founded by German immigrant Frederick August Otto Schwarz in 1862 and is now the flagship store for over 40 U.S. locations. Kids love looking, but be prepared to be wheeled into a purchase. ⚅ *767 5th Avenue at 58th St • Map H3*

F.A.O. Schwartz

7 Coney Island/ New York Aquarium

Although a bit frayed since its early 1900s heyday, Coney Island is still home to the landmark ferris wheel and roller-coaster rides, and the long sandy beach and beachside boardwalk. The excellent New York Aquarium, along the boardwalk, is an indoor and outdoor complex where whales, walruses, and dolphins play, and finny creatures range from sharks to seahorses. Worth the trip, this is a great family day's outing *(see p155)*.

8 Tall Ship Cruises

A boat ride in Manhattan harbor is always a thrill, and what better way to go to sea than aboard the 1885 Schooner Pioneer at South Street Seaport? Ninety-minute lunch sails are good for those with short attention spans; two-hour cruises depart afternoon and evening. ⚅ *South Street Seaport Museum: Pier 16 at South Street Seaport • Map Q4 • Thu–Sun May–Sep • Admission charge*

9 The Circus

New York's own non-profit Big Apple Circus, with a delightful one-ring show, pitches its tent each November in Damrosch Park at Lincoln Center for the holiday season. Those who want the traditional three-ring extravaganza will find Ringling Bros. and Barnum & Bailey in town each year in April. ⚅ *Big Apple Circus, Lincoln Center Plaza; Ringling Bros./Barnum & Bailey, Madison Square Garden, 7th Avenue at 32nd St • Map H2 & K3 • Admission charge*

10 Children's Museum of the Arts

When little ones get fed up with sightseeing, bring them to this SoHo stop where children can enjoy interactive exhibits. Those under the age of ten can create their own works of art using paint, collage, chalk, or you name it, and work off energy in the play areas. Under-fives have their own WEE (wondrous experimenting and exploring) Artists Drop-In section. Children's art from other nations is on show. ⚅ *182 Lafayette Street, between Broome & Grand sts • Map P4 • Open noon–5pm Thu–Sun, noon–7pm Wed • Admission charge*

Left **Upper West Side restaurant** Right **Nobu**

🔟 Restaurants

1 Union Square Café

Danny Meyer's first restaurant has been one of New York's most popular since 1985, loved for delicious fare served by friendly staff in comfortable surroundings. Chef Michael Romano's new

Union Square Café

takes on American standards include the freshest ingredients from the neighboring Union Square Greenmarket *(see p115)*.

2 Gotham Bar and Grill

A perennial favorite. Alfred Portale was one of the first with "vertical food," delicious layers so artfully stacked you can hardly bear to disturb them. The new American fare is elegant, and the lofty, columned space is sophisticated and casual. The $20 three-course lunch is a great buy. ◈ *12 East 12th Street, between 5th Av & University Pl • Map M3 • 212 620 4020 • $$$*

3 Nobu

Reservations are hard to come by for Nobu Matsuhisa's Japanese/Peruvian fusion that produces inspired dishes. Say "Omakase" ("I leave it to you") and let the waiter choose among the surprising and always sublime offerings. David Rockwell's whimsical setting adds to the experience. Casual Nobu Next Door needs no reservations *(see p103)*.

4 Jean Georges

Already a culinary star from his earlier Jo Jo and Vong restaurants, Jean-Georges Vongerichten in his namesake restaurant turns out food that is among the very best in New York, transformed by the French master's delicate sauces and creative combinations. Designer Adam Tihany has created a polished, almost austere, setting that does not upstage the four-star chef *(see p137)*.

5 Daniel

Another luminary of the food world, Daniel Boulud now has a flower-filled, Venetian Renaissance-inspired dining room worthy of his extraordinary talents. Seasonal menus with choices such as roasted squab with spiced pineapple or black truffle-crusted cod are divine. Lunch is a less expensive opportunity to sample the master *(see p131)*.

6 Danube

The chemistry is just right at David Bouley's unusual TriBeCa restaurant, offering light as air, "nouveau Austrian" food in an intimate, sensuous new spin on an old-world setting that includes Klimt-style paintings. It's all so warm and wonderful, nobody wants to leave. Wiener schnitzel and spaetzle never had it so good *(see p103)*.

7 Le Cirque 2000
Some love the bright neon and Adam Tihany's playful, curving furniture, some find it jarring amid the gilded, old-world splendor of the landmark Villard Houses. No one doubts that Le Cirque is one of the city's better French restaurants and for many the place to see and be seen *(see p129)*.

8 Le Bernardin
Seafood doesn't come any better than at this quietly luxurious French restaurant lauded for revolutionizing the way fish is served in New York. Chef Eric Lipert seems to have no critics. Of course, perfection has its price and you'll pay dearly, but the meal will be memorable *(see p129)*.

9 Gramercy Tavern
Another Danny Meyer success, this is perhaps New York's most unpretentious fine dining. Tom Colicchio's inventive American cuisine is universally praised. No reservations are needed for the less expensive Tavern area *(see p115)*.

10 Four Seasons
Restaurants come and go but this New York institution with landmark decor by Philip Johnson seems to go on forever, and it is always among the top-rated for Continental food. The Grill Room is still the prime place for power lunches, and the Pool Room is a perfect setting for special occasion dinners *(see p129)*.

Top 10 Cheap Eats

1 Lombardi's Pizza
On everybody's list of best-in-town for its thin crust, coal oven pizza *(see p87)*.

2 Salaam Bombay
A top-ranked Indian restaurant with bargain lunch and brunch. ◎ *319 Greenwich Street • Map Q3 • 212 226 9400*

3 The Elephant
Café with Thai/ French fusion menu. ◎ *58 East 1st Street • Map N4 • 212 505 7739*

4 Nyonya
Good Malaysian fast food. ◎ *194 Grand Street • Map P4 • 212 334 3669*

5 Sweet-n-Tart
Asian snacks, dinners, tea drinks, and soups; Tong shui, the house soup, is said to balance ying and yang. ◎ *20 Mott Street • Map P4 • 212 964 0380*

6 Flor de Mayo
Peruvian/Cuban/Chinese mix; Peruvian-style rotisserie chicken is a specialty. ◎ *2651 Broadway • Map D2 • 212 595 2525*

7 Republic
Lots of noodle dishes and noise at this Pan-Asian. ◎ *37 Union Square West • Map M4 • 212 627 7168*

8 Il Bagatto
Even uptowners head for this East Village Italian with good food and prices. ◎ *192 East 2nd Street • Map N5 • 212 228 0977*

9 La Bonne Soupe
Midtown's best bet for onion soup, fondue, and other bistro specialties *(see p125)*.

10 Pomaire
This cheerful Chilean restaurant is the Theater District's best deal. ◎ *371 West 46th Street • Map J2 • 212 956 3056*

For more restaurants and a key to price categories **See pages 77, 83, 89, 95, 103, 109, 115, 121, 129, 137, 143, 149, and 157**

AROUND TOWN

NEW YORK'S TOP 10

Left **Federal Reserve Bank** Center **Federal Hall National Memorial** Right **Battery Park City**

Lower Manhattan

OLD AND NEW NEW YORK *meet at the tip of the island. The city was born here under Dutch rule and became the nation's first capital after the Revolutionary War (1775–83). At the intersection of Broad and Wall streets are the Federal Hall National Memorial, marking the site where George Washington was sworn in as president in 1789, and the New York Stock Exchange, the financial giant founded in 1817, whose influence is felt worldwide. The 20th-century skyscraper era added drama to the skyline. The* 2001 leveling of the World Trade Center towers damaged but certainly did not destroy lower Manhattan. Historic buildings, exciting architecture, outdoor sculptures, and waterfront promenades remain unscathed. Numerous museums and galleries add to the area's appeal.

Battery Park City esplanade

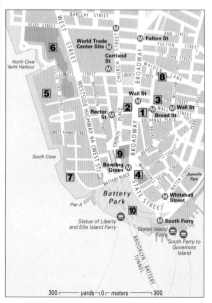

🔟 Sights

1. New York Stock Exchange
2. Trinity Church
3. Federal Hall National Memorial
4. U.S. Custom House
5. Battery Park City
6. World Financial Center
7. Museum of Jewish Heritage
8. Federal Reserve Bank
9. Cunard Building
10. Battery Park

1 New York Stock Exchange

Behind the Neo-Classical façade is the financial heart of the U.S., grown from a local exchange to a global enterprise. Over 200 million shares are traded daily for more than 2,000 companies. Although the action is much calmer now that everything is computerized, visitors can watch the trading floor from a balcony gallery where signs explain what is happening in the trading posts below. Each post has 22 sections of traders handling the stock of up to 10 companies. Ⓝ *20 Broad Street at Wall St • Map R4 • Open 9:15am–4pm Mon–Fri (last admission 3.30pm) • Free*

New York Stock Exchange

2 Trinity Church

This much-admired Gothic building is the third church on this site for one of the U.S.'s oldest Anglican parishes, founded in 1697. The church has had notable additions since completion in 1846, including the sacristy, chapel, and Manhattan wing; the bronze doors were donated as a memorial to John Jacob Astor III. Trinity is known for its musical programs, with concerts each Thursday at 1pm and occasional Sunday concerts by the full choir. Trinity also oversees the programs at St. Paul's Chapel *(see p80)*. Ⓝ *Broadway at Wall St • Map R6 • Open 7am–6pm Mon–Fri, 8am–4pm Sat, 7am–4pm Sun; tours daily and after 11.15am Sun service • Free*

3 Federal Hall National Memorial

Although the bronze statue of George Washington on the steps marks the site where the nation's first president took his oath of office, the original building was replaced by this handsome, columned Greek Revival structure in 1842. It served as the U.S. Custom House and a branch of the Federal Reserve Bank before becoming a museum in 1955, with exhibits of the Constitution and the Bill of Rights. An introductory video and talks detail the historic events that occurred here. Ⓝ *26 Wall Street at Nassau St • Map R4 • Open Jul & Aug: 9am–5pm daily • Free*

Left **New York Stock Exchange** Right **Trinity Church**

4 U.S. Custom House

A renovation in 1994 installed gleaming galleries that circle the grand rotunda of this classic building. It is now the George Gustav Haye Center of the Smithsonian National Museum of the American Indian, with changing exhibits of Native American life, including costumes and fine crafts. Baskets of ceremonial objects, toys, and musical instruments in the research room can be examined and researched further on the computer installed there *(see p47).*
🐦 *1 Bowling Green, between State & Whitehall sts • Map R4 • Open 10am–5pm Fri–Wed, 10am–8pm Thu • Free*

5 Battery Park City

Several prestigious architects were involved in this extension of Manhattan, a commercial and residential enclave built on a 92-acre landfill created with earth displaced by excavation for the World Trade Center. A 2-mile (3-km) esplanade offers grand Statue of Liberty views. Parts of the complex were damaged by the Trade Center collapse but a brighter future is forecast since the opening of the posh Ritz-Carlton Hotel and the new Skyscraper Museum.
🐦 *Off West Street, Battery Place to Chambers St, bounded by the Hudson River • Map Q3*

George Washington in New York

A statue at the Federal Hall National Memorial *(see p73)* where George Washington was sworn into office is testament to the time the president spent in New York City. So too is the pew where he worshipped at St. Paul's Chapel *(see p80),* and the museum at Fraunces Tavern where he said farewell to his officers in 1789.

6 World Financial Center

Some of the top U.S. financial companies have headquarters in the World Financial Center, which was damaged in the September 11 attack. The center of the complex is the Winter Garden, with a 120-ft (37-m) atrium, palms and marble steps *(see p45).*
🐦 *Battery Park City at West St • Map Q3 • Open daily*

7 Museum of Jewish Heritage

A memorable experience for all faiths is this chronicle of the 20th-century Jewish experience before, during, and after the Holocaust, told with over 2,000 photographs, hundreds of artifacts, and original documentary films.
🐦 *First Place at Battery Place, Battery Park City • Map Q3 • Open 10am–5.45pm Sun–Wed, 10am–8pm Thu, 10am–5pm Fri & Jewish holiday eves • Admission charge*

Left **Federal Hall interior** Center **Federal Reserve Bank** Right **U.S. Custom House**

Cunard Building

8 Federal Reserve Bank

Although gold is no longer transferred in payments between nations, much of the world's gold reserve remains stored in the five-story vault below this building. All bank notes from this branch have the letter B in the Federal Reserve seal. ✎ *33 Liberty Street, between William & Nassau sts • Map Q4 • Tours 9.30, 10.30, 11:30am, 1:30, 2.30pm, Mon–Fri • Free, reserve ahead*

9 Cunard Building

Brass doors and wrought iron gates lead into a U.S. Post Office in one of New York's grandest interiors; a Great Hall with murals, frescoes and an elaborate domed ceiling. It was once the ticket office for the Queen Mary and Cunard's other great ocean liners. ✎ *25 Broadway • Map R3 • Open during business hours*

10 Battery Park

Built largely on 18th- and 19th-century landfill, this park at New York harbor is usually visited for Castle Clinton, the 1807 fort that is now the embarkation point for Ellis Island and Statue of Liberty ferries. This welcome swath of green is of interest for its many monuments and statues. ✎ *Broadway and Battery Place • Map R3–4 • Open daily • Free*

A Day Exploring Lower Manhattan

Morning

Begin at **Battery Park** for a view of the waterfront, and look into **Castle Clinton** *(see p16)*, an 1807 fort, to see dioramas of a changing New York. Then visit the **Museum of the American Indian** at the **U.S. Custom House**. Cross to **Bowling Green**, the city's first park, then turn right on Whitehall, and left on Pearl Street for the **Fraunces Tavern Museum**, a restoration of the 1719 building where George Washington bade farewell to his troops.

Continue on Pearl Street and turn left to Broad Street to join Wall Street denizens at a favorite lunching spot, the lively **Wall Street Kitchen and Bar** *(see p77)*.

Afternoon

Head up Broad Street to Wall Street to the **New York Stock Exchange**, where there is chaos on the trading floor, close by **Federal Hall** *(see p73)*.

Continue uptown on Nassau Street (a continuation of Broad) to see **Chase Plaza** and its famous sculptures. At the end of the Plaza on Liberty Street is the ornate **Federal Reserve Bank** and then Louise Nevelson Square, featuring the artist's *Shadows and Flags.*

Go back on Liberty and turn downtown on Broadway to find **Trinity Church** *(see p73)* and the **Cunard Building**. End the day with drinks or dinner at the scenic **American Park at the Battery** *(see p77)*.

Left **The Immigrants** Center **The Four Continents** Right **Group of Four Trees**

Outdoor Sculptures

1 The Immigrants
Reflecting the diversity of newcomers to the U.S. from 1855–90, Luis Sanguino's 1973 work includes an African, a Jew, a family, a priest, and a worker.
◈ *Battery Park • Map R3*

2 Giovanni da Verrazzano
The first European to sail into New York Harbor in 1524 was honored by fellow Italians with this 1909 statue by Ettore Ximenes.
◈ *Battery Park • Map R3*

3 The Four Continents
Sculptor Daniel Chester French reflects 18th-century U.S. views – meditative Asia and exotic Africa to the sides, regal Europe and a dynamic U.S. in the center.
◈ *U.S. Custom House, 1 Bowling Green • Map R4*

4 Shadows and Flags
Louise Nevelson's 1977 figures enliven the traffic island they inhabit. The largest is rooted to the ground, others are on stilts.
◈ *Between Maiden Lane, William, & Liberty streets • Map Q4*

5 Sunken Garden
The spray from a central fountain covers the floor of the recessed circular garden. Isamu Noguchi's 1960s work suggests rocks rising from the sea. ◈ *Chase Manhattan Bank Plaza, between Nassau & Liberty sts • Map R4*

6 Group of Four Trees
Jean Dubuffet's 1972 mushroom-like sculptures hover over pedestrians nearby and bring a reason to smile in this busy area.
◈ *1 Chase Manhattan Plaza, between Nassau & Liberty sts • Map R4*

7 George Washington
Designed and cast in 1883, a bronze Washington on a massive granite pedestal lifts his hand from the Bible after being sworn in.
◈ *Federal Hall National Memorial, 26 Wall Street • Map R4*

8 Red Cube
Isamu Noguchi's 1967 red, 28-ft (9-m) high, metal cube balances on a corner defying gravity.
◈ *Marine Midland Plaza, 140 Broadway • Map Q4*

9 Double Check
The briefcase of J. Seward Johnson, Jr.'s 1982 seated bronze figure contains a stapler, calculator, and an occasional sandwich provided by a passerby. ◈ *Liberty Plaza, between Broadway & Church St • Map Q4*

10 Yu Yu Yang Sculpture
This untitled sculpture by artist Yu Yu Yang creates intriguing patterns with an L-shaped steel slab pierced by a circular disk. ◈ *Orient Overseas Building, 88 Pine Street • Map R4*

For a three-course meal for one with half a bottle of wine (or equivalent meal), taxes and extra charges.

$ under $25
$$ $25–$50
$$$ $50–$80
$$$$ over $80

Left **American Park** Right **Wall St Kitchen & Bar**

 # Restaurants

1 American Park at the Battery

At the tip of the Battery, location and harbor views are the draw. An American menu includes seafood. ◈ *Battery Park, nr Bridge St and Whitehall St • Map R4 • 212 809 5508 • $$$*

2 Gigino's Wagner Park

Gigino's delivers excellent Italian food from the Amalfi coast and dazzling views from the sophisticated dining room and the waterfront terrace. ◈ *20 Battery Place, next to the Jewish Heritage Museum • Map R3 • 212 528 2228 • $$$*

3 14 Wall Street

A handsome setting for fine French cuisine. Service is impeccable and there's a convivial bar. ◈ *14 Wall Street, between New St and Nassau St • Map R4 • 212 233 2780 • $$$*

4 Vine

A good wine list accompanies American dishes served in this airy room. The building is an 1898 Beaux Arts landmark. ◈ *25 Broad Street at Exchange Place • Map R4 • 212 344 8463 • $$$*

5 Wall Street Kitchen & Bar

Bistro fare and a bar with 50 beers on tap make this bustling spot in a former bank building a neighborhood favorite. ◈ *70 Broad Street at Beaver Street • Map R4 • 212 797 7070 • $$*

6 St. Maggie's Café

An oasis in the busy financial district, the menu features American standards. ◈ *120 Wall Street, between Front and South sts • Map R4 • 212 943 9050 • $$$*

7 Bayards

Located in the restored former N.Y. Cotton Exchange. The chef uses the freshest ingredients and the wine list is good. ◈ *1 Hanover Square at Pearl St • Map R4 • 212 514 9454 • $$$$*

8 55 Wall Street

Corinthian columns set the scene for elegant dining on American dishes with continental touches. ◈ *Regent Wall Street Hotel 55 Wall Street, between Hanover and William sts • Map R4 • 212 699 5555 • $$$$*

9 Joseph's

When Wall Streeters require Italian food, they often head for Joseph's. The menu includes linguine with clam sauce and fried calamari. ◈ *3 Hanover Square • Map R4 • 212 747 1300 • $$$*

10 Harry's at Hanover Square

A fixture in the financial district since 1875, Harry's is known for its bountiful wine cellar, steaks, and other American fare. ◈ *1 Hanover Square, between Pearl and Stone sts • Map R4 • 212 425 3412 • $$$*

Note: *Unless otherwise stated, all restaurants accept credit cards and serve vegetarian meals*

Left **Surrogate's Court** Center **Relief detail, the former AT&T Building** Right **Police Plaza**

Civic Center and South Street Seaport

*S*OME OF NEW YORK'S *finest architecture is found at its Civic Center, the headquarters for city government. Buildings here span the centuries, from the 18th-century St. Paul's Chapel to the pioneering 20th-century Woolworth Building. Nearby is the famous Brooklyn Bridge, and the old maritime center of the city, South Street Seaport, its piers and buildings now restored as a lively hub of cafés, restaurants, and museums.*

Sights

1. South Street Seaport
2. Brooklyn Bridge
3. Woolworth Building
4. AT&T Building
5. St. Paul's Chapel
6. City Hall
7. Municipal Building
8. New York County Courthouse
9. Surrogate's Court/ Hall of Records
10. Police Plaza

Woolworth Building

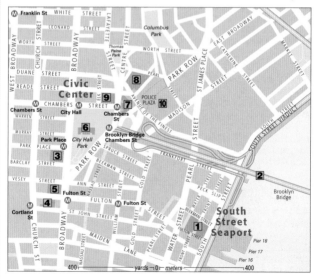

South Street Seaport

1 The cobbled streets, buildings, and piers that were the center of New York's 19th-century seafaring activity (known as "the street of sails") have been restored as a tourist center. There are shops, food stalls, restaurants, a museum with many seafaring exhibits, a fleet of tall ships for boarding, and plenty of outdoor entertainment. ◎ *Museum 207 Front Street • Map Q4 • Open 10am–6pm Fri–Wed, 10am–8pm Thu • Admission charge*

Brooklyn Bridge

2 When it was completed in 1883 linking Manhattan and Brooklyn, this was the largest suspension bridge in the world and the first to be built of steel. It took 600 workmen and 16 years to build, and claimed 20 lives, including that of the designing engineer, John A. Roebling. It is now a symbol of New York, and those who walk the 1-mile (1.8-km) span are rewarded with fabulous views of city towers seen through the artistic wire cablework. ◎ *(Manhattan side) Park Row near Municipal Building • Map Q4 • Free*

Woolworth Building

3 Step inside to see one of New York's great interiors; marble walls, bronze filigree, a mosaic ceiling, and stained glass combine to magical effect. Architect Cass Gilbert also had a sense of humor – sculptures include Five and Dime mogul Woolworth counting nickels and Gilbert himself cradling a model of the building. It set the standard for the skyscrapers that followed in the 1920s and 1930s *(see p44)*. ◎ *Broadway, between Park Pl & Barclay St • Map Q4 • Open office hours • Free*

AT&T Building

4 Built in 1922, this is a monument to excess but fun to see nevertheless. The façade is said to have more columns than any other building in the world, and the vast lobby is a forest of marble pillars. Close by at 120 Broadway, the former Equitable Building, built in 1915, is of note for another excess: the immense bulk of the building was responsible for the nation's first skyscraper zoning regulations. ◎ *195 Broadway • Map Q4 • Open office hours • Free*

Left **Brooklyn Bridge** Right **Bas-relief caricature of architect Cass Gilbert, the Woolworth Building**

5 St. Paul's Chapel
Manhattan's oldest church was built in 1766 as an "uptown" chapel for Trinity Church and took on added importance while Trinity was being rebuilt after the great fire of 1776. The chapel was modeled after London's St. Martin-in-the-Fields and has been kept as close as possible to its original form. ◈ Broadway, between Fulton & Vesey sts • Map Q4 • Episcopal service 8am Sun • Concerts 1pm Mon, $2 donation

6 City Hall
The seat of city government since 1812, City Hall is considered one of the most beautiful early 19th-century public buildings in the U.S. The design, by architects Mangin and McComb, Jr., won a competition held in 1802. A statue of Justice, dating from 1887, crowns the top of the structure. The rear of the building, facing north, was not clad in marble until 1954, since the architects never expected the city to develop further north. ◈ Broadway and Park Row • Map Q4 • Open 9am–5pm Mon-Fri • Free

City Hall

The "Boss Tweed" Courthouse
The first New York County Courthouse at 52 Chambers Street (completed in 1881) was built by Boss Tweed (see p48), a corrupt politicain who spent fortunes on this grand marble monument to himself. The elaborate interior and octagonal rotunda are being restored, though its future use is uncertain.

7 Municipal Building
This building dominating the Civic Center area, straddling Chambers Street, was the first "skyscraper" by McKim, Mead, and White, a 25-story structure completed in 1914. The top is a veritable wedding-cake fantasy of towers and spires topped by Adulph Wienman's famous statue, Civic Fame. The intricate terra-cotta vaulting above the street is modeled on the entrance of the Palazzo Farnese in Rome, and the subway entrance at the south end, an arcaded plaza, is a dramatic vault of Guastavino tiles. ◈ Center Street and Chambers Street • Map Q4

Left **Interior, St. Paul's Chapel** Right **Municipal Building**

8 New York County Courthouse

Ascend the wide staircase of the 1926 New York County Courthouse (adjacent to the 31-story, pyramid-topped U.S. Courthouse dating from 1933) and enter to admire the marble columned rotunda with Tiffany lighting fixtures. Note, too, the ceiling murals depicting Law and Justice. The hexagonal building has a courtroom in each of its six wings. ◎ 60 Center Street • Map P4 • Open 9am–5pm Mon–Fri • Free

9 Surrogate's Court/ Hall of Records

An interior inspired by the Paris Opéra is one of the glories of this 1907 Beaux Arts beauty, boasting a magnificent central hall with marble stairways and ceiling mosaics. The façade features statues representing justice, the seasons, commerce, and notable New Yorkers, as well as figures depicting the stages of life. ◎ 31 Chambers Street • Map Q4 • Open 10am–3pm Mon–Fri • Free

10 Police Plaza

Constructed in 1973, the city's police headquarters can be found on a spacious pedestrian plaza, a welcome area in a district with very few public spaces. The 75-ton Tony Rosenthal abstract sculpture, Five in One, made of five sloping interlocked discs, symbolizes the city's five boroughs. ◎ Park Row at Pearl St • Map Q4

A Walk Through Civic Center and South Street Seaport

Morning

Most subway routes lead to the Civic Center. When you come up to street level, walk down Broadway to see the lobbies of the **Woolworth** (see p79) and the former **AT&T Building** (see p79) and the Georgian interior of **St. Paul's Chapel**.

Return via Park Row, once known as Newspaper Row because it was lined with their offices. Printing House Square has a statue of Benjamin Franklin with his Pennsylvania Gazette. West of the Row lies City Hall Park, where the Declaration of Independence was read to George Washington's troops in July 1776. The park was recently restored and has a new granite time wheel telling the city's history.

A walk along Center and Chambers streets takes you past the ornate **Municipal Building**.

Afternoon

At midday, head west for a seafood lunch at the **Bridge Café** (see p83), housed in a 1794 wood-framed building. From here the East River is a short stroll away, offering excellent views of lower Manhattan.

Spend the afternoon at **South Street Seaport** (see p79), visiting the museum and maritime crafts center, perhaps taking a cruise on one of the ships. Have dinner on Pier 17, enjoying Caribbean fare at the lively **Cabana** (see p83), or New American fare at **Harbour Lights** (see p83).

Left **Schermerhorn Row** Center **Fulton Market** Right **Pier 17**

TOP10 Maritime Sights

1 South Street Seaport Museum

The city's maritime heritage is celebrated in art, photographs, workshops, and ships. The Police Museum is nearby. ⊗ *207 Front St • Map Q4 • Open 10am–6pm Fri–Wed, 10am–8pm Thu • Admission charge*

2 Schermerhorn Row

Federal-style houses built by Peter Schermerhorn in 1811–12 have restaurants and shops. They will house the World Port New York exhibition. ⊗ *Fulton St, between Front & South sts • Map Q4 • Free*

3 Historic Ships

Seven classic ships, several open for boarding, include the 1885 square-rigger *Wavertree*, and the landmark, four-masted *Peking*, built in 1911. ⊗ *Piers 15, 16, South Street Seaport • Map Q4 • Open 10am–6pm daily • Admission charge*

4 Bowne & Company

Recreation of a 19th-century print shop with working printing presses. ⊗ *211 Water Street • Map Q4 • Open 10am–5pm Tue–Sat • Free*

5 Maritime Crafts Center

Marvel at the skill of woodcarvers at work, creating model ships and figureheads. ⊗ *Pier 15, South Street Seaport • Map Q4 • Open 10am–6pm daily • Free*

6 Pilot House

The South Street Seaport ticket and information center is housed in this pilot house, taken from a steam tugboat built in 1923 by the New York Central Railroad. ⊗ *South Street Seaport • Map Q4 • Open 10am–6pm daily*

7 Pier 17

A pier with three floors of restaurants, food stands and sweeping views of the East River and Brooklyn Bridge. ⊗ *South Street Seaport • Map Q5*

8 Harbor Excursions

The 1885 schooner *Pioneer* offers 90-minute family sails and two-hour cruises in the afternoon and evening. ⊗ *Pier 16, South Street Seaport • Map Q4 • Admission charge*

9 Fulton Market

Rise at dawn and catch the action at this busy market, which may eventually move to the Bronx. ⊗ *Fulton Street at South St • Map Q4 • Open midnight–9am daily • Free*

10 Seaman's Church Institute

Established in 1834, the institute is in a stunning 1991 building with a gallery plus water views. ⊗ *241 Water Street, between Beekman St & Peck Slip • Map Q4 • Free*

Left **Bridge Café** Right **Little Italy Pizza**

🔟 Restaurants

1 Bridge Café
A quaint building, checked tablecloths, and a surprisingly sophisticated American menu. ⊗ *279 Water Steet at Dover St • Map Q4 • 212 227 3344 • $$*

2 Harbour Lights
Peerless views of the harbor and bridge account for the crowds, although the seafood-oriented fare is only average. ⊗ *Pier 17, South Street Seaport • Map Q5 • 212 227 2800 • $$$*

3 Sequoia
Nautical décor and harbor views make this informal American a top choice. ⊗ *Pier 17, South Street Seaport • Map Q5 • 212 732 9090 • $$*

4 Quartino
Convivial Italian wine bar with a big selection of wines by the *quartino* (carafe). ⊗ *Peck Slip • Map Q4 • 212 349 4433 • $$*

5 Cabana at the Seaport
A Latin flavor enlivens this Seaport favorite, serving a Cuban/Caribbean menu. ⊗ *Pier 17, South Street Seaport • Map Q5 • 212 406 1155 • $$*

6 Gators Southern Seafood
Fun decor sets an informal mood for Southern specialties like oysters, steamed shrimp, Louisiana gumbo, crabcakes, and Cajun/blackened dishes. ⊗ *Pier 17, 1st level, 89 South Street • Map Q5 • 212 571 4199 • $$*

7 Cosi Sandwich Bar
Pita bread warm from the oven laden with your choice of fillings, including ham, chicken, or roasted peppers. Part of a chain. ⊗ *54 Pine Street at William St • Map Q4 • 212 809 2674 • $*

8 Café Europa
Another chain found all over the city, this café offers soups, salads, sandwiches, and pizzas. ⊗ *199 Water Street, between Fulton & St. John sts • Map Q4 • 212 422 0070 • $*

9 Red
Wall Street suits and tourists alike can be found enjoying the famous blood orange margaritas at this busy Tex-Mex spot. ⊗ *19 Fulton Street, between Front & Water sts • Map Q4 • 212 571 5900 • $*

10 Sgarlato's Café
Many Italian favorites plus seafood with an Italian accent make this a Seaport standby. Try the seafood fettuccine alfredo or maybe the homemade lobster ravioli. ⊗ *Pier 17, 3rd level, 89 South Street • Map Q5 • 212 619 5226 • $$*

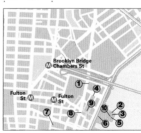

Left **Police Headquarters Building** Center **Church of the Transfiguration** Right **Food shopping**

Chinatown and Little Italy

THESE TWO ETHNIC ENCLAVES *are among the most colorful parts of the city. Each was settled by early immigrants, who preserved their own language, customs, and food in the midst of the new and foreign land. Little Italy has dwindled to a few blocks, but it is still an atmospheric center of authentic Italian food and shops, especially on a warm night, when cafés set out sidewalk tables and the songs of Napoli fill the air. Chinatown, however, continues to grow. More than 200,000 Chinese live there, in crowded quarters. The shops and sidewalk markets overflow with exotic foods and herbs, as well as gifts ranging from backscratchers to fine antiques; and it has been estimated that Chinatown contains an astounding 200 restaurants.*

Street scene, Chinatown

Sights

1. Mulberry Street
2. Police Headquarters Building
3. Museum of Chinese in the Americas
4. Mott Street General Store
5. Mott Street Shopping
6. Pearl River Chinese Products Emporium
7. Eastern States Buddhist Temple
8. Church of the Transfiguration
9. Columbus Park
10. Bloody Angle

Il Palazzo, Little Italy *(see p89)*

1 Mulberry Street

There are many trendy shops on Mulberry Street from Houston down to Spring Street and though Chinatown is overrunning much of Little Italy, the block between Broome and Canal remains strictly Italian. It is filled with restaurants, coffee shops with tempting Italian pastries, and stores selling pasta implements, statues of saints, and T-shirts saying "Kiss Me, I'm Italian." The Feast of San Gennaro packs the street each September *(see p62)*. ✪ *Mulberry Street, between Broom & Canal sts • Map P4*

2 Police Headquarters Building

After the boroughs merged into Greater New York in 1898, the city's police department expanded rapidly. This 1905 headquarters near Little Italy was the result, a monumental, columned Baroque structure fit for "New York's Finest," with an ornate dome tall enough to be seen from City Hall. The strange shape of the building

fits a wedge-shaped lot. Empty for more than a decade after the department relocated in 1973, the building has since been converted into luxury cooperatives, the Police Building Apartments.
✪ *Center Street • Map P4*
• Closed to public

3 Museum of Chinese in the Americas

Small but fascinating, this first floor museum, devoted to the Chinese experience in the West, features an exhibit called "Where is Home?," with personal stories, photographs, mementos, and poetry culled from the community. Among the topics explored are women's roles, religion, and the "bachelor society." Changing exhibits range from art to the experience of gay Chinese. Books, area guides, and free flyers on cultural events are available.
✪ *70 Mulberry Street at Bayard St*
• Map P4 • Open 10:30am–5pm Tue–Sun
• Admission charge

4 Mott Street General Store

Originally known as Quong Yeun Shing & Company, this is the oldest store in Chinatown, established in 1891. The wood-paneled interior and tin ceiling have hardly changed, and the store sells a bit of everything, from woks to wood cabinets.
✪ *32 Mott Street • Map P4*

Left **Detail, Police Headquarters Building** Right **Museum of Chinese in the Americas**

Around Town – Chinatown & Little Italy

5 Mott Street Shopping

Clustered on this block are shops with a wonderful selection of Chinese goods. China Silk and Handicrafts has vases, figurines, bowls, tea sets, and Buddhas by the dozen. Lamps made from attractive Oriental vases are the specialty of Pearl of the Orient Gallery, while New Age Designer makes clothing to order in your choice of jewel-hued silks. Serious antiques collectors should head to the Sinotique Gallery. ✈ *China Silk and Handicrafts: 18 Mott Street • Sinotique Gallery: 19A Mott Street • Pearl of the Orient Gallery: 36 Mott Street • New Age Designer: 38 Mott Street • Map P4 for all*

6 Pearl River Chinese Products Emporium

The largest department store in Chinatown has two locations and a fascinating potpourri of goods for sale. There are Chinese musical instruments, paper lanterns, kites, dried herbs, embroidered silk tops, dresses and pajamas with mandarin collars, purses, dolls, pillows, and sandalwood and jasmine soaps. ✈ *277 Canal Street at Broadway & 200 Grand Street • Map P4*

7 Eastern States Buddhist Temple

Step into the incense-scented interior, where offerings of fresh fruit are piled high, and more than 100 gold Buddhas gleam in

the candlelight. The temple takes advantage of Chinatown's tourist traffic by offering $1 fortunes for sale near the front. ✈ *64B Mott Street • Map P4 • Open 9am–8pm daily • Free*

8 Church of the Transfiguration

Built by the English Lutheran Church in 1801 and sold to the Roman Catholic Church of the Transfiguration in 1853, this Georgian-style stone church with Gothic windows is typical of the influence of successive influxes of immigrants in New York. The church has changed with the nationalities of the community it serves, first Irish, then Italian, and now Chinese. As the focal point of today's Chinese Roman Catholic community, it offers classes and services to help newcomers and holds services in Cantonese and Mandarin. ✈ *Mott Street • Map P4 • Open 7:30–9am & 11:30am–1pm daily, 5:30–7pm Sat, 8am–2pm Sun • Free*

Left **Pearl River Chinese Products Emporium** Right **Eastern States Buddhist Temple**

Bloody Angle, Chinatown

9 Columbus Park

Chinatown's only park was created in the late 1890s as a result of the campaigning of newspaper reporter Jacob Riis and other social reformers. It filled a stretch of the city that at the time was New York's worst slum, where Riis reported a stabbing or shooting at least once a week. Though it features more concrete than greenery, the park is popular today, filled with Chinese kids at play, *mah jong* players, and people practicing *tai chi* and martial arts. On the weekends, Chinese fortune-tellers sometimes set up shop in the park. ◈ *Bayard and Mulberry sts • Map P4*

10 Bloody Angle

The name for this sharp curve on Doyers Street was coined by a newspaper because this was the site of so many gangland ambushes during the 1920s. It was a period when the Hip Sing and On Leong *tongs*, groups similar to criminal gangs, were fighting for control of the opium trade and gambling rackets in Chinatown. The *tong* wars continued off and on until at least the 1940s, and their rivalries continue in the present-day youth gangs. ◈ *Doyers Street near Pell St • Map P4*

A Stroll Around Chinatown and Little Italy

Morning

⏱ Take the No. 6 train to Spring Street, walk past Lafayette, and turn down Mulberry Street *(see p85)* for a stroll through Little Italy. Don't miss the old-fashioned food shops on Grand Street, such as cheese specialist Alleva Dairy (188 Mulberry Street at Grand) and Piemonte Homemade Ravioli (190 Grand Street), where two dozen shapes and varieties of pasta can be bought. At 206 Grand is DiPalo Dairy, where you can watch fresh mozzarella being made. Take a break at a classic Italian café, like Caffè Roma, 385 Broome Street, or Ferrara's, 195–201 Grand Street.

Continue on Mulberry to Bayard, and you'll find an introduction to what's ahead, the **Museum of Chinese in the Americas** *(see p85)*. Walk east one block to Mott Street, the center of Chinatown. Enjoy a dim sum lunch at **Jing Fong** or the **Golden Unicorn** *(see p89)*.

Afternoon

Remaining on Mott Street, spend some time browsing the many shops, exotic food stores, markets, and galleries that line the street. Step into Saint's Alp Teahouse, 51 Mott Street, to sample a current fad imported from Taiwan: tall glasses of flavored teas served with "pearls" of tapioca in the bottom.

End the afternoon with a visit to the golden Buddhas of the **Eastern States Buddhist Temple** and have your fortune read.

Left **Street market** Center **Ten Ren Tea & Ginseng Company** Right **Chinatown Ice Cream Factory**

🔟 Chinatown Food Shops

1 Street Markets
Canal Street and Hester Street are among the many blocks crowded with outdoor stands selling exotic Chinese vegetables, fruits, and dried foods. ◈ *Chinatown, including Canal & Hester sts • Map P4*

2 Egg Cake Lady
Constant lines attest to the talents of Cecilia Tam, who sells the neighborhood's best custard cakes at a little red street stand. ◈ *Mott Street at Mosco St • Map P4*

3 Kamwo Herb and Tea
One of the better-known shops offering Chinese herbs said to cure anything from arthritis to impotence. Ginseng is available in teas or supplement form. ◈ *209–11 Grand Street • Map P4*

4 Fay Da Bakery
Sample a delicious soft bun filled with roasted pork or beef for less than $1, then try almond cookies, red bean cakes, custard tarts, or cream buns for dessert. ◈ *214–16 Grand Street • Map P4*

5 Ten Ren Tea & Ginseng Company
An array of golden canisters holds many varieties of Chinese teas; knowledgeable clerks will explain the properties of each and how to brew them properly. ◈ *75 Mott Street • Map P4*

6 Kam Man Food Products
One of the largest food emporiums in Chinatown stocks tonics, teas, jellies, ginseng, vegetables of every shape, and row upon row of sauces. ◈ *200 Canal Street • Map P4*

7 Dynasty Supermarket
This calm, modern market is in marked contrast to the raucous street scene, a place for comfortable browsing where all the strange vegetables you've seen elsewhere are neatly labeled. ◈ *68 Elizabeth Street • Map P4*

8 Kam Kuo Food Corp.
Another wide selection of foods and an upstairs laden with woks, kitchen tools, steamers, teapots, and other utensils. ◈ *7 Mott Street • Map P4*

9 May May Gourmet Chinese Bakery
On one of the streets of old Chinatown is this cheerful, modern shop best known for dim sum, to be enjoyed on the spot or to go. ◈ *35 Pell Street • Map P4*

🔟 Chinatown Ice Cream Factory
Ginger, lychee, pumpkin, mango, and red bean are among the flavors that can be sampled at this popular dessert stop, a favorite with young visitors. ◈ *65 Bayard Street at Mott St • Map P4*

Left **New York Noodle Town** Right **Golden Unicorn**

Price Categories

For a three-course meal for one with half a bottle of wine (or equivalent meal), taxes and extra charges.

$	under $25
$$	$25–$50
$$$	$50–$80
$$$$	over $80

TOP10 Restaurants

1 New York Noodle Town
The decor is simple and so is the menu, with wonderful soups, noodles, meat dishes, and creative ways with seafood. ⊗ 28½ Bowery Street at Bayard St • Map P4 • 212 349 0923 • No credit cards • $

2 Joe's Shanghai
The Chinatown branch of the Flushing restaurant famous for its soup dumplings (look for steamed buns on the menu). ⊗ 9 Pell Street at Bowery • Map P4 • 212 233 8888 • No credit cards • $$

3 Grand Sichuan
For the spicy flavors of China's Sichuan province, this is a no-frills bargain storefront with authentic specialties. ⊗ 125 Canal Street at Broadway • Map P4 • 212 625 9212 • No credit cards • $$

4 Vegetarian Paradise 3
The name says it all. Try veggie "beef" balls of mushroom and arrowroot, or iron "steak" made with Chinese yams, and you'll never miss the meat. ⊗ 33 Mott Street at Pell St • Map P4 • 212 406 6988 • No credit cards • $

5 Golden Unicorn
Dim sum is the star but all the dishes are well prepared in this crowded, third-floor restaurant. Go in a large group to enable more sampling. ⊗ 18 East Broadway at Catherine St • Map P4 • 212 941 0911 • $

6 Jing Fong
This enormous, glittery room is packed on weekends for the amazing selection of dim sum. Point at your choices as the carts roll by and ignore the din. ⊗ 20 Elizabeth Street, between Bayard & Canal sts • Map P4 • 212 964 5256 • $$

7 Canton
Cantonese food at its best lures locals even though the prices are high for Chinatown. ⊗ 45 Division Street at Bowery St • Map P4 • 212 226 4441 • No credit cards • $$$

8 Lombardi's
Pizza doesn't come much better than at this unpretentious old-timer that turns out delectable thin-crust pies. ⊗ 32 Spring Street, between Mott & Mulberry sts • Map P4 • 212 941 7994 • No credit cards • $

9 Da Nico
A rustic setting and a wonderful courtyard garden make this family-run restaurant with 16 kinds of pizza a favorite. ⊗ 164 Mulberry Street, between Broome & Grand sts • Map P4 • 212 343 1212 • $$

10 Il Palazzo
One of the better choices on Mulberry Street; cozy, candlelit, non-touristy. The menu includes all the Italian favorites, and the garden is a summer delight. ⊗ 51 Mulberry Street at Grand St • Map P4 • 212 343 7000 • $$

> **Note:** Unless otherwise stated, all restaurants accept credit cards and serve vegetarian meals

Left **Orchard Street** Right **Street Scene**

Lower East Side and East Village

THE LOWER EAST SIDE IS ALIVE *with memories, a neighbor-hood still seeming to echo the calls of immigrants crowded into tenements, peddlers hawking wares from pushcarts, and children playing in the streets, the only open spaces to be found. Early churches became synagogues for the Jews who came in record numbers between 1880 and 1920. Some remain, but in recent years, Latinos and Chinese have moved in, adding to the area's rich history. Meanwhile, Orchard Street tempts with bargains, and a hip, young generation is rediscovering the old neighborhood. Nearby, the East Village has its own layers of history, an early Dutch enclave that changed from German to Jewish before becoming a 1960s haven for hippies and the place where punk rock was born. A Ukrainian community has remained through most of these changes, including recent gentrification.*

Painting, Ukrainian Museum

🔟 Sights

1. Lower East Side Tenement Museum
2. Orchard Street
3. Bialystoker Synagogue
4. Eldridge Street Synagogue
5. Beth Hamedrash Hagodol Synagogue
6. Guss' Pickles
7. St Mark's Place
8. St Mark's-in-the-Bowery Church
9. Renwick Triangle
10. Ukrainian Museum

Street vendor's pushcart, Tenement Museum

1 Lower East Side Tenement Museum

Guided tours inside a tenement building give the visitor an insight into the carefully researched lives of three families who lived here; a German-Jewish seamstress in 1874, an orthodox Jewish family from Lithuania in 1918, and a Sicilian Catholic family during the Depression in the 1930s. ◎ 90 Orchard Street • Map N5 • Open for tours 1pm–4pm Tue–Fri, 11am–4:30pm Sat, Sun • Admission charge

2 Orchard Street

The heart of bargain shopping, Orchard Street became a street of shops in 1940, when Mayor Fiorello La Guardia outlawed pushcarts in the city. Many merchants still put some of their wares on the sidewalk on Sundays, their busiest day, and lure customers with 20 to 30 percent off brand names. The Lower East Side Visitor Center offers free tours each Sunday.

◎ Lower East Side Visitor Center, 261 Broome Street • Map P4 • 888 825 8374 • Open 10am–4pm Sun–Fri

3 Bialystoker Synagogue

Built in 1826 as a Methodist Episcopal Church, the fieldstone building was acquired in 1905 to house a congregation from the Polish community of Bialystok. A recent two-year restoration has revealed an interior of glowing beauty, painted in bold colors, with Moorish motifs, biblical scenes, and the signs of the zodiac, which are found in some Jewish scriptures. As in all Orthodox synagogues, only men are allowed on the main floor; women are seated in the gallery upstairs. ◎ 7–11 Willett Street • Map P6 • Open during Sat services, or by appointment • Free

4 Eldridge Street Synagogue

A National Historic Landmark. This 1887 Moorish-style synagogue was the first house of worship built in the U.S. by Jewish immigrants from Eastern Europe, from where 80 percent of American Jews come. As many as 1,000 people attended services here at the turn of the century. As congregants left the

Left **Art for sale, Orchard Street** Right **Stained glass, Eldridge Street Synagogue**

neighborhood, attendance waned, and the temple closed in the 1950s. The Eldridge Project has been at work for several years to restore the magnificent sanctuary. ⊗ *12 Eldridge Street • Map P5 • Open for tours 11am & 2:30pm Tue & Thu, 11am–3pm Sun • Admission charge*

5 Beth Hamedrash Hagodol Synagogue

Artists can often be seen sketching this small, picturesque building. It was constructed in 1850 as the Norfolk Street Baptist Church, but as the neighborhood changed, the membership moved uptown, and in 1885 the structure was converted to a synagogue by America's oldest Russian, Orthodox Jewish congregation. Gothic woodwork and the iron fence from the original church remain. ⊗ *60–64 Norfolk Street • Map P5 • Open 10am–5:50pm Mon–Sat, 11am–5:50pm Sun • Free*

6 Guss' Pickles

One of the survivors from the old days of the Jewish Lower East Side, and a fixture for more than 80 years, Guss' was even featured in the movie, *Crossing Delancey*. Fans stand in line on weekends for their fix from the barrels on the sidewalk filled with pickles – sour and half-sour. Guss' also does a thriving

The Changing Scene

Proving that change is the rule in New York, the Lower East Side has emerged as the newest trendy area for clubs, restaurants, and hip boutiques. Some residents are even moving into the tenement buildings their great-grandparents fought to escape from. Ludlow Street is one of the best streets to get a feel for the current scene.

business by mail, shipping all over the U.S. ⊗ *35 Essex Street • Map P5 • Open 9am–6pm Sun–Thu, 9am–3:30pm Fri*

7 St. Mark's Place

Once the heart of hippie-dom, this block still has a counter-culture feel and is headquarters for the East Village youth scene. Sidewalks are crowded until late into the night with patrons of funky, punky bars and shops selling music, books, T-shirts, vintage clothing, beads, posters, and black leather everything. The place to get pierced or tattooed. ⊗ *East 8th Street, between 3rd Av & Av A • Map M4*

8 St. Mark's-in-the-Bowery Church

The second-oldest church in New York stands on land where Peter Stuyvesant, governor of Dutch New York in the 1600s, had his

Left **Beth Hamedrash Hagodol Synagogue** Center **Guss' Pickles** Right **Renwick Triangle**

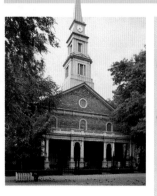

private chapel. Stuyvesant is also buried here. In the 1960s it served as one of the city's most politically committed congregations and continues to be on the avant-garde edge. ◈ *131 East 10th Street • Map M4 • Open 10am–5:50pm Mon–Sat, 11am–5:50pm Sun • Free*

9 Renwick Triangle

This handsome group of townhouses was created in 1861 by James Renwick, Jr., a prominent architect of the day. The houses are on land that was once Peter Stuyvesant's farm, developed by his descendants as a stylish residential area. ◈ *114–128 East 10th Street, 23–25 Stuyvesant Street, between 2nd & 3rd avs • Map M4*

10 Ukrainian Museum

Tucked away behind a gate is this tiny gem. Four floors of small galleries contain a beguiling collection of Ukrainian costumes, lavishly embroidered peasant blouses, colorful sashes, fancy sheepskin and fur vests, wedding wreaths of yarn and ribbons. There are also ceramics, jewelry, and the intricately designed Ukrainian Easter eggs known as *pysanky*. ◈ *203 2nd Avenue near 12th St • Map M4 • Open 1–5pm Wed–Sun • Admission charge*

East Side Exploration

Morning

Start at the Delancey Street subway stop at **Ratner's** *(see p95)*, where you can have coffee and a bagel. Or continue to Grand Street and Kossar's Bialystocker Bakery, 367 Grand, famous for chewy, onion-flavored rolls, or the Doughnut Plant, 379 Grand, where the oversize cakes achieve gourmet status. Walk east for two historic houses of worship, the **Beth Hamedrash Hagodol Synagogue** and the **Bialystoker Synagogue** *(see p91)*.

Return along East Broadway, passing the Henry Street Settlement at No. 281, in three restored Federal buildings. The gallery at the Educational Alliance, No. 197, has good art and photography exhibits. Walk to Essex for **Guss' Pickles**, then turn down Grand to Orchard Street for bargain shopping. Continue to East Houston Street, and have lunch at **Katz's Delicatessen** *(p95)*, a New York institution.

Afternoon

After lunch, walk uptown on 2nd Avenue, and turn down **St. Mark's Place**, browsing through the funky shops and bars, and then walk east again on Stuyvesant Street, admiring the landmark townhouses of the **Renwick Triangle** and **St. Mark's-in-the-Bowery Church**, one of the oldest in the city, where you can pay your respects to Peter Stuyvesant's grave. Continue north on Second Avenue to the **Ukrainian Museum**, a small and hidden gem of costumes and culture.

Around Town – Lower East Side & East Village

Left **Lismore Hosiery Co.** Right **Kleins of Monticello**

⁙⁰ Bargain Stores

1 Harry Zarin Fabric Warehouse
Since 1936 this mammoth showroom and workshop has provided fabrics and upholstery to the public at wholesale prices. ✎ *318 Grand Street • Map P5*

2 Fishkin Knitwear
Women's knits, clothing, and shoes by American, Italian, and French designers sold at discount. ✎ *314 Grand Street at Allen St • Map P5*

3 Forman's
Whatever your size, you will find it at these adjacent shops stocking brand-name women's fashions at discount prices. ✎ *78, 82, 94 and Orchard Street • Map P5*

4 Kleins of Monticello
One of the most attractive shops on the block offers well-tailored business and casual wear by American and European designers. ✎ *105 Orchard Street • Map N5*

5 Fine & Klein
Well-known for its wide selection of high quality handbags and accessories, most at a discount. ✎ *119 Orchard Street • Map N5*

6 Giselle Sportswear
Designer clothing by European names such as Valentino, Escada, and Ungaro, promising 20 to 30 percent off retail. ✎ *143 Orchard Street • Map N5*

7 Lismore Hosiery Co.
Stored away in boxes stacked floor to ceiling are name brands in underwear and socks for men and women at bargain prices. To take advantage of the savings, know the brand and size you need. ✎ *334 Grand Street • Map P5*

8 Salwen's Umbrellas
Need a really good umbrella, one that won't give in the first gust of wind? This merchant has been selling quality gear to ward off the weather at sunny prices since 1902. ✎ *45 Orchard Street • Map P5*

9 Altman Luggage
From computer cases to carry-ons, brand names like Lark, TravelPro, and American Tourister are sold for less at this well-stocked emporium. ✎ *135 Orchard Street • Map N5*

10 Harris Levy
One of the last survivors of what used to be rows of discount stores selling linens for table, bed, and bath. European linens and home accessories are a specialty at this store. ✎ *278 Grand Street • Map P5*

Katz's Delicatessen

Price Categories

For a three-course meal for one with half a botttle of wine (or equivalent meal), taxes and extra charges.

$	under $25
$$	$25–$50
$$$	$50–$80
$$$$	over $80

🔟 Restaurants

1 Ratner's and Lansky Lounge & Grill

The 100-year-old Ratner's serves blintzes by day, while Lansky's, once a speakeasy, now offers steak and chops to a hip crowd. ⓢ 138 Delancey Street at Norfolk St & 104 Norfolk St • Map N5 • 212 677 5588 & 212 677 9489 • $ & $$

2 Katz's Delicatessen

Savor a pastrami sandwich on rye here, and you'll understand why New York delis are famous. ⓢ 205 East Houston Street at Ludlow St • Map N5 • 212 254 2246 • $

3 Sammy's Roumanian

It looks like a Jewish wedding every night. Chopped liver and shmaltz will freak your cholesterol level, but you'll enjoy every minute. ⓢ 157 Chrystie Street • Map N4 • 212 673 0330 • No vegetarian options • $$

4 71 Clinton Fresh Food

A hip, foodie café famous for the exciting creations of chef Wylie Dufresne. Be prepared to wait. ⓢ 71 Clinton Street, between Rivington & Stanton sts • Map N5 • 212 614 6960 • $$

5 Le Père Pinard

A fine place to relax with wine and French bistro fare in the heated garden out back. ⓢ 175 Ludlow Street, between Houston & Stanton sts • Map N5 • 212 777 4917 • $$

6 Veselka

A funky Ukrainian diner serving borscht, blintzes, and pierogis for a pittance. Tables at the back are quieter. ⓢ 144 2nd Avenue at 9th St • Map M4 • 212 228 9682 • No credit cards • $

7 Daily Chow

A big Pan-Asian diner offering specialties from all of Asia and potent cocktails in the busy bar. ⓢ 2 East 2nd Street at the Bowery • Map N4 • 212 254 7887 • $

8 Jeollado

Korean pancakes or imaginative Japanese sushi keep this cavernous East Village hangout humming. ⓢ 116 East 4th Street at 1st Av • Map N5 • 212 260 7696 • No credit cards • $$

9 First

A late-opening café, where the continental dishes are creative, and the Sunday Sopranos special is an Italian feast. ⓢ 87 1st Avenue, between East 5th & 6th sts • Map N5 • 212 674 3823 • $$

10 Teresa's

Polish comfort food, guaranteed to fill you up without emptying your pockets. The pierogis and potato pancakes are perfection. ⓢ 103 1st Avenue, between East 6th & 7th sts • Map N5 • 212 228 0604 • No credit cards • $

Note: Unless otherwise stated, all restaurants accept credit cards and serve vegetarian meals

Left **Mural, Greene Street** Right **Haughwout Building**

SoHo and TriBeCa

<p>

UNTIL RECENTLY, THE AREA NAMED *for its shape (TRIangle BElow CAnal) consisted mostly of abandoned warehouses. Then Robert De Niro set up his Tribeca Film Center, stylish restaurants began to open, and the big loft spaces started to draw celebrity residents. Now TriBeCa is one of New York's hottest neighborhoods, the center of the city's movie industry with a TriBeCa Film Festival and plenty of nightlife. SoHo (South of Houston) has also come full circle. The empty loft spaces first drew artists, then galleries, then crowds of* browsers and the restaurants to serve them. The new chic image quickly drove up rents and drove out many galleries. Some remain, and the streets are lined with designer clothing and home furnishing boutiques, maintaining SoHo's lure as the city's favorite Sunday brunch-and-browse neighborhood. Both areas boast the cast-iron architecture that is a New York specialty.

Gallery, White Street

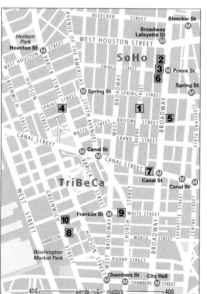

🔟 Sights

1 Greene Street
2 New Museum of Contemporary Art
3 Prada
4 New York City Fire Museum
5 Haughwout Building
6 "Little" Singer Building
7 Canal Street
8 Harrison Street
9 White Street
10 TriBeCa Film Center

Preceding pages **New York skyline at night**

1 Greene Street
Cast-iron architecture flourished in New York in the late 19th century, as a way to produce decorative elements such as columns and arches and create impressive buildings inexpensively. Greene Street, between Canal and Grand streets, and between Broome and Spring streets, has 50 of these beauties, rows of columned façades creating a striking streetscape. ◈ • Map N4

2 New Museum of Contemporary Art
This provocative and recently renovated museum in a SoHo cast-iron building is dedicated to work by living artists. Since its founding in 1977, it has mounted shows featuring experimental work that other museums often overlook, particularly new multi-media forms, which sometimes extend into intriguing window displays. ◈ Broadway, between Houston & Prince streets • Map N4 • Open noon–8pm Thu–Sat, noon–6pm Wed & Sun • Admission charge, free Thu after 6pm

3 Prada
The sign reads "Guggenheim SoHo" but the new occupant of the building is an extraordinary $40 million flagship store for trend-setting Italian retailer Prada, a sign of SoHo's shift from art to fashion. Dutch architect Rem Kookhaas is responsible for the ultra-hip floating stairs, undulating walls, futuristic elevators and hi-tech dressing rooms. The entire Prada line is on sale. ◈ 575 Broadway at Prince St • Map N4 • Open 11am–7pm Mon–Sat, 12–6pm Sun.

4 New York City Fire Museum
A nostalgic treasure housed in a 1904 firehouse, this splendid collection includes the city's fire-fighting engines, equipment, garb and memorabilia from the 18th century to the present. A moving photo display depicts the World Trade Centre attack and honors the hundreds of firefighters lost there. ◈ 278 Spring Street • Map N3 • Open 10am–5pm Tue–Sat, 10am–4pm Sun • Admission charge

Left **New Museum of Contemporary Art** Right **Prada**

5 Haughwout Building

A cast-iron masterpiece, this structure was built to house a fashionable china and glassware emporium. The design of colonnaded arches flanked by taller Corinthian columns was adapted from the façade of the Sansovino Library in Venice. This motif is repeated 92 times across the front of the building. A 1995 restoration removed grime and restored the elegant original pale color. This building boasted the first Otis safety elevator, an innovation that made the skyscraper possible.
Ⓢ 490 Broadway at Broome St • Map P4

6 "Little" Singer Building

By the early 1900s, cast iron was giving way to steel-framed brick and terra-cotta. One notable example is Ernest Flagg's "Little" Singer Building (to distinguish it from a taller tower also built for Singer). Influenced by Parisian architecture of the period, it has a charming 12-story façade and graceful cast-iron balconies. Ⓢ 561–3 Broadway, between Prince & Spring sts • Map N4

Haughwout Building

TriBeCa's Movie Business

TriBeCa is known as Hollywood East, and although much of its movie business is behind the scenes, many screenings take place. Big name stars have been sighted heading for the Grand Screen Room at the TriBeCa Grand Hotel (see p177).
The TriBeCa Film Festival, begun in 2002, promises to be a further star-spotting event.

7 Canal Street

The end of SoHo, the beginning of TriBeCa, and a world of its own, no street better shows the contrasts of New York. Canal Street is crowded with peddlers selling fake Rolex watches and Gucci bags, electronics that may or may not be new, and bargain stores offering sneakers, jeans, and flea-market finds. Keep walking east into Chinatown, and the sidewalk goods shift to vegetables and displays of fish. Ⓢ Map P3–4

8 Harrison Street

This rare group of Federal townhouses, built between 1796 and 1828, did not exist as a row until 1975, when the houses

Left "Little" Singer Building Right Canal Street

Harrison Street

were moved to this site to be saved from the urban renewal that razed much of the area. At the end of the block (No. 6) is the former New York Mercantile Exchange, a Queen Anne building dating from 1884 and in use until 1977 when the Exchange moved to the World Financial Center (see p45). 🔗 Map P3

9 White Street

The best example of cast-iron architecture in TriBeCa is a sampling of several styles. No. 2 has Federal features and a gambrel roof; Nos. 8–10, designed by Henry Fernbach in 1869, sport Tuscan columns and arches and use the Neo-Renaissance device of building shorter upper stories to give an illusion of height. There is a complete change of pace at No. 38, which houses neon artist Rudi Stern's gallery, Let There Be Neon. 🔗 Map P3–4

10 TriBeCa Film Center

A turn-of-the-century coffee warehouse has been converted into office space for the film and entertainment industry. The guiding spirit was Robert De Niro, whose TriBeCa Productions was founded in 1988. Miramax has set up offices here and the building is also home to the TriBeCa Grill, owned by De Niro and restaurateur Drew Nieporent. The restaurant has managed to maintain its star appeal for over a decade. 🔗 375 Greenwich Street • Map P3

A Stroll Around SoHo and TriBeCa

Morning

🕐 The Bleecker Street subway stop is a good starting point to explore SoHo's shops and galleries. **Greene Street** (see p99) has a number of interesting boutiques, such as Plein Sud, Helmut Lang, and Vivienne Tam. Galleries worth a visit in this area are Beizel, No. 102, Kent, No. 67 Prince Street, and Haller, No. 560, and Ross, No. 568 Broadway.

The Drawing Center (see p43) exhibits work from emerging artists and is great for poetry readings. This is also a prime area for photography galleries. The most interesting are Ariel Meyerowitz, No. 580, Janet Borden, No. 560 Broadway, and Howard Greenberg and 292 Gallery at 120 Wooster Street. Stop for a pancake lunch at Palacinka, 28 Grand Street, between 6th Avenue and Thompson Street.

Afternoon

Drop in on designer boutiques Miu Miu, 100 Prince Street, and Anna Sui, 113 Greene Street, before proceeding to TriBeCa. Take a stroll along **White** and **Harrison** streets to view the historic architecture and stop for a drink at the **Church Lounge** (see p102).

Spend the rest of the afternoon taking in the exhibits at the Apex Art Gallery, 291 Church Street, and the Ace Gallery, 275 Hudson Street, a cavernous space showing large-scale art. Make your way to **Dylan Prime** (see p102) for an early evening cocktail then head for **The Screening Room** (see p102) for dinner followed by a film in the bar's intimate theater.

Left **The Screening Room** Center **Dylan Prime** Right **Temple Bar**

Nightlife

1 The Screening Room
The ultimate movie date. Enjoy chic bistro dining, then head for the intimate theater showing a mix of current films and revivals. ◎ *54 Varick Street at Laight St • Map N3 • 212 334 2100*

2 Church Lounge
Almost the entire ground floor of the hotel is devoted to this popular bar with plush seats and a dramatic eight-story atrium. ◎ *TriBeCa Grand Hotel, 2 Sixth Avenue • Map N3 • 212 519 6600*

3 Dylan Prime
An extensive cocktail menu, and an attractive space with lofty ceilings help make this a current hotspot. ◎ *62 Laight Street, between Greenwich & Collister sts • Map P3 • 212 334 4783*

4 Liquor Store Bar
The building dates to 1804 and was once a liquor store, but now it's a comfortable, low-key place to have a beer. ◎ *235 West Broadway at White St • Map P3 • 212 226 7121*

5 The Sporting Club
You'll never miss a game in this popular, memorabilia-filled sports lounge crammed with giant TV screens. ◎ *99 Hudson Street, between Franklin & Leonard sts • Map P3 • 212 219 0900*

6 Puck Fair
At this cosy multi-level pub you can settle in to enjoy a pint along with tasty Irish snacks. ◎ *289 Lafayette Street, between Houston & Prince sts • Map N4 • 212 431 1200*

7 Grand Bar
Like its sister TriBeCa Grand, the SoHo Grand is a neighborhood nightlife mecca, comfortable, softly lit, with food if you want it, and filled with beautiful people. ◎ *SoHo Grand Hotel, 310 West Broadway, between Canal & Grand sts • Map P3 • 212 965 3000*

8 Merc Bar
This trendy SoHo meeting place attracts all manner of sophisticates who dig the mountain lodge decor. ◎ *151 Mercer Street, between Houston & Prince sts • Map N4 • 212 966 2727*

9 Temple Bar
Dark, swanky, sexy, and pricey, but the martinis are mammoth. A good place to bring a date – or find one. ◎ *332 Lafayette Street, between Bleeker & East Houston sts • Map N4 • 212 925 4242*

10 The Room
The Room is a friendly, candle-lit place with no hard liquor, but 60 kinds of beer and 20 wines. ◎ *144 Sullivan Street, between Prince & Houston sts • Map N3 • 212 477 2102*

For more New York bars and lounges See pp54–5

Price Categories

For a three-course meal for one with half a bottle of wine (or equivalent meal), taxes and extra charges.

$	under $25
$$	$25–$50
$$$	$50–$80
$$$$	over $80

Left **Montrachet** Right **Balthazar**

⁑ Restaurants

1 Danube
Light as air "nouveau Austrian" food at David Bouley's warm and wonderful TriBeCa restaurant *(see p68)*. ✆ 30 *Hudson Street • Map P3 • 212 791 3771 • $$$$*

2 Nobu
Nobu Matsuhisa's sublime Japanese/Peruvian fusion fare in a whimsical setting *(see p68)*. ✆ *105 Hudson Street • Map P3 • 212 219 0500 • $$$$*

3 Nobu Next Door
The no-reservations policy at this restaurant means you might get to taste the famous Nobu black cod with miso. ✆ *106 Hudson Street at Franklin St • Map P3 • 212 334 4445 • $$$*

4 Bouley Bakery
David Bouley can't go wrong when it comes to food. The room isn't memorable, but the New French cuisine is heavenly. ✆ *120 West Broadway at Duane St • Map P3 • 212 964 2525 • $$$*

5 Montrachet
The first of Drew Nieporent's restaurant empire still ranks among the city's best, known for its casual decor, modern French cuisine, and exceptional wine list. ✆ *239 West Broadway, nr West Broadway & North Moore sts • Map P3 • 212 219 2777 • $$$$*

6 Le Zinc
The proprietors of the very haute Chanterelle have opened a welcome informal bistro, which is open until 4am. Onion fritters and skate are recommended. ✆ *139 Duane Street, between Church St & West Broadway • Map P3 • 212 513 0001 • $$*

7 Balthazar
As close to a Parisian bistro as you're likely to find in SoHo, Balthazar's only problem is its popularity. A buzzing scene. ✆ *80 Spring Street at Broadway • Map N3 • 212 965 1414 • $$$*

8 Raoul's
Another bit of the Left Bank in SoHo, with an updated French menu and a great garden. ✆ *180 Prince Street, between Sullivan & Thompson sts • Map N4 • 212 966 3518 • $$$*

9 The Odeon
Art Deco decor, consistently good food, and a star-studded crowd keeps the vibe right, even after 20 years. ✆ *145 Broadway at Thomas Street • Map P3 • 212 233 0507 • $$$*

10 Hampton Chutney Co.
Perfect for an inexpensive snack of *dosas*: crêpes stuffed with creative combinations. ✆ *68 Prince Street • Map N4 • 212 226 9996 • $*

Note: Unless otherwise stated, all restaurants accept credit cards and serve vegetarian meals

Left **Washington Square Park** Center **Jefferson Market Courthouse** Right **Bar on Bleecker Street**

Greenwich Village

IT WAS DIFFERENT FROM THE START, *a crazy pattern of streets that broke from the city's grid plan, reflecting the boundaries of a rural village. As a bohemian haven, the leafy lanes of the Village have been home to artists and writers. Jazz musicians, beat poets, and performers like the young Bob Dylan found their places here. Later it became popular with gays, and today cafés and funky shops attract the young from all over the city. The village really comes to life at night, when cafés, theaters, and clubs beckon at every turn.*

Sights

1. Washington Square Park
2. MacDougal Alley
3. Washington Mews
4. Grove Court
5. Jefferson Market Courthouse
6. Cherry Lane Theater
7. Bleecker Street
8. New York University
9. Judson Memorial Church
10. 75½ Bedford Street

Balconies, Greenwich Village

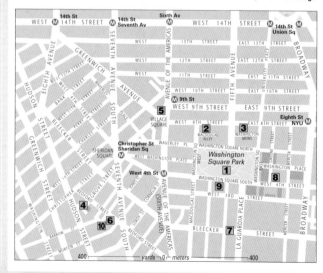

1 Washington Square Park

In 1826, a marshy area was filled to form this popular park. The marble arch by Stanford White went up in 1895, replacing a wooden version that marked the centenary of George Washington's inauguration. Mothers with strollers, chess players, and young lovers now occupy benches where drug dealers once reigned. The fountain in the center is where Bob Dylan sang his first folk songs. ⬡ *5th Avenue, between Waverly Pl & 4th St • Map N3*

2 MacDougal Alley

These 19th-century stables for the fine homes on Washington Square North were converted into studios by artists early in the 20th century, causing the street to be known as "Art Alley de Luxe." Among the residents were painter Guy Pene du Bois and sculptor Gertrude Vanderbilt Whitney, who established the first Whitney Museum in 1914 at 8 West 8th Street, adjoining her studio. ⬡ *East of MacDougal Street, between 8th St & Waverly Pl • Map M3*

3 Washington Mews

Another group of stables turned into houses around 1900, the Mews attracted both writers and artists. No. 14A housed, at various times, author John Dos Passos and artists Edward Hopper, William Glackens, and Rockwell Kent. Writer Sherwood Anderson often stayed at No. 54 with his friend and patron, Mary Emmett. In contrast to the modern buildings in much of Manhattan, this type of quaint enclave is the reason many find the Village so appealing. ⬡ *University Place to 5th Avenue • Map M3*

4 Grove Court

This group of six townhouses in a bend in the street was developed by grocer Samuel Cocks, who thought that having residents nearby would help his business at No. 18. But while such private courts are prized today, they were not considered respectable in the 1850s, and the disreputable types who moved in earned it the nickname "Mixed Ale Alley." O. Henry used the block as the setting for *The Last Leaf*. ⬡ *Grove Street near Bedford St • Map N3*

Left **MacDougal Street** Right **Grove Court**

5 Jefferson Market Courthouse

The site was a market in 1833, named after the former president, Thomas Jefferson. The fire lookout tower had a giant bell that alerted volunteer firefighters. When the courthouse was built in 1877, the bell was installed in its clock tower. The building became a treasured Village landmark, and, after the market had moved and court sessions were discontinued, it was eventually saved from demolition after a spirited local campaign and converted into a branch of the New York Public Library *(see p124)* in the 1950s. ✪ *425 6th Avenue, between 9th & 10th sts • Map M3 • Open noon–8pm Mon, Wed, 10am–6pm Tue,Thu, noon–6pm Fri, 10am–5pm Sat • Free*

6 Cherry Lane Theatre

In 1924, a warehouse was converted into one of the first Off-Broadway theaters and showcased plays by the likes of Edward Albee, Eugene Ionesco, David Mamet, and Harold Pinter. Today, the "Cherry Lane Alternative" uses established playwrights to mentor talented newcomers. ✪ *38 Commerce Street, between Bedford & Barrow sts • Map N3 • 212 989 2020*

7 Bleecker Street

The present line-up of ordin-ary shops and restaurants belies the history of this street. James

The Halloween Parade

Anything goes in this wildly gaudy annual parade of cross-dressers and amazing costumes. It draws 25,000 marchers and many times that many spectators. The parade route goes up 6th Avenue, from the Village to 23rd Street, starting at 7pm.

Fenimore Cooper lived at No. 145 in 1833, Theodore Dreiser stayed at No. 160 when he came to New York in 1895, and James Agee lived at No. 172 from 1941 to 1951. The café at No. 189, the corner of Bleecker and MacDougal, was the San Remo bar, the favorite gathering place for William Burroughs, Allen Ginsberg, Gregory Corso, and Jack Kerouac, leading lights of the beat generation. ✪ *Between 6th Avenue & West Broadway • Map N3*

8 New York University

Founded in 1831, N.Y.U. enlarged the scope of early 19th-century study from its previous concentration on Greek and Latin to contemporary subjects: a "rational and practical education" for those aspiring to careers in business, industry, science, and the arts, as well as in law, medicine, and the ministry. It has grown into the largest private university in America and now occupies many blocks around Washington Square. ✪ *Washington Square • Map N4*

Left **Cherry Lane Theater** Right **Bleecker Street**

9 Judson Memorial Church

An elegant work in Romanesque style by Stanford White, with stained glass by John La Farge, the church was built in 1888–93 as a memorial to Adoniram Judson, the first American Baptist missionary in Asia. John D. Rockefeller, Jr. *(see p48)* contributed to the construction. White's use of mottled yellow brick and white terra-cotta trim introduced light coloration into American church architecture. ◈ *55 Washington Square South • Map N3 • Open for services 11am Sun • Free*

10 75½ Bedford Street

Ever quirky, New York's narrowest home, just 9.5 ft (3 m) wide, was built in 1893 in a passageway in the Village. Poet Edna St. Vincent Millay lived here, as did actors John Barrymore and, later, Cary Grant. No. 77 Bedford Street is the oldest house in the Village, dating from around 1799, and at No. 103 is the house known as "Twin Peaks," an 1830 structure remodeled in 1925 by Clifford Reed Daily to house artists and writers, who would presumably be inspired by the whimsical architecture. ◈ *Between Morton & Barrow sts • Map N3*

A Village Stroll

Morning

Begin at **Washington Square** *(p108)* and the elegant townhouse row where Edith Wharton and Henry James once lived. Find the charming houses of **Washington Mews** and **MacDougal Alley** *(p105)*, then follow 6th Avenue, past Balducci's famous gourmet market, to West 10th Street.

Stroll down the passageway at the front of the Alexander Onassis Center for Hellenic Studies. This walkway once led up to the Tile Club, a gathering place for the artists of the Tenth Street Studio, where Augustus Saint-Gaudens, John La Farge, and Winslow Homer lived and worked. Continue along Waverly Place, Grove Steet, and Bedford Street, each with its share of prize townhouse architecture. Have lunch at a typical Village bistro like **Café Loup** *(see p109)*.

Afternoon

After lunch, spend a few hours in the local shops. Vintage clothing can be admired at specialty shops such as Antique Boutique, 712 Broadway at Waverly, and Cheap Jack's, 841 Broadway between 13th and 14th streets, while across the street at No. 840 is Forbidden Planet, a nirvana for comic book fanatics.

West 8th Street and West 4th Street are also crammed with shops, and several coffeehouses are great for people-watching. Try Caffe Reggio, 119 MacDougal Street, where the literary lights of the beat generation used to read their poetry.

Left **Washington Mews** Center **Chumley's** Right **White Horse Tavern**

Literary Landmarks

1 Washington Square
Prominent figures who lived here include Edith Wharton at No. 7 in 1882. Henry James was born at No. 21 in 1843. 🔗 *Map N3*

2 St. Luke's Place
Poet Marianne Moore lived here, and Theodore Dreiser wrote *An American Tragedy* at No. 16. 🔗 *Between Hudson Street & 7th Avenue South • Map N3*

3 Patchin Place
A charming pocket of 19th-century houses that later attracted ee cummings, John Masefield, and Eugene O'Neill, among others. 🔗 *West 10th Street • Map N3*

4 Chumley's
Book covers of Steinbeck, Hemingway, Faulkner, and others who drank here adorn the walls of this prohibition-era speakeasy. 🔗 *86 Bedford Street • Map N3*

5 White Horse Tavern
Favorite hangout of Norman Mailer and Dylan Thomas, who announced one night in 1953, "I've had 18 straight whiskeys," and passed out. He died the next day. 🔗 *567 Hudson Street at 11th St • Map N3*

6 Willa Cather Residence
Willa Cather wrote six novels here and her Friday "at homes" were attended by the likes of D. H. Lawrence. 🔗 *5 Bank Street, between West & Greenwich sts • Map N3 • Closed to public*

7 Mark Twain Residence
A plaque marks the home (1904–08) of Mark Twain, designed by James Renwick, Jr., architect of St. Patrick's Cathedral. Twain received guests while propped up in a huge carved bed. 🔗 *21 Fifth Avenue at 9th St • Map M3 • Closed to public*

8 William Styron Residence
This was Styron's first "tiny but rather nice" apartment after writing *Lie Down in Darkness* aged 23. 🔗 *43 Greenwich Avenue • Map M3 • Closed to public*

9 Edward Albee Residence
Albee wrote *The Zoo Story* here. He first saw the words "Who's Afraid of Virginia Woolf?" written in soap on a saloon mirror nearby. 🔗 *238 West 4th Street • Map N3 • Closed to public*

10 West 10th Street
Mark Twain lived at No. 14 in 1900–1, Hart Crane at No. 54 in 1917, and Edward Albee lived in the carriage house at No. 50 during the 1960s. 🔗 *Map M3 • Closed to public*

For more on figures in New York history See pp48–9

Left **Babbo** Right **Blue Ribbon Bakery**

Price Categories

For a three-course meal for one with half a bottle of wine (or equivalent meal), taxes and extra charges.

$	under $25
$$	$25–$50
$$$	$50–$80
$$$$	over $80

🔟 Restaurants

1 Babbo
An attractive setting and the inventive Italian fare make this very popular; reserve in advance. ✆ *110 Waverly Place • Map N3 • 212 777 0303 • $$$*

2 Il Mulino
Another top Italian. Quality is consistent, portions large, the brick-walled room inviting. ✆ *86 West 3rd Street, between Sullivan & Thompson sts • Map N3 • 212 673 3783 • $$$*

3 Blue Hill
Highly praised New American fare served in intimate, elegant surroundings. ✆ *75 Washington Place at MacDougal St • Map N3 • 212 539 1776 • $$$*

4 Blue Ribbon Bakery
A casual Village favorite with an enormous, eclectic menu of comfort foods, including the signature fried chicken. ✆ *33 Downing Street at Bedford St • Map N3 • 212 337 0404 • $$*

5 Cafe de Bruxelles
Mussels, frites, and fabulous Belgian beer can't be beat at this comfortable restaurant. ✆ *118 Greenwich Avenue • Map M3 • 212 206 1830 • $$*

6 Cafe Loup
An agreeable French bistro, where favorite dishes include tuna carpaccio, steak, and roast chicken. ✆ *105 West 13th Street • Map M3 • 212 255 4746 • $$*

7 Da Silvano
Watch the celebrities come and go from a table outside. The northern Italian fare here is consistent, and the buzz even better. ✆ *260 Sixth Avenue, between Bleecker & West Houston sts • Map N3 • 212 982 2343 • $$$*

8 Home
Food like Mom used to make (provided she was a terrific cook) keeps this narrow café crowded. The patio provides a breath of fresh air. ✆ *20 Cornelia Street, between Bleeker St & 6th Avenue • Map N3 • 212 243 9579 • $$*

9 Pastis
Hot, hot, hot is this straight-out-of-Paris café; order steak frites or escargots, and get into the spirit of things. ✆ *9 9th Avenue at Little West 12th St • Map M2 • 212 929 4844 • $$$*

🔟 Rio Mar
There are free tapas at the bar, and seafood paella, sangria, and a cozy, rustic setting upstairs. ✆ *7 9th Avenue at Little West 12th St • Map M2 • 212 243 9105 • $$*

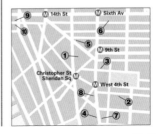

Note: Unless otherwise stated, all restaurants accept credit cards and serve vegetarian meals

Left **Gramercy Park** Center foreground **Metropolitan Life Tower** Right **Rooftops on Broadway**

Union Square, Gramercy Park, and Flatiron

CHANGE IS IN THE AIR *in this flourishing section of Manhattan. Union Square, once a hangout for drug dealers and scene of protest rallies, has been renovated and transformed. A Greenmarket fills the square with fresh produce four times a week, drawing patrons from all over the city, and the neighborhood around the square is attracting an increasing number of new apartments, shops, and restaurants. The shops and lively eating places now extend up Fifth Avenue into the once-neglected Flatiron District, named for the building at the intersection of Fifth Avenue and Broadway at 23rd Street. Quiet Madison Square, opposite the Flatiron Building, recently became the site of two of the city's hottest restaurants and is receiving its own restoration. No change was needed in Gramercy Park, the most European of the city's neighborhoods.*

Fantasy Fountain, Greg Wyatt, Gramercy Park

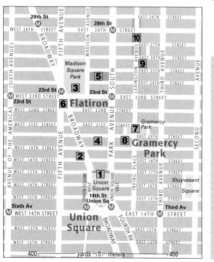

🔟 Sights

1. **Union Square Greenmarket**
2. **ABC Carpet & Home**
3. **Madison Square**
4. **Theodore Roosevelt Birthplace**
5. **Metropolitan Life Tower**
6. **Flatiron Building**
7. **Gramercy Park**
8. **National Arts Club**
9. **69th Regiment Armory**
10. **"Curry Hill"**

Union Square Greenmarket

Herbs and berries, miniature vegetables, fresh flowers and home-baked pastries, newly woven yarns, hams, honey – all of these and more can be found at the bountiful Greenmarket that fills Union Square each Monday, Wednesday, Friday, and Saturday. More than 200 regional farmers take part in the market, each offering only goods that they have grown or made. A colorful New York scene not to be missed. ⊗ *At Broadway & 14th Street • Map M4*

ABC Carpet & Home

The city's most eclectic emporium, two landmark buildings that are part flea market, part antiques fair, and part Middle Eastern bazaar. Offerings include fancy French or rugged Mexican furniture, antiques and reproductions, fabrics and accessories, linens, bedding, flowers, foods, and a whole building for rugs. There are two dining places: Chicama *(see pp115)* and Pipa. ⊗ *881 & 888 Broadway at East 19th St • Map L4*

Madison Square

The square opened in 1847 at the center of a fine residential area where politician Theodore Roosevelt and writer Edith Wharton were born. The original Madison Square Garden was here, at Madison Avenue and 26th Street. Later office development brought distinguished sites such as the Flatiron and Metropolitan Life buildings. Today the statue-filled park is being renovated and the area rediscovered. ⊗ *23rd to 26th sts, between Broadway & Madison Av • Map L3*

Theodore Roosevelt Birthplace

The boyhood home where the colorful 26th President was born in 1858 has been reconstructed. Exhibits trace his political career as well as his explorations, displaying everything from toys to campaign buttons, and emblems of the trademark "Rough Rider" hat Roosevelt wore in the Spanish-American war. The house offers a rare glimpse of a privileged 19th-century New York lifestyle. ⊗ *28 East 20th Street, between Broadway & Park Av South • Map L4 • Open 9am–5pm Mon–Fri • Admission charge*

Left **Madison Square** Right **Theodore Roosevelt Birthplace**

5 Metropolitan Life Tower

This 54-story tower, built along the east side of Madison Square in 1909, was the world's tallest building at that time, an appropriate corporate symbol for the world's largest insurance company. Designed by Napoleon Le Brun and Sons, the tower follows the form of the campanile in the Piazza San Marco in Venice. Although it was altered in the 1960s, when the entire structure was renovated, the ornate four-faced clock and crowning cupola remain, a familiar landmark on the New York skyline. ◈ *1 Madison Avenue, near 24th St • Map L4 • Open during office hours • Free*

6 Flatiron Building

Though dwarfed by countless taller structures today, this unusual building – its shape conforming to a triangular plot of land – remains striking, a symbol of the beginning of the skyscraper era. Its slim, rounded façade is as proud as a ship's prow sailing up the avenue. Completed in 1903, it anchored the north end of the prestigious Ladies' Mile shopping district, located between Union and Madison squares. The designer, famous Chicago architect Daniel Burnham, included detailed Italian Renaissance decoration on the building from top to bottom, much of it in terra-cotta. ◈ *175 Fifth Avenue at Broadway & 23rd St • Map L3 • Open office hours • Free*

Flatiron Building

7 Gramercy Park

Samuel Ruggles laid out this neighborhood around a private park in the 1830s. It remains the city's only private park and a desirable place to live. Stanford White remodeled No. 16 in 1888 for Edwin Booth, who founded the Players Club here. His statue stands in the park *(see pp114).* ◈ *Lexington Avenue, between 20th & 21st sts • Map L4 • Closed to public*

8 National Arts Club

Originally the home of Samuel Tilden, a governor of New York and opponent of the notorious Boss Tweed *(see pp48–9).* The Gothic Revival brownstone was designed by Calvert Vaux, of Central Park fame. The National Arts Club, whose members have included leading American artists since the 1800s, bought the building in 1906. Each member is asked to donate a work to the club. Its galleries are open to the public. ◈ *15 Gramercy Park South • Map L4*

Writers' faces, National Arts Club

9 69th Regiment Armory

This Beaux Arts building was used as the drill hall and offices of a military unit privately formed in 1848. In 1913, the controversial exhibition of modern art known as the Armory Show was held here, including works by Van Gogh, Duchamp, and Brancusi. The show was widely panned in the press, but it brought modern art to New York on a large scale and had a profound and lasting affect on American art. ⊗ *Lexington Avenue, between 25th & 26th sts • Map L4 • Closed to public*

10 "Curry Hill"

Despite changes around it, this three-block corridor just south of Murray Hill remains filled with Indian shops selling saris and gifts, and is lined with restaurants that are a boon for diners (particularly vegetarians) in search of interesting food at reasonable prices. Kalustyan's, 123 Lexington Avenue, is a treasure trove of fragrant spices and grains and features some 31 different kinds of rice.
⊗ *Lexington Avenue, between 26th & 29th sts • Map L4*

Exploring Gramercy Park and Flatiron

Morning

🕐 Book-lovers should start on 12th Street, where the city's biggest used bookstore, the Strand, is located at No. 828. From here, head north up Broadway to Union Square, visiting the **Greenmarket** *(see p111)*. Continuing up Broadway brings you to the Paragon Sports superstore, 867 Broadway at 18th Street, and Fishs Eddy, 889 Broadway at 19th, selling all but indestructible vintage and new china. The fascinating **ABC Carpet & Home** awaits at No. 888 *(see p111)*.

At the **Flatiron Building**, turn east to **Madison Square** *(p111)*, then have lunch at **Tabla** or the gourmet **11 Madison Park** *(p115)*. Several restaurants on **"Curry Hill"** also offer inexpensive lunches, Including Pongal, No. 110, and Chatkhara Kebab House, No. 103.

Afternoon

🕐 While you are in the neighborhood, check out the intriguing spices at Kalustyan's, 123 Lexington Avenue.

More shops can be found on Fifth Avenue between 14th and 23rd streets, including Emporio Armani, No. 110, between 16th & 17th and Daffy's, No. 111, a discount store offering designer finds.

End your day in the civilized oasis of the **Gramercy Park** neighborhood. Be sure to stroll East 19th Street, known as the "Block Beautiful," for its handsome 1920s houses.

Left **Farragut Monument** Center **George Washington** Right **Marquis de Lafayette**

Statues and Monuments

1 George Washington
The city's first major outdoor statue was created in 1856 by Henry Kirke Brown. The statue is a 14-foot (4.26-metre) equestrian figure on a granite pedestal. ✪ *Union Square facing 14th St • Map M4*

2 Abraham Lincoln
This pensive figure by Henry Kirke Brown was commissioned shortly after the president's assassination in 1865. ✪ *North end of Union Square near 16th St • Map M4*

3 Marquis de Lafayette
A larger-than-life 1873 statue of Lafayette pledging his heart to the American Revolution by Frédéric-Auguste Bartholdi, creator of the Statue of Liberty. ✪ *Madison Square • Map L3–4*

4 Mohandas K (Mahatma) Gandhi
The site for this 1986 statue of the hero of Indian independence was chosen because the park was frequently the site of protest gatherings. ✪ *Union Square • Map M4*

5 Edwin Booth as Hamlet
The founder of the Players Club is shown in his most famous role, about to give Hamlet's soliloquy. The 1917 statue faces his former house. ✪ *Gramercy Park • Map L4*

6 Fantasy Fountain
Greg Wyatt's 1983 smiling sun and moon flanked by dancing giraffes, from whose mouths water flows in warm weather. ✪ *Southeast corner of Gramercy Park • Map L4*

7 Worth Monument
An 1850s obelisk marks the grave of the only public figure buried under the streets of Manhattan, General Worth, hero of the Mexican Wars. ✪ *Traffic Island, 23rd Street & Broadway • Map L3*

8 Farragut Monument
This 1880 memorial to a naval hero established Augustus Saint-Gaudens as the nation's foremost sculptor; Stanford White designed the base. ✪ *Madison Square • Map L3–4*

9 Chester Alan Arthur
Arthur became the 21st President when James Garfield was assassinated. George Edwin Bissell sculpted him in 1898, standing in front of an elaborate chair. ✪ *Madison Square • Map L3–4*

10 William Seward
In 1876 Randolph Rogers immortalized the secretary of state under Lincoln, best remembered for his much-criticized purchase of Alaska in 1867. ✪ *Madison Square • Map L3–4*

Around Town – Union Square, Gramercy Park, & Flatiron

Price Categories

For a three-course meal for one with half a bottle of wine (or equivalent meal), taxes and extra charges.

$	under $25
$$	$25–$50
$$$	$50–$80
$$$$	over $80

Tabla, Madison Avenue

🔟 Restaurants

1 Union Square Café
One of New York's most popular restaurants uses ingredients from the neighboring Union Square Greenmarket *(see p68)*. ◈ *21 East 16th Street at Union Square West • Map M4 • 212 243 4020 • $$$*

2 Gramercy Tavern
Unpretentious fine dining where the inventive American cuisine is universally praised. Great desserts *(see p69)*. ◈ *42 East 20th Street at Broadway • Map L4 • $$$*

3 11 Madison Park
Danny Meyer has made 11 Madison Square chic with his imaginative New American cuisine in an elegant Art Deco setting. ◈ *Madison Avenue at East 24th St • Map L4 • 212 889 0905 • $$$*

4 AZ
Magical American/Asian fusion; every dish is delicious, and the rooftop space heavenly. ◈ *21 West 17th Street at 5th Av • Map M3 • 212 691 8888 • $$$*

5 Tabla and Tabla Bread Bar
Another Danny Meyer success on Madison Square; New American with Indian seasonings, served in colorful surroundings. ◈ *11 Madison Avenue at East 25th St • Map L4 • 212 889 0667 • Tabla $$$$ Bread Bar $$*

6 Union Pacific
The dramatic setting and Rocco DiSpirito's bold menu help make this a neighborhood hotspot. ◈ *111 East 22nd Street, between Park Av South & Lexington Av • Map L4 • 212 995 8500 • $$$$*

7 Patria
Latin American gone gourmet; creative dishes are beautifully presented here in a festive setting. Prices are lower at lunchtime. ◈ *250 Park Avenue South at East 20th St • Map L4 • 212 777 6211 • $$$*

8 Veritas
An amazing wine list is the big draw, but the New American cuisine is also outstanding. Reserve ahead. ◈ *43 East 20th Street, between Broadway & Park Av South • Map L4 • 212 353 3700 • $$$$*

9 Chicama
A bold, pan-Latin menu is served in a rustic wood-beamed room with cheerful decor. ◈ *35 East 18th Street at Broadway • Map M4 • 212 505 2233 • $$$*

10 Mavalli Palace
This "Curry Hill" favorite, with walls lined with carvings, serves some interesting South Indian vegetarian dishes. ◈ *46 East 29th Street at Madison Av • Map L4 • 212 679 5535 • $$*

➤ **Note:** *Unless otherwise stated, all restaurants accept credit cards and serve vegetarian meals*

115

Left **Macy's façade** Center **Ornamental clock, Herald Square** Right **Chelsea Piers**

Chelsea and Herald Square

A NEIGHBORHOOD that has seen a great deal of recent change, Chelsea was a quiet enclave of 19th-century brownstones that never made it as a fashionable address. Now it is a hub for gay New Yorkers and center for the city's avant-garde art galleries. Buildings along 6th Avenue are now occupied by superstores and discount outlets, and to the west, Chelsea Piers has transformed the waterfront. Uptown, the Garment District begins around 27th Street, with Herald Square and Macy's at the heart of the city's busiest shopping area.

🔟 Sights

1. 6th Avenue Shopping
2. Annex Antiques and Flea Market
3. Flower District
4. Chelsea Hotel
5. Chelsea Historic District
6. General Theological Seminary
7. Chelsea Piers
8. Fashion Institute of Technology (F.I.T.)
9. Herald Square
10. Macy's

Cheerleaders at Macy's

1 6th Avenue Shopping

Anchored by Macy's, which opened in 1858, this was once a popular district known as "Fashion Row". The 1876 cast-iron façade of the Hugh O'Neill Dry Goods Store at Nos. 655–71 exemplifies the era, when the arrival of the 6th Avenue elevated line provided easy access to the area. As Manhattan's commercial center moved northward, these cast-iron palaces were left deserted until recently, when they found new life as bargain fashion outlets and superstores. ✆ *6th Avenue, 18th to 23rd sts • Map L3*

2 Annex Antiques and Flea Market

On weekends, year-round, an empty parking lot becomes one of the city's most popular outdoor markets. A tradition for more than 30 years, some 600 dealers, from Maine to Maryland, set up booths selling clothing, silver, jewelry, furniture, art, and "junktiques" from old tools to vintage eyeglasses. Many prize antiques can be discovered at The Garage, an indoor market just around the corner at 112 West 25th Street, and at The Showplace, 40 West 25th Street, with 135 dealers on three floors. ✆ *6th Avenue at 25th St • Map L3 • Open sunrise to sunset • Admission charge*

3 Flower District

Here, at the heart of the city's wholesale flower district, you can hardly see the sidewalk for the masses of greenery, shrubs, and flowers. Manhattan's largest concentration of shops selling houseplants, trees, blooming plants, and all manner of flowers, fresh, dried, and artificial can be found here; if you can't find what you want, it probably doesn't exist. The district extends along 6th Avenue roughly from 25th to 30th streets. ✆ *6th Avenue at 27th St • Map L3*

Facade, Chelsea Hotel

4 Chelsea Hotel

Seedy it is, yet there's a definite mystique to this 1884 building bedecked with wrought-iron balconies. Once a fancy apartment, it became a hotel favored by musicians, artists, and writers. Former guests, commemorated on brass plaques outside, include Tennessee Williams, Mark Twain, Jack Kerouac, and Brendan Behan. Dylan Thomas spent his last years here. Notoriously, it was also the place where punk rocker Sid Vicious killed his girlfriend Nancy Spungeon in 1978. Step into the lobby and take a look at the wild artwork, and soak up the ambience at the bar. ✆ *212 West 23rd Street, between 7th & 8th avs • Map L3*

Left **The Flower District** Right **Chelsea Hotel, cast-iron stairwell**

5 Chelsea Historic District

Clement Moore, author of *A Visit from St. Nicholas*, developed this land in the 1830s. The finest of the townhouses built here are the seven known as "Cushman Row," Nos. 406–18 West 20th Street, which are among the city's best examples of Greek Revival architecture. Houses at Nos. 446–50 West 20th are in the Italianate style, for which Chelsea is also known. ✈ *Between 9th & 10th avenues, 20th & 21st sts • Map L2*

6 General Theological Seminary

America's oldest Episcopal seminary was founded in 1819. This campus was built around two quadrangles in the 1830s, on a site donated by Clement Moore, who taught at the seminary. The main building, added in 1960, includes a library with the largest collection of Latin Bibles in the world. There are lovely inner gardens (9th Avenue entrance). ✈ *20th to 21st streets • Map L2 • Open noon–3pm Mon–Fri, 11am–3pm Sat • Free*

7 Chelsea Piers

Four neglected piers have been turned into a 30-acre sports and recreation complex, and Manhattan's largest venue for

The World's Largest Store

Macy's is more than a store to most New Yorkers. It is a major part of the city, sponsoring the famous Thanksgiving Day Parade, the city's Fourth of July fireworks and everything from an annual spring flower show filling the main floor, to Tap-O-Mania, when thousands of tap dancers converge on Herald Square.

film and TV production. Sports facilities include ice skating, inline skating and skateboarding, batting cages, playing fields, a basketball court, bowling alley, golf driving ranges, and a marina offering harbor cruises and sailing instruction. Pier Park is a place to relax with a water view. ✈ *23rd Street at the Hudson River • Map L2 • Open 6am–11pm Mon–Fri, 8am–9pm Sat & Sun • Admission charge*

8 Fashion Institute of Technology (F.I.T.)

Founded in 1944 and now a branch of the State University of New York, the Fashion Institute of Technology is a prestigious school teaching art, fashion design, and marketing, and boasts famous alumni, including Calvin Klein, Norma Kamali, and David Chu. Students have the benefit of internships with New

Left **Chelsea Piers** Center **"Cushman Row", Chelsea Historic District** Right **Herald Square**

34th Street entrance, Macy's

York's leading stores and designers. Of greatest interest to the public is the gallery, which has changing exhibits, often from their collection of clothing and textiles. ✸ *7th Avenue at West 27th St • Map L3 • Open noon–8pm Tue-Fri, 10am–5pm Sat • Free*

9 Herald Square

The center of a rowdy theater district known as the Tenderloin in the 1870s and 80s, until it was reformed. The Manhattan Opera House was razed in 1901 to make way for Macy's, and other stores soon followed. The clock on the island where Broadway meets 6th Avenue is all that is left of the building occupied by the *New York Herald* until 1921. ✸ *Broadway at 6th Av • Map K3*

10 Macy's

Former whaler R. H. Macy founded the store in 1858 on 6th Avenue and 14th Street; the red star logo was from his tattoo, a souvenir of sailing days. Innovations included pricing goods a few cents below a full dollar and offering a money-back guarantee. The store was sold in 1888 and moved to the present building *(see p64).* ✸ *151 West 34th Street at 6th Av • Map K3*

A Day Around Chelsea

Morning

🕐 Wend your way through Chelsea, starting with the megastores now occupying former "Fashion Row," on **6th Avenue** *(p117)* between 18th and 23rd streets. Walk up 16th Street to 9th Avenue and Chelsea Market, a one-time Nabisco factory where the first Oreo cookies were made, now a block-long line of stalls offering all manner of food. The Food Network tapes its TV shows in a street-level studio here

Continue up 9th to 20th Street, for the **Chelsea Historic District** and **General Theological Seminary**. Then head for the ever-expanding "Gallery Row," from 21st to 24th streets, 10th to 11th avenues. A good lunch bet in the neighborhood is **The Red Cat**, offering Mediterranean fare *(see p121).*

Afternoon

Walk east on 23rd Street to the **Chelsea Hotel** *(see p117),* and when you get to 6th Avenue, turn uptown for the big antiques market and the colorful **Flower District** *(see p117).* A stroll one block further west on 27th brings you to the **Fashion Institute of Technology**, where the gallery usually has interesting displays.

Head for one of the great hidden treasures in this area, St. John the Baptist Church, at 210 East 31st Street, whose dingy façade belies a glowing Gothic interior. Continue to 34th Street for **Herald Square** and **Macy's**.

Left **Dia Center for the Arts** Right **Marlborough**

🔟 Chelsea Galleries

1 Dia Center for the Arts
The Dia Center for the Arts is the heart of the Chelsea scene. Its spacious galleries support projects that could not be accommodated elsewhere. Unmissable *(see p43)*. ⊛ *545 and 548 West 22nd Street at 10th Av • Map L2 • Open noon–6pm Wed–Sun • Admission charge*

2 Matthew Marks
Of the two galleries, the original shows large-scale works, while the second specializes in new work *(see p43)*. ⊛ *522 West 22nd Street at 10th Av; 523 West 24th Street at 10th Av • Map L2 • Open 10am–5:30pm Tue–Sat • Free*

3 Paula Cooper
The lofty setting itself is worth a visit. Many of Cooper's shows are controversial *(see p43)*. ⊛ *534 West 21st Street at 10th Av • Map L2 • Open 10am–6pm Tue–Sat • Free*

4 Paul Kasmin
Son of a British art dealer, Kasmin has nurtured many talented newcomers *(see p43)*. ⊛ *293 10th Avenue at 27th St • Map M2 • Open 10am–6pm Tue–Sat • Free*

5 Barbara Gladstone
A dramatic backdrop for large-scale pieces, video pioneers, and photography. ⊛ *515 West 24th Street at 10th Av • Map L2 • Open 10am–6pm Tue–Sat • Free*

6 Andrea Rosen
Since leaving SoHo for Chelsea, Rosen's eclectic shows have made this one of the area's most visited galleries. ⊛ *525 West 24th Street at 10th Av • Map L2 • Open 10am–6pm Tue–Sat • Free*

7 Marlborough, Chelsea
The 57th Street gallery shows established luminaries, while this downtown satellite has new sculpture and painting *(see p42)*. ⊛ *211 West 19th Street at 7th Av • Map L3 • Open 10am–6pm Tue–Sat • Free*

8 Robert Miller
This gallery shows big names like Diane Arbus, Walker Evans, Andy Warhol, and Jacob Epstein. ⊛ *526 West 26th Street at 10th Av • Map L2 • Open 10am–6pm Tue–Sat • Free*

9 Sonnabend
A power in the art world, representing early pop artists, and still on the lookout for new trends. ⊛ *536 West 22nd Street at 10th Av • Map L2 • Open 10am–6pm Tue–Sat • Free*

🔟 Pat Hern
A pioneer who continues to show talented contemporary art. ⊛ *530 West 22nd Street at 10th Av • Map L2 • Open 11am–6pm Tue–Sat • Free*

 For more on New York galleries See pp42–3

Left **Rocking Horse** Right **Empire Diner**

Price Categories

For a three-course meal for one with half a bottttle of wine (or equivalent meal), taxes and extra charges.

$	under $25
$$	$25–$50
$$$	$50–$80
$$$$	over $80

🔟 Places to Eat

1 Da Umberto
Popular over the years for sophisticated Tuscan fare and a long list of daily specials. ◉ *107 West 17th Street, between 6th & 7th avs • Map M3 • 212 989 0303 • $$$*

2 Periyali
A billowing canopy and white walls set the scene for classy Greek dining; creative dishes put the food in gourmet territory.
◉ *35 West 20th Street, between 5th & 6th avs • Map L3 • 212 463 7890 • $$$*

3 The Red Cat
This warm neighborhood place serves first-rate American fare; don't miss the Parmesan frites with mustard aioli. ◉ *227 10th Avenue, between 23rd & 24th sts • Map L2 • 212 242 1122 • $$*

4 Chelsea Bistro & Bar
A romantic bit of Paris in Chelsea, with a candlelit terrace and sophisticated bistro menu.
◉ *358 West 23rd Street, between 8th & 9th avs • Map L2 • 212 727 2026 • $$*

5 Le Madri
Northern Italian cooking attracts a well-heeled crowd who enjoy the *osso buco* and extensive Italian wine list. ◉ *168 West 18th Street at 7th Av • Map M3 • 212 727 8022 • $$$*

6 Cafe Mexicano
Always packed with diners who come for the great margaritas and excellent Mexican food at reasonable prices.
◉ *182 Eighth Avenue, between 19th & 20th sts • Map L2 • 212 463 9511 • $$*

7 El Cid
Tapas, paella, sangria, and all the other Spanish favorites are on hand at this friendly restaurant.
◉ *322 West 15th Street, between 8th & 9th avs • Map M2 • 212 929 9332 • $$*

8 Gus' Figs Bistro
Fashion types come to this pleasant café with a creative bistro menu near F.I.T. *(see p118)* ◉ *250 West 27th Street, between 7th & 8th avs • Map L3 • 212 352 8822 • $$*

9 Bottino
Thanks to the booming gallery scene, this attracts a stylish crowd for good northern Italian fare and a lovely garden.
◉ *246 10th Avenue, between 24th & 25th sts • Map L2 • 212 206 6766 • $$*

10 Empire Diner
The door is always open at this rail car converted to a 24-hour Art Deco diner. The best people-watching comes after midnight.
◉ *210 10th Avenue at 22nd St • Map L2 • 212 924 0012 • $*

Note: *Unless otherwise stated, all restaurants accept credit cards and serve vegetarian meals*

121

Left **Prometheus, Rockefeller Center** Center **Grand Central Terminal** Right **Chrysler Building**

Midtown

THE LIGHTS OF TIMES SQUARE, THE SPIRES *of the Empire State and Chrysler buildings, Rockefeller Center, the United Nations Headquarters, stores on 5th Avenue, museums, theaters, and grand buildings galore – all are found in the midtown area between 34th and 59th streets, extending from the East River as far as Broadway. The concentration of attractions makes this the*

most important area of the city for visitors, and many a day can be spent taking in the sights. Fifth Avenue, the dividing line between the East and West sides, is in many ways the Main Street of Manhattan, and in itself offers a generous sampling of the city's riches, from architecture to commerce. Midtown also reflects the city's characteristic diversity, with attractions that range from the bustling retail of the Diamond District, to the stately halls of the New York Public Library.

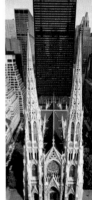

St. Patrick's Cathedral

Sights

1. Times Square
2. Empire State Building
3. Rockefeller Center
4. Chrysler Building
5. Grand Central Terminal
6. New York Public Library
7. St. Patrick's Cathedral
8. United Nations Headquarters
9. Diamond District
10. Carnegie Hall

1 Times Square
The city's most famous intersection, and symbol of the lively surrounding theater district *(see pp22-5)*.

2 Empire State Building
New York's most famous, and tallest, skyscraper is an Art Deco classic. Since it was completed in 1931 more than 120 million visitors have looked down on the city from its observatories *(see pp8–9)*.

3 Rockefeller Center
Rockefeller Center is the hub of midtown New York, alive with activity day and night, integrating shops, gardens, dining and office space, and countless works of art *(see pp12–15)*.

4 Chrysler Building
The unmistakable shimmering spire of the Chrysler Building is one of New York's great landmarks. The grand Art Deco lobby, once used as a showroom for Chrysler cars, has been restored to show off its lavish marbles and granite, and a vast painted ceiling depicts transportation scenes of the late 1920s *(see p44)*. ◎ *405 Lexington Avenue at 42nd St • Map K4 • Open (lobby only) 8:30am–5:30pm Mon–Fri • Free*

5 Grand Central Terminal
One of the world's great rail terminals, the outstanding Beaux Arts building *(see p47)* is New York's most visited, with 500,000 people passing through it daily. Since the recent restoration, its admirers are no longer limited to travelers. Grand Central has become an attraction in its own right, with 15 restaurants, over 40 shops, the New York City Transit Museum and its own gourmet food market. ◎ *42nd Street, between Park & Lexington avs • Map J–K4 • Open 5:30am–1:30am daily • Free*

Left **Empire State Building** Center **Rockefeller Center** Right **Chrysler Building**

6 New York Public Library

Carrère and Hastings won a competition for the design of this great Beaux Arts building. Their genius reached its height in the Main Reading Room, a paneled space as majestic as a cathedral, extending almost two city blocks, with enormous arched windows, 18 grand chandeliers, and an elaborately decorated, vaulted ceiling *(see p47)*. ◈ *5th Avenue at 42nd St • Map K3 • Open 10am–6pm Mon, Thu–Sat, 11am–7:30pm Tue & Wed • Free*

7 St. Patrick's Cathedral

America's largest Catholic cathedral is a place where more than 5,000 people worship every Sunday. When Archbishop John Hughes decided to build a cathedral here in 1850, many criticized the choice of a site so far from the city's center at the time. Today his foresight has given the church one of the best locations in Manhattan *(see p46)*. ◈ *5th Avenue, between 50th & 51 sts • Map J3 • Open 7am–9:45pm daily • Free*

William O. Partridge's Pieta, St. Patrick's Cathedral

Time for Tea

Taking tea is an increasingly popular custom in New York. Among the top places are the elegant Palm Court at the Plaza Hotel, 59th and 5th, the Tea Box Café at Takashimaya *(see p126)*, the tea room at the St. Regis Hotel *(see p172)*, and the *salon de thé* at Fauchon, 442 Park Avenue at 56th.

8 United Nations Headquarters

John D. Rockefeller, Jr. donated $8.5 million to purchase the 18-acre East River site, and American Wallace Harrison worked with international consultants to create this striking headquarters. The United Nations was formed in 1945, to work for peace and economic and social well-being around the globe. Currently, 189 members meet in the General Assembly, the closest thing to a world parliament. Guided tours allow visitors to see the various council chambers, the General

Left **New York Public Library** Right **St. Patrick's Cathedral**

Assembly Hall, and many of the works by prominent artists, including Marc Chagall and Henry Moore. ✪ *First Avenue at 46th St • Map J5 • Open for tours) 9:30am–4:45pm daily Admission charge*

9 Diamond District

Jewels glisten in every window of this block, the center of the city's retail and wholesale trade. It handles 80 percent of the diamonds coming into the U.S. Developed largely by Orthodox Jews, the district grew in importance during the World War II when thousands fled the diamond centers of Antwerp and Amsterdam to settle in New York. Above the shops are offices and workshops where the stones are cut and set. ✪ *47th Street, between 5th & 6th avs Map J3*

10 Carnegie Hall

New York almost lost its most famous concert hall when the New York Philharmonic moved to the newly built Lincoln Center in the 1950s. However, a coalition, led by violinist Isaac Stern, successfully fought to save the building from demolition. It was bought by the city in 1960 and became a National Historic Landmark in 1964. A major 1986 renovation restored much of the original appearance while updating technical facilities and preserving the hall's famous acoustics. Musical memorabilia fills the halls and the Rose Museum *(see p46).* ✪ *West 57th treet at 7th Av • Map H3 • Open 11am–6pm Mon–Sat, noon–6pm Sun Admission charge*

A Day Exploring Midtown

Morning

Start at the **Morgan Library** *(see p41)*, and see Morgan's opulent study, then proceed to 42nd Street and turn east for a tour through **Grand Central Terminal** *(see p123)*. Continue east, stopping to look at the outstanding lobbies of the **Chrysler Building** *(see p123)*, the **Daily News Building**, and the **Ford Foundation**, and climbing the stairs to see the **Tudor City** complex *(see p127)*.

End the morning with a tour of the **United Nations HQ**. If you reserve ahead, you can have lunch in the very special delegate's dining room, opposite the museum (212 963 7625).

Afternoon

Take the 42nd Street crosstown bus back to Fifth Avenue and visit the **New York Public Library**. Walk uptown to 47th Street and turn west for the **Diamond District**, then pay a quick visit to the **Museum of Television and Radio** *(see p128)* on 52nd Street between Fifth and Sixth avenues. Pop in to the new home of the **American Museum of Folk Art** *(see p139)* and stop for a coffee in the museum's café before taking in the exhibits of traditional art.

Return to 5th Avenue where the uptown shops include **Tiffany and Company**'s *(see p10)* windows of jewels, **Bergdorf Goodman**'s *(see p10)* stylish displays, and F.A.O Schwarz. Round the day off at the Plaza Hotel at 59th Street, perfect for a refreshing cocktail in a landmark setting.

Left **H&M** Center **Henri Bendel** Right **Niketown**

🔟 Places to Shop

1 Department Stores
Bountiful stocks of beautiful clothing await at Bergdorf Goodman, Saks Fifth Avenue, Lord & Taylor, and Bloomingdales. ⊗ *5th Avenue, between 38th & 58th sts • Map K3–H3*

2 H&M
Flagship store of the Swedish retailer known for great young fashion with small price tags *(see p65).* ⊗ *5th Avenue at 51st St • Map J3*

3 Henri Bendel
This is one of the most attractive stores in the city, featuring designer fashions and a notable selection of cosmetics *(see p64).* ⊗ *712 5th Avenue at 55th St • Map H3*

4 Takashimaya
Tasteful New York home of a leading Japanese department store, filled with the finest clothing, home accessories, and art *(see p64).* ⊗ *5th Avenue, between 54th & 55th sts • Map H3*

5 Felissimo
A five-story, Japanese-owned townhouse filled with unusual and tasteful jewelry, clothing, home furnishings and accessories. ⊗ *West 56th Street, between 5th & 6th avs • Map H3*

6 Museum of Modern Art Design Shop
Lamps, furniture, toys, jewelry, posters – whatever the item here, you can be sure it will be the epitome of good design. ⊗ *44 West 53rd Street, between 5th & 6th avs • Map J3*

7 Designer Boutiques
Many designers have moved north, but 57th Street between 5th and Madison remains impressive, with Burberry, Hermes, Chanel, and Dior. Prada is at No. 724 5th Avenue. ⊗ *57th Street, between 5th & Madison avs • Map H4*

8 Fortunoff's
If Tiffany is out of your league, try this retailer specializing in fine jewelry at more reasonable prices. ⊗ *5th Avenue at 54th St • Map H3*

9 Niketown
Commercial, high-tech shopping fun, all to entice you to buy sneakers and sportswear. ⊗ *6 East 57th Street, between 5th & Madison avs • Map H4*

10 Trump Tower
An over-the-top mall of expensive boutiques, the Trump Tower is worth visiting for the pink marble-with-waterfall surroundings even if you don't buy. ⊗ *725 5th Avenue at 56th St • Map H3*

Left **Ford Foundation Building** Center **Lever House** Right **Tudor City**

🔟 Midtown Architecture

1 Lever House
This 24-story building of glass and steel by Gordon Bunshaft was the first "glass box" in New York (see p44). ◈ 390 Park Avenue • Map H4 • Lobby open during office hours

2 General Electric Building
This 1931 Art Deco building has a clock whose arms grasp at lightning bolts. ◈ 570 Lexington Avenue • Map H4 • Lobby open during office hours

3 Chanin Building
One of the great early Art Deco skyscrapers (c.1929) notable for its terra-cotta frieze and bronze and illustrating the theory of evolution. ◈ 122 East 42nd Street • Map K4 • Lobby open during office hours

4 Daily News Building
The Daily News has moved on, but this fine 1930 building is still an Art Deco classic. Step inside and marvel at the revolving globe. ◈ 220 East 42nd Street at 2nd Av • Map K4 • Lobby open during office hours

5 Ford Foundation
Considered one of the city's best modern designs (1967). Every office opens onto a skylit, 12-story atrium with lush landscaping and a pond. ◈ 320 East 43rd Street at 1st Av • Map J4 • Lobby open during office hours

6 Fred F. French Building
Built for the best-known real estate firm of its day, this 1927 building is opulent inside and out. Don't miss the lobby. ◈ 521 5th Av • Map J3 • Lobby open during office hours

7 Tudor City
Fred R. French created this mock-Tudor enclave, designed to prove that middle-class housing could succeed in Midtown. ◈ 1st to 2nd Avenues, 40th to 43rd sts • Map J4–K4 • Lobby open during office hours

8 NY Yacht Club
The window bays of this 1899 private club are the carved sterns of ships, sailing on a sea of sculpted waves. ◈ 37 West 44th Street at 5th Av • Map J3 • Closed to public

9 American Standard Building
Raymond Hood's first New York skyscraper is an ornate black tower built in 1924, now a hotel. ◈ 40 West 40th Street • Map K3 • Lobby open during office hours

🔟 Condé Nast Building
The 48-story tower, built in 1999, is striking and environmentally friendly, with photovoltaic cells on the façade and integrated recycling chutes. ◈ 4 Times Square • Map J3 • Lobby open during office hours

For more on architecture **See pp46–7**

Left **Morgan Library** Center **Museum of Television and Radio** Right **New York Public Library**

🔟 Midtown Museums

1 Morgan Library
A café has been added and the intimate private collection expanded *(see p41)*. ◈ *29 East 36th Street at Madison Av • Map K4 • Open 10:30am–5pm Tue–Thu, 10:30am–8pm Fri, 10:30am–6pm Sat, noon–6pm Sun • Admission charge*

2 Museum of Modern Art
Re-opening in 2005, the new building will be worthy of this outstanding collection *(see p40)*. Some works can meantime be seen at MOMA Queens *(see p154)*. ◈ *11 West 53rd Street at 5th Av • Map H3*

3 American Museum of Folk Art
The new museum quadruples the space for this extensive collection of folk art *(see p139)*.

4 American Craft Museum
The Craft Council's showcase, with several changing exhibitions each year. ◈ *40 West 53rd Street at 5th Av • Map H3 • Open 10am–6pm Tue–Sun (10am–8pm Thu) • Admission charge*

5 International Center of Photography
Two floors of retrospectives and changing exhibits. ◈ *1133 6th Avenue • Map J3 • Open 10am–5pm Tue–Thu, 10am–8pm Fri, 10am–6pm Sat & Sun • Admission charge*

6 Museum of Television and Radio
Watch your favorites from over 60,000 radio and TV programs, plus special exhibits and classic screenings. ◈ *25 West 52nd Street between 5th & 6th avs • Map J3 • Open noon–6pm Tue, Wed, Sat, Sun, noon–8pm Thu, noon–9pm Fri (theaters only) • Admission charge*

7 Whitney Museum at Philip Morris
A midtown branch of the museum used for small shows from its contemporary collection. ◈ *120 Park Avenue at 42nd St • Map K4 • Open during office hours • Free*

8 New York Public Library Galleries
Rare prints, paintings, and changing exhibitions. ◈ *5th Avenue at 42nd St • Map K3 • Open 10am–6pm Mon–Sat • Free*

9 Dahesh Museum of Art
A private collection of 2,000 works of 19th- and 20th-century art. ◈ *601 5th Avenue at 48th St • Map J3 • Open 11am–6pm Wed–Fri • Free*

🔟 Municipal Art Society Galleries
Changing exhibits covering the city's architecture and neighborhoods. ◈ *457 Madison Avenue • Map J4 • Open 11am–5pm Mon–Wed, Fri & Sat • Free*

Price Categories

For a three-course meal for one with half a bottle of wine (or equivalent meal), taxes and extra charges.

$	under $25
$$	$25–$50
$$$	$50–$80
$$$$	over $80

Left **Le Cirque** Right **Le Colonial**

🔟 Restaurants

1 Four Seasons
A New York institution with landmark decor (see p69). ◈ 99 East 52nd Street at Park Av • Map J4 • 212 754 9494 • $$$

2 Le Bernardin
Seafood doesn't come any better than this (see p69). ◈ 155 West 51st Street at 6th Av • Map J3 • 212 489 1515 • $$$$

3 Le Cirque 2000
See and be seen at one of the city's top French restaurants (see p69). ◈ 455 Madison Avenue, Palace Hotel, at 50th St • Map J4 • 212 303 7788 • $$$

4 Lespinasse
Opulent Louis XV surroundings and sumptuous formal French fare put this firmly in the top ranks, but the final tab can be painful. Jackets required. ◈ 2 East 55th Street, St. Regis Hotel, between 5th & Madison avs • Map H4 • 212 339 6719 • $$$$

5 Le Colonial
Sultry decor straight from 1930s Saigon sets the scene for a Vietnamese/French menu full of delicate contrasts and combinations. Relax with an after-dinner drink in the lounge upstairs.◈ 149 East 57th Street at Lexington Av • Map H4 • 212 752 0808 • $$$

6 Osteria del Circo
The sons of Le Cirque's owner have created their own whimsical circus, serving traditional Tuscan fare. ◈ 120 West 55th Street at 6th Av • Map H3 • 212 265 3636 • $$$

7 The Oyster Bar and Restaurant
A New York classic, this bustling restaurant serves only the freshest seafood. ◈ Grand Central Terminal, lower level, 42nd Street at Lexington Av • Map K4 • 212 490 6650 • $$

8 The Brasserie
Newly remodeled with sleek, high-tech decor and an updated bistro menu that still features a few classics. ◈ 100 East 53rd Street at Lexington Av • Map J4 • 212 751 4840 • $$

9 Russian Tea Room
Opulent decor in glitzy red and gold, this reincarnated old favorite has a talented new chef. ◈ 150 West 52nd Street, between 6th & 7th avs • Map J3 • 212 757 0168 • $$$

10 La Bonne Soupe
A midtown haven for the thrifty, with comfortable, old-fashioned, French bistro charm. ◈ 48 West 55th Street, between 5th & 6th avs • Map H3 • 212 586 7650 • $$

Left **Toward Roosevelt Island** *(see p134)* Right **River promenade, Carl Schurz Park** *(see p135)*

Upper East Side

WHEN NEW YORK'S UPPER CRUST *moved uptown a century ago, their destination was the Upper East Side, and it is still the address of choice for many wealthy families. Most of the older Beaux Arts mansions around 5th Avenue are now occupied by embassies or museums; today's elite live in the solid apartment buildings that went up on 5th and Park Avenues, convenient for patronizing the boutiques on Madison, the city's most exclusive shop-*ping street. Only churches and a few restaurants remain of German Yorkville or the Hungarian and Czech neighborhoods that used to fill the blocks east of Lexington. Young families now occupy the newer buildings in this area. For visitors, the Upper East Side is home to many of the city's best museums.*

Mount Vernon *(see p135)*

🔟 Sights

1. Central Park
2. Metropolitan Museum of Art
3. Solomon R. Guggenheim Museum
4. Museum Mile
5. Bridgemarket
6. Roosevelt Island
7. Seventh Regiment Armory
8. Henderson Place Historic District
9. Gracie Mansion and Carl Schurz Park
10. Mount Vernon Hotel Museum and Gardens

Preceding pages **Central Park skaters**

June. Participants include the Metropolitan Museum of Art, National Academy of Fine Arts, Cooper-Hewitt National Design Museum, Soloman R. Guggenheim Museum, Jewish Museum, Neue Gallery for German and Austrian Art, Museum of the City of New York *(see p41)*, and El Museo del Barrio. ⊛ • *5th Avenue from 82nd to 104th sts • Map F4–D • Opening times vary*

1 Central Park
The 843-acre swathe of green that provides recreation and beauty for more than two million visitors each year *(see pp26–7)*.

2 Metropolitan Museum of Art
More a collection of museums, spanning 5,000 years of global culture *(see pp28–31)*.

3 Solomon R. Guggenheim Museum
A notable collection of modern art set in Frank Lloyd Wright's only New York building *(see pp32–3)*.

4 Museum Mile
Nine museums are situated within one convenient mile. They unite for a free open house day in

5 Bridgemarket
Britain's Sir Terence Conran was a major player in the development of this cathedral-like space beneath the 59th Street bridge. The vaults are among the most dramatic works by Rafael Guastavino, a Spanish architect noted for his use of Catalan-style tiling. Beneath the grand ceilings are Guastavino's restaurant *(see p137)* and a Food Emporium market. The complex, which is responsible for the rapid revitalization of the neighborhood, also includes the Conran Shop for high-end home decor, and a public plaza. ⊛ *59th Street, between 1st & York avs • Map H5*

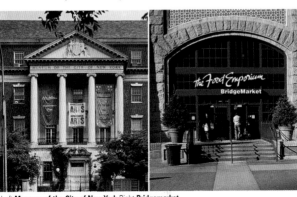

Left **Museum of the City of New York** Right **Bridgemarket**

For New York's Top 10 museums **See pp40–41**

133

6 Roosevelt Island

A four-minute tram ride is the route to this East River enclave. Once known as "Welfare Island," when it was home to a prison, poor house, and hospital for the insane, the 147-acre island was renamed and redeveloped in the 1970s according to a master plan drawn up by Philip Johnson and John Burgee, intended to create a quiet, almost traffic-free residential community. The plan has not been fully developed, although more than 3,000 apartments have been built, and while there is a subway stop from Manhattan, the only auto access is via a bridge in Queens. ◈ *Trams every 15 mins from TramPlaza, 2nd Avenue at 59th St • Map H5*

7 Seventh Regiment Armory

The socially prominent members of the Seventh Regiment, formed in 1806, had the wherewithal to construct a remarkable armory in 1877–89, with a drill room 200 by 300 feet (60 by 90 m) and 100 feet (30 m) high, and an administration building in the form of a medieval fortress. Interior decoration was by Louis Comfort Tiffany, Stanford White, and others, and the result is opulent rooms with lavish Victorian furnishings. The drill room is used for the prestigious

St. Nicholas Russian Orthodox Cathedral

An unexpected bit of Russia, this building was constructed in 1902 in Muscovite Baroque style with a façade of red brick, white stone, and blue and yellow tiles. The incense-filled interior has marble columns and an altar enclosed by wooden screens trimmed with gold. Mass is still said in Russian. It is located at 15 East 97th Street.

Winter Antiques Show every January, as well as for many society charity balls. ◈ *Park Avenue at 66th St • Map G4 • 212 452 3067 • Open by appointment only*

8 Henderson Place Historic District

Built in 1881 by the developer John C. Henderson for "persons of moderate means," these winning Queen Anne houses made of brick and stone are embellished with towers, bays, gables, dormers, and slate roofs. They were an investment and remained in Henderson's family until the 20th century. Today they are unique in the city and rank among the most desirable places to live. Each block front was composed as a unit, with small towers at the end. Twenty-four of the original 32 units remain. ◈ *East End Avenue, between 86th & 87th sts • Map F5*

Left **Seventh Regiment Armory** Right **Henderson Place Historic District**

Gracie Mansion and Carl Schurz Park

The balconied, wooden, country home built by merchant Archibald Gracie in 1799 was the original home of the Museum of the City of New York and became the official residence of Mayor under Fiorello LaGuardia in 1942. It is located at the northern end of a park laid out in 1891, with a wide promenade that stretches along the East River. The park was named for a prominent statesman and newspaper editor who lived in the neighborhood.
ⓢ East End Avenue at 88th St • Map E5 • 212 570 4751 • Open Apr–mid Nov, tours at 10am, 11am, 1pm, 2pm; Wed for pre-booked tours • Admission charge

Mount Vernon Hotel Museum and Gardens

A rare bit of old New York, this was the stone carriage house of a 1799 estate. When the house burned in 1826, the carriage house was converted into an inn and became a fashionable resort for New Yorkers who wanted to escape to what was then still countryside. The building and garden have been restored by the Colonial Dames of America and furnished with historic objects. Guides are on hand to explain the unique history of the attraction. ⓢ 421 East 61st Street • Map H5 • Open 11am–4pm Tue–Sun, closed August, public holidays • Admission charge

A Day Exploring the Upper East Side

Morning

Start at the **Guggenheim** (see pp32–3) and admire Frank Lloyd Wright's great architectural achievement before seeing the fine modern art collection. "Must sees" include Chagall's *Paris Through the Window*, Modigliani's *Nude*, and Picasso's *Woman Ironing*. Stop for coffee at the café on the main floor of the museum before leaving.

Head east along 92nd Street to see two rare remaining wooden houses, No. 120, built in 1859, and No. 122, in 1871. Continue east for **Gracie Mansion** and **Henderson Place** and rest on a bench with a river view in **Carl Schurz Park**. One block west on York Avenue, a 31 bus will take you to the spectacular **Bridgemarket** (see p133). Have lunch at **Guastavino's** (see p137), and admire the great ceilings.

Afternoon

Take the 57th Street crosstown bus back to Madison Avenue and head uptown, browsing the designer boutiques. Detour on any of the side streets in the upper 60s and 70s to see the townhouses of affluent New Yorkers. Pay a quick visit to the **Frick Collection** (see p41) then stop for coffee at one of the cafés on Madison Avenue.

Spend the rest of the afternoon at the **Metropolitan Musuem of Art** (see pp28–31), a New York "must," and see Rembrandt's *Self-portrait*, *Cypresses* by Van Gogh, and Michelangelo's Sistine Chapel studies. End the day with a candlelit meal at **Erminia** (see p137).

Left **Giorgio Armani** Right **Yves Saint Laurent**

TOP 10 Madison Avenue Boutiques

1 Bottega Veneta
The first in the uptown Madison Avenue boutique line-up, known for luxury leather goods, shoes, and fashion. ◈ 635 Madison Avenue, between 59th & 60th sts • Map H4

2 Shanghai Tang
The colorful townhouse home of a well-known Hong Kong retailer, selling luxury fashions and home furnishings. ◈ 714 Madison Avenue, between 63rd & 64th sts • Map H4

3 Valentino
If you can afford it, join the rich and famous; many of his gowns are worn at the Oscars. ◈ 760 Madison Avenue at 65th St • Map G4

4 Giorgio Armani
The New York flagship of the Italian master, known for his superb tailoring, offers a good range from his collection. ◈ 760 Madison Avenue at 65th St • Map G4

5 BCBG Max Azria
"Bon chic, bon genre," (good style, good attitude), is the motto of this hot designer. Fans of his sexy fashions include many young Hollywood stars. ◈ 770 Madison Avenue at 66th St • Map G4

6 Moschino
An other-worldly setting provides the backdrop for whimsical, with-it clothing, continuing the legacy of the late Italian designer. ◈ 803 Madison Avenue, between 67th & 68th sts • Map G4

7 Dolce & Gabbana
Spot the celebrities at this chic Italian outpost – one of the hot labels of the moment. ◈ 816 Madison Avenue, between 68th & 69th sts • Map G4

8 Chloe
The French house continues the hip look acquired under Stella McCartney – this store carries the full line. ◈ 850 Madison Avenue at 70th St • Map G4

9 Yves Saint Laurent
The legacy of the legendary French couturier lingers, with a particular appeal to the young. ◈ 855-59 Madison Avenue, between 70th & 71st sts • Map G4

10 Polo Ralph Lauren
The 1898 Rhinelander Mansion is the backdrop for the king of preppy fashion, who spent $14 million renovating the old mansion. Sportswear is in a separate shop across the street. ◈ 867 Madison Avenue at 72nd St • Map G4

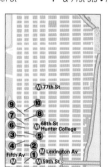

For more on shopping in New York See p165

Left **Guastavino's** Right **Orsay**

Restaurants

1 Daniel
A flower-filled dining room provides the setting for Daniel Boulud's superb seasonal menus *(see p68)*. ◈ 60 East 65th Street at Park Av • Map G4 • 212 288 0033 • $$$

2 Guastavino's
A great setting, beneath the 59th Street bridge, with formal French dining in the upstairs club and a huge brasserie downstairs. ◈ 409 East 59th Street at 1st Av • Map H5 • 212 980 2455 • $$$

3 The Dining Room
Excellent American cuisine in a comfortable setting makes this a prime choice. The glazed red snapper is a favorite. ◈ 154 East 79th Street at Lexington Av • Map F4 • 212 327 2500 • $$$

4 Café Boulud
Since Daniel *(above)* opened, Boulud's first restaurant has become more casual. But the French menu and tab are serious. ◈ 20 East 76th Street at 5th Av • Map G4 • 212 772 2600 • $$$

5 Butterfield 81
There's an intimate feel to this paneled, dimly lit dining room. The American menu includes many grill specialties. ◈ 170 East 81st Street, between Lexington & 3rd avs • Map F4 • 212 288 2700 • $$$

6 Erminia
They don't come more romantic than this tiny, candlelit Italian with beamed ceilings and a menu of well-prepared classics. ◈ 250 East 83rd Street, between 2nd & 3rd avs • Map F4 • 212 879 4284 • $$$

7 Etats-Unis
Despite the French name, the inventive menu is New American and draws a loyal following. ◈ 242 East 81st Street, between 2nd & 3rd avs • Map F4 • 212 517 8826 • $$$

8 Orsay
Replacing society hangout Mortimer's isn't easy, but this chic French café has succeeded, serving authentic bistro fare. ◈ 1057–59 Lexington Avenue at 75th St • Map G4 • 212 517 6400 • $$$

9 Cello
The dinner crowd is elegantly turned out, but lunch is the best way to sample Laurent Tourondel's superb seafood without breaking the bank. ◈ 53 East 77th Street at Madison Av • Map F4 • 212 517 1200 • $$$$

10 E.J.'s Luncheonette
A family-friendly diner with heaping portions of well-prepared American food. Great pancakes are served all day. ◈ 1271 Third Avenue at 73rd St • Map G4 • 212 472 0600 • No credit cards • $

Note: Unless otherwise stated, all restaurants accept credit cards and serve vegetarian meals

137

Left **Monument, Riverside Park** Center **Riverside Gardens** Right **Apartment buildings**

Upper West Side

THIS AREA DID NOT BEGIN TO DEVELOP *until the 1870s, when the 9th Avenue El went up, making it possible to commute to midtown. When the Dakota, New York's first luxury apartment building, was completed in 1884, it was followed by others on Central Park West and Broadway, while side streets were filled with handsome brownstones. The West Side remains a desirable neighborhood with a reputation for attracting intellectuals, and much of the city's best residential architecture.* The creation of Lincoln Center in the 1950s was a great boost, and the American Museum of Natural History is also a draw.

Mask, Natural History Museum

🔟 Sights

1. American Museum of Natural History
2. Lincoln Center for the Performing Arts
3. New York Historical Society
4. American Museum of Folk Art
5. Pomander Walk
6. Riverside Park
7. Riverside Drive/West End Historic District
8. Children's Museum of Manhattan
9. Zabar's
10. Green Flea Market/ 77th Street Flea Market

1 American Museum of Natural History

The mammoth museum whose holdings include 32 million artifacts *(see pp34-7)*.

2 Lincoln Center for the Performing Arts

Built on 15 acres in the 1950s, transforming slums into a giant cultural complex, Lincoln Center houses the Metropolitan Opera, the New York City Opera and Ballet, the New York Philharmonic, the Lincoln Center and Walter Reade theaters, Avery Fisher and Alice Tully halls, and the Julliard School. In the summer, popular Mostly Mozart concerts take place, the central fountain plaza becomes a dance floor, and free concerts are held in the adjacent park *(see p50)*. ◈ *Columbus to Amsterdam avs, between 62nd & 66th sts • Map G2 • Tours 10:30am, 12:30pm, 2:30pm, & 4:30pm daily • Admission charge*

Copper weathervane, Museum of American Folk Art

3 New-York Historical Society

New York's oldest museum, founded in 1804, has organized much of its vast collection into the 4th floor Henry Luce III Center, which displays 40,000 objects divided into areas such as paintings, sculpture, furniture, silver, tools, and, notably, Tiffany lamps. Other galleries are used for changing exhibits. The society also maintains a research library. ◈ *2 West 77th Street at Central Park West • Map G2 • Open 10am–5pm Tue–Sun; Library 10am–5pm Tues–Sun (Tue–Fri in summer) • Admission charge*

4 American Museum of Folk Art

The Museum marks its 40th anniversary with the opening of a spacious new building in midtown *(see p128)*, but this gallery will remain as a showcase for a collection that encompasses some 4,000 objects, from traditional folk art of the 18th and 19th centuries to the work of contemporary artists. Paintings, sculptures, weathervanes, whirligigs, and toys are among the objects on display. ◈ *2 Lincoln Square at Columbus Av • Map H2 • Open 11:30am–7:30pm Tue–Sun • Free*

Lincoln Center for the Performing Arts

5 Pomander Walk

This double row of small brick and stucco, timbered, Tudoresque townhouses, hidden on a private street, is one of the many delightful surprises to be discovered in Manhattan. The developer, a restaurateur named Thomas Healy, took his inspiration in 1921 from the sets used for a popular play by Lewis Parker called *Pomander Walk*, hoping to recreate the village atmosphere depicted in the play. Gloria Swanson, Rosalind Russell, and Humphrey Bogart are among the players who have lived here. ◈ *261–7 West 94th Street, between Broadway & West End Av • Map E2*

6 Riverside Park

Another example of the landscape genius of Frederick Law Olmsted, a woodsy, hilly band of green planned in 1873, following curving Riverside Drive for 70 blocks and hiding the abandoned railroad tracks below. Playgrounds, sports fields, a promenade, and monuments were added later. The impressive 1902 marble Soldiers' and Sailors' monument at 89th Street, a memorial to those who died in the Civil War, was modeled after the Monument of Lysicrates in Athens. ◈ *Riverside Drive, 72nd to 155th sts • Map C1 • Open 6am–1am daily • Free*

Soldiers' and Sailors' monument

7 Riverside Drive/ West End Historic District

A walk through this area shows the late 19th-century townhouses that characterize the Upper West Side. West 88th Street is a good example. The earliest, Nos. 267–71, were built in 1884. Nos. 302–38, from the early 1890s, have stepped gables and Roman brick, while Nos. 315–23, circa 1896, have bow fronts in brown or white stone. The Yeshiva Ketana School, at 346 West 89th Street, begun in 1901 by Herts and Tallant, occupies one of only two survivors of the mansions that once lined Riverside Drive. ◈ *Between Riverside Drive & West End Av, 85th & 95th sts • Map E1*

8 Children's Museum of Manhattan

Founded in 1973, in a former school building, this is a museum dedicated to the principal that children learn best through

Upper West Side Architecture

The Upper West Side's side streets are lined with fine rows of the brownstones favored by New York's 19th-century middle classes. Built of inexpensive, local, brown sandstone, the narrow buildings are typically three or four stories high, and have a flight of steps called a "stoop" leading to the living floors.

Left House façade, Pomander Walk **Right** Children's Museum of Manhattan

self-discovery. It uses a variety of participatory activities and fantasy world environments to engage its young visitors in learning that is fun. The Tisch Building, as the museum is known, has been renovated in a $6.5 million expansion headed by the museum chairman, Laurie Tisch Sussman. The museum's many activities include exhibits to intrigue older children, while Word Play is an enticing environment for newborns to four year olds *(see p66)*.

Ⓢ *212 West 83rd Street at Broadway* • *Map F2* • *Open 10am–5pm Wed–Sun* • *Admission charge*

9 Zabar's

A monument to New York's mania for finding the best foods and a landmark since 1934, this always-crowded market sells smoked salmon, sturgeon, and other Jewish delicacies, wonderful bread, desserts, coffee, and cheeses, and big selections of oils, vinegars, and gourmet gift baskets. The second floor is filled with cooking equipment, and a coffee counter at the 80th Street corner lets you taste the delicious baked goods. Ⓢ *2245 Broadway at 80th St* • *Map F2*

10 Green Flea Market/ 77th Street Flea Market

Flea market junkies throng this school yard every Sunday, hoping for finds from among the piles of vintage clothing, crafts, books, jewelry, prints and all manner of memorabilia. Less glamorous, new merchandise, from socks to T-shirts, is also sold here. On a good day as many as 300 booths crowd the premises. A weekly green market shares the same space. Ⓢ *I.S.44, 77th Street at Columbus Av* • *Map F2*

Walk on the West Side

Morning

🕐 Begin at **Lincoln Center** *(see p139)* and admire the plaza, the Chagall windows at the Metropolitan Opera, and the Henry Moore statue in front of Lincoln Center Theater. The New York Public Library for the Performing Arts on Amsterdam Avenue, behind the theater, is notable for its enormous collection of books on the performing arts.

🕐 Make your way up Broadway, window shopping and noting some of the landmark buildings such as the **Apthorp Apartments** *(see p142)* and the **Ansonia Hotel** *(p142)*, and the West Side's gastronomic palaces, such as Fairway, at 75th Street, and **Zabar's**. Almost any of the side streets will reveal examples of the area's great line-up of brownstone townhouses. Finally, head east to Columbus Avenue and **Calle Ocho** *(p143)* for a Cuban lunch.

Afternoon

The **American Museum of Natural History** *(see pp34–7)* can easily fill an entire afternoon, and the **New York Historical Society** *(p139)* has an amazing collection on show.

Stroll down Central Park West and admire the landmark **apartment buildings** *(p142)* that can be seen here, and then head for **Central Park** *(pp26-7)*, the city's vast "backyard". Take a boat out on the lake, or enjoy a gondola ride around it, followed by refreshments at the Loeb Boathouse, the perfect end to an afternoon.

Left **Detail, Dakota** Center left **Balcony, Dorilton** Center right **San Remo** Right **Hotel des Artistes**

🔟 Apartment Buildings

1 Dakota
Famous as the site where John Lennon was shot, the block was thought so far west in 1884, it might as well be in Dakota. ⊗ *1 West 72nd Street at Central Park West • Map G2 • Closed to public*

2 Dorilton
One of the most flamboyant examples of the Beaux Arts era, this 1902 apartment house has an iron gate fit for a palace. ⊗ *171 West 71st Street at Broadway • Map G2 • Closed to public*

3 Ansonia Hotel
This 1908 apartment-hotel included soundproof partitions, a feature that has attracted many distinguished musicians. ⊗ *2109 Broadway, between 73rd & 74th sts • Map G2*

4 Apthorp Apartments
Modeled after an Italian Renaissance palazzo, this luxury 1908 building includes a huge interior courtyard. ⊗ *Broadway, between 78th & 79th sts • Map F2*

5 Belnord
Even larger than the Apthorp, this 1908 Renaissance Revival structure is where Nobel Prize-winning author Isaac Bashevis Singer lived and wrote. ⊗ *225 West 86th Street, at Amsterdam Av • Map F2 • Closed to public*

6 Majestic
The first of Irwin Chanin's two 1931 landmarks, one of the original four twin towers that dominate the West Side skyline. ⊗ *115 Central Park West, between 71st & 72nd sts • Map G2 • Closed to public*

7 Century
Irwin Chanin's second twin tower, the tallest on the block, and an Art Deco icon. ⊗ *25 Central Park West, between 62nd & 63rd sts • Map H2 • Closed to public*

8 San Remo
Emery Roth's 1930 Art Deco masterpiece is a sophisticated adaptation of Renaissance forms. The twin towers hide water tanks. ⊗ *145–6 Central Park West, between 74th & 75th sts • Map G2 • Closed to public*

9 Eldorado
Another Art Deco Roth design. Groucho Marx and Marilyn Monroe were once tenants. ⊗ *300 Central Park West, between 90th & 91st sts • Map E2*

10 Hotel des Artistes
Built in 1918 to serve as artists' studios and apartments, the lofty spaces are much coveted. Residents have included Noel Coward, Isadora Duncan, and Joel Grey. ⊗ *West 67th Street, between Central Park West & Columbus Av • Map G2*

For more historic New York buildings See pp46–7

142

Price Categories

For a three-course meal for one with half a bottle of wine (or equivalent meal), taxes and extra charges.	**$**	under $25
	$$	$25–$50
	$$$	$50–$80
	$$$$	over $80

Left **Shun Lee Cafe** Right **Rosa Mexicano**

🔟 Restaurants

1 Jean Georges
Jean-Georges Vongerichten's namesake restaurant is among the best in New York *(see p68)*.
⌾ 1 Central Park West, Trump International Hotel • Map H2 • 212 299 3900 • $$$$

2 Picholine
For fine dining in the Lincoln Center area, it's hard to beat Terrance Brennan's elegant Mediterranean restaurant.
⌾ 35 West 64th Street at Broadway
• Map H2 • 212 724 8585 • $$$

3 Shun Lee Café
This clean-lined, black-and-white dim sum café is arguably the best north of Chinatown.
⌾ 43 West 65th Street at Columbus Av
• Map G2 • 212 769 3888 • $$

4 Cafe Fiorello
The bountiful antipasto bar is good enough reason to visit, but the thin-crust pizzas and Italian menu are equally tempting.
⌾ 1900 Broadway, between 63rd & 64th sts • Map H2 • 212 595 5330 • $$

5 O'Neal's
Casual and comfortable, this attractive pub/restaurant is a neighborhood standby, always packed with Lincoln Center patrons.
⌾ 49 West 64th Street, between Central Park West & Broadway • Map H2
• 212 787 4663 • $$

6 Gabriel's
Sophisticated Tuscan food keeps this stylish room filled with Lincoln Center-goers at night.
⌾ 11 West 60th Street at Columbus Av
• Map H2 • 212 956 4600 • $$$

7 Rosa Mexicano
A branch of New York's top Mexican restaurant, famous for its guacamole made to order and power-packed margaritas.
⌾ 61 Columbus Avenue at 62nd St • Map H2 • 212 977 7700 • $$$

8 Café Luxembourg
A classic Parisian bistro with a zinc-topped bar and a hip clientele. The steak frites can't be beat.
⌾ 200 West 70th Street at Amsterdam Av
• Map G2 • 212 873 7411 • $$$

9 Calle Ocho
Every night feels like a Latin party here; modern dishes from the Cuban chef are inspired by cuisine from Peru to Puerto Rico.
⌾ 446 Columbus Avenue, between 81st & 82nd sts • Map F2 • 212 873 5025 • $$

🔟 Gennaro
Fans say this tiny café serves the best Italian food on the Upper West Side, at the most reasonable prices, which explains the constant lines.
⌾ 665 Amsterdam Avenue, between 92nd & 93rd sts
• Map E2 • 212 665 5348
• No credit cards • $$

Note: Unless otherwise stated, all restaurants accept credit cards and serve vegetarian meals

Left **Columbia University** Center **Rose Window, St. John the Divine** Right **Streetside Musicians**

Morningside Heights and Harlem

THE AREA BETWEEN MORNINGSIDE PARK *and the Hudson River, from 110th–125th streets, is dominated by Columbia University and two important churches. Further west and extending north is Harlem, America's best-known African-American community. In the 1880s, when rail connected the neighborhood to Midtown, the large townhouses were occupied by Irish, Italian, and Jewish families, but by the 1920s black families predominated. The Harlem Renaissance, when nightclubs with black entertainers were frequented by whites, ended with the Depression. Nevertheless, recent development is reviving the area, causing some to declare a second Renaissance.*

🔟 Sights

1. Columbia University
2. Cathedral Church of St. John the Divine
3. Riverside Church
4. Hamilton Heights Historic District
5. St. Nicholas Historic District (Strivers' Row)
6. Abyssinian Baptist Church
7. Marcus Garvey Park
8. Studio Museum in Harlem
9. Schomburg Center for Research in Black Culture
10. Malcolm Shabazz Mosque/Harlem Market

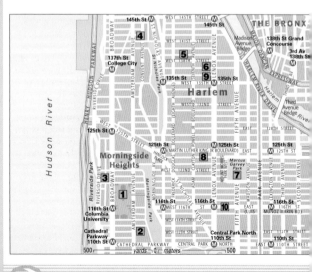

Columbia University
1 One of America's oldest universities, noted for its law, medicine, and journalism schools, Columbia was founded in 1754 as King's College. It moved in 1897 to its present campus, designed by Charles McKim with lawns and plazas on a serene terrace set apart from the street. Notable buildings include McKim's 1898 Low Library, and St. Paul's Chapel with three windows by La Farge.
Ⓢ West 116th Street at Broadway
• Map C3

Cathedral Church of St. John the Divine
2 The mother church of the Episcopal Diocese of New York, begun in 1892 and still incomplete, is the largest cathedral in the world. Over 600 feet (180m) long and 146 feet (45m) wide, the church is a mix of Romanesque and Gothic styles. Its most impressive features include the west entrance, the rose window, bay altars, and the Peace Fountain on the south lawn. The medieval stone carving techniques used on the building are taught in workshops for disadvantaged youths (see p46).

Ⓢ 1047 Amsterdam Avenue at 112th St
• Map C3 • Open 10am–2pm Mon–Fri, 9am–5pm Sat & Sun • Free

Riverside Church
3 This skyscraper Gothic church modeled on Chartres cathedral and financed by John D. Rockefeller Jr. in 1930, has a 21-story tower with wonderful Hudson River views. Inside the tower is the largest carillon in the world, dedicated to Rockefeller's mother. The brilliant stained-glass windows are copies of those at Chartres with four notable exceptions – the early 16th-century Flemish windows on the east wall. The congregation has long been active in liberal social causes.
Ⓢ 490 Riverside Drive at 122nd St
• Map C1 • Open 10:30am–5pm Tue–Sun
• Admission charge

Hamilton Heights Historic District
4 Once part of the country estates of the wealthy, like Alexander Hamilton whose 1802 home, Hamilton Grange, is here, this location on a hill above Harlem became desirable in the 1880s when an elevated rail line was built. Fine residences went up between 1886 and 1906, and in the 1920s and 30s they attracted Harlem's elite, when the area was dubbed Sugar Hill. Chief Justice Thurgood Marshall and musicians Count Basie, Duke Ellington, and Cab Calloway were among those who lived here.
Ⓢ West 141st to West 145th streets
• Map A2

Riverside Church

5 St. Nicholas Historic District (Strivers' Row)

These fine houses, originally known as the King Model Houses, went up in 1891 when Harlem was a neighborhood for the gentry. Three architects, including McKim, Mead, and White, managed to blend Renaissance, Georgian, and Victorian styles and create a harmonious whole. Successful African-Americans moved here in the 1920s and 30s, giving rise to the nickname Strivers' Row. ◈ *202–250 West 138th Street, between 7th & 8th avs • Map A3*

6 Abyssinian Baptist Church

One of the oldest and most influential African-American churches in the U.S. was organ-ized in 1808 by a group protesting segregation within the Baptist church. The congregation became politically active under such leaders as congressman Adam Clayton Powell, Jr. Today the church is widely attended on Sundays by many who come to hear the wonderful gospel choir. ◈ *132 West 138th Street, between 7th Lenox avs • Map A3 • Sunday services 9am & 11am*

7 Marcus Garvey Park

A black nationalist who encouraged emigration to Africa, Garvey became a hero of the Black Pride movement, and the park's name was changed from Mount Morris in 1973 to honor him. It adjoins the Mount Morris Historical District of handsome houses and churches from an earlier, affluent, German-Jewish era. In the 1920s, as Harlem became mostly African-American, the synagogues became churches, and the houses were divided up. ◈ *West 119th to West 124th streets, between Lenox & 5th avs • Map B3*

8 Studio Museum in Harlem

Opened in 1967 as an artists' studio, the organization expanded to become an important center for work by black artists. A local bank donated space for the present building, which opened in 1982 and is undergoing a major expansion that will add more gallery space, an enlarged sculpture garden, an auditorium, and a café. ◈ *144 West 125th Street, between 7th & Lenox avs • Map B3 • Open noon–6pm Wed & Thu, noon–8pm Fri, 10am–6pm Sat & Sun • Admission charge*

Studio Museum, Harlem

Harlem Market

9 Schomburg Center for Research in Black Culture

A complex opened in 1991 houses the largest research center for African and African-American culture in the U.S. The immense collection was assembled by the late Arthur Schomburg, who became curator when the collection was given to the New York Public Library. The original building was the unofficial meeting place for writers in the black literary renaissance of the 1920s, and the present building includes a theater and two art galleries. ◎ 515 Lenox Avenue at 135th St • Map A3 • Open 10am–6pm Mon–Sat, 1–5pm Sun • Free

10 Malcolm Shabazz Mosque/Harlem Market

The mosque, Masjid Malcolm Shabazz, was the ministry of the late Malcolm X, and the area around it has become the center of an active Muslim community. Local shops sell books, tapes, and Muslim clothing, and restaurants serve Sengalese cuisine. Street vendors who used to crowd the sidewalks of 125th Street have been moved into an organized complex of market stalls selling African art, dolls, drums, masks, dashiki shirts, and fabrics in African prints. ◎ Mosque, 102 West 116th Street at Lenox Av • Map C3 • Open 9am–5pm daily • Free • Harlem Market, 52–60 West 116th Street, between 5th & Lenox avs • Map C3 • Open 10am–6pm daily • Free

A Day in Harlem and Morningside Heights

Morning

Begin late Sunday morning and take the No. 2 or No. 3 subway uptown to 135th Street and Lenox Avenue. Walk to 138th Street and turn west to hear the fabulous choir at the **Abyssinian Baptist Church**.

Continue west along 138th Street to see the fine 1890s homes of the **St. Nicholas Historic District** and stop on 8th Avenue to enjoy a gospel brunch at **Londel's Supper Club** (see p148).

Afternoon

Retrace your steps to Lennox Avenue and head downtown to 125th Street to peruse the shops. Turn west for the famous **Apollo Theater** (see p148) and excellent displays of African-American art at the **Studio Museum in Harlem**. Afterwards, stop for coffee at the Starbucks on Lennox Avenue at 125th Street.

Take the M100 bus west to Riverside Drive. Walk down to **Riverside Church** (see p145) for fine views over the Hudson River from the bell tower. Across the street is the monument honoring the 18th U.S. president, Ulysses S. Grant. At 116th Street, head east two blocks to Broadway and the main entrance to **Columbia University** (see p145). One block east on Amsterdam Avenue is the **Cathedral Church of St. John the Divine** (see p145) with its immense interior. End the day with some good southern cooking at **Miss Mamie's** (see p149) and return to Broadway for the No. 1 or No. 9 subway back downtown.

Around Town – Morningside Heights & Harlem

Left **Gospel at Sylvia's** Right **Apollo Theater**

TOP 10 Places for Music

1 Lenox Lounge
A standby for 50 years, the lounge has a new retro look and features the latest sounds in jazz as well as more traditional numbers. ◈ *288 Malcolm X Blvd, between 124th & 125th sts• Map B3*

2 Showman's
Live jazz is the lure on Monday, Thursday, and Saturday nights at this club, where the vibes and people are as cool as the music. ◈ *375 West 125th Street, between St. Nicholas & Morningside Dr • Map B2*

3 Londel's Supper Club
Part of the new Harlem, with upscale ambience, waiters in tuxedos, delicious Southern fare, and good live jazz on weekends. ◈ *2620 Frederick Douglass Blvd, between 139th & 140th sts • Map A3*

4 St. Nick's Pub
Savion Glover and Ray Charles have been known to drop by at this popular venue. Live jazz can be heard six nights a week. ◈ *773 St. Nicholas Avenue at 149th St • Subway line A, B, C, or D to 145th Street*

5 Sylvia's
The place is jammed for Saturday and Sunday gospel brunches, and always fun despite the tour groups. ◈ *328 Lenox Avenue, between 126th & 127th sts • Map B3*

6 Cotton Club
Duke Ellington and Cab Calloway are long gone, and the location has changed, but the famous club of the 1920s is currently making a comeback. ◈ *656 West 125th St nr West 125th and Dr Martin Luther King Jr Blvd • Map B2*

7 Apollo Theater
This theater is Harlem's famous showcase, where Ella Fitzgerald and James Brown launched their careers. ◈ *253 West 125th Street, between 7th & 8th avs • Map B3*

8 Aaron Davis Hall
Home to jazz series, as well as ballet, opera, and the Harlem Film Festival. ◈ *City College campus, West 135th St & Convent Av • Map A2*

9 Miller Theatre
Columbia's main performance venue runs the musical gamut, with jazz an important part. ◈ *Columbia University, 116th Street & Broadway • Map C2*

10 Smoke
Columbia students and jazz lovers of all ages congregate at this intimate club to hear top notch jazz groups every weekend. ◈ *2751 Broadway at 106th St • Map D2*

Price Categories

For a three-course meal for one with half a botttle of wine (or equivalent meal), taxes and extra charges.

$	under $25
$$	$25–$50
$$$	$50–$80
$$$$	over $80

Left **Charles' Southern Style Kitchen** Right **Terrace in the Sky**

🔟 Restaurants

1 Charles' Southern Style Kitchen
Famous fried chicken, ribs, and collard greens can't be beat at this tiny no-frills and very popular spot. ◎ *2841 Frederick Douglass Blvd, between 151st & 152nd sts • Subway line C or E to 155th Street • 212 926 4313 • $*

2 Sugar Shack
Top-rated Southern soul food is served in a comfortable setting. ◎ *2611 Frederick Douglass Blvd at 139th St • Map A3 • 212 491 4422 • $*

3 Miss Maude's/Miss Mamie's
Down-home, cheerful cafés run by Norma Jean Darden, who knows her Southern cooking. ◎ *Miss Maude's, 547 Lenox Avenue at 137th St • 212 690 3100 • Miss Mamie's, 366 Cathedral Pkwy between Manhattan Av and Columbus Av • 212 865 744 • Map A3, D2 • Both $*

4 Copeland's
Take your pick of Southern classics at this popular spot; don't miss the Sunday gospel brunch. ◎ *547 West 145th Street, at Broadway • Map A2 • 212 234 2357 • $*

5 Bayou
Cajun is a specialty of Steve Manning, who spent 10 years in New Orleans perfecting crawfish *étouffé.* ◎ *547 145th Street between Amsterdam and Broadway • Map B3 • 212 234 2357 • No disabled access • $$*

6 Café Largo
Spanish dishes are served in hearty portions in this friendly neighborhood café, with occasional poetry readings or live music. ◎ *3387 Broadway at 137th St • 212 862 8142 • Map A2 • $*

7 Amy Ruth's
A cheerful café with an up-dated slant on Southern classics. Waffles are a house specialty. ◎ *113 West 116th Street, between Powell & Lenox avs • Map C3 • 212 280 8779 • $$*

8 Le Baobab
The Senegalese cooking and the tab are both agreeable here. ◎ *120 West 116th Street at Lenox Av • Map C3 • 212 864 4700 • No credit cards • $$*

9 Toast
Sandwiches are the forte of this informal café, and the home-fries unmissable. ◎ *3157 Broadway, between Tiemann Pl & LaSalle St • Map B2 • 212 662 1144 • $*

10 Terrace in the Sky
This elegant, rooftop restaurant is so romantic, weddings are held here. The continental fare lives up to the setting. ◎ *400 West 119th Street at Amsterdam Av • Map C2 • 212 666 9490 • $$$*

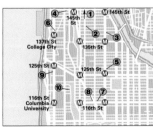

Note: *Unless otherwise stated, all restaurants accept credit cards and serve vegetarian meals*

Left **New York Botanical Garden** Center **Wildlife Conservation Park** Right **Park Slope Historic District**

The Outer Boroughs

MANHATTAN IS JUST ONE of New York's five boroughs, each of which has
its own unique attractions. Brooklyn alone, with its fine brownstone
neighborhoods and numerous top-class sights, would be one of the largest
cities in the U.S. The Bronx, to the north, boasts one of New York's finest zoos,
plus the New York Botanical Garden and Yankee Stadium, while Queens,
a veritable melting pot of nationalities, is famous for its museums, ethnic
dining, and numerous sports events. The ferry to Staten Island leads to
New York's only restored historic village.

🔟 Sights

1. Bronx Zoo/Wildlife Conservation Park
2. New York Botanical Garden
3. Brooklyn Botanic Garden
4. Brooklyn Heights Historic District
5. Prospect Park
6. Park Slope Historic District
7. Flushing Meadow-Corona Park
8. Yankee Stadium
9. Richmondtown Restoration
10. City Island/North Wind Institute Museum

Brooklyn Bridge

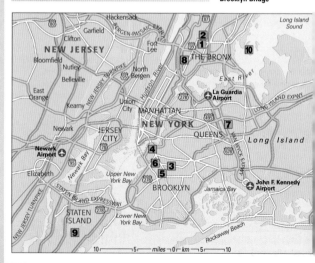

Haupt Conservancy, a restored Victorian glass house, offers plants of misty tropical rain forests and arid deserts, and changing special exhibits. A tram makes it easy to see the highlights, and many guided tours are offered. ⊗ *Kazimiroff Boulevard, Bronx • Subway Bedford Park Blvd • Open Apr–Oct: 10am–6pm Tue–Sun, holiday Mon; Nov–Mar: 10am–4pm Tue–Sun • Admission charge*

1 Bronx Zoo/Wildlife Conservation Park

Well past its 100th birthday, this sprawling zoo on 265 acres gets better all the time. The newest exhibit, the 6.5-acre Congo Gorilla Forest, an authentic world of forests, lakes, and meadows, uses walls and tunnels of glass to bring visitors nose to nose with the inhabitants. The unusual World of Darkness shows nocturnal animals like bats in action *(see p64)*. ⊗ *2300 Southern Boulevard, Bronx • Subway Pelham Pkwy • Open Apr–Oct: 10am–5pm Mon–Fri, 10am–5:30pm Sat & Sun; Nov–Mar: 10am–4:30pm daily • Admission charge*

2 New York Botanical Garden

One of the oldest and largest botanical gardens in the world, this National Historic Landmark covers 250 acres and includes 48 gardens and plant collections and 50 acres of forest, the only remains of woods that once covered New York. The Enid A.

3 Brooklyn Botanic Garden

A small but magnificent oasis, this 52-acre garden designed by the Olmsted brothers in 1910 is home to more than 12,000 plantings. It is best known for the Cranford Rose Gardens where thousands of roses cascade down arches, climb lattices, and fill formal beds, and the authentic Japanese Hill-and-Pond Garden, planted in 1915. It is also known for its Cherry Esplanade and Cherry Walk, one of the foremost cherry-blossom sites outside Japan. The Steinhardt Conservatory houses tropical and desert plants and one of America's largest bonsai collections. ⊗ *1000 Washington Avenue, Brooklyn • Subway Eastern Pkwy • Open Apr–Sep: 8am–6pm Tue–Fri, 10am–6pm Sat, Sun, & hols; Oct–Mar: 8am–4:30pm Tue–Fri, 10am–4:30pm Sat, Sun, & hols • Admission charge*

Brooklyn Botanic Garden

4 Brooklyn Heights Historic District

Overlooking the East River and lower Manhattan skyline, the Brooklyn Heights Historic District is an enclave of old-world charm. Along its quaint streets are preserved, Federal, wooden and brick townhouses of the 1820s and even grander Greek Revival homes of the following decades. ◈ *Court Street to Furman Street, between Fulton & State sts • Subway Clark St*

5 Prospect Park

Frederic Olmsted and Calvert Vaux considered this park, completed in 1877, to be their masterpiece. The 90-acre Long Meadow is the longest unbroken green space in the city. The pools and weeping willows of the Vale of Cashmere are particularly fine, along with Vaux's Oriental Pavilion and Concert Grove. ◈ *Between Eastern Parkway & Parkside Avenue, Brooklyn • Subway Grand Army Plaza*

Carousel horse, Prospect Park

6 Park Slope Historic District

These blocks on the western edge of Prospect Park became desirable places to live after the opening of the Brooklyn Bridge in 1883. The Victorian brownstones from the late 19th and early 20th centuries are outstanding U.S. Romanesque Revival and Queen Anne residences. ◈ *Prospect Park*

Train to Queens

This subway route, dubbed the International Express, serves New York's most varied ethnic communities. Take 61st Street, Woodside for Irish pubs, 46th Street for the Middle East, 69th Street for the Philippines. A $1 guide is available from Queens Council on the Arts, 79-01 Park Lane South, Woodhaven, NY 11421.

West to 7th Avenue, between 14th St & St. John's Pl, Brooklyn • Subway 9th St

7 Flushing Meadow-Corona Park

The site of two World Fairs, this is now a spacious park with picnic areas, fields for cricket and soccer, paths for bikers and skaters, boating lakes, and many other attractions. The New York Mets' Shea Stadium, the U.S. Tennis Center, the New York Hall of Science, and the Queens Museum of Art are also here. The Unisphere, the symbol of the 1964 World Fair, still stands. ◈ *Queens • Subway 111th St*

8 Yankee Stadium

A sports shrine, built in 1923 and known as "The House that Ruth Built" for the legions of fans who came to see superhero Babe Ruth. Other legendary heroes of

Left **World's Fair Unisphere, Flushing Meadow-Corona Park** Right **Yankee Stadium**

ichmondtown Restoration

merica's most winning baseball
eam include Joe DiMaggio and
Mickey Mantle. The legendary
4,000-seat stadium was updated
n the 1970s, but a new modern
omplex may appear in the
uture. ⊗ *161st St and River Avenue,
ronx • Subway 161st St-River Avenue
• Opening times vary • Admission charge*

9 Richmondtown Restoration

his restored village has 27 build-
ngs from the town of Richmond,
taten Island's seat of govern-
nent from 1729. Other historic
uildings were moved here from
ther sites. The Dutch-style Voor-
ezer's House (1695) is the island's
ldest home on its original site.
⊗ *441 Clarke Avenue, Staten Island • Ferry
o Staten Is • Open Sept–Jun: 1–5pm
Ved–Sun; Jul–Aug: 10am–5pm Wed–Sat,
–5pm Sun • Admission charge*

10 City Island/North Wind Institute Museum

his tiny Bronx outpost on Long
sland Sound was founded in
685. The boatyards are a forest
f masts, and the main street is
ned with seafood restaurants
nd nautical bars. The North
Vind Institute Museum is full of
autical lore. ⊗ *North Wind Institute
Museum, 610 City Island Avenue, City
sland, Bronx • Subway Pelham Pkwy
Bx29 bus to City Island • Open
0am–5pm Mon–Fri, noon–5pm Sat
Sun • Admission charge*

A Day Out in Brooklyn

Morning

Take the No. 2 or 3
subway train to Eastern
Parkway – Brooklyn
Museum, for the world-
class **Brooklyn Museum
of Art** *(see p41)*. The
museum is part of a civic
complex that includes the
stately Grand Army Plaza,
the **Brooklyn Botanic
Garden** *(see p151)*, with
its well-known Japanese
garden, and neighboring
Prospect Park.

Along the western edge
of Prospect Park is the
beautiful **Park Slope
Historic District**. Stop
for coffee at Ozzie's, 57
7th Avenue, before taking
in the area's historic resi-
dences. Browse the hip
line-up of small shops
along 7th Avenue, and
stop for lunch at one of
the many cafés here.

Afternoon

Return by train to Borough
Hall and head for the
**Brooklyn Heights Historic
District**. Walk along Pierre-
pont, Willow, and Cranberry
streets to see some 19th
century houses; Truman
Capote wrote *Breakfast at
Tiffany's* in the basement
of No. 70 Willow, and
Arthur Miller once owned
the property at No. 155.

A short walk east brings
you to **Atlantic Avenue**
(see p156). Look in on the
spice shops here, and
stop for refreshments at
the Waterfront Ale House,
155 Atlantic Avenue. Head
back to the Brooklyn
Bridge, stopping at the
Brooklyn Heights Prom-
enade for dramatic vistas
of Lower Manhattan's
towers. End the day with
dinner at the romantic
River Café *(see p157)*.

Left **Brooklyn Museum of Art** Center **Hall of Science** Right **Museum of the Moving Image**

🔟 Museums

1 Brooklyn Museum of Art
The permanent collection has objects from ancient Egyptian to contemporary art *(see p41)*. 🚇 *200 Eastern Parkway, Brooklyn • Subway Eastern Pkwy • Open 10am–5pm Wed–Fri, 11am–6pm Sat & Sun; 11am–11pm first Sat of month • Admission charge*

2 Isamu Noguchi Garden Museum
Thirteen galleries and a serene Japanese garden house this sculptor's work. 🚇 *3237 Vernon Blvd, Queens • Bus 104 to Vernon Blvd • Open Apr–Oct: 10am–5pm Wed–Fri, 11am–6pm Sat & Sun • Admission charge*

3 American Museum of the Moving Image
Artifacts and film screenings show the history and techniques of film, TV, and digital media. 🚇 *35th Avenue at 36th St, Queens • Train to Steinway St • Open noon–5pm Tue–Fri, 11am–6pm Sat, Sun. Screenings 6.30pm Sat, Sun • Admission charge*

4 New York Hall of Science
A science and technology museum with hands-on exhibits and outdoor play area. 🚇 *4701 111th St, Queens • Subway 111th St • Open Jul & Aug: 9.30am–5pm Tue–Sun, Wed, 9:30am–2pm Mon; Sep–Jun: 9.30am–2pm Tue, Wed, 9.30–5pm Thu–Sun • Admission charge*

5 Queens Museum of Art
The New York Panorama scale model has 800,000 buildings. 🚇 *New York City Building, Queens • Subway 111th St • Open 10am–5pm Tue–Fri, noon–5pm Sat & Sun • Admission charge*

6 P.S. 1 Contemporary Art Center
Since 1976 this center has displayed contemporary art and provided studio space for artists. 🚇 *2225 Jackson Avenue at 46th Av, Queens • Subway 23rd St-Ely Ave • Open noon–6pm Wed–Sun • Admission charge*

7 MOMA Queens
This former factory is a temporary home for the most famous paintings from the Museum of Modern Art *(see p40)*. 🚇 *3500 47th Avenue, Queens • Subway 33rd St • Open 10am–5pm Sun–Thu, 10am–7.45 Fri • Admission charge*

8 Jacques Marchais Museum of Tibetan Art
A collection of Tibetan art in a mountain temple with an altar and garden. 🚇 *383 Lighthouse Avenue, Staten Island • Bus S74 from ferry • Open 1–5pm daily • Admission charge*

9 Staten Island Historical Society Museum
In historic Richmondtown is a museum housed in the County Clerk's office, built in 1848. 🚇 *441 Clarke Street, Staten Island • Bus S74 from ferry • Opening times vary • Admission charge*

10 Snug Harbor Cultural Center
Chinese garden, performance spaces, art center, children's museum, and a maritime collection. 🚇 *1000 Richmond Terrace, Staten Island • Bus S70 from ferry • Opening times vary • Admission charge*

Around Town – The Outer Boroughs

154   *For more on New York's museums See pp40–41*

Left **New York Aquarium** Center **Staten Island Ferry** Right **Staten Island Children's Museum**

⁀10 Family Adventures

1 New York Aquarium
Walk through a swamp and stay dry beneath a waterfall *(see p067).* ◐ Surf Avenue, Brooklyn • Subway W 8th St • Open 10am–6pm Mon–Fri, 10am–7pm Sat, Sun; last tickets 45 min before closing • Admission charge

2 Brooklyn Children's Museum
A permanent collections and changing exhibits. ◐ 145 Brooklyn Av at St. Marks Pl, Brooklyn • Subway Grand Army Plaza • Open 2–5pm Wed–Fri, 10am–5pm Sat & Sun; summer: 10am–5pm Wed–Fri • Admission charge

3 Prospect Park Wildlife Center
Tunnel through a prairie dog town, master baboon language, leap-frog across lily pads. ◐ 450 Flatbush Avenue, Brooklyn • Subway Eastern Pkwy • Open Apr–May: noon–5pm Sat, Sun; May 25–Labor day: 11am–3pm Thu–Fri • Rides 50 cents, Apr–Oct

4 Prospect Park Carousel
This 1912 carousel with hand-carved animals was moved here from Coney Island in 1950. ◐ Prospect Park, Brooklyn • Subway Flatbush-7th Av • Open Apr 6–May 19: 12–5pm; May 25–Labor Day 11am–3pm Thu, Fri, 12–6pm Sat, Sun • Admission charge

5 Lefferts Homestead Children's House Museum
A rare 18th-century Dutch Colonial farmhouse shows early farm life. ◐ Prospect Park, Brooklyn • Subway Flatbush–7th Av • Open Apr–Nov: 1–4pm Thu & Fri, 1–5pm Sat & Sun • Free

6 Puppetworks
Hand-carved marionettes are used to present children's classics. ◐ 338 6th Avenue at 4th St, Brooklyn • Subway 7th Avenue (Brooklyn) • Performances 12:30pm, 2:30pm Sat & Sun • Admission charge, reservations required.

7 Sheepshead Bay Fishing Boats
A fishing fleet takes passengers for day and evening excursions. ◐ Eamons Avenue, Brooklyn • Subway to Sheepshead Bay • Boats leave 6:30–9am, 1pm, & 7pm, or can be chartered • Charge

8 Staten Island Children's Museum
A 6-ft (2-m) kinetic porpoise welcomes you to this interactive playground exploring water, insects, and visual and performing arts. ◐ 1000 Richmond Terrace, Staten Island • Bus S48 from ferry • Open summer: 11am–5pm daily; winter: noon–5pm daily • Admission charge

9 Staten Island Zoo
The African Savannah at Twilight is a highlight. Other top sights include the Tropical Forest and Serpentarium. ◐ 614 Broadway, Staten Island • Bus S48 from ferry • Open 10am–4:45pm daily • Admission charge

10 Staten Island Ferry
A free ride with fabulous views of Manhattan. St. George Terminal buses go to Staten Island's sights *(see p59).* ◐ Bus to St. George Terminal, Staten Island • Boats every 15 mins–1 hr, 24 hours daily from Whitehall and South sts • Free

For more family days out in New York **See pp66–7**

Left **Designer shoes, Madison Avenue** Right **Household goods on display**

TOP 10 Ethnic Shopping

1 Broadway, Astoria
Astoria has the largest Greek community outside Greece, with restaurants, coffee shops, and bakeries on Broadway. ◎ *Broadway, Astoria, Queens • Subway Broadway*

2 Main Street, Flushing
Flushing's Chinatown offers bakeries, food, gifts, restaurants, herbal remedies, and acupuncture. Queensborough Library has material in 40 languages. ◎ *Main Street, Flushing, Queens • Subway Main St*

3 74th Street, Jackson Heights
New York's Indian community's shop windows are filled with ornate gold jewelry and rich saris. Food stores are redolent with spices. ◎ *74th Street, Jackson Heights, Queens • Subway Roosevelt Av*

4 Roosevelt Avenue, Jackson Heights
Around the corner from Indian 74th Street, loudspeakers play Latin American rhythms, street vendors sell hot *churros* (fried dough), and shops offer music, foods, gaucho boots, hats, and piñatas. ◎ *Roosevelt Avenue, Jackson Heights, Queens • Subway Roosevelt Av*

5 Arthur Avenue, Bronx
In this Italian neighborhood, dozens of small, family-run stores sell everything from Italian wines, handmade pastas, and sausages to rosaries and votive candles. ◎ *Arthur Avenue, Bronx • Subway Fordham Rd*

6 Nassau Avenue, Greenpoint
Shops in America's largest Polish community are laden with home-made *kielbasas* and *babkas*, statues of saints, Polish books, music and cosmetics. ◎ *Nassau Avenue, Greenpoint, Brooklyn • Train to Nassau A*

7 Brighton Beach Avenue, Brooklyn
Known as "Little Odessa," Russian is the first language on this busy street selling everything from smoked fish to Russian dolls. A boardwalk stroll by the sea is a bonus. ◎ *Brighton Beach Avenue, Brooklyn • Subway 55th St*

8 13th Avenue, Borough Park
The main street of Borough Park, home to America's largest Orthodox Jewish community, bustles with shops filled with religious articles, tempting baked goods, children's clothing, and linens. ◎ *13th Avenue, Borough Park, Brooklyn • Subway 55th St*

9 18th Avenue, Bensonhurst
Headquarters of an old-world Italian community, the street is lined with coffee shops, bakeries and delis. ◎ *18th Avenue, Bensonhurst, Brooklyn • Subway 18th Av*

10 Atlantic Avenue, Brooklyn
New York's Middle-Eastern shopping center offers baklava, varieties of olives, dried fruits, spices, and traditional clothing. ◎ *Atlantic Avenue, Brooklyn • Subway Court St*

For more on shopping in New York **See p165**

Price Categories

For a three-course meal for one with half a bottle of wine (or equivalent meal), taxes and extra charges.

$	under $25
$$	$25–$50
$$$	$50–$80
$$$$	over $80

River Café

10 Restaurants

1 River Café

Lobster, duck, and seafood are among many specialties. The Chocolate Duo dessert includes a mini chocolate Brooklyn Bridge (see p58). ❄ 1 Water Street, Brooklyn • Subway High St • 718 522 5200 • Men require jackets after 5pm • $$$$

2 Gage & Tollner

Established in 1879, Gage & Tollner's reliable menu features seafood and steak, with a few contemporary additions. The crabcakes are legendary. ❄ 372 Fulton Street, Brooklyn • Subway Jay St • 718 875 5181 • $$$

3 Peter Luger Steak House

Beef lovers flock to Peter Luger's gritty, beer hall-style location for what has long been considered New York's best steaks. Reservations are necessary. ❄ 178 Broadway, Brooklyn • Subway Marcy Av • 718 387 7400 • $$$

4 Al Di La Trattoria

This cozy, northern Italian trattoria serves regional dishes like hanger steak, mussels in tomato sauce, and wonderful pastas. ❄ 248 5th Avenue, Brooklyn • Subway Union St • 718 636 8888 • $$

5 Dominick's Restaurant

Stand in line, join a table, and feast on homemade Southern Italian food at its best. There's no menu; order your favorite or trust the waiter's choice. ❄ 2335 Arthur Avenue, Bronx • Subway Fordham Road • 718 733 2807 • No credit cards • $$

6 S'Agapo

Greek for "I love you," the name is apt for this cheerful, unpretentious spot with wonderful Greek food, weekend music, and a summer terrace. ❄ 3421 34th Avenue, Queens • Subway Broadway N • 718 626 0303 • $$

7 Kum Gang San

The place to sample Korean stews, noodle dishes, or do-it-yourself Korean barbecue cooked at the table. Meals begin with Panchan, small dishes of hot and cold, sweet and sour foods. ❄ 138–28 Northern Boulvard, Queens • Subway Main St • 718 461 0909 • $$

8 Joe's Shanghai

The original of this Chinese café chain is popular for its pork or crab soup dumplings, or "steamed buns." There's also a menu of Shanghai specialties. ❄ 136–21 37th Avenue, Queens• Subway Main St • 718 539 3838 • No credit cards • $

9 Jackson Diner

No ambience, but one of New York's best Indian restaurants, complete with an all-you-can eat buffet lunch. ❄ 37–47 74th Street, Queens • Subway Roosevelt Avenue • 718 672 1232 • No credit cards • $

10 Denino's

A family pizzeria with all the favorites and some adventurous alternatives at the right price. ❄ 524 Port Richmond Avenue, Staten Island • Bus 44 from ferry • 718 442 9401 • No credit cards • $

Note: Unless otherwise stated, all restaurants accept credit cards and serve vegetarian meals

STREETSMART

NEW YORK'S TOP 10

Left **Umbrella** Center left **Comfortable shoes** Center Right **Sunglasses** Right **Seasonal clothing**

TOP 10 Planning Your Trip

1 Seasonal Clothing
New York has distinct seasons with average temperatures ranging from 26–38° F (-3–3° C) in the winter to 67–84° F (19–29° C) in the summer Despite the averages New York weather is predictably unpredictable. Layers are the solution – a short-sleeved knitted shirt, long-sleeved cotton shirt, and sweater will see you through most changes, plus a warm coat for winter.

2 Umbrella and a Raincoat
The months of March and August have the heaviest rainfall, but an umbrella and raincoat are useful all year round.

3 Walking Shoes
Midtown streets are often clogged with traffic, meaning that walking is not only the most pleasant, but often the fastest, way to get around. Invest in a pair of sturdy walking shoes, and break them in before you leave home to avoid developing blisters.

4 Dark Colors
Dry cleaning is expensive in New York, and laundromats are scarce in midtown where most visitors stay. The practical solution is to pack dark clothing, preferably in fast-drying, drip-dry fabrics that can be rinsed out overnight.

5 Hat and Sun-Glasses
Most visitors are more than likely to undertake a lot of walking in New York. Don't make the mistake of thinking that those tall buildings shut out the sun; if anything, it seems intensified in the city. So come prepared with a hat and sunglasses, and don't forget to pack the suntan lotion.

6 Electric Current Adapter
The U.S. uses a 115–120V current, rather than the 220V current used in Europe and elsewhere. Some hair dryers are equipped with an automatic conversion switch, but most 220V appliances will need an adapter, available in airport shops and some department stores. The U.S also uses two-pin plugs, and you will therefore need a two-pin plug adapter.

7 Metric Conversion Chart
Unlike most of the world, the U.S. does not use the metric system. A conversion chart or electronic pocket converter makes it simple to convert miles into kilometers for distances, ounces into litres for capacity measurements, kilograms to pounds for weight, and celcius into fahrenheit for the weather.

8 Student or Senior ID
Subways and buses, movie houses, most major attractions, and many hotels offer discounted rates for seniors over the age of 65. But proof of age is sometimes requested, so bring along a valid photo identification to take advantage of the discounts. Most museums and sightseeing attractions also offer discounted rates for students, again on presentation of the relevant ID. The minimum age for entry into bars and clubs in the U.S is 21 and proof of age will be required on entry.

9 Pocket Calculator
To save having to do laborious calculations in your head to convert the price of goods from dollars into pounds or euros when out shopping, bring a pocket calculator with you. Some are almost as small as a credit card, and fit easily into a wallet or pocket.

10 Driving Licence
If you plan on any out-of-New York trips with a rented car, be sure to bring a valid driving licence with you. You will also need to show official identification with a photograph and signature, such as a passport. A credit card will also be required when renting a car.

Left **Arriving by air** Center **Arriving by ship** Right **Arriving by bus**

🔟 Arriving in New York

1 Arriving by air
Most international flights land at John F. Kennedy Airport and some at Newark. La Guardia Airport serves domestic flights. Cab fares to the city are a fixed $35 from Kennedy Airport, $34–$43 from Newark, and $19–$22 from LaGuardia, plus $3.50 toll and tips.

2 Limousine service
Several limousine companies offer private door-to-door services by appointment, to or from the airports, rail, or ship terminals, at pre-arranged rates averaging $5-$10 more than taxi fares. Reputable services include Carmel and Tel Aviv. 🄫 *Carmel: 212 666 6666 • Tel Aviv: 212 777 7777*

3 Supershuttle
Supershuttle vans operate door-to-door and are less like limousines or taxis. They pick up passengers so allow plenty of time. Prices around $19 according to zip code. 🄫 *Supershuttle: 212 258 3826*

4 Coach companies
Coaches from the airports to central midtown points cost $8–$13. Shared minibuses with hotel drop-offs cost $13–$19. Transportation information is available at the baggage checkout areas in all airports. 🄫 *Advance information: 800 247 7433 • NY-NJ Port Authority: www.panynj.gov*

5 Arriving by train
Amtrak trains from all parts of the U.S. arrive at Pennsylvania Station, 7th Avenue and 33rd Street. Long Island Railroad and New Jersey Transit commuter trains also use Penn station, and Metro-North regional trains use Grand Central Terminal, at Lexington Avenue and 42nd Street. Cabs are widely available at all terminal entrances. 🄫 *Amtrak trains: 800 872 7245 • Long Island Railroad: 718 217 5477 • New Jersey Transit: 973 762 5100 • MetroNorth: 212 532 4900*

6 Arriving by bus
Buses are the least expensive way to travel in the U.S. Intercity bus and commuter lines arrive at the Port Authority Bus Terminal. Cabs wait at the 8th Avenue entrance. 🄫 *Port Authority Bus Terminal: 8th Avenue at 42nd Street • 212 564 8484*

7 Arriving by ship
Cruise ships arrive in New York at the spacious, modern NYC Passenger Ship Terminal. Customs and immigration officials are on duty to process passengers on overseas cruises. Cabs are found outside the terminal. 🄫 *NYC Passenger Ship Terminal: 711 10th Avenue • 212 246 5450*

8 Arriving by car
Cars are a liability in midtown, where parking spaces are nonexistent and parking expenses can run to more than $30 a day. Check in advance with your hotel over the availability and cost of parking, and, if necessary, consider using a suburban motel located near convenient transportation into Manhattan.

9 Customs allowances
$100 worth of gifts ($400 for U.S. citizens), one carton of 200 cigarettes (or 50 cigars), and one litre of liquor may be brought into the U.S. without incurring customs fees. No meat, seeds, growing plants, or fresh fruit may be brought in. Prescription drugs should be clearly marked. A receipt for any cameras or laptops will pre-empt any queries when you leave. 🄫 *U.S Customs Service: 800 697 3662. For general information: 877 CUSTOMS*

10 Immigration
Landing cards and customs declaration forms are usually distributed on the plane, to be filled out ready for U.S. customs and immigration. Foreign nationals will have to join a separate (and usually long) line to have their passport inspected at immigration. Most UK and Canadian passport holders do not need visas if staying in the U.S. for 90 days or less; always check with your embassy.

Left **The Visitors Bureau** Center **New York taxi** Right **Student Card**

🔟 Useful Information

1 Tourist Information

NYC & Company, the New York Convention & Visitors Bureau, operates a Visitor Information Center with multilingual counselors and free information. ◈ *Visitor Information Center: 810 Seventh Avenue at 53rd St • Map J3 • www. nycvisit.com • 8am–6pm Mon–Fri, 9am–5pm Sat & Sun*

2 New York Newspapers

The *New York Times* is read nationally for its extensive international coverage. The city's tabloids, the *New York Post* and *New York Daily News*, are known for their attention-grabbing headlines and a number of pages of sports coverage. Many young New Yorkers read the free weekly *Village Voice* and rival *New York Press*.

3 Out-of-Town Newspapers

Foreign and out-of-town newspapers may be found at branches of Barnes & Noble bookstore, and many Sunday papers are carried at the Universal News Stand. If you can't find what you want, Hotalings News Agency, a wholesaler, may be able to help. ◈ *Universal News Stand: 234 West 42nd Street. Map K3 • Hotalings News Agency: 212 974 9419*

4 Entertainment Listings

The Friday *New York Times* arts section, *Time Out New York*, the *New Yorker*, and *New York Magazine* are all comprehensive weekly sources of current happenings in the city, readily available at any newsstand.

5 Museum/ Gallery Guides

Besides listings in the entertainment magazines, *Museums New York* is a quarterly publication ($4.95) available at most newsstands, with write-ups of current museum and gallery exhibitions. The *Art Now Gallery Guide*, free in most galleries, details current offerings around the city. ◈ *Museums New York: 212 604 0877*

6 Opening Hours

Most stores and sightseeing attractions are open daily (see p165); banks close on weekends, although ATMs are always available (see p169); post offices close on Sundays with the exception of the General Post Office (see p169). Many museums close on Mondays and major holidays – check with individual venues for their specific times.

7 Tipping

A tip of at least 15 percent is usual for meals, taxis, and personal services such as haircuts or massages.

Bellboys at hotels usually receive $1 per bag, and bartenders $1 per drink. Many diners find it easiest to calculate a tip by simply doubling the tax (8.25 percent) on a restaurant bill.

8 Taxes

Be sure to factor in taxes when you calculate costs in New York. Sales tax is an extra 8.25 percent on every purchase, except for clothing or shoes under $110. Hotel taxes add 13.25 percent to the bill, plus an extra $2 per night occupancy tax.

9 Big Apple Greeters

Visitors might like to try an afternoon with a Big Apple Greeter, a volunteer New York guide who will take you on a tour of any neighborhood of your choice or give you an insider's view of the city. ◈ *Big Apple Greeter: 212 669 8159 • www. bigapplegreeter.org*

10 Restrooms

Hotels (see pp172–9) and department stores (see p64) are the best places for restrooms. Most fast-food restaurants, such as McDonald's, and coffee shops such as Starbucks, also have restrooms and although intended for patrons, these are usually available if you ask for the key.

Left **Traffic control** Center **Staten Island Ferry** Right **Traffic signs**

🔟 Getting Around

1 The Street Plan

Above Greenwich Village, Manhattan is laid out on a straight grid plan, with the avenues running to the north and south, and the streets crossing east to west. All are one-way, alternating the direction with each block, except for Park Avenue, which runs both ways. 5th Avenue is the dividing line between the East and West sides.

2 Finding an Address

To locate the nearest cross street for avenue addresses in Manhattan, drop the last digit of the street number, divide by 2 and add these key numbers:

1st Avenue	3
2nd Avenue	3
3rd Avenue	10
8th Avenue	9
Lexington Avenue	22
Madison Avenue	27

For further address formulas, check the Yellow Pages.

3 Traffic Signs

Traffic lights show red for stop, yellow for caution, and green for go for vehicles, and spell out "walk" and "don't walk" for pedestrians. The "don't walk" sign blinks when the lights are about to change; given the aggressive traffic, it's wise not to attempt to beat the light.

4 Subway Routes

Subways run north and south up and down the city on Lexington Avenue, 6th Avenue, 7th Avenue/ Broadway, and 8th Avenue. The N, R, E, F and W trains to Queens run east to west, crossing Manhattan. A free copy of the current subway map is available at any station booth. ◎ passenger information: *718 330 1234 • www.mta.info*

5 Bus Routes

Manhattan buses run on every north-south artery except on Park and West End avenues. The most useful crosstown buses run on 96th, 86th, 79th, 67th, 57th, 49/50th, 42nd, 34th, 23rd, and 14th streets. Route numbers are posted on a lighted strip above the front windshield. Free maps are available on most buses.

6 The Metrocard

Metrocards are sold in subways and in shops displaying the sign. Denominations starting at $6 are good for subways and buses. Each ride deducts one $1.50 fare from the card; transfers within two hours are free on buses or subways.

7 Taxi Know-how

Manhattan yellow taxis can be hailed anywhere you spy one. Lights atop the cab go on when the car is available, or to show that the driver is off-duty. Hotel cab stands are good places to look for a cab. ◎ *For taxi complaints: 212 221 8294*

8 Car rentals

Rentals offices are found throughout the city; drivers must be over 25, and have a valid license and major credit card. Weekends are heavily booked, so phone in advance. ◎ *Hertz: 800 654 3131 • Avis: 800 831 2847 • National: 800 227 7368 • Enterprise: 800 736 8222*

9 Parking Rules and Penalties

Street parking is not available midtown and is scarce elsewhere. Some avenues have curb meters allowing 15- to 60-minute stays; overstaying means a ticket or having your car towed away, both of which are extremely expensive. Side streets have "alternate side" regulations banning cars, during certain hours and on alternate days, from parking on alternate sides of the street.

10 Ferries

New York Waterways ferries connect Manhattan with New Jersey and provide transportation to New York Yankee and Mets baseball games. ◎ *For ferry schedules: 800 533 3779 • Staten Island ferry information: see p59.*

Left **Circle Line boat** Center **Touring by bus** Right **Carriage in Central Park**

🔟 Guided Tours

1 Neighborhood Walking Tours
The best way to see New York is on foot with a knowledgeable guide. Top leaders include: Big Onion Walking Tours (history oriented), Joyce Gold History Tours, and the 92nd Street Y (Jewish oriented). ✪ *Big Onion Walking Tours: 212 439 1090 • Joyce Gold History Tours: 212 242 5762 • 92nd Street Y: 212 439 1090*

2 Architectural Tours
The Municipal Art Society, dedicated to preservation and excellence in urban design, offers enlightening "Discover New York" tours highlighting the city's buildings and neighborhoods, led by architectural historians. ✪ *Municipal Art Society: 212 935 3960*

3 Boat Tours
Circle Line offers two- or three-hour cruises around Manhattan, as well as Harbor Lights evening cruises and one-hour sails from South Street Seaport. New York Waterways has 90-minute harbor trips. ✪ *South Street Seaport: Pier 16 & Pier 83, 212 563 3200 • New York Waterways: 800 533 3779*

4 Bus Tours
Gray Line offers two- to ten-hour double-decker and motorcoach Manhattan sightseeing trips with multilingual guides, plus Brooklyn tours and Harlem gospel tours. An all-day tour costs $60 including a bonus Statue of Liberty boat ticket and one-day subway/bus pass ✪ *Gray Line Bus Tours: 212 397 2600.*

5 Backstage Tours
Among the insider's offerings are Lincoln Center *(see p137)*, the Metropolitan Opera, Radio City Music Hall *(see p13)*, NBC Studios *(see p12)*, Carnegie Hall *(see p125)*, Madison Square Garden, Grand Central Terminal *(see p123)*, Gracie Mansion *(see p135)*, and the New York Public Library *(see p124)*. ✪ *Lincoln Center: 212 875 5350 • Metropolitan Opera: 212 769 7020 • Radio City Music Hall: 212 246 4600 • NBC Studios: 212 664 3700 • Carnegie Hall: 212 247 7800 • Madison Square Garden: 212 465 6080 • Grand Central Terminal: 212 935 3960 • Gracie Mansion: 212 570 4751 • New York Public Library: 212 340 0849*

6 Park Tours
See the glories of Central Park with Urban Park Rangers or volunteer guides from the Park Conservancy. Free programs are held most weekends and some Wednesdays. ✪ *Park Conservancy schedules, 212-360-2727 • Urban Rangers, 866-692-4295*

7 Bicycle Tours
A leisurely, two-hour spin around Central Park takes in all the important sights, with a break for refreshments. Tours cost $20, or $30 with bike rental. ✪ *2 Columbus Circle, 59th St & Broadway • Map H2 • 212 541 8759*

8 Garden Tours
The New York Botanical Garden (718 817 8700) holds various tours. ✪ *Highlight tours (1pm Wed, Sat, Sun), conservatory tours (1pm Tue), forest tours (3pm Tue, 1pm Thur, noon Sat & Sun) • Tickets are free with garden admission • Tram tours run every 20 minutes ($2 adults, $1 children, see p151)*

9 Museum Tours
The Metropolitan Museum of Art *(see p133)* offers 20 different guided tours daily in several languages, covering the highlights of the museum as well as specific galleries; tours are included with the price of admission. The Guggenheim Museum *(see p133)* offers family tours of museum highlights, also free with the price of admission.

10 Carriage Tours
Horse-drawn cabs take passengers on a short, old-fashioned ride through Central Park *(see p26–7)*. Rides cost $40. ✪ *Central Park South at 59th St • Map H3*

Left **Givenchy** Center **Gourmet shopping** Center **Barnes & Noble bookstore**

Streetsmart

🔟 Shopping Tips

1 Store Hours

Most stores operate 10am–7pm Mon–Sat, until 8pm Thu, and 11am or noon to 6pm or 7pm Sun. Many stay open on holidays but all close for Christmas and Easter.

2 Credit Cards

MasterCard and Visa are accepted everywhere; American Express and Discover in most places.

3 Women's Clothing

Department stores have the widest selections (see p64), Madison Avenue has the designer names (p136), and SoHo the best trendy fashions (see p65). For discounts, try Orchard Street (p91), Century 21, and Daffy's. ◈ *Century 21: 22 Cortlandt Street, Map Q4 • Daffy's: 125 East 57th Street & 111 5th Avenue, Map H4 & L3*

4 Men's Clothing

For designer fashion go to Barneys, traditional styles Brooks Brothers or Paul Stuart, and Moe Ginsburg for Italian designs; Today's Man has affordable prices. ◈ *Barneys: 660 Madison Avenue, Map K4 • Brooks Brothers: 345 Madison Avenue, Map L4 • Paul Stuart: Madison Avenue at 45th St, Map J4 • Moe Ginsburg: 162 5th Avenue, Map L3 • Today's Man: 625 6th Avenue, Map L3*

5 Books

Barnes & Noble carries a huge range; Rizzoli specializes in art and general books, Murder, Ink in mysteries, Bank Street in children's books, and the Strand used books. ◈ *Barnes & Noble: 1960 Broadway, Map G2 • Rizzoli: 31 West 57th Street, Map H2 • Murder, Ink: 2486 Broadway, Map E2 • Bank Street Book Store: 610 West 112th St, Map C2 • Strand Book Store: 828 Broadway, Map M4*

6 Gourmet Food

Among the city's gastronomic palaces, Zabar's is the best known (see p141), but Dean & DeLuca, the Gourmet Garage, Citarella, and Agata & Valentina have their devotees. ◈ *Dean & DeLuca: 560 Broadway, Map M4 • Gourmet Garage: 2567 Broadway, Map E2 • Citarella: 2135 Broadway, Map G2 • Agata & Valentina: 1505 1st Avenue, Map F5*

7 Crafts and Antiques

Manhattan Art & Antiques and Chelsea Antiques carry a little of everything. For American folk, try Susan Parrish or Kelter-Malce, fine American furniture Israel Sack, and contemporary crafts the American Craftsman. ◈ *Manhattan Art & Antiques: 1050 2nd Avenue, Map G4 • Chelsea Antiques: 110 West 25th Street, Map L2 • Susan Parrish: 309 Bleecker Street, Map N3 • Kelter-Malce: 74 Jane Street, Map M2 • Israel Sack: 730 5th Avenue, Map H3 • American Craftsman: 317 Bleecker Street, Map N3*

8 Toys and Children's Clothes

F. A. O. Schwarz is amazing (see p66), but less overwhelming is the Enchanted Forest and the Children's General Store. There is beautiful clothing at Bonpoint, cool choices at Space Kiddets, and affordable outfits at Children's Place. ◈ *Enchanted Forest: 85 Mercer Street, Map N4 • Children's General Store: 2473 Broadway, Map E2 • Bonpoint: 1269 Madison Avenue, Map K3 • Space Kiddets: 46 East 21st Street, Map L4 • Children's Place: 1460 Broadway, Map K3*

9 Music

Megastores Tower, HMV, and Virgin will satisfy all tastes. Opera lovers should head for the Metropolitan Opera, and vintage collectors the House of Oldies. ◈ *Tower Records: 692 Broadway, Map N4 • Virgin Megastore: 1540 Broadway, Map 3J • HMV: 565 5th Avenue, Map J3 • Metropolitan Opera Shop: 136 West 65 Street, Map G2 • House of Oldies: 35 Carmine Street, Map N3*

10 Perfumes and Cosmetics

Creed, the English perfume shop, stocks hundreds of fragrances, and Kiehl's has quality skin products. Aveda features natural products made from plant extracts. ◈ *Creed: 9 Bond Street, Map N4 • Kiehl's: 109 3rd Avenue, Map L4 • Aveda: 233 Spring Street, Map N3*

Streetsmart

Left **TKTS booth** Right **Gotham Bar and Grill**

🔟 New York on a Budget

1 TKTS Booths
Tickets for Broadway and off-Broadway shows are sold at a 25 to 50 percent discount (plus a small service charge) on the day of the show at TKTS booths. Payment is in cash or travelers' checks only. Queues get very long very quickly so it is advisable to arrive early. ⬦ *South Street Seaport. Map Q4. Open 11am–5.30pm Mon–Fri, 11am–3.30pm Sat*

2 Free TV Shows
Watch your favorite show for free – if you can get in a request early enough. For more information, call the individual networks. Same-day tickets are sometimes available at the Tourist Information Center *(see p162)* or from the NBC lobby desk. ⬦ *ABC: 212 456 3054 • CBS: 212 975 2476 • NBC: 212 664 4000*

3 Free Events
There are regular free performances, exhibits, and festivals in the Winter Garden at the World Financial Center in Battery Park City (212 945 2699). Free masterclasses and excellent concerts are also held by faculty and talented students at the Julliard School (212 799 5000).

4 Free Summer Venues
Metropolitan Opera performances, New York Philharmonic concerts, Shakespeare in the Park at the Delacorte Theater in Central Park, and outdoor performances at Lincoln Center's Damrosch Park – all free – are among the reasons why New Yorkers love summer. Contact NYC & Company (212 484 1222) for a current schedule.

5 Saving on Transit
The best transit deal is the $4 Fun Pass, a Metrocard that allows unlimited subway and bus rides from the first ride until 3am the next morning. If you are staying in the city longer, a $15 Metrocard includes one free ride, and a $17 card will buy you unlimited rides for one full week.

6 Cheap Eats
Pre-theater prix fixe dinners are good value, but lunch menus are usually even better. During Restaurant Week, the third week in January and again in June, New York's best restaurants offer three-course lunches priced according to the year: $20.02, $20.03 and so on. Several, including Union Pacific *(see p115)* and Gotham Bar and Grill *(p68)*, keep this option going all year.

7 Changing Money
You can save money by using your bank card at ATMs (Automated Teller Machines). Many accept Plus or Cirrus network cards and will debit your account and pay you in dollars. The transaction fees are less than those at Currency Exchanges, and you get the wholesale exchange rate used between banks *(see p169)*.

8 Bargain Buys
CityPass will buy you admission to seven top attractions for $38, half the usual price. You can buy it at participating sites, including the Empire State Building, the Guggenheim Museum, the American Museum of Natural History, the Whitney Museum of American Art, and the Intrepid Sea Air Space Museum.

9 Sale Periods
White sales on linens are held in January and August, coat sales are featured during the November Veteran's Day and February George Washington's Birthday holidays. Bathing suits go on sale after the 4th of July and everything is on sale after Christmas.

10 Discount Malls
Round trips are available seven times a day to Woodbury Common Premium Outlets, a one-hour drive to a mall of 220 discount outlets carrying top name brands such as Armani, Gucci, and Burberry. Tickets cost $33. ⬦ *Short Line Bus Tours: Port Authority Bus Terminal, 800 631 8405*

New York Subway

Things to Avoid

1 Unlicensed Cabs
Unregulated cars whose drivers solicit passengers at airports or in front of hotels have no safety regulations and no metered limits on what they can charge you. Be patient, and stand in line for a licensed yellow cab instead. (For tips on taxi know-how *see p163*.)

2 "Going Out of Business" Signs
The "lost our lease" or "going out of business" signs you might see in shops – particularly along 5th Avenue or on Broadway – have been up there for years. The signs are intended to lure unwary customers into stores with, typically, overpriced electronics.

3 Pickpockets
Just as in most large cities around the world, New York has its share of pickpockets hoping to take advantage of distracted visitors. Be especially alert in crowds and when getting on and off crowded buses and subway trains. Even better, use hidden travel wallets to keep your money secure at all times. Leave your valuable jewelry at home or back at the hotel, and never stop to count your money on the street.

4 Ticket Scalpers
You may be more than happy to pay the extra price for tickets to sold-out sporting events or shows, but be aware of the risk you run; sometimes the tickets peddled by scalpers turn out to be counterfeit, and you could wind up with no money and no seat.

5 Three-card Monte Games
You'll see these card games on the street, especially around Broadway. Sometimes it seems as though a player has won big, but be warned – the winner is usually an assistant. You will only win these games if the dealer wants you to.

6 Rush Hour on the Subway
Most workers have no choice and have to ride the subway at its busiest hours. But you do not need to get caught in the crush; avoid the rush hours between 7am and 9am, and between 4.30pm and 6.30pm, and you'll have a much pleasanter ride. (For information on subway routes *see p163*.)

7 Hotel Phone Charges
Unfortunately there is no regulation on what hotels can charge for telephone calls made by their guests. Read carefully the card that explains your hotel's phone surcharges, since they can be hefty, even if you use a credit card. You can save money by patronizing the telephone booth in the lobby or sometimes by buying a phone card (*see p169*).

8 Hotel Breakfasts
Hotels notoriously overcharge for their breakfasts, counting on the fact that their guests will find it easier and pleasanter to stay in. But you can save more than half – and often have a better breakfast – just by seeking out a coffee shop down the block.

9 Luggage Hassles
One tip that might help you to avoid luggage hassles: Discourage break-ins by making it harder for thieves; use tape to seal your bags shut and make any tampering obvious. You can also put your travel itinerary inside any bags, so that if they go astray, the airline will be able to track you down. ◐ *Lost and Found for bus and subway services: 718 625 6200* • *Lost and Found for taxis: 212 222 8294*

10 Jaywalking
It may seem tempting to save a few minutes by cutting across traffic in the middle of the street rather than crossing at the traffic lights on the corner, but it could cost you dearly if a speeding, inattentive New York driver comes along. It is much better to follow the city slogan, "Cross at the green, not in-between."

Left **New York city bus "kneeling" to help the elderly** Center **Wheelchair access** Right **Tour bus**

🔟 Special Needs

1 Information Sources

Hospital Audiences, Inc, publishes Access for All ($5), a guide to available resources at all New York's cultural institutions. The Mayor's Office for People with Disabilities provides services to residents and also has information on city facilities. ⑥ *Hospital Audiences, Inc: 212 575 7660 • People with Disabilities: 212 788 2830*

2 Accommodation for the Disabled

New York city law requires that all facilities built after 1987 provide entrances and accessible restroom facilities for the disabled. All city buses now have rear steps that can be lowered to allow wheelchair access, and most street corners also have curb cuts for wheelchairs.

3 Special Tours

Hands On is an organization devoted to the hearing-impaired, and publishes a calendar of information on museum and backstage tours, performances, films, and other events available with sign language interpretation. ⑥ *Hands On: 212 822 8550*

4 Aids for the Hearing-Impaired

All Broadway shows have free amplification devices for the hearing-impaired, and sign language interpretation can be arranged with the Theater Access Project or Hands On.

⑥ *Theater Access Project: 212 221 1103 • Hands On: 212 822 8550*

5 Aids for the Sight-impaired

Lighthouse International is an organization devoted to enabling the vision-impaired to cope through rehabilitation and education. It offers tips for travelers, and also lends receivers so that you can hear the new talking traffic signs at 59th Street and Lexington Avenue. ⑥ *Lighthouse International: 111 East 59th Street, between Park & Lexington avs • Map H4 • 212 821 9200*

6 Facilities for Infants and Toddlers

Department stores are equipped with diaper changing stations (*see p64*); because space is so tight in New York, other facilities tend to be scarce. Most restaurants do have highchairs these days, but it is always wise to call and check what facilities they have for children before you set out.

7 Babysitting

The Babysitter's Guild, established over 60 years ago, is a reliable source for babysitting. Staff can accommodate 16 different languages and rates are $15 per hour, for a four-hour minimum, plus $4.50 for transportation ($7 after midnight). *212 682 0227* ⑥ *The Babysitter's Guild: 212 682 0227*

8 Legal Assistance

The Legal Aid Society offers free advice and referrals; Legal Services for New York City , a non-profit referral service, also offers assistance to those with legal problems. ⑥ *The Legal Aid Society: 212 577 3300 • Legal Services for New York City: 212 431 7200*

9 Other Useful Numbers

Help is at hand in the city for various eventualities. ⑥ Clothing repairs *Raymond's Tailor Shop: 212 226 0747* All-night drugstores *Duane Reade: 212 541 970 • Genovese: 212 772 0104* Emergency car repairs *Citywide Towing: 212 924 8104* Lost and found for buses and subways *212 712 4500* Lost and found for taxis *212 221 8294.*

10 Student Identification

Foreign students will benefit from having an International Student Identity Card (ISIC) which can help to secure discounts on transportation, rental cars, hotels, and various attractions in New York and across the U.S. The cards cost $22 and are available from the Council on International Educational Exchange (CIEE). ⑥ *CIEE: 205 East 42nd Street, between 2nd & 3rd avs • Map K4 • 212 822 2700.*

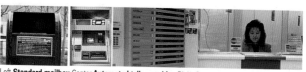

Left **Standard mailbox** Center **Automated teller machine** Right **Currency exchange counter**

🔟 Banking and Communications

1 Banking Hours
Most New York banks are open from Monday through Friday, 9am–3pm, though individual branches may have longer opening hours. Only larger banks are equipped to exchange foreign currency. Be prepared to show a passport or other photo identification when changing currency.

2 Currency Exchange Locations
People's Foreign Exchange offers currency exchange with no commission charge. Thomas Cook Currency Service charges a fee. ⊗ *People's Foreign Exchange: 575 5th Avenue at 47th St. Map K3. 212 883 0550 • Thomas Cook Currency Services: 1590 Broadway at 48th St. Map J3. 212 265 6063*

3 Automated Teller Machines (ATMs)
ATM machines can be found at almost all banks and are open 24 hours a day. They accept most common bank cards and credit cards, although they usually charge a small service fee. ⊗ *For banks accepting Cirrus bank cards: 800 424 7787 • Plus cards: 800 843 7587.*

4 Credit Cards
Cash advances can be obtained from ATM machines using Master-Card and Visa cards;

Banks accepting Cirrus (see ATM section) take MasterCard; Plus card banks (see ATM section) accept Visa. American Express members can also withdraw cash with their credit card at American Express offices.

5 Cashing Checks
Travelers' checks in dollars issued by well-known organizations such as American Express or Thomas Cook are widely accepted in the U.S. in restaurants, banks, and stores, although personal checks on a foreign bank are not. American Express offices will also cash checks for their cardholders.

6 Telephones
Public telephones are found on many street corners, in hotel lobbies, and in restaurants and department stores. You will need 25 cents in coins to make a local three-minute call, and more if you talk longer. You can buy prepaid telephone cards at many newsstands, which conveniently eliminate the need for coins.

7 Internet Access
Many hotels now have free dataport connections for laptop Internet access. In addition, free access to the Internet is available for members of the public at the Science and Business branch of the

New York Public Library ⊗ *188 Madison Avenue at 34th St • Map K4 • 212 592 7000.*

8 Sending Mail
Postage for letters sent within the U.S. costs 34 cents for the first ounce, and 23 cents for additional ounces; stamps for postcards cost 21 cents. To send mail internationally, post-cards cost 70 cents, and letters start at 80 cents for the first half-ounce.

9 Post Office Hours
All city post offices are open from 9am to 5pm Monday to Saturday; the General Post Office stays open 24 hours a day. Most hotels sell stamps and will mail letters for their guests. ⊗ *General Post Office: 421 Eighth Avenue at 33rd St. Map K2. 212 967 8585 • For branch locations: 800 725 2161*

🔟 Express and Courier Delivery
The U.S. Post Office Express Mail next-day delivery service starts at $12.25 for up to 8 ounces; global 2- to 3-day delivery costs from $20. Next-day delivery is also available from Federal Express and United Parcel Service; both include pick-up services in their charges. ⊗ *Federal Express: 800 247 4747 • United Parcel Service: 800 742 5877*

169

Left **Sign for public payphones** Center **Kaufman's Pharmacy** Right **New York ambulance**

🔟 Security and Health

1 Discouraging Thieves

Pickpockets are on the lookout for tourists, who usually have substantial amounts of cash on them. Don't flaunt jewelry or advertise your status by wearing a waistpack and sporting your camera around your neck. A local grocery store bag is a good, inconspicuous place for cameras.

2 Avoiding Scams

Beware of distractions in front of you when boarding buses or subways; a pickpocket's accomplice behind you may be after your wallet.

If you buy electronics from street peddlers for next to nothing, you may find next to nothing of value inside the box when you open it.

3 Locations to Avoid

New York's crime rate is way down, but it makes little sense to take chances. Most city parks are delightful during the day, but after dark are not safe places to explore; nor are low-income neighborhoods very safe places for visitors to roam late at night.

4 Hotel Room Safety

Don't advertise your empty hotel room by putting out the "please make up this room" sign. Leave the lights on if you think you will be returning late. Other than the maids, don't admit strangers to your room; if necessary, phone the desk to verify someone who claims to be an employee of the hotel.

5 Walk-in Medical Clinics

The D.O.C.S clinics, affiliated with the Beth Israel Medical Center, offer convenient by appointment or walk-in services for adults and children. ⑤ *55 East 34th Street, between Madison & Park avs. Map K4. 212 252 6022. Open 8am–8pm Mon–Thu; 8am–7pm Fri; 9am–3pm Sat; 9am–2pm Sun • 1555 3rd Avenue at 88th St. Map E4. 212 828 2300 • 202 West 23rd Street at 7th Av. Map L3. 212 352 2600*

6 Hospital Emergency Rooms

Emergency treatment is available 24 hours a day; if you are able, call the number on your policy first, and check which hospitals your insurance company deals with. ⑤ *Roosevelt Hospital: 428 West 59th Street at 9th Av. Map H2. 212 523 4000 • St. Vincent's Hospital: 153 West 11th Street at 7th Av. Map M3. 212 604 7998*

7 Dental Emergencies

For dental crises, D.O.C.S has walk-in clinics. You can also contact N.Y.U. Dental Care for urgent treatment. ⑤ *N.Y.U. Dental Care: 345 East 24th Street, between 1st & 2nd avs • Map L4 • 212 988 9487, 212 988 9828 weekend & out of hours*

8 Travel Insurance

Most U.S. insurance is effective throughout the country, but those with foreign insurance coverage should take out comprehensive medical travel insurance before arriving in the U.S. Should you need any treatment, you will be expected to pay for it at the time of service and the bill can be an extremely steep one.

9 Smoking

Smoking is illegal in almost all public places in New York, including subways, movie theaters, and any restaurant with more than 35 seats. The fines are stiff, $100 and up.

10 Telephone Helplines

Various helplines are available to call in a crisis. ⑤ *Suicide Help Line: 212 532 2400 • Sex Crimes Report Line: 212 267 7273 • Victim Services Agency: 212 577 7777 • Travelers' Aid: 212 944 0013*

Emergency Numbers

Police, fire, and Medical Emergencies
911
N.Y. Hotel Urgent Medical Services
212 737 1212

Sunbathers basking at Jones Beach

⚙10 Excursions from New York

1 Jones Beach State Park

Miles of ocean beaches, pools, a boardwalk with games, miniature golf, and entertainment are all part of this exceptional recreational center on Long Island's south shore. A great day's outing from the city. ◈ *Long Island Railroad connects with buses • LIRR: 212 718 217 • 90 mins from Manhattan*

2 Fire Island

An escapist's dream. No cars are allowed on this tranquil island off Long Island, rimmed with 26 miles (42 km) of beach. Visitors get around on foot or bike, and shop or dine in tiny, village centers. ◈ *Long Island Railroad to Bayshore ferry boats • LIRR: 212 718 217 • 2 hrs, 30 mins from Manhattan*

3 The Hamptons

Celebrity-watching is a favorite sport in the sophisticated Hamptons on eastern Long Island, where society and entertainment names gather to enjoy the miles of beach and beautiful old colonial towns such as Southampton and Easthampton. ◈ *Long Island Railroad • LIRR: 212 718 217 • 2 hrs, 30 mins from Manhattan*

4 New Jersey Shore

With the Atlantic Ocean beaches stretching the length of the state, the New Jersey shore is ideal for families. It offers lively boardwalks, laidback beach escapes, and Victorian towns like Spring Lake and Cape May, filled with romantic inns. ◈ *New Jersey Transit trains: 201 762 5100 • 90 mins from Manhattan*

5 Hyde Park

F. D. Roosevelt's estate and presidential library, the lavish Vanderbilt mansion, a chance to preview the work of future great chefs at the Culinary Institute of America, and scenic river views are among the lures of this Hudson River valley town. By car, Rhinebeck, 10 miles (16 km) away, is a good overnight base. ◈ *Metro North trains: 212 532 4900 • Short Line buses: 212 736 4700 • 2 hrs from Manhattan*

6 Buck's County, PA

This bucolic enclave of hills, streams, covered bridges, and mellow stone farmhouses offers visitors cozy, country inns, fine dining, choice antiquing, and gallery hopping. New Hope, a charming art colony, is the place to stay. ◈ *Trans-Bridge Line buses: 800 962 9135 • 2 hrs from Manhattan*

7 Princeton, NJ

Home to one of the oldest and most elite universities in America, Princeton is also a lovely town filled with fine 18th-century homes. On campus are Nassau Hall, the 1783 U.S. Capitol, and a museum of sculpture. ◈ *New Jersey Transit trains to Princeton: 201 762 5100 • 90 mins from Manhattan*

8 Philadelphia, PA

Boasting Independence Hall, colonial neighborhoods, a lively riverfront, and more than 100 museums, including some noted collections of Impressionist art, Philadelphia is a great addition to a visit to New York. ◈ *Amtrak trains: 800 USA RAIL • 1 hr, 45 mins from Manhattan*

9 Caramoor, Katonah

The 100-acre Caramoor estate, in northern Westchester County, includes a museum of room settings brought from European palaces, and a Venetian theater that hosts an outdoor summer music festival. ◈ *Metro North "Caramoor Specials": 212 532 4900 • 75 mins from Manhattan*

10 Tarrytown Mansions

Kykuit, the Rockefeller mansion overlooking the Hudson River, is the major draw, but Tarrytown also offers Philipsburg Manor, a restored Dutch farm estate. A little farther south in Irvington is Sunnyside, home of author Washington Irving, and Lyndhurst, palace of financier Jay Gould. ◈ *Metro North trains: 212 532 4900. 1 hr from Manhattan • New York Waterway river cruises to Kykuit: 800 533 3779*

Left **The Four Seasons** Center **The Carlyle** Right **The Pierre**

Best Hotels in New York

1 Four Seasons
For luxury in a modern mode, this dramatic, pale-hued tower by I.M. Pei is the ultimate, with rooms among the city's largest, and every amenity. The bar and restaurant draws the city's elite. ❧ *57 East 57th Street, New York, NY 10022 • Map H4 • 212 758 5700 • www.fourseasons. com • $$$$$*

2 Carlyle
Antiques set the stage for an uptown, luxury lair that has long attracted the famous with its hushed European ambience and spacious quarters in understated good taste. Café Carlyle is the city's poshest cabaret. ❧ *35 East 75th Street, New York, NY 10021 • Map G4 • 212 744 1600 • www.dir-dd. com/the-carlyle.html • $$$$$*

3 New York Palace
Fresh from lavish refurbishment, the hotel straddles the opulent 1882 Villard Houses and a 55-story tower, with a choice of traditional or contemporary room decor. Room service is from the legendary Le Cirque 2000. ❧ *455 Madison Avenue at 50th Street, New York, NY 10022 • Map J4 • 212 888 7000 • www. newyorkpalace.com • $$$$$*

4 Trump International Hotel and Towers
High ceilings and tall windows mean fabulous city and Central Park views, and the amenities are equally bountiful – jacuzzis, personal business cards, room service from Jean Georges *(see p68)*, or a chef to cook for you. ❧ *1 Central Park West, New York, NY 10023 • Map H2 • 212 299 1000 • www. trumpintl.com • $$$$$*

5 Peninsula
The Hong Kong hotel group has done itself proud, turning a 1905 classic into a state-of-the-art luxury lodging. Rooms are contemporary with Art Nouveau accents and bedside controls for the many gadgets. The health club with pool is superb. ❧ *700 5th Avenue, New York, NY 10019 • Map H3 • 212 956 2888 • www. peninsula.com • $$$$$*

6 Pierre
A landmark opposite Central Park since the 1930s, the Pierre, part of the Four Seasons group, is a bastion of old-world elegance. Personal service is a hallmark that draws many of the elite. ❧ *2 East 61st Street, New York, NY 10021 • Map H3 • 212 838 8000 • www. fourseasons.com/pierre • $$$$$*

7 St. Regis
Rooms come with Louis XVI furnishings, silk wall coverings, chandeliers, and a butler tending to your every need at this Beaux Arts beauty. French restaurant Lespinasse *(see p129)* is attached. ❧ *2 East 55th Street, New York, NY 10022 • Map H4 • 212 753 4500 • www. stregis.com • $$$$$*

8 The Mark
Discreetly elegant, this member of the prestigious Mandarin group is a contemporary sanctuary. It draws an international clientele who appreciate the Biedemeier furnishings, antique prints, luxury linens, and conveniences such as cordless phones. ❧ *25 East 77th Street, New York, NY 10021 • Map F3 • 212 744 4300 • www.themarkhotel.com • $$$$$*

9 Hotel Plaza Athénée
An intimate, 152-room Parisian outpost located on a quiet upper East Side street. Modern facilities include a fitness center and staff waiting to attend to your every need. ❧ *37 East 64th Street, New York, NY 10021 • Map H4 • 212 734 9100 • www.plaza-athenee.com • $$$$$*

10 Regency Hotel
A gilt and mirrored sanctuary favored by show business moguls, the hotel has Regency decor that inspired the name and oversize suites. The restaurant, 540, a power breakfast favorite, turns into Feinstein's club *(see p56)* at night. ❧ *549 Park Avenue, New York, NY 10021 • Map H4 • 212 759 4100 • www.loewshotels. com/regency • $$$$-$$$$$*

 Note: Unless otherwise stated, all hotels accept credit cards, and have en-suite bathrooms and air conditioning

Price Categories

For a standard, double room per night (with breakfast if included), taxes and extra charges.

$	under $150
$$	$150-$250
$$$	$250-$350
$$$$	$350-$450
$$$$$	over $450

Left **Rihga Royal** Center **Renaissance New York** Right **Le Parker Meridien**

TOP 10 Deluxe Hotels

1 Stanhope
Museum-goers favor this elegant, 185-room Hyatt Hotel, across from the Metropolitan Museum of Art *(see pp28–31)*, and recently upgraded by new management with old-world grace and new technology. ◉ 995 5th Avenue, New York, NY 10028 • Map F3 • 212 774 1234 • www.hyatt.com • $$$$-$$$$$

2 Renaissance New York
An upscale oasis in the Theater District, with an elegant lobby, handsome traditional furnishings, and deep tubs in the bathrooms. The hotel's restaurant offers a dazzling Times Square view. ◉ 714 7th Avenue, New York, NY 10026 • Map J3 • 212 765 7676 • www.renaissance hotels.com • $$$-$$$$

3 Michelangelo
A handsome, New York outpost of an Italian hotel, with unusually spacious rooms in a choice of Art Deco, French Country, or Neo-Classical styles. ◉ 152 West 51st Street, New York, NY 10019 • Map J3 • 212 765 1900 • www. michelangelohotel.com • $$$$

4 Rihga Royal
Space is the main attraction of this striking, 54-story skyscraper, recently added to the Marriott chain. Every room is a well appointed suite

with a bay-windowed living room. The location is ideal for both theater and shopping. ◉ 151 West 54th Street, New York, NY 10019 • Map H3 • 212 307 5000 • www.go.marriott. com/nyc • $$$-$$$$

5 Ritz-Carlton New York, Battery Park
Towering 39 stories above the harbor with wide-angle views over Manhattan and Ellis Island (harbor-side rooms are equipped with telescopes), this downtown newcomer offers sleek modern decor and luxury amenities for business or leisure travel. ◉ 2 West Street, New York, NY10004 • Map R3 • 212 344 0800 • www.ritzcarlton. com • $$$$$

6 Le Parker Meridien
The soaring public spaces, fitness facilities, and rooftop pool are assets of this lively hotel. Newly designed, compact guest rooms in modern cherry and cedar offer ergonomic chairs, giant TVs, and DVD/CD players. ◉ 118 West 57th Street, New York, NY 10019 • Map H3 • 212 245 5000 • www.parkermeridien.com • $$$$

7 Doral Park Avenue
A small, sophisticated haven, the Doral has smart decor and newly decorated rooms with Neo-Classical furnishings and a rich, gold and green color scheme. Other features include guest

privileges at the well-equipped Doral Fitness Center. ◉ 70 Park Avenue, New York, NY 10016 • Map K4 • 212 687 7050 • www. doralparkavenue.com • $$$

8 The Plaza
The grande dame of New York hotels, this 19-story, French Renaissance building opened in 1907 as a residence for the wealthy and is now a National Historic Landmark. The 805 rooms vary greatly; the better ones have original fireplaces and crystal chandeliers. ◉ 5th Avenue at Central Park South, New York, NY 10019 • Map H3 • 212 759 3000 • www.fairmont.com • $$$$-$$$$$

9 U.N. Plaza Hotel
Kevin Roche's soaring tower attracts an international clientele from the nearby United Nations. They enjoy panoramic views from rooms beginning on the 28th floor, a glass-enclosed swimming pool, and New York's only indoor hotel tennis court. ◉ U.N. Plaza, 1st Avenue & 44th St, New York, NY 10017 • Map J5 • 212 758 1234 • www.unplaza.com • $$$$

10 Waldorf-Astoria
An Art Deco landmark with a magnificent lobby, the 1,407-room Waldorf offers a variety of rooms, some grand and some disappointing. ◉ 301 Park Avenue, New York NY 10017 • Map J4 • 212 355 3000 • www.waldorfastoria.com

Left **The Warwick Hotel** Center **The Mansfield Hotel** Right **Roger Williams Hotel**

TOP 10 Mid-Range Hotels

1 Roger Smith Hotel
An art-filled and artful change of pace, the Roger Smith is owned by sculptor/designer James Knowles who has filled it with art exhibits. Rooms are contemporary with antique accents, and breakfast is included. ◎ 501 Lexington Avenue, New York, NY 10022 • Map J4 • 212 755 1400 • www. rogersmith.com • $$$

2 Warwick Hotel
William Randolph Hearst built the hotel in 1927, with large rooms and ample closets, and celebrities have been coming ever since. The lobby is small; rooms have traditional furnishings and mahogany armoires. ◎ 65 West 54th Street, New York, NY 10019 • Map J3 • 212 247 2700 • www. warwickhotels.com • $$$–$$$$

3 Mansfield Hotel
A distinctive Theater District hotel, the Mansfield features a soaring lobby, copper-domed salon for free continental breakfast and afternoon tea, and original Elie Nadelman drawings in the library. Rooms have sleigh beds. ◎ 12 West 44th Street, New York, NY 10036 • Map J4 • 212 944 6050 • www.boutiquehg. com • $$$

4 Algonquin Hotel
A literary landmark, famous for the New Yorker "Round Table," the

Algonquin remains an oasis of civility, with antique lighting fixtures and New Yorker cartoon wallpaper in the halls. Rooms are small but have charm. ◎ 59 West 44th Street, New York, NY 10019 • Map J3 • 212 840 6800 • www. camberleyhotels.com • $$$

5 Salisbury Hotel
Well-placed for visits to Carnegie Hall, shops, and theaters, the Salisbury was once an apartment-hotel and still has a quiet, low-key, ambience, with traditional American decor, good-sized accommodations, and a pleasant new breakfast room. ◎ 123 West 57th Street, New York, NY 10019 • Map H3 • 212 246 1300 • www. nycsalisbury.com • $$$

6 Roger Williams Hotel
An atrium with floor-to-ceiling windows, fluted zinc columns, ultra-modern maple furniture, and a mezzanine lounge for complimentary breakfast are among the features that have transformed this hotel. ◎ 131 Madison Avenue, New York, NY 10016 • Map L4 • 212 448 7000 • www. boutiquehg.com • $$$

7 Hotel Elysée
The Elysée has the warmth of a small inn, serving not only breakfast, but wine and hors d'oeuvres in the evening.

Room service is from the legendary Monkey Bar & Restaurant. ◎ 60 East 54th Street, New York, NY 10022 • Map J4 • 212 753 1066 • www.members.aol.com/ elysee • $$$–$$$$

8 Gorham
The cosmopolitan mood begins in the Art Deco lobby with clocks showing the time around the world. Contemporary rooms have red lacquer furnishings and kitchenettes. ◎ 136 West 55th Street, New York, NY 10019 • Map H3 • 212 245 1800 • www. gorhamhotel.com • $$$

9 Shoreham
A thoroughly modern makeover has included custom cabinetry, creative use of light and textures, and guest rooms in pale tones. Complimentary breakfast and all-day refreshments included. ◎ 33 West 55th Street, New York, NY 10019 • Map H3 • 212 247 6700 • www. shorehamhotel. com • $$$

10 Doubletree Guest Suites
The price of an ordinary hotel room will buy you two comfortable rooms (one with a sofabed), two TVs, and a kitchenette at this Theater District hotel. Kids stay free and have their own playroom. ◎ 1560 Broadway, New York, NY 10036 • Map J3 • 212 719 1600 • www. doubletreehotels.com • $$$

Note: Unless otherwise stated, all hotels accept credit cards, and have en-suite bathrooms and air conditioning

Price Categories

For a standard, double room per night (with breakfast if included), taxes and extra charges.

$	under $150
$$	$150-$250
$$$	$250-$350
$$$$	$350-£450
$$$$$	over $450

Left **Hotel Edison** Right **Carlton Arms**

🔟 Budget Accommodations

1 Wyndham Hotel

Reserve well ahead if you hope to snag one of the large, comfortable rooms here – among the city's best buys. Furnishings are a bit threadbare, but this only adds to the home-like atmosphere. ⊗ 42 West 58th Street, New York, NY 10019 • Map H3 • 212 753 3500 • $$

2 Pickwick Arms

Rooms may be small and spare, but the lobby is pleasant and the central location cannot be beat. Rooms have TV and there is a rooftop sitting area. Single rooms with shared baths are under $100. ⊗ 230 East 51st, New York, NY 10022 • Map J4 • 212 355 0300 • $

3 Gershwin Hotel

The bright red façade adorned with huge white abstract forms tells you that this is an arty, budget choice, popular with young visitors. Don't expect frills, but rooms do offer TV and private baths. ⊗ 7 East 27th Street, New York, NY 10016 • Map L3 • 212 545 8000 • www. gershwinhotel.com • $$

4 Herald Square Hotel

A tiny, budget hideaway renovated with taste. The small rooms have been nicely decorated and baths are new. The cherub over the front door remains from the days when this Beaux Arts building was the first home of *LIFE* magazine, and vintage covers line the hallway. ⊗ 19 West 31st Street, New York, NY 10001 • Map K3 • 212 279 4017 • www. heraldsquarehotel.com • $

5 Hotel Edison

Although the rates have gone up in recent years, this remains good value in the Theater District. It features a stunning Art Deco lobby and small but well decorated rooms with updated bathrooms. The hotel's café is a long-time, favorite, inexpensive pre-theater choice. ⊗ 228 West 47th Street, New York, NY 10036 • Map J3 • 212 840 5000 • www. edisonhotelnyc.com • $$

6 Best Western Manhattan

On a midtown block known for its Korean restaurants, this is one of several Apple Core hotels – renovated buildings offering comfortable lodging, new bathrooms, and first-class services at reasonable rates. ⊗ 17 West 32nd Street, New York, NY 10001 • Map K3 • 212 736 1600 • www. applecorehotels.com • $–$$$

7 Habitat Hotel

A great midtown location for a budget hotel, one recently renovated with care and some sophistication. Rooms are small but have modern furniture, TV, and Internet access. Those sharing baths have a sink. ⊗ 130 East 57th Street, New York, NY 10022 • Map H4 • 212 753 8841 • www. stayinny.com • $

8 Carlton Arms

There's no TV or phone, but this budget haven is popular with young visitors for its hip spirit and funky halls with walls painted by young artists. Private baths are available in 20 of the 54 colorful rooms. ⊗ 160 East 25th Street, New York, NY 10010 • Map L4 • 212 679 0680 • www.carltonarms. com • No air conditioning • $

9 Hostelling International

Although run by American Youth Hostels, all ages are welcome to share the clean, safe rooms, with 4 to 12 beds at budget prices. This 628-bed facility offers a coffee bar, cafeteria, and self-service kitchen. ⊗ 891 Amsterdam Avenue, New York, NY 10025 • Map D2 • 212 932 2300 • www. hinewyork.org • No en-suite bathrooms • $

10 A Hospitality Company

This company offers furnished studios to 3-bedroom apartments around the city. Refrigerators are stocked with breakfast fixings. Great value, but be sure locations are near transit lines. ⊗ 247 West 35th Street, New York, NY 10012 • Map K3 • 212 965 1102 • www. hospitality company.com • $–$$$

Left **The Muse** Center **Inn at Irving Place** Right **The Iroquois**

TOP 10 Boutique Hotels

1 Library Hotel
Books fill this 60-room themed hotel. Each floor is devoted to a Dewey Decimal System category, like the Arts or Philosophy, with appropriate volumes in each room. Includes a rooftop sitting room and terrace. ✆ *290 Madison Avenue, New York, NY 10017 • Map K4 • 212 983 4500 • www.libraryhotel. com • $$$-$$$$*

2 The Muse
A new Theater District boutique, the Muse inspires with a smart lobby decorated with Matisse-like murals and good-size rooms painted in pale colors, with bright bedcovers. Offers personalized business cards for guests. ✆ *130 West 46th Street, New York, NY 10036 • Map J3 • 212 485 2400 • $$$*

3 Inn at Irving Place
Two Greek Revival townhouses form an elegant, 12-room inn straight from a Jane Austen novel. Rooms have fireplaces and antiques; only the VCRs and CD players bring them up to date. ✆ *56 Irving Place, New York, NY 10002 • Map M4 • 212 533 4600 • www. innatirving. com • $$$*

4 Hotel Wales
There is a European feel to the genteel Wales. Fresh from renovation, the hotel has stylish, traditional furnishings and a panoramic, rooftop deck.

Breakfast and tea are served in a room lined with illustrations from children's books. ✆ *1295 Madison Avenue, New York, NY 10128 • Map E4 • 212 876 6000 • www. boutique.com • $$$*

5 Lowell
Luxurious and intimate, the Lowell exudes old-world charm in rooms and suites with wood-burning fireplaces, libraries, flowers, marble baths, and kitchens. Decor is an eclectic mix of French, Deco, and Oriental. ✆ *East 63rd Street, New York, NY 10021 • Map H4 • 212 838 1400 • www. preferredhotels.com • $$$$-$$$$$*

6 Iroquois
A suite is named for James Dean, who lived here from 1951 to 1953; other Hollywood guests have included Sandra Bullock and Johnny Depp. Rooms are modestly sized but deluxe, with French decor. Packages offer excellent rates. ✆ *49 West 44th Street, New York, NY 10036 • Map J3 • 212 840 3080 • www.iroquoisny. com • $$$*

7 Casablanca
A Moroccan theme, complete with tiles, arches, and ceiling fans, sets this 48-room Theater District hotel apart. Rooms are small but well furnished. Continental breakfast is served in (what else?) Rick's Café.

✆ *147 West 43rd Street, New York, NY 10036 • Map J3 • 212 869 1212 • www. casablancahotel.com • $$$*

8 Hotel Giraffe
A sunny glass-walled lobby leads to this newly constructed, 73-room hotel, with stylish Retro decor and a delightful roof terrace. Indulgent rooms, just seven per floor, even feature bedside controls for the shades. Breakfast, snacks, evening cheese, wine, and champagne are all complimentary. ✆ *Park Avenue South, New York, NY 10016 • Map L4 • 212 685 7700 • www. hotelgiraffe.com • $$$-$$$$*

9 Dylan
Although the 1903 façade has been faithfully restored, the former Chemists' Club has been transformed with serene Zen decor. The great hall is now the Virot restaurant. ✆ *52 East 41st Street, New York, NY 10017 • Map K4 • 212 338 0500 • www. dylanhotel.com • $$$-$$$$$*

10 Bryant Park
Raymond Hood's 1924 American Radiator Building has become an ultra-contemporary hotel, with giant glass windows, bold, red-lacquered lobby desks, and pale-hued rooms that are the last word in minimalist decor. ✆ *40 West 40th Street, New York, NY 10018 • Map K3 • 212 869 0100 • www. bryantparkhotel.com • $$$$$*

Note: *Unless otherwise stated, all hotels accept credit cards, and have en-suite bathrooms and air conditioning*

Price Categories

For a standard, double room per night (with breakfast if included), taxes and extra charges.

$	under $150
$$	$150-$250
$$$	$250-$350
$$$$	$350-£450
$$$$$	over $450

Left **Tribeca Grand Hotel** Right **Soho Grand Hotel**

TOP 10 Hip Hotels

1 Soho Grand Hotel
Perfectly suited to its artistic neighborhood, the hotel is housed in a landmark cast-iron building. The surroundings are dramatic and contemporary, and the Grand Bar is always hopping. ◎ *310 West Broadway, New York, NY 10013 • Map R4 • 212 965 3000 • www. sohogrand.com • $$$$-$$$$$*

2 TriBeCa Grand Hotel
TriBeCa's first hotel is a hit. All the neighborhood gathers at the Church Lounge, the dramatic lobby/bar with 70 translucent columns of light. Rooms are a calm counterpoint with an array of high-tech toys. ◎ *2 6th Avenue, New York, NY 10013 • Map P3 • 212 519 6600 • www. tribeca grand.com • $$$$-$$$$$*

3 W Union Square
Designer David Rockwell has turned a Beaux Arts building into a contemporary showstopper, complete with floating staircase. Trademark W features include a lobby with books and chess sets, and rooms with pillow-top beds. ◎ *201 Park Avenue South, New York, NY 10003 • Map M4 • 212 253 9119 • www. whotels.com • $$$-$$$$$*

4 Morgans Hotel
Ian Schrager's understated first New York hotel still has loyal fans for its clean, uncluttered look and clever, functional built-ins in the small but trendy rooms. Celebrity favorite restaurant Asia de Cuba adjoins the lobby. ◎ *237 Madison Avenue, New York, NY 10016 • Map K4 • 212 686 0300 • $$-$$$*

5 Royalton
Media and fashion folk flock to this collaboration between Ian Schrager and Philippe Starck, with a space-age lobby, curving hallways, rooms as compact as a ship's, and totally cool bathrooms. Celebs are the norm in the bar and restaurant. ◎ *44 West 44th Street, New York, NY 10036 • Map J3 • 212 869 4400 • $$$-$$$$*

6 Paramount
Appropriately in the Theater District, this hotel is like a theater, thanks to Philippe Starck's spectacular stairway and lofty lobby. Ian Schrager created the hotel for the young and hip, and they come in abundance, despite rooms that disguise their minute size with playful design. ◎ *235 West 46th Street, New York, NY 10036 • Map J2 • 212 764 5500 • $$$*

7 Hudson Hotel
The Schrager-Starck team pulled out all the stops for this 1,000 room extravaganza, a melting pot of styles described as "organized chaos." Tiny rooms were billed low-budget, but rates went up when the hotel became a hit. ◎ *356 West 58th St, New York, NY 10019 • Map H2 • 212 554 6000 • www. hudsonhotel. com • $$*

8 Time Hotel
Bold red, bright yellow, or blue? Each of the 200 rooms in this new hotel is awash in color, courtesy of hot designer Adam Tihany. Take the glass and chrome elevator to the peaceful second-floor bar. ◎ *224 West 49th Street, New York, NY 10036 • Map J3 • 212 320 2900 • www.thetimeny.com • $$$*

9 Mercer Hotel
A hit from day one with Hollywood luminaries, the Mercer is housed in an 1890 structure built for John Jacob Astor II, and makes good use of lofty spaces and a voguish, shabby-chic look. ◎ *147 Mercer Street, New York, NY 10012 • Map N4 • 212 966 66060 • $$$$-$$$$$*

10 W New York
The W Hotel group has a winning formula, turning an ordinary hotel into a hip sanctuary. It features a big, open lobby, plenty of light and clever use of contemporary furnishings in a limited space. ◎ *541 Lexington Av, New York, NY 10022 • Map J4 • 212 755 1200. • W Times Square, 1567 Broadway and 47th St, New York, NY 10036 • 212 930 7400 • Map J3 • www. whotels.com • $$$-$$$$$*

Streetsmart

177

Left **Benjamin** Center **Regent Wall Street** Right **Hotel Metro**

🔟 Business Hotels

1 Hilton New York
The quintessential business hotel, the 2,040-room Hilton has a central location, huge ballroom, and extensive meeting facilities. A redesign has transformed the lobby, upgraded rooms, and added a large fitness club and spa. ⊗ *1335 6th Avenue, New York, NY 10019 • Map J3 • 212 586 7000 • www. hilton.com • $$$-$$$$*

2 Millennium Broadway
A postmodern skyscraper, encompassing a theater, the Millennium is sleek and streamlined. Compact rooms are well appointed with high-tech features that include voicemail in four languages. ⊗ *145 West 44th Street, New York, NY 10036 • Map J3 • 212 768 4400 • www. millbdwy. com • $$$$*

3 Benjamin
A 1927 landmark by Emery Roth has been converted to an all-suite hotel designed for executives, with all the requisite high-tech gadgetry and the popular An American Place restaurant. ⊗ *125 East 50th Street, New York, NY 10022 • Map J4 • 212 715 2500 • www. thebenjamin. com • $$$-$$$$*

4 Beekman Tower Hotel
The Beekman is an Art Deco gem. Suites are roomy and provide

kitchenettes; the 26th floor Top of the Tower lounge is the perfect unwinding place. ⊗ *3 Mitchell Place, 49th Street, New York, NY 10017 • Map J5 • 212 753 9366 & 800 ME-Suite • www. mesuite.com • $$$-$$$$*

5 Metropolitan
Newly refurbished, this mid-range property offers 722 comfortable rooms and good value suites. Amenities include a fitness center and business facilities. ⊗ *509 Lexington Avenue, New York, NY 10128 • Map J4 • 212 752 7000 & 800 836 6471 • www.loews. com • $$$*

6 Hotel Metro
Popular with the fashion industry, and good value, the Metro has a sophisticated Deco feel and good-sized rooms. Public spaces include a library, rooftop terrace, and spacious dining room. ⊗ *45 East 35th Street, New York, NY 10001 • Map K3 • 212 947 2500 • www. hotelmetronyc • $$*

7 The Drake Swissotel
Business travelers appreciate the prime location, fitness center, spa, meeting facilities, and well-equipped business center of this recently refurbished 495-room hotel. Rooms have high-speed internet access, voice mail, call waiting and fax machines. ⊗ *440 Park Avenue, New York, NY*

10022 • Map H4 • 212 421-0900 & 800 372 5369 • www.swissotel.com • $$$

8 Sheraton Manhattan
An indoor pool, sauna, and free continental breakfast are among the features of this 22-story hotel, a quieter sibling and neighbor of the Sheraton New York, a major convention venue. The theater district is steps away. ⊗ *790 7th Avenue, New York, NY 10019 • Map J3 • 212 581 3300 & 800 223 6550 • www.sheraton. com • $$$-$$$$$*

9 Holiday Inn Wall Street
High-tech heaven, this was New York's first hotel with T-1 Internet access, plus check-in computers that dispense key cards. Comfortable rooms come with ergonomic workspaces, a PC with DVD/CD and MS Office applications. ⊗ *15 Gold Street, New York, NY 10038 • Map Q4 • 212 232 7700 & 800 465 4329 • www. holidaynnwsd.com • $$-$$$*

10 Regent Wall Street
The 1842 Merchants' Exchange has been transformed into a five-star property, with elegant, rooms furnished in a modern take on traditional Italian style. No amenity is lacking. ⊗ *55 Wall Street, New York, NY • Map R4 • 212 845 8600 • www. regenthotels.com • $$$$$*

Note: *Unless otherwise stated, all hotels accept credit cards, and have en-suite bathrooms and air conditioning*

Price Categories

For a standard,	**$**	under $150
double room per	**$$**	$150-$250
night (with breakfast	**$$$**	$250–$350
if included), taxes	**$$$$**	$350–£450
and extra charges.	**$$$$$**	over $450

Left **The Lucerne** Right **The Mayflower**

10 Neighborhood Hotels

1 Lucerne
The Upper West Side offers excellent value, and the Lucerne, housed in a 1903 building, is top of the list. It has a comfortable lobby, business and fitness centers, a rooftop terrace, and tasteful rooms with many amenities. ◎ 201 West 79th St, New York, NY 10024 • Map F2 • 212 875 1000 • www. newyorkhotel. com • $$$

2 Excelsior
A lavish, old-world lobby fronts a recently refurbished, well-appointed hotel with traditional decor, many suites, and facilities such as in-room computers and fax machines. A breakfast room, library, outdoor decks, and media room are among other features. ◎ 45 West 81st Street, New York, NY 10024 • Map F2 • 212 362 9200 & 800 368 4575 • $$

3 Hotel Beacon
Named for the famous theater next door (see p52), the Beacon is a relaxed, comfortable hotel, with generous looks with standard decor, and, a big plus, kitchenettes with refrigerators and microwaves. ◎ 2130 Broadway, New York, NY 10023 • Map G2 • 212 787 1100 • www. beaconhotel. com • $$

4 Mayflower
The location, a short walk from Lincoln Center, is a big attraction, drawing performers to this long-time standby.

The hotel is overdue for refurbishment, but the rooms are comfortable enough and offer kitchenettes. Views from those facing the park are prime. ◎ 15 Central Park West, New York, NY 10023 • Map H2 • 212 265 0060 • $$

5 Empire Hotel
Lincoln Center is across the street from this refurbished hotel with an impressive lobby and small but decently decorated rooms. There's a tape and CD library for in-room players, plus a café, good for pre-concert dining. ◎ 44 West 63rd Street, New York, NY 10023 • Map H2 • 212 265 7000 • www. empirehotel. com • $$-$$$

6 Franklin
The most affordable lodging on the Upper East Side, the Franklin offers style rather than size, with sleek furnishings that make good use of the compact rooms. The hotel serves complimentary breakfast and cappuccino, espresso, and tea all day. ◎ 164 East 87th Street, New York, NY 10128 • Map F4 • 212 369 1000 & 877 847 4444 • www. franklinhotel.com • $$$

7 Chelsea Savoy
An excellent neighborhood lodging, close to Chelsea's shops, flea markets, cafés, and galleries. Pleasantly furnished rooms are a decent size, with all the necessary amenities, and

the bathrooms are new. ◎ 204 West 23rd Street, New York, NY 10011 • Map L2 • 212 929 9353 • www. chelseasavoy.com • $$

8 Best Western Seaport Inn
Close to South Street Seaport, this restored 19th-century building has the predictable rooms of a chain hotel, but a cozy lobby. All 72 rooms have VCRs and refrigerators, and breakfast is included. ◎ 33 Peck Slip, New York, NY 10038 • Map Q4 • 212 766 6600 & 800 468 3569 • www. bestwestern.com • $$

9 Washington Square Hotel
A haven in the heart of Greenwich Village. Rooms are tiny, hallways painfully narrow, but the decor is pleasant, continental breakfast is included, and you can say you stayed where Bob Dylan and Joan Baez once hung out. ◎ 103 Waverly Place, New York, NY 10011 • Map N3 • 212 777 9515 • www. wshotel.com • $$

10 60 Thompson
SoHo's new, 12-story luxury hotel has 100 rooms, elegantly decked out with custom furnishings. Guests can enjoy the view from the roof garden or watch the neighborhood scene from the sidewalk café. ◎ 60 Thompson Street, New York, NY 10012 • Map N3 • 212 431 0400 • www. 60thompson.com • $$$$

General Index

Index

Acknowledgements

The Author
Eleanor Berman is a widely published travel writer whose journeys have spanned 59 countries and six continents. A long-time New Yorker, she is New York correspondent for the Expedia travel web site, main contributor to the *DK Eyewitness New York Travel Guide* (winner, Thomas Cook award 1994), and author of *New York Neighborhoods* (winner, Independent Publishers award, 2000) and nine additional travel guides.

Project Editors Felicity Crowe, Marianne Petrou
Art Editor Gillian Andrews
Senior Editor Marcus Hardy
Senior Art Editor Marisa Renzullo
Senior Publishing Manager Louise Lang
Publishing Manager Kate Poole
Art Director Gillian Allan

Photographers David King, Tim Knox

Illustrator Chris Orr & Associates

Cartography Casper Morris

Maps John Plumer

Editor Caroline Taverne

Researcher Vivienne Foley

Picture Research Jenny Silkstone, Lilly Sellar

Proofreader Stephanie Driver

Indexer Hilary Bird

DTP
Jason Little

Production
Joanna Bull, Marie Ingledew

Design and Editorial Assistance
Tessa Bindloss, Gadi Farfour, James Hall, David Saldanha, Melanie Simmonds, Hayley Smith, Rachael Symons, Andrew Szudek

Additional Photography
Tony Foo, Edvard Huember, Dave King, Norman McGrath, Michael Moran, Paul Solomon, Chuck Spang, Chris Stevens.

Picture Credits
t-top, tl-top left, tlc-top left centre, tc-top centre, tr-top right, cla-centre left above, ca- centre above, cra- centre right above, cl-centre left, c- centre, cr- centre right, clb- centre left below, cb-centre below, crb-centreright below, bl-bottom left, b-bottom, bc-bottom centre, bcl-bottom centre left, br-bottom right, d-detail

Works of art have been reproduced with the permission of the following copyright holders: *'Untitled'* Christian Boltanski (c) ADAGP, Paris and DACS, London 2002 99bl.

The publishers would like to thank the following individuals, companies and picture libraries for their kind permission to reproduce their photographs.

AMERICAN FOLK ART MUSEUM, New York: John

arnell 19c; AMERICAN
MUSEUM OF NATURAL
HISTORY, Courtesy Department
f Library Services: 35c, 35b,
5t, 37c, 37b, 138cr; D. Finnin
6tl, 36tc, 36tr, 36c; AMERICAN
ARK AT THE BATTERY: 77tl;
SSOCIATED PRESS AP:
tephen J Boitano 49b; AXA
INANCIAL, INC.: 'City Building'
om America Today, Thomas Hart
enton, 1931. Distemper and
gg tempera on gessoed linen
vith oil glaze 92 x 117 in.
ollection AXA Financial, Inc.
hrough its subsidiary The
quitable Life Assurance Society
f the U.S (c) T. H. Benton and R.
Benton Testamentary Trusts/
AGA, New York/DACS, London
002 14tl; MARY BOONE
ALLERY: Eric Fischl Installation
999) ZINDMAN/FREMONT,
.Y.C. 42tl; THE BOUTIQUE
OTEL GROUP: 174tc, 174tr;
HE BROOKLYN MUSEUM OF
RT, NEW YORK: 154tl.

ENTRAL PARK CONSERVANCY:
ara Cedar Miller 26b, 27b;
OACH USA: 164tc;
OLORIFIC: Black Star 18b;
AULA COOPER GALLERY:
ospective Retrospective by
arl Andre 43c, Adam Reich 42tr.
ORBIS: 17cr, 48c, 48ca, 158-
9; Bettman 19t, 20tl, 20c, 20b;
5t, 48tl, 49t; Bill Ross 16t; Bob
ist 168tr; Charles O'Rear 38-
; Dave Houser 62c; David
tzenstein 62b; Duomo 63c,
uomo / Chris Trotman 63t; Gail
ooney 9t; 18cl, 22c, 64b,
8tc; James Marshall 157t;
seph Sohm; ChromoSohm Inc

4-5; Kelly Mooney 116cr, 119t;
Kit Kittle 128tr; Lawrence 70-71;
Lee Snider 10cl, 74br; Lynn
Goldsmith 10-11c; Michael S.
Yamashita 3bl, 131; Museum of
the City of New York 48tc;
Nathan Benn 45cl; Patrik
Giardino 167t.
DEPARTMENT: 170TR; DIA
CENTER FOR THE ARTS: Cathy
Carver 120tl.

HOTEL EDISON: 175tl.
THE SOLOMON R. GUGGENHEIM
FOUNDATION, NEW YORK:
'Before the Mirror' Edouard
Manet, 1876, Thannhauser
Collection, Gift Justin K
Thannhauser 1978, photo David
Heald 33t; 'Black Lines' Wassily
Kandinsky, 1913, Gift Solomon R.
Guggenheim 1937, photo David
Heald (c) ADAGP, Paris and
DACS, London 2002 33b; 'Haere
Mai' Paul Gauguin, Thannhauser
Collection, Gift Justin K.
Thannhauser 1978 33r; 'The
Hermitage at Pontoise' Camille
Pissaro, Thannhauser Collection,
Gift Justin K Thannhauser 1978
32c; 'Woman with Yellow Hair'
Pablo Picasso, December 1931,
Thannhauser Collection. Gift
Justin K Thannhauser, photo
David Heald (c) Succession
Picasso/DACS 2002 32b.

HULTON GETTY ARCHIVE: 20tr;
Ernst Haas 20tc.

THE IMAGE BANK/GETTY
IMAGES: 59cl; IMAGE STATE:
AGE Fotostock 96-97; THE
IRVING PLACE: Roy J. Wright
176tc.

Acknowledgements

JOAN MARCUS: 23b, 25c, 25b; NY CITY MARRIOTT HOTELS: 173tl. THE METROPOLITAN MUSEUM OF ART, NY: The Metropolitan Museum of Art, New York: 28b, 29cb; 'Cypresses' Vincent van Gogh, 1889, Rogers Fund 1949 30b; 'Gertrude Stein', Pablo Picasso, 1905-6, Bequest of Gertrude Stein 1946 (c) Succession Picasso/DACS 2002 30tr; 'The Card Players', Paul Cezanne, Bequest of Stephen C. Clark 1960 30tl; 'Washington Crossing the Delaware' Emanuel Gottlieb Leutze, 1851, Bequest of John S. Kennedy 29t; 'Young Woman with Water Jug', Johannes Vermeer, 1664-5, Marquand Collection, Gift of Henry G. Marquand 1889 7c and 30c; 'Garden at Sainte-Adresse' Claude Monet, 1867, Monet Purchase, special contributions and funds given or bequeathed by friends of the Museum (c) ADAGP, Paris and DACS, London 2002 30tc; The Cloisters Collection/Mick Hales 31crb; Purchase The Costume Institute Fund in memory of Polaire Weissman 1989 29ca; 'Triptych with Annunciation', Robert Campin, 1425, The Cloisters Collection 1956 31b; The Cloisters Collection 1937 31t; The Cloisters Collection Gift of John D. Rockefeller 1937 31cl.

THE MUSE HOTEL: 176tl. NEW YORK CITY FIRE DEPARTMENT: 170tr. PACE WILDENSTEIN: Ellen Page Wilson 'Cornflake Girl', Mel Ramos (c) Mel Ramos/VAGA, New York/DACS, London 2002 42c. PRADA: 99br

REGENT HOTELS: 178tc; RENAISSANCE NEW YORK: 173tc. ROCKEFELLER CENTER ARCHIVE: 14tr, 15c, John D Rockefeller Jr 48tr; SOHO GRAND HOTEL: 177tr.

TRIBECA GRAND HOTEL: Michael Kleinberg 177tl.

WALL STREET KITCHEN & BAR: 77tc.

COVER: All photographs specially commissioned except: CORBIS: front tc; Bruce Burkhardt front blb; Joseph Sohm; ChromoSohm Inc back tl; Lawrence Manning front ca; Mortin Beebe, S.F front bl.

All other images are © Dorling Kindersley. For further information see www.dkimages.com.